BACKPACKING
WASHINGTON

A curious mountain goat at the upper Enchantment Lakes (Trip 43)

Previous page: Gypsy Peak, Eastern Washington's highest summit, as seen from the Salmo-Divide Trail (Trip 67)

Upper Ice Lake in late August (Trip 49)

Opposite: Wildflowers add brilliant color to Mount Saint Helens' blast zone. (Trip 15)

A hiker marvels at giant ancient Alaska yellow cedars on the Laughingwater Trail, Mount Rainier National Park. (Trip 28)

Opposite: Evening dinner at Toleak Point (Trip 2)

Rocky and difficult going around Cape Johnson (Trip 1)

Autumn at South Pass in the Sawtooth Range (Trip 60)

Opposite: Evening reflections on Aurora Lake at Klapatche Park (Trip 24)

Approaching Bogachiel Peak in late September (Trip 4)

BACKPACKING
WASHINGTON

Overnight and Multiday Routes

Craig Romano

THE MOUNTAINEERS BOOKS

THE MOUNTAINEERS BOOKS
is the nonprofit publishing arm of The Mountaineers,
an organization founded in 1906 and dedicated to the exploration,
preservation, and enjoyment of outdoor and wilderness areas.

1001 SW Klickitat Way, Suite 201, Seattle, WA 98134

© 2011 by Craig Romano

Distributed in the United Kingdom by Cordee, www.cordee.co.uk

Manufactured in the United States of America

Copy Editor: Julie Van Pelt
Cover, book design, and layout: Peggy Egerdahl
Cartographer: Pease Press Cartography
All photographs by author unless otherwise noted.
Maps shown in this book were produced using National Geographic's TOPO! software. For more information go to www.nationalgeographic.com/topo.

Cover photograph: *Pacific Crest Trail* (Trip 28)
Frontispiece: *Upper Robin Lake embraced by Granite Mountain* (Trip 36)

Library of Congress Cataloging-in-Publication Data
  Romano, Craig.
    Backpacking Washington : overnight and multiday routes / by Craig Romano. — 1st ed.
    p. cm.
    ISBN 978-1-59485-110-0 (pbk.) — ISBN 978-1-59485-413-2 (ebook)
    1. Backpacking—Washington (State)—Guidebooks. 2. Hiking—Washington (State)—Guidebooks. 3. Trails—Washington (State)—Guidebooks. 4. Washington (State)—Guidebooks. I. Title.
  GV199.42.W2R63 2010
  796.5109797—dc22
                 2011005310

ISBN (paperback): 978-1-59485-110-0
ISBN (e-book): 978-1-59485-413-2

Contents

Trips at a Glance   8
Acknowledgments   14
Preface   15
Introduction   17

Olympic Peninsula

1. Olympic Coast North:
   The Shipwreck Coast   38
2. Olympic Coast South:
   The Wildcatter Coast   42
3. Enchanted Valley   46
4. High Divide   49
5. Happy Lake Ridge   54
6. Press Expedition Traverse:
   Elwha to North Fork
   Quinault   56
7. Home Lake and
   Constance Pass   61
8. Anderson Glacier   64
9. Flapjack and Black and
   White Lakes   68
10. Lake La Crosse   71
11. Upper Lena Lake   74

South Cascades

12. Trapper Creek and
    Observation Peak   78
13. Indian Heaven
    Wilderness Lakes   81
14. Mount Adams: Devils
    Gardens   85
15. Mount Margaret
    Backcountry Lakes   88
16. Green River and Goat
    Mountain   91
17. Goat Rocks: Cispus Basin   95
18. Fryingpan Lake   97
19. American Ridge   100
20. Crow Creek Lake   104
21. Big Crow Basin   106

Mount Rainier

22. Ipsut Creek and
    Seattle Park   113
23. Sunset Park and
    Golden Lakes   116
24. Klapatche Park   119
25. Emerald Ridge   122
26. Northern Loop   125
27. Huckleberry Creek   128
28. Cougar Lakes and
    Three Lakes   132

Snoqualmie Region

29. Snoqualmie Lake   138
30. Williams Lake   141
31. Kaleetan Lake   145
32. Wildcat Lakes   149
33. Spectacle Lake   152
34. Waptus Lake   155
35. Deep Lake   158
36. Tuck and Robin Lakes   161
37. Marmot Lake   164

Central Cascades

38. Dishpan Gap   170
39. Necklace Valley   173
40. Chain and Doelle Lakes   176
41. Ladies Pass and Chiwaukum
    Lakes   179
42. Lake Augusta and the
    Badlands   183
43. Enchantment Lakes   187
44. Napeequa Valley via Boulder
    Pass   191
45. Buck Creek Pass   195

46. Lyman Lakes via Spider Gap   199
47. Image Lake   203
48. Mad Lake   207
49. Ice Lakes   210
50. Pyramid Mountain   214

North Cascades

51. Twin Lakes   218
52. Blue Lake   221
53. Glacier Peak Meadows   224
54. Copper Ridge   228
55. Horseshoe Basin (Stehekin)   232
56. Little Beaver and Big Beaver Creeks   235
57. East Bank Trail and Desolation Peak   240

58. Devils Dome and Jackita Ridge   243
59. Snowy Lakes   247
60. Twisp Pass–South Pass   250
61. Oval Lakes   254
62. Cooney Lake   257
63. Corral Lake   260
64. Horseshoe Basin and Windy Peak (Pasayten)   264

Eastern Washington

65. Kettle Crest South   270
66. Kettle Crest North   273
67. Little Snowy Top Mountain   278
68. Shedroof Divide   281
69. Mount Misery Highline   284
70. Oregon Butte   287

Appendix I: Recommended Reading   290
Appendix II: Conservation and Trails Organizations   292
Appendix III: Short Backpacking Trips   294
Index   298

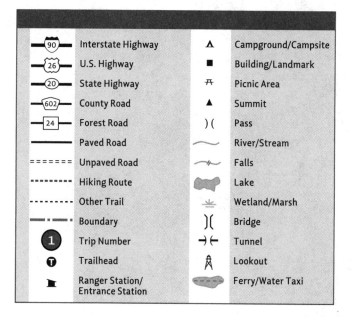

Symbol	Description	Symbol	Description
90	Interstate Highway	▲	Campground/Campsite
26	U.S. Highway	■	Building/Landmark
20	State Highway	⊼	Picnic Area
602	County Road	▲	Summit
24	Forest Road	) (	Pass
	Paved Road		River/Stream
=======	Unpaved Road		Falls
········	Hiking Route		Lake
--------	Other Trail		Wetland/Marsh
	Boundary	)(	Bridge
1	Trip Number	→←←	Tunnel
T	Trailhead	𝐀	Lookout
▪	Ranger Station/Entrance Station		Ferry/Water Taxi

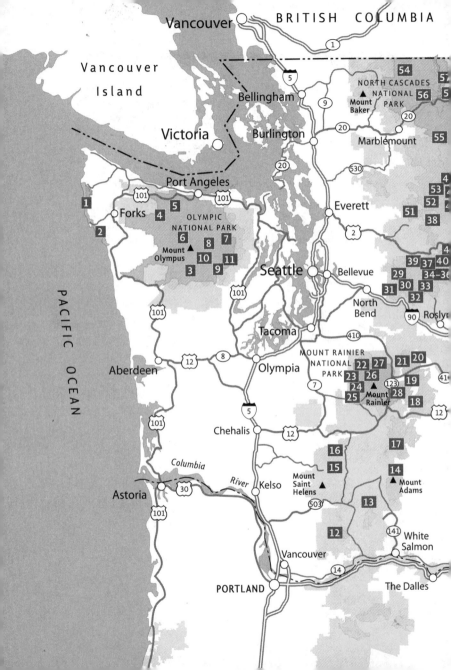

Trips at a Glance

TRIP	DISTANCE (miles)	TYPE	DIFFICULTY	ELEVATION GAIN (feet)	
OLYMPIC PENINSULA					
1. Olympic Coast North: The Shipwreck Coast	20.2	one-way	4	260	
2. Olympic Coast South: The Wildcatter Coast	17.5	one-way	5	1900	
3. Enchanted Valley	26.4	out and back	1	1900	
4. High Divide	20.5	loop	3	4175	
5. Happy Lake Ridge	18	loop	3	4400	
6. Press Expedition Traverse: Elwha to North Fork Quinault	44.5	one-way	3	3500	
7. Home Lake and Constance Pass	22	out and back	4	6300	
8. Anderson Glacier	33.2	out and back	3	4800	
9. Flapjack and Black and White Lakes	18.3	loop	3	4200	
10. Lake La Crosse	41	out and back	5	8100	
11. Upper Lena Lake	15	out and back	4	4000	
SOUTH CASCADES					
12. Trapper Creek and Observation Peak	13.8	loop	3	3400	
13. Indian Heaven Wilderness Lakes	14	loop	1	2150	
14. Mount Adams: Devils Gardens	18.6	out and back	4	3300	
15. Mount Margaret Backcountry Lakes	16.4	out and back	4	3825	
16. Green River and Goat Mountain	20	loop	3	3500	
17. Goat Rocks: Cispus Basin	14.4	out and back	2	1950	
18. Fryingpan Lake	14.6	loop	1	2200	
19. American Ridge	18.3	loop	5	4900	
20. Crow Creek Lake	16	out and back	3	4000	
21. Big Crow Basin	20.7	loop	3	4125	
MOUNT RAINIER					
22. Ipsut Creek and Seattle Park	16.2	loop	3	4375	
23. Sunset Park and Golden Lakes	20.6	out and back	3	3650	
24. Klapatche Park	21.4	out and back	4	4600	
25. Emerald Ridge	13.6	loop	3	3150	
26. Northern Loop	36.3	loop	5	9000	
27. Huckleberry Creek	15	out and back	3	2750	
28. Cougar Lakes and Three Lakes	23.4	one-way	3	2600	

SEASON	OVERNIGHT PERMIT REQUIRED	KID-FRIENDLY	DOG-FRIENDLY	SOLITUDE	WILD-FLOWERS	OLD GROWTH	CAMPFIRES PERMITTED	CAR CAMPING NEARBY
year-round	x						x	x
year-round	x						x	
Mar–Nov	x	x			x	x	x	x
late Jul–Oct	x	x			x	x		x
late Jun–Oct	x			x	x	x		
Jun–Oct	x	x				x	x	x
mid-Jul–Oct	x	x	part		x	x		
Jul–Oct	x	x			x	x	part	
late Jun–Oct	x	x			x	x		x
late Jul–Oct	x			x	x	x		x
late Jul–Oct	x				x	x		x
Jun–Nov	x	x	x	x		x	x	
Jul–late Oct	x	x	x		x	x	x	x
late Jul–Oct	x			x	x		x	x
late Jul–Oct	x				x			
Jul–Oct			x	x	x	x	x	x
mid-Jul–Oct	x	x	x		x			
Jul–Oct	x	x			x	x	x	x
Jul–Oct	x			x	x		x	x
mid-Jun–Nov	x		x	x		x	x	x
mid-Jun–Nov	x	x	x		x		x	
mid-Jul–Oct	x	x			x	x		
Jul–Oct	x			x	x	x		
mid-Jul–Oct	x			x	x	x		
Jul–Oct	x			x	x	x		
mid-Jul–Oct	x				x	x		x
Jul–Oct	x	x		x		x		
mid-Jul–Oct	x	x		x	x	x		x

TRIP	DISTANCE (miles)	TYPE	DIFFICULTY	ELEVATION GAIN (feet)
SNOQUALMIE REGION				
29. Snoqualmie Lake	17	out and back	2	2100
30. Williams Lake	30	out and back	4	3600
31. Kaleetan Lake	22.2	out and back	4	5185
32. Wildcat Lakes	17	out and back	3	4020
33. Spectacle Lake	19.8	out and back	2	1760
34. Waptus Lake	18	out and back	1	900
35. Deep Lake	16	out and back	3	3400
36. Tuck and Robin Lakes	14.4	out and back	5	3000
37. Marmot Lake	18.8	out and back	3	2975
CENTRAL CASCADES				
38. Dishpan Gap	22	loop	3	3500
39. Necklace Valley	18	out and back	3	3200
40. Chain and Doelle Lakes	25	out and back	4	6200
41. Ladies Pass and Chiwaukum Lakes	25	out and back	4	4500
42. Lake Augusta and the Badlands	21	loop	4	6400
43. Enchantment Lakes	26	out and back	5	6500
44. Napeequa Valley via Boulder Pass	36	out and back	5	6500
45. Buck Creek Pass	19.2	out and back	3	3150
46. Lyman Lakes via Spider Gap	34.6	loop	5	7335
47. Image Lake	42.4	out and back	5	7550
48. Mad Lake	17	out and back	1	1500
49. Ice Lakes	30.6	out and back	5	4325
50. Pyramid Mountain	19	out and back	4	4540
NORTH CASCADES				
51. Twin Lakes	17	out and back	4	3900
52. Blue Lake	27.3	loop	4	5725
53. Glacier Peak Meadows	25	out and back	4	5325
54. Copper Ridge	20.4	out and back	4	5485
55. Horseshoe Basin (Stehekin)	17.6	out and back	3	4550
56. Little Beaver and Big Beaver Creeks	37	loop	3	3100
57. East Bank Trail and Desolation Peak	45.6	out and back	4	6500
58. Devils Dome and Jackita Ridge	28.1	loop	5	8150
59. Snowy Lakes	20.2	out and back	3	3550
60. Twisp Pass–South Pass	25.4	loop	3	5475
61. Oval Lakes	20.4	loop	4	5900

SEASON	OVERNIGHT PERMIT REQUIRED	KID-FRIENDLY	DOG-FRIENDLY	SOLITUDE	WILD-FLOWERS	OLD GROWTH	CAMPFIRES PERMITTED	CAR CAMPING NEARBY
Jun–Nov	x	x	x			x	x	x
Jul–Oct	x		x	x	x			
Jul–Oct	x	x	x	x	x			
mid-Jul–Oct	x				x			
Jul–Oct	x	x	x		x			x
late Jun–Nov	x	x	x				x	x
late Jul–Oct	x	x	x		x			
late Jul–Oct	x				x			
late Jul–Oct	x	x	x	x	x			
mid-Jul–Oct			x		x	x		x
mid-Jul–Oct	x		x		x			
mid-Jul–Oct	x		x	x	x			
Jul–Oct	x		x		x			
Jul–Oct	x		x		x			x
Jul–Oct	x				x			
late Jul–mid-Oct			x	x	x	x	x	x
Jul–Oct		x	x		x		x	x
late Jul–Oct					x			x
mid-Jul–Oct			x		x			x
late Jun–Oct		x	x		x		x	
late Jul–Oct					x			x
Jul–Oct			x	x	x		x	x
late Jul–Oct					x	x		
late Jul–Oct				x	x	x		x
mid-Jul–Oct			x		x	x		x
late Jul–Oct	x				x			x
mid-Jul–Oct	x	x			x			
late Jun–Oct	x			x	x	x	x	
late Jun–Oct	x				x		x	
late Jul–Oct					x		x	
late Jul–Oct		x	x		x			
Jul–Oct	x			x	x	x		x
Jul–Oct			x		x		x	x

TRIP	DISTANCE (miles)	TYPE	DIFFICULTY	ELEVATION GAIN (feet)
NORTH CASCADES CONTINUED				
62. Cooney Lake	16	loop	3	4440
63. Corral Lake	33.4	out and back	4	6810
64. Horseshoe Basin and Windy Peak (Pasayten)	19.5	loop	3	3400
EASTERN WASHINGTON				
65. Kettle Crest South	13.5	one-way	2	2900
66. Kettle Crest North	30.5	one-way	3	4600
67. Little Snowy Top Mountain	19	loop	3	3650
68. Shedroof Divide	19	one-way	3	3200
69. Mount Misery Highline	17.8	out and back	2	1900
70. Oregon Butte	17.4	loop	3	3400

SEASON	OVERNIGHT PERMIT REQUIRED	KID-FRIENDLY	DOG-FRIENDLY	SOLITUDE	WILD-FLOWERS	OLD GROWTH	CAMPFIRES PERMITTED	CAR CAMPING NEARBY
Jul–Oct			x	x	x		x	x
Jul–Oct	x		x	x	x		x	x
late Jun–Oct	x	x	x		x			x
late Jun–Nov			x	x	x		x	x
mid-Jun–late Oct			x	x	x		x	x
Jul–mid-Oct			x	x	x	x	x	
mid-Jul–mid-Oct			x	x	x	x	x	
mid-Jun–Nov		x	x	x	x		x	
Jun–Nov			x	x	x	x	x	x

Acknowledgments

I have worked for two years on *Backpacking Washington* and it has been my most challenging book. I could have never completed the 1500 miles of researched trails and the 80,000-word manuscript without the help and support of friends and colleagues. I am also deeply thankful to God for watching over me while I trudged through Washington's spectacular wilderness areas, which can sometimes be unforgiving. I had more than a few cathartic moments along the way, including being caught in a forest fire.

I am deeply proud of this book and proud of all the folks who supported and encouraged me along this two-year, 1500-mile journey! I never tire of thanking all the great people at The Mountaineers Books, especially publisher Helen Cherullo and editor-in-chief Kate Rogers for continuing to support and believe in me. And I never tire of thanking my project manager, Mary Metz, for her encouragement and sympathetic ear. To all three of you, I also extend a heartfelt thank you for your patience and understanding while I missed deadline after deadline for this incredible volume.

I want to especially acknowledge my editor, Julie Van Pelt. I am deeply grateful to work with such a professional. Not only are you an amazing editor, but you're also an amazing backpacker—someone who can not only correct my dangling modifiers but who also knows the trails and backcountry and can offer suggestions so that my descriptions are clear, concise, and correct.

I hiked with a wonderful and varied bunch of folks while researching this book, and I thank them all for their company on many a wilderness mile and night. Thanks to Terry Wood, Steve Tischler, Ted Evans, Kim Brown, Douglas Romano, Jeffrey Romano, Christian Carver, Kent Wright, Alan Bauer, Karen Sykes, Bob Morthorst, Barbara Rossing, Jirka Matula, and Katka Matula.

I want to especially thank Kevin Hinchen for shuttling me up and down the Olympic Coast and Don and Chris Hanson for not only accompanying me on some of the best trips in this book but for the many pre- and après backpacking accommodations and hearty meals. All three of you made my work so much easier and I would have had a difficult time without your generosity. Thank you!

And lastly, but most importantly, I want to thank my loving wife, Heather, for once again believing in me and supporting me while I worked on yet another guidebook. Your patience and understanding know no bounds. Thanks for hiking with me, too, to some of the special places in this book. I love spending time in the backcountry with you and look forward to many more days and miles of exploring together. *Mille grazie mia amore—ti voglio bene!*

Preface

I first stepped foot (actually wheel) in Washington State in April of 1980. I had bicycled across the country from my home state, New Hampshire, entering the Evergreen State in Pacific County. I immediately fell in love with the raw beauty and expansive tidal flats of Willapa Bay. The Washington that I first experienced was the Washington I had always imagined—emerald ridges cloaked in big timber, big powerful rivers, and a big wild coastline.

In July 1985, I returned to the Evergreen State to hike the Cascades. My very first trip—along the Pacific Crest Trail to Cutthroat Pass—yielded stunning alpine views and an up-close-and-personal encounter with four mountain goats. I fell in love with these wild and awesome mountains. But it wasn't until

Pack securely and wisely.

September 1989, three months after moving to the Northwest, that I truly discovered the allure of Washington's wild and expansive backcountry.

That solo backpacking trip to the High Divide in Olympic National Park affected me as no other experience in my life had done. Never before had I felt so alive, so full of purpose, so at ease with myself and the world around me as in that special corner of the Olympic wilderness. I watched a black bear sow and her cub splash in a tarn, elk bugling and foraging in a high subalpine basin, a curious young coyote sniff out my campsite. And I sat under a blood-red evening sky by an alpine lake listening to a marmot pierce the stillness of the air with his high-pitched whistles. My vivid memories of this trip are forever etched in my mind.

Since the summer of 1989, I have logged over 14,000 miles of hiking on Washington's trails. And since my solo backpacking sojourn on the High Divide, I have backpacked scores of equally stunning and magical places throughout the Evergreen State. This book captures 70 of the very best overnight hiking destinations in the state—from the wild misty Olympic Coast in the west, to snowy volcanoes and resplendent alpine meadows in the Cascades, to the wide sun-scorched canyons of the Blue Mountains in the east. I'm excited to share these great backpacking trips with you!

And with that, it's time once again for my battle cry, the one I have been proclaiming since my *Day Hiking: Olympic Peninsula* debuted in the spring of 2007. As our world continues to urbanize, as we grow more sedentary, materialistic, and disconnected from the natural world, life for many has lost its real meaning. Nature may need us to protect it from becoming paved over, but we need nature to protect us from the encroaching world of consumption and shallow pursuits. Henry David Thoreau proclaimed, "In wildness is the preservation of the world." And I would like to add, "In wildness is also the salvation of our souls, the meaning of life, and the preservation of our humanness." You don't need to go looking for it in the mountains of Nepal or Peru—it's right here in our backyards. So, shun the mall, turn off the TV, ditch the smart phone, and hit the trail! I've lined up 70 magnificent multiday hikes to help you celebrate nature, life, the incredible wild places of Washington State, and you. Yes, you! Go take a hike! Celebrate life and return from the natural world a more content person. You don't need a lot of money or fancy equipment—just a little energy, direction, and wanderlust.

If I'm preaching to the choir, then help me introduce new disciples to the sacred world of nature. While we sometimes relish our solitude on the trail, we need more like-minded souls to help us keep what little wildlands remain. Help nature by introducing family members, coworkers, your neighbors, children, and politicians to our wonderful trails. I'm convinced that a society that hikes is not only good for our wild and natural places (people will be willing to protect them) but is also good for us (it helps us live healthy and connected lives).

Enjoy this book. I've enjoyed writing it. I'm convinced that we can change our world for the better, one hike at a time. I hope to see you on the trail.

Introduction

Backpacking Washington will give you all the information you need to find and enjoy your backpacking adventure, but it leaves enough room for you to make your own discoveries. And when paired with the other books in the Day Hiking series, *Backpacking Washington* simply overflows with possibilities. I have hiked every mile of trail described in these books, so you can follow my directions and advice with confidence.

WHAT'S IN THIS BOOK
In *Backpacking Washington* you'll find 70 destinations throughout the state that make for fine overnight and multiday backpacking trips. The trips reflect the amazing diversity of hiking options in Washington State—from the wild Olympic Coast to the lonely Selkirks and Blue Mountains in eastern Washington. Though not meant to be comprehensive, this guidebook will lead you to the popular "must-see" places as well as introducing you to some destinations you've probably never heard of. Choosing what to include wasn't easy, but in making my selections I wanted the following:

• A wide arrange of destinations reflecting Washington State's diverse regions and landscapes
• Trips that generally can be done in 2 to 4 days
• Trips that generally don't require long and complicated car shuttles between trailheads
• Trips that provide for exceptional scenery, wildlife observations, and/or wilderness experiences
• Trips that are accessible from generally good roads so that most vehicles can reach the trailheads

WHAT'S NOT IN THIS BOOK
The trips in *Backpacking Washington* range from 14 to 45 miles, with most in the 18–25 mile range. This book is meant to be a guide for weekend and multiday getaways, not for long-distance trekking. For instance, you'll not find complete descriptions for Washington's segment of the Pacific Crest Trail or the Pacific Northwest Trail, or for Mount Rainier's Wonderland Trail. You will, however, find exceptional shorter trips on those long-distance trails, allowing you to experience part of the allure, grandeur, and beauty of those great trails.

Neither will you find destinations shorter than 14 miles. Those hikes are thoroughly covered in the multivolume Day Hiking series. Appendix III: Short Backpacking Trips recommends hikes from the Day Hiking series that would make wonderful overnight trips. Refer to *Day Hiking: Olympic Peninsula, Day Hiking: Columbia River Gorge, Day Hiking: South Cascades, Day Hiking: Mount Rainier, Day Hiking: Snoqualmie Region, Day Hiking: Central Cascades,* and *Day Hiking: North Cascades.* You'll never run out of places to explore!

Since one of the selection factors for trips in *Backpacking Washington* is ease of access, you also won't find hikes radiating from roads like the Suiattle and White Chuck that have long since washed out. Not only are most hikers unwilling or uninterested in hiking (or biking) many miles on these closed roads to get to trails, but nearly all of the trails taking off from these roads have not been maintained in years, creating all kinds of hazards, from washed-out tread and bridges to choking brush. In a similar vein, you won't find Mount Saint Helens' Loowit Trail, which sustained

major washout damage several years ago, rendering it unsafe to hike for years. The good news is that the Washington Trails Association recently has begun rehabilitating this exceptionally scenic path through the blast zone.

We are in real danger of losing many of our trails, and I encourage you to write and call your elected representatives (both state and federal) as well as to join a trail advocacy group or two (like the Washington Trails Association and The Mountaineers) to help maintain and sustain our trails and access roads. If some of these roads eventually get reopened and the trails they serve once again are maintained, I have every intention of including them in future editions of this book.

WHAT THE RATINGS MEAN

Each trip in this book starts with two subjective ratings: a **rating** of 3 to 5 stars for overall appeal, and numerical score of 1 to 5 for each route's **difficulty**. This is purely subjective, based on my impressions of each hike. But these assessments do follow a formula of sorts.

The overall **rating** is based on scenic beauty, natural wonder, and other unique qualities, such as solitude potential and wildlife-viewing opportunities.

*****   Unmatched backpacking adventure, great scenic beauty, and wonderful trail experience

****   Excellent experience, sure to please all

***   A great backpacking trip, with one or more fabulous features to enjoy

Why only 3 to 5 stars? Because the trips in this book are the stand-outs in the state. For their less superlative cousins—perfectly lovely hikes all, just more pedestrian—the Day Hiking series includes hikes with 1 and 2 stars.

The **difficulty** score is based on trip length, overall elevation gain, steepness, trail conditions, and other features such as river fords and snowfields. Generally, trails that are rated more difficult (4 or 5) are longer, steeper, and consist of more cumulative elevation gain than average. But it's not a simple equation. A shorter, steep trail over talus slopes or a coastal route over slippery rocks and ledges may be rated a 4 or 5, while a long, smooth trail with little elevation gain may be rated a 1 or 2.

5   Extremely difficult: A trip consisting of long mileage and excessive elevation gain and/or one that traverses extremely difficult terrain. A trip with bragging rights!

4   Difficult: A challenging trip, usually with sufficient mileage and elevation gain, but generally consisting of less difficult trail conditions than those rated 5.

3   Moderate: A good backpacking trip consisting of decent mileage and elevation gain and generally few special trail concerns.

2   Moderately easy: A trip that is generally of moderate length and overall elevation gain.

1   Easy: A trip on good trail, with generally gentle grade, ideal for beginner backpackers.

To help explain the difficulty score, you'll also find the **round-trip mileage** (unless otherwise noted as one-way), total **elevation gain**, and **high point**. While I have measured most of the trails using GPS and maps, and I have consulted the governing land agencies for all trips in this book, a trip's distance may not be exact but it'll be pretty close. The elevation gain measures the *cumulative* amount that you'll go up on a hike—not only the difference between the

Opposite: Sand ladders aid passage over steep headlands.

A well-behaved, well-conditioned dog can be a good backpacking partner.

high and low points, but also all other significant changes in elevation along the way. As for a hike's high point, it's worth noting that not all high points are at the end of a trail—a route may run over a high ridge before dropping to a lake basin.

The recommended **season** is another tool meant to help you choose a trip. Many trails can be enjoyed from the time they lose their winter snowpack right up until they are buried in fresh snow the following fall. But the snowpack varies from year to year, so a trail that is open in May one year may be snow covered until mid-July the next. The hiking season for each trip is an estimate. Contact land managers for current conditions.

The **maps** noted for each trip are either USGS maps, Green Trails maps, or, for the Olympic Peninsula, Custom Correct maps. Green Trails maps are available at most outdoor retailers in the state as well as at many National Park Service and U.S. Forest Service visitors centers (Custom Correct maps are usually available at outdoor retailers on the peninsula). Each trip then lists the land-management agency to **contact** for current information; **permits/regulations** required, including any fees, reservations, regulations governing campfires, bear canisters, and the like; **special features** that make a trip worth-while; **special concerns** to be aware of, such as difficult fords, lingering snowfields, and rough road access; and trailhead **GPS coordinates** to help you get back to your car if you wander off-trail.

Finally, **icons** at the start of each hike description give a quick overview of what each backpacking trip has to offer. **Kid-friendly** trips are generally easier and, in *Backpacking Washington*, refer to trips good for *older* children who have experience hiking, if not backpacking (kid-friendly hikes in the Day Hiking series and in Appendix III are for younger children). A **dog-friendly** trip is one where dogs are not only allowed but that is easy on the paws, with adequate shade and water. Lightly traveled routes where you can enjoy exceptional **solitude** are noted. Trips with especially abundant seasonal **wildflowers** are also highlighted. **Historical** trips take you through the region's human story of First Peoples and early European settlement. **Endangered Trails** are threatened due to lack of maintenance, motorized encroachment, or other actions detrimental to their existence.

 Kid-friendly

 Dog-friendly

 Solitude

🔲 Wildflowers

🏠 Historical

❌ Endangered Trail

The route descriptions themselves provide detailed descriptions of what you might find on your backpacking trip, including geographic features, water sources, where to set up camp, flora and fauna potential, and more. Thorough driving directions from the nearest large town or geographic feature will get you to the trailhead, and options for extending your outing round out each trip so that, if you want, you can add more miles or even days to your adventure. Each description also includes a **Trip Planner** with milepoints for features and where campsites can be found, so you can decide how far you want to go each day.

Of course, you'll need some information long before you leave home. So, as you plan your trips consider the following issues.

PERMITS, REGULATIONS, AND FEES

As our public lands have become increasingly popular, and as both state and federal funding have continued to decline, regulations and permits have become necessary components in managing our natural heritage. It's important that you know, understand, and abide by them. To help keep our wilderness areas wild and our trails safe and well-maintained, land managers—especially the National Park Service and U.S. Forest Service—have implemented a sometimes complex set of rules and regulations governing use of these lands.

Generally, most developed trailheads in Washington and Oregon national forests fall under the Region 6 forest pass program. Simply stated, in order to park legally at these designated trailheads, you must display a Northwest Forest Pass in your windshield. These sell for $5 per day or $30 for an annual pass good throughout Region 6.

In Washington's national parks, popular access points usually require a park entrance fee. Your best bet if you hike a lot in both national parks and forests is to buy an

WILDERNESS REGULATIONS

Areas officially designated as wilderness come with a set of rules that apply. And even areas that aren't officially wilderness sometimes adopt these regulations to preserve flora, fauna, and your hiking experience. According to the U.S. Forest Service:

* Party size is limited to twelve, including people and horses.
* Cutting switchbacks is prohibited.
* Campfires are restricted in certain areas, such as at lakeshores and higher elevations.
* Caching supplies is prohibited.
* All wheeled conveyances (except wheelchairs)—including motorized equipment, mechanized equipment, bicycles, wagons, carts, and wheelbarrows—are prohibited.
* Aircraft (except at designated airstrips) and hang gliders are prohibited.
* Commercial activities are banned, except for outfitters and guides operating under a permit.
* Permanent structures are prohibited except for those of historical value.
* There are additional regulations for backcountry stock users.

Now, not all of these rules will apply to you as a backpacker—you weren't planning on taking your plane, were you? Or building a getaway cabin? But it's good to know what you can and can't do, for your own good and the good of the land.

America the Beautiful Pass (http://store.usgs .gov/pass) for $80. This pass grants you and three other adults in your vehicle access to all federal recreation sites that charge a day-use fee (children under sixteen are admitted free). These include national parks, national forests, national wildlife refuges, and Bureau of Land Management areas not only here in Washington but throughout the country.

CAMPING

When choosing a place to set up camp for the night, always use established sites if available. If there are none stay well away from lakeshores and creekbeds (at least 200 feet). Meadows, too, should be avoided. Instead, seek sheltered, wooded sites at meadow's edge. Never camp in areas closed for rehabilitation, and always adhere to rules and regulations (particularly, those related to permits and group size). In some less visited areas you are pretty free to camp where you please (though please do follow

Leave No Trace principles). Other areas are strictly regulated, requiring reservations and assigned camping sites.

In general, most destinations on national forest land require either no permit to camp or a self-issued permit available at the trailhead. The exception is the Enchantment Lakes in the Okanogan-Wenatchee National Forest, which requires a complicated Enchantment Permit for overnight visits from June 15 to October 15 (see Trip 43).

Washington's three national parks all require permits for backcountry camping, and each park issues them differently.

Mount Rainier National Park: During summer months, obtain permits at any ranger station in the park during open hours. Permits are free and issued the day of your trip or up to one day before. Reservations are not required but are highly recommended if you plan on visiting popular places during the summer and on weekends. Seventy percent of Mount Rainier's wilderness camping permits are available through the reservation system and can be secured several months in advance. There is a fee for reserving. Visit www.nps.gov/mora for details.

North Cascades National Park: Permits are required year-round for all backcountry camping in the park, including the Ross Lake and Lake Chelan national recreation areas managed by the park. Permits are issued according to a site or a cross-country zone, and there is no cost. Permits are issued in person on the first day of your trip or up to one day before. There are no reservations. They are available at the Wilderness Information Center in Marblemount. If you won't be passing through Marblemount, obtain your permit at the closest ranger station en route to your destination trailhead. Visit www.nps.gov/noca for details.

Olympic National Park: Backcountry camping permits are required and require a fee, payable in advance or the day of your trip. The cost is $5 per group (up to twelve people), plus $2 per person per night. There is no charge for youths fifteen years old or younger. Annual passes are also available for frequent wilderness visitors. Popular areas such as the High Divide and Cape Alava require reservations and permits are limited. Permits may be picked up at the Wilderness Information Center in Port Angeles as well as at other ranger stations within the park. In some instances, permits can be filled out at the trailhead, where you'll find envelopes with printed instructions. Visit www.nps.gov/olym for details.

Backcountry permits have their plusses and minuses. They allow land managers to limit numbers, reducing pressure in fragile areas and enabling you to have a better wilderness experience. On the other hand, they don't allow for spontaneity and can really frustrate you, limiting where and when you can camp. Of Washington's three national parks, I find the Olympic's system is the best and most convenient.

WEATHER

Mountain weather in general is famously unpredictable, and in the Cascades, Olympics, Blue Mountains, and Selkirks you can expect all kinds of interesting weather events, from high winds and thunderstorms to summer snowstorms. Weather patterns are radically different in the west and east ends of the state. The west side is influenced more by Pacific Ocean currents, creating a more temperate climate with a copious amount of rainfall, heavy from November to April. Summers are generally mild, with extended periods of no or low rainfall. July through early October is generally a delightful time to hike the western region.

In the east, weather patterns are representative of a continental climate, with cold winters and hot, dry summers. Snowfall is usually light due to the Cascades' rainshadow effect. But higher elevations see ample snowfall, as storm clouds move eastward and are pushed up over the mountains, cooling and releasing their moisture. Heaviest rains usually occur along the Olympic Mountains' western front. Heaviest snows usually occur at or near the Cascade crest. And in eastern Washington, the heaviest precipitation occurs in the state's northeast corner.

Plan your hike according to your weather preference. But no matter where you hike in the region, always pack raingear. Being caught in a sudden rain and wind storm without adequate clothing can lead to hypothermia (loss of body temperature), which is deadly if not immediately treated. Most hikers who die of such exposure do so, not in winter, but during the milder months when a sudden change of temperature accompanied by winds and rain sneak up on them. Always carry extra clothing layers, including rain and wind protection.

While snow blankets the high country primarily from November through May, it can occur anytime of year. Be prepared. Lightning is rare in the Olympics and along the west slope of the Cascades but is quite common during summer months on the eastern slope of the Cascades and in eastern Washington mountain ranges. If you hear thunder, waste no time getting off of summits and away from water. Take shelter, but not under big trees or rock ledges. If caught in an electrical storm, crouch down making minimal contact with the ground and wait for the boomer to pass. Remove your metal-framed pack and ditch the trekking poles! For more detailed information and fascinating reading on this subject, refer to Jeff Renner's excellent book, *Lightning Strikes: Staying Safe Under Stormy Skies.*

Other weather-induced hazards you should be aware of result from past episodes of rain and snow. River and creek crossings can be extremely dangerous after periods of heavy rain or snowmelt. Always use caution and sound judgment when fording. Also be aware of snowfields left over from the previous winter. Depending on the severity of the past winter, and the weather conditions of the spring and early summer, some trails may not

WHOSE LAND IS THIS?

All of the hikes in this book are on public land. That is, they belong to you and me and the rest of the citizenry. What's confusing however, is just who exactly is in charge of this public trust.

The majority of trips in this book are in national forests administered by the U.S. Forest Service. A division of the Department of Agriculture, the Forest Service strives to "sustain the health, diversity, and productivity of the Nation's forests and grasslands to meet the needs of present and future generations." The agency purports to do this under the doctrine of "multiple-use," in which lands are managed for wildlife preservation and timber harvest, foot traffic and motorbikes. However, supplying timber products, managing wildlife habitat, and developing motorized and nonmotorized recreation options have a tendency to conflict with each other. Some of these uses may not exactly sustain the health of the land either. Several areas administered by the Forest Service have been afforded stringent protections as federal wilderness (see "Untrammeled Washington" in the South Cascades section), barring development, roads, and motorized recreation.

The National Park Service, a division of the Department of the Interior, manages hundreds of thousands of acres of land within Washington. The Park Service's primary objective is quite different from that of the Forest Service. The agency mandate is "to conserve the scenery and natural and historic objects and the wildlife therein and to provide for the enjoyment of the same in such a manner and by such means as will leave them unimpaired for the enjoyment of future generations." In other words, the primary focus of the Park Service is preservation.

It's important that you know what agency manages the land where you'll be backpacking, for each has its own fees and rules (like for dogs: generally no in national parks and national wildlife refuges, yes in national forests, and yes but on-leash in popular national forest areas). Confusing, yes? But it's our land and we should understand how it's managed for us. And remember that we have a say in how our lands are managed, too, and can let the agencies know whether we like what they're doing or not.

melt out until well into summer. In addition to treacherous footing and difficulties in route-finding, lingering snowfields can be prone to avalanches or slides. Use caution crossing them. Finally, strong winds are another concern. Avoid hiking during extreme windy periods, which can fell trees and branches. And be aware of forest fires and impending trail closures due to them.

ROAD AND TRAIL CONDITIONS

In general, trails change little year to year. But change can and does occur, sometimes very quickly. A heavy storm can cause a river to jump its channel, washing out sections of trail or access road in moments. Windstorms can blow down trees by the hundreds across trails, making paths unhikeable. And snow can bury trails well into the summer. Avalanches, landslides, and forest fires can also bring serious damage and obliteration to our trails. Lack of funding plays a role in trail neglect and degradation as well.

With this in mind, each trip in this book lists the land manager's contact information so you can phone the agency prior to your trip and ensure that your chosen road and trail are open and safe to travel.

On the topic of trail conditions, it is vital that we thank the countless volunteers who donate tens of thousands of hours to trail maintenance each year. The Washington Trails Association (WTA) alone coordinates upward of 100,000 hours of volunteer trail maintenance annually.

As enormous as the volunteer efforts have become, there is always a need for more. Our trail system faces ever-increasing threats, including (but by no means limited to) ever-shrinking trail funding, inappropriate trail uses, and conflicting land-management policies and practices. Decades ago, the biggest threat to our trails was the overharvesting of timber and the wanton building of roads

to access it. Ironically, as timber harvesting has all but ceased in much of our federal forests, one of the biggest threats to our trails now is access. Many roads once used for hauling timber (and by hikers to get to trailheads) are no longer maintained. Many of these roads are slumping and growing over and are becoming downright dangerous to drive. Many, too, are washing out, severing access. While this author supports the decommissioning of many of the trunk roads that go "nowhere" as both economically and environmentally prudent, I am deeply disturbed by the number of main roads that are falling into disrepair. Once a road has been closed for several years, the trails radiating from it often receive no maintenance, which often leads them to becoming unhikeable.

On the other end of the threat scale is the increased motorized use of many of our trails. Despite also being open to hiking, motorized vehicles on trails tend to discourage hikers—the noise, speed, and negative impact on the natural environment are not compatible with quiet, muscle-powered modes of backcountry travel. Even when motorized users obey rules and regulations—and most do—wheels tear up tread far more than boots do. This is especially true in the high country, where fragile soils and lush meadows are easily damaged. While the majority of motorcyclists are decent people and I have shared trails with them, hiking with them is simply not a wilderness experience. And while I support the rights of motorized recreation users to have access to public lands, many of the trails currently open to them should never have allowed them. Only two trips in this book (and one just seasonally) are open to motorcycles.

This guide includes several trails that are threatened and in danger of becoming unhikeable due to motorized use, access problems, and other issues. These Endangered Trails are marked with a special icon.

On the other side of the coin, we've had some great trail successes in recent years, thanks in large part to a massive volunteer movement spearheaded by WTA and other organizations.

WILDERNESS ETHICS

As wonderful as volunteer trail maintenance programs are, they aren't the only way to help save our trails. Indeed, these on-the-ground efforts provide quality trails today, but to ensure the long-term survival of our trails—and more specifically, to preserve the wildlands they cross—we must embrace and practice a sound wilderness ethic.

A strong, positive wilderness ethic includes making sure you leave the wilderness as good as (or even better than) you found it. But a sound wilderness ethic goes deeper than simply picking up after ourselves (and others) when we go for a hike. It must carry over into our daily lives. We need to ensure that our elected officials and public land managers recognize and respond to our wilderness needs and desires. Get involved with groups and organizations that safeguard, watchdog, and advocate for land protection. And get on the phone and keyboard and let land managers and public officials know how important protecting lands and trails is to you.

CARRYING ON AN OUTDOOR LEGACY

I grew up in rural New Hampshire and was introduced to hiking and respect for our wildlands at a young age. I grew to admire the men and women responsible for saving and protecting many of our trails and wilderness areas as I became more aware of the often tumultuous history behind the preservation efforts.

When I moved to Washington in 1989, I immediately gained a respect for Harvey Manning and Ira Spring. Through their pioneering 100 Hikes guidebooks, I was introduced to and fell in love with the Washington backcountry. I joined the Mountaineers Club, the Washington Trails Association, Conservation Northwest, and other local trail and conservation organizations so that I could help protect these places and carry on this legacy to future generations.

WHAT'S YOUR HIKING FOOTPRINT? LEAVING NO TRACE

All of us who recreate in Washington's natural areas have a moral obligation to respect and protect our natural heritage. Everything we do on the planet has an impact—and when we take to the woods, we should strive to have the least negative impact possible. The Leave No Trace Center for Outdoors Ethics is an educational, nonprofit, apolitical organization that promotes responsible enjoyment and active stewardship of the outdoors.

According to the center, "Leave No Trace is best understood as an educational and ethical program, not as a set of rules and regulations." And their message is framed by these seven principles:

1. Plan ahead and prepare.
2. Travel and camp on durable surfaces.
3. Dispose of waste properly.
4. Leave what you find.
5. Minimize campfire impacts.
6. Respect wildlife.
7. Be considerate of other visitors.

It's a no-nonsense code that we all should follow. Visit www.lnt.org to learn more.

I believe 100 percent in what Ira Spring termed "green bonding." We must, in Ira's words, "get people onto trails. They need to bond with the wilderness." This is essential in building public support for trails and trail funding. When hikers get complacent, trails suffer.

When you get home from the trails, write a letter to your congressperson or state representative, asking for better trail and public lands funding. Call your local Forest Service office and let them know how you feel about converting wilderness trails into motorized trails.

If you're not already a member, consider joining an organization devoted to wilderness, backcountry trails, or other wild-country issues. Organizations like the Mountaineers Club, Washington Trails Association, Mountains to Sound Greenway, Friends of the Columbia River Gorge, and countless others help leverage individual contributions and efforts to ensure the future of our trails and the wonderful wilderness legacy we've inherited. Buy a specialty license plate for Washington's national parks and let everybody on the way to the trailhead see what you value and support.

TRAIL ETIQUETTE

We need to not only be sensitive to the environment surrounding our trails but to other trail users as well. Many of the trails in this book are open to an array of trail users. Some are hiker-only, but others allow equestrians and mountain bikers too.

When you encounter other trail users—whether they are hikers, climbers, runners, bicyclists, or horse riders—the only hard-and-fast rule is to follow common sense and exercise simple courtesy. It's hard to overstate just how vital these two things—common sense and courtesy—are to maintaining an enjoyable, safe, and friendly situation when

Use only stoves in the high country.

different types of trail users meet.

With this Golden Rule of Trail Etiquette firmly in mind, here are other things you can do during trail encounters to make everyone's trip more enjoyable:

- **Right-of-way.** When meeting other hikers, the uphill group has the right-of-way. There are two general reasons for this. First, on steep ascents, hikers may be watching the trail and might not notice the approach of descending hikers until they're face-to-face. More importantly, it's easier for descending hikers to break stride and step off-trail than it is for those who have gotten into a good climbing rhythm. But by all means, if you're the uphill trekker and you wish to grant passage to oncoming hikers, go right ahead with this act of trail kindness.

- **Moving off-trail.** When meeting other user groups (like bicyclists and horseback riders), the hiker should move off the trail. This is because hikers are more mobile and flexible than other users, making it easier for them to step off the trail.

- **Encountering horses.** When meeting horseback riders, the hiker should step off the downhill side of the trail unless the terrain makes this difficult or dangerous. In that case, move to the uphill side of the trail, but crouch down a bit so you don't tower over the horses' heads. Also, make yourself visible so as not to spook the big beastie, and talk in a normal voice to the riders. This calms the horses. If hiking with a dog, keep your buddy under control.

- **Stay on trails,** and practice minimum impact. Don't cut switchbacks, take shortcuts, or make new trails. If your destination is off-trail, stick to snow and rock when possible so as not to damage fragile alpine meadows. Spread out when traveling off-trail; don't

Treat all backcountry water sources.

hike in line if in a group, as this greatly increases the chance of compacting thin soils and crushing delicate plant environments.

- **Obey the rules** specific to the trail you're visiting. Many trails are closed to certain types of use, including hiking with dogs and travel by mountain bike.

- **Hiking with dogs.** Hikers who take dogs on the trails should have their dog on a leash or under very strict voice command at all times. And if leashes are required, then this *does* apply to you. Too many dog owners flagrantly disregard this regulation, setting themselves up for tickets, hostile words from fellow hikers, and the possibility of losing the right to bring Fido out on that trail in the future. One of the most contentious issues in hiking circles is whether dogs should be allowed on trails. Far too many hikers (this author, who happens to love dogs, included) have had very negative trail encounters with dogs (actually, the dog owners). Remember that many hikers are not fond of dogs on the trail (and some are actually afraid of your pet). Respect their right not to be approached by your loveable lab. A well-behaved leashed dog, however, can certainly help warm up these hikers to your buddy.

- **Avoid disturbing wildlife.** Observe from a distance, resisting the urge to move closer to wildlife (use your telephoto lens). This not only keeps you safer, but it prevents the animal from having to exert itself unnecessarily fleeing from you.

- **Take only photographs.** Leave all natural things, features, and historical artifacts as you found them for others to enjoy.

- **Never roll rocks off trails or cliffs.** You risk endangering lives below you.

These are just a few of the things you can do to maintain a safe and harmonious trail environment. And while not every situation is addressed by these rules, you can avoid

THE DEFECATION PROCLAMATION

Another important Leave No Trace principle focuses on the business of taking care of business. So here is some privy information for you.

The first rule of backcountry bathroom etiquette says that if an outhouse exists, use it. They help keep backcountry water supplies free of contamination and the surrounding countryside free of human waste decorated with toilet-paper flowers. Composting privies can actually improve the environment. I once spent a summer as a backcountry ranger in which one of my duties was composting the duty. Once the "stew" was sterile, we spread it on damaged alpine meadows, helping to restore the turf.

When privies aren't provided, however, the key factor to consider is location. Choose a site at least 200 feet from water, campsites, and the trail. Dig a cat hole (a trowel comes in handy). Once you're done, bury your waste with organic duff and place a "Microbes at Work" sign over it (just kidding about the sign—but making an X marks the spot with a couple of sticks is a fine idea).

problems by always remembering that *common sense and courtesy are in order.*

"Leave only footprints, take only pictures" is a worthy slogan to live by when visiting the wilderness.

WATER

As a general rule you should assume that all backcountry water sources are contaminated with *Giardia* (a waterborne parasite) or other aquatic nasties. Treating water can be as simple as boiling it, chemically purifying it (adding tiny iodine tablets), or pumping it through a water filter and purifier. (Note: Pump units labeled as filters generally remove everything but viruses, which are too small to be filtered out. Pumps labeled as purifiers use a chemical element, usually iodine, to render viruses inactive after filtering all the other bugs out.)

CAMPFIRES

Sometimes, nothing is as comforting in the backcountry as sitting around a campfire. Unfortunately, often nothing is as devastating—especially in popular areas where downed wood has been picked cleaned and vegetation trampled.

If you plan on making a fire, first be sure that it's allowed. In many popular lake basins and high-altitude areas, fires are not permitted. In general, fires are not permitted in the Mount Rainier National Park backcountry or above 3500 feet in Olympic National Park.

Also be sure to stay abreast of fire closures, as areas that usually permit campfires often ban them during extended dry periods. If you plan on having a fire, stick to established fire rings and keep your fire small. Always plan on using a stove for your cooking, as wood may not be available and conditions (such as a storm) may render a campfire unfeasible.

COOKING AND CLEANING UP

When washing up, rinse as much as you can in plain water first. If you still feel the need for a soapy wash, collect a pot of water from a lake or stream and move at least 100 feet away. Apply a small amount of biodegradable soap to your hands, and lather up. Use a bandanna or towel to wipe away most of the soap; then rinse with the water in the pot. Follow the same procedure with your pots and pans, making sure you eat all the food first (never dump leftover food in the water or on the ground). If you can't eat it, pack it into a plastic bag and pack it out!

Remember, too, that anything you pack in must be packed out, even biodegradable items like orange peels and pistachio shells. Burn paper if you have a fire; but do not attempt to burn foil and other noncombustible items. Folks have been trying for hundreds of years with the same results—a dirty, unsightly fire pit.

HUNTING

Many of our public lands are seasonally open to hunting. The dates vary, but generally big game hunting begins in early August and ends in late November. While backpacking in areas frequented by hunters, it's best to make yourself visible by donning an orange cap and vest. If your dog is with you, your buddy should wear an orange vest too. The vast majority of hunters are

responsible, decent folks (and are conservationists who also support our public lands), so you should have little concern when encountering them in the backcountry. Still, if being around outdoors people schlepping rifles is unnerving to you, then stick to hiking in national parks where hunting is prohibited.

THE BEAR ESSENTIALS

Washington State (particularly Olympic National Park and the North Cascades) harbors a healthy population of black bears, and your chances of eventually seeing one are pretty good. The North Cascades and Columbia Highlands of northeastern Washington also support a small population of grizzly bears. Your chances of seeing one of these guys are slim. Your ursine encounters will most likely be with black bears, and you'll usually just catch a glimpse of its bear behind. But occasionally the bruin may actually want to get a look at *you*. In very rare cases (and I repeat, rare), a bear may act aggressively (usually during berry failures, meaning that bears become hungry and malnourished; or if a sow feels her cubs are threatened).

To avoid an un-*bear*-able encounter, heed the following advice compliments of fellow guidebook writer Dan Nelson:

* **Respect a bear's need for personal space.** If you see a bear in the distance, make a wide detour around it. If that's not possible, leave the area.
* **Remain calm** if you do encounter a bear at close range. Do not run, as this may trigger a predatory-prey reaction from the bear.
* **Talk in a low-voiced, calm manner** to the bear to help identify yourself as a human.
* **Hold your arms out from your body,** and if wearing a jacket hold open the front so you appear as big as possible.

Freshly scratched trees indicate bear presence.

- **Don't stare directly at the bear**—the bear may interpret this as a direct threat or challenge. Watch the animal without making direct eye-to-eye contact.
- **Slowly move upwind** of the bear if you can do so without crowding the bear. The bear's strongest sense is its sense of smell, and if it can sniff you and identify you as human, it may retreat.
- **Know how to interpret bear actions.** A nervous bear will often rumble in its chest, clack its teeth, and "pop" its jaw. It may paw the ground and swing its head violently side to side. If the bear does this, watch it closely (without staring directly at it). Continue to speak low and calmly.
- **A bear may bluff-charge**—run at you but stop well before reaching you—to try and intimidate you. Resist the urge to run, as that would turn the bluff into a real charge and you will *not* be able to outrun the bear (black bears can run at speeds up to 35 miles per hour through log-strewn forests).
- If you surprise a bear and it does charge from close range, **lie down and play dead.** A surprised bear will leave you once the perceived threat is neutralized. However, if the bear wasn't attacking because it was surprised—if it charges from a long distance, or if it has had a chance to identify you and still attacks—you should fight back. A bear in this situation is behaving in a predatory manner (as opposed to the defensive attack of a surprised bear) and is looking at you as food. Kick, stab, punch at the bear. If it knows you will fight back, it may leave you and search for easier prey.
- **Carry a 12-ounce (or larger) can of pepper spray bear deterrent.** The spray—a high concentration of oils from hot peppers—should fire out at least 20 or 30 feet in a broad mist. Don't use the spray unless a bear is actually charging and is in range of the spray.

THIS IS COUGAR COUNTRY

Very few hikers ever see cougars in the wild. I've been tracked by them, but in all of my hiking throughout North and South America I have only seen one of these elusive kitties, and it was while doing research for this book in the Blue Mountains. Washington supports healthy populations of the shy and solitary *Felix concolor*. While cougar encounters are extremely rare, they do occur. To make sure the encounter is a positive one (at least for you), you need to understand these wildcats.

Cougars are curious (after all, they're cats). They will follow hikers simply to see what kind of beasts we are, but they rarely (almost never) attack adult humans. If you do encounter one, remember that cougars rely on prey that can't, or won't fight back. Fellow guidebook writer Dan Nelson offers the following advice should you run into one of these cats:

- **Do not run!** Running may trigger a cougar's attack instinct.
- **Stand up and face it.** Virtually every recorded cougar attack of humans has been a predator-prey attack. If you appear as another aggressive predator rather than as prey, the cougar will back down.
- **Try to appear large.** Wave your arms or a jacket over your head.
- **Pick up children and small dogs.**
- **Maintain eye contact** with the animal. The cougar will interpret this as a show of dominance on your part.
- **Back away slowly** if you can safely do so.
- **Do not turn your back** or take your eyes off the cougar. Remain standing.
- **Throw things,** provided you don't have to bend over to pick them up. If you have a water bottle on your belt, chuck it at the cat. Wave your trekking pole, and if the cat gets close enough, whack it *hard* with your pole.
- **Shout loudly.**
- **Fight back** aggressively.

And you can minimize the already slim chances of having a negative cougar encounter by doing the following:

- **Do not hike or run alone** (runners look like fleeing prey to a predator).
- **Keep children within sight** and close at all times.
- **Avoid dead animals.**
- **Keep dogs on-leash and under control.** A cougar may attack a loose, solitary dog, but a leashed dog next to you makes two foes for the cougar to deal with—and cougars are too smart to take on two aggressive animals at once.

NERVOUS TICKS AND RATTLED NERVES

Compared with other parts of the world, natural nuisances in Washington State are minimal. Two that you should be concerned with, and only minimally at that, are snakes that rattle and arachnids that hitch a ride.

Rattlesnakes: There's no need for concern on the wet west side of the Cascades or in the Olympics. But on the east side of the Cascade crest—in particular, in low-elevation, dry canyon areas—northern Pacific rattlesnakes may be found. A viper that is as intent on avoiding you as you are it, rattlesnakes generally keep to themselves. But if you get too close, they'll set off an alarm by rattling their tails. Should this happen, walk away, allowing the snake to retreat. Never, ever try to catch, provoke, or pursue one. Rattlesnake bites in Washington are extremely rare; deaths by rattlesnake bites even rarer. If bit, however, remain calm. Wash the bite. Immobilize the limb. Apply a wet wrap. Seek medical attention immediately.

Ticks: This nuisance you should be far more concerned with. Other than the fact that most people (this author included) find these hard-shelled arachnids disgusting (and fascinating too, I admit), it's ticks' role as a disease vector that raises alarm. Ticks are parasites that live off the blood of their host. Hikers make great hosts, and ticks will cling to them if given the opportunity. Generally active in the spring on the lower slopes of the east side of the Cascades and throughout eastern Washington, ticks inhabit shrubs and tall grasses. When you brush up against these plants, the tick gets an opportunity to hitch a ride. During tick season wear long sleeves and tuck pant legs into socks. Be sure to check yourself after hiking, particularly at waist and sock lines. And if one of the little buggers has fastened itself to you, get out your tweezers. Gently squeeze its head until it lets go (try not to break the head off, or it may become lodged and infected). Wash and disinfect the bite area. Most ticks in the Northwest do not carry Lyme disease. Still, it's best to monitor the bite. If a rash develops, immediately seek medical help.

GEAR

While a full description of all available gear is beyond the scope of this book (which is about where to backpack, not how to backpack) it's worth noting a few pointers here. No backpacker should venture far up a trail without being properly equipped.

Starting with your feet, a good pair of boots can make all the difference between a wonderful trip and a blistering affair. Keep your feet happy and you'll be happy. Every hiker will swear by different brands and types of boots, so your best bet is to be fit by a professional and to try a bunch out—see what works for you.

For clothing, wear whatever is most comfortable, unless it's cotton. Cotton is a wonderful fabric but not the best to hike in. When it gets wet, it stays wet and lacks any insulation value. In fact, wet cotton sucks away body heat, leaving you susceptible to hypothermia. Think synthetics and layering.

As far as what goes in your backpack, you need to weigh (literally) everything out, trying to balance comfort and convenience without overloading. There's an old adage that goes something like this: Travel light, enjoy the hike. Travel heavy, enjoy the night. With today's affordable lightweight equipment, there is no reason to schlepp 60 pounds worth of gear on a one- or two-night trip.

As a general rule, you should not carry more than 25 percent of your body weight. If you're 150 pounds, that means a pack weighing no more than 38 pounds. I usually carry 30 to 40 pounds of gear on a one- to three-night trip and am able to cover 15 miles a day without discomfort. Of course, there are plenty of backpackers that think I carry too much. These ultralight disciples travel with minimal gear, which may or may not be for you.

MY BACKPACKING MASTER LIST

Those items marked with an asterisk (*) are for comfort, while all other items I consider essential.

Pack
Pack cover
Tent
Ground cloth
Space blanket
Sleeping bag
Sleeping pad
Headlamp
Batteries
*Stool
*Collapsible water bucket
Stove
Fuel
Dishes and cup
Utensils
Matches
Food bag and food
Boots
Socks (2 pairs) and liners
Shorts
Briefs (2 pairs)
Thermal shirt
Long-sleeve shirt
Short-sleeve shirt
Fleece vest
Long pants
Rain jacket, shell, or poncho
Rain pants
Rain hat

Cap
Sunglasses
Gloves
*Camp shoes
Bandanna
Map and compass
Notebook and pen
Safety pins
Garbage bag
Resealable plastic bags
Rope
Jackknife
Collapsible water bottles (2)
*Collapsible wine bag
Duct tape
*Trekking poles
First-aid kit
Toiletries
Toilet paper and hand sanitizer
Ibuprofen
*Magazine/book
Sunscreen
Bug dope
Water tablets
*Washcloth and towel
*Camera
*GPS unit
*Small lantern (in fall)

Be sure you have proper permits.

While the list of what you pack will vary, there are a few items everyone should have in their packs every trip: the Ten Essentials. I've also included my own backpacking master list, which I more or less adhere to on every trip, making minor adjustments for weather and trail conditions.

TRAILHEAD CONCERNS

Sadly, the topic of trailhead and trail crime must be addressed. As urban areas encroach upon our green spaces, societal ills follow along. While violent crime is extremely rare (practically absent on most of our public lands, thankfully), it is a grim reminder that we are never truly free from the worst elements of society.

By and large our hiking trails are safe places—far safer than most city streets. Common sense and vigilance, however, are still in order. This is true for all backpackers, but particularly so for solo backpackers. Be aware of your surroundings at all times. Leave your itinerary with someone back home. If something doesn't feel right, it probably isn't. Take action by leaving the place or situation immediately. But remember, most hikers are friendly, decent people. Some may be a little introverted, but that's no cause for worry.

By far your biggest concern should be with trailhead theft. Car break-ins are far too common at some of our trailheads, especially along the I-90 corridor and Mountain Loop Highway. Do not—absolutely under no circumstances—leave anything of value in your vehicle while out hiking. Take your wallet, cell phone, and listening devices with you—or better yet, don't bring them along in the first place. Consider taking your registration with you too. Don't leave anything in your car that may appear valuable. A duffle bag on the back seat may contain dirty T-shirts, but a thief may think there's a laptop in it. Save yourself the hassle of returning to a busted window by not giving criminals a reason to clout your car.

If you arrive at a trailhead and someone looks suspicious, don't discount your intuition. Take notes on the person and his or her vehicle. Record the license plate and report the behavior to the authorities. Do not confront the person. Leave and go to another trail.

While most car break-ins are crimes of opportunity by drug addicts looking for loot to support their fix, organized gangs intent on stealing IDs have also been known to target parked cars at trailheads. While some trailheads are regularly targeted, and others rarely if at all, there's no sure way of preventing this from happening to you other than being dropped off at the trailhead or taking the bus (rarely an option, either way). But you

THE TEN ESSENTIALS

1. **Navigation (map and compass):** Carry a topographic map of the area you plan to be in and know how to read it. Likewise bring a compass—again, make sure you know how to use it.

2. **Sun protection (sunglasses and sunscreen):** Even on wet days, carry sunscreen and sunglasses; you never know when the clouds will lift. At higher elevations your exposure to UV rays is much more intense than at sea level. You can easily burn on snow and near water.

3. **Insulation (extra clothing):** Storms can and do blow in rapidly. In the high country it can snow anytime of year. Be sure to carry raingear, wind gear, and extra layers.

4. **Illumination (flashlight/headlamp):** Carry extra batteries too.

5. **First-aid supplies:** At the very least your kit should include bandages, gauze, scissors, tape, tweezers, pain relievers, antiseptics, and perhaps a small manual. Consider first-aid training through a program such as MOFA (Mountaineering Oriented First Aid).

6. **Fire (firestarter and matches):** Be sure you keep your matches dry. Resealable plastic bags do the trick.

7. **Repair kit and tools (including a knife):** A knife is helpful; a multitool is better. You never know when you might need a small pair of pliers or scissors, both of which are commonly found on compact multitools. A basic repair kit should include such things as nylon cord, a small roll of duct tape, some 1-inch webbing and extra webbing buckles (to fix broken pack straps), and a small tube of superglue. A handful of safety pins can do wonders too.

8. **Nutrition (extra food):** Always pack more food than what you need for your hike. Better to have extra and not need it than the other way around. Pack energy bars for emergency pick-me-ups. I swear by chocolate-covered espresso beans!

9. **Hydration (extra water):** Carry two full 32-ounce water bottles, unless you're hiking entirely along a water source. You'll need to carry iodine tablets or a filter too, so as not to catch any waterborne nasties like *Giardia*.

10. **Emergency shelter:** This can be as simple as a garbage bag or something more efficient like a reflective space blanket. A poncho can double as an emergency tarp.

can make your car less of a target by not leaving anything of value in it. And contact your government officials and demand that law enforcement be a priority on our public lands. We taxpayers have a right to recreate safely in our parks and forests.

ENJOY THE TRAILS

Most importantly, though, be safe and enjoy the trails in this book. They exist for our enjoyment and for the enjoyment of future generations of hikers. We can use them and protect them at the same time if we're careful with our actions and forthright in demanding that our state and federal representatives continue and further the protection of our wildlands.

Throughout the last century, wilderness lovers helped secure protection for many of the lands we enjoy today. President Theodore Roosevelt was visionary in establishing the national forest system and in greatly expanding our public lands (by over 40 million acres). President Franklin Roosevelt was ingenious in stimulating infrastructure on our public lands and also in expanding our parks and preserves.

Republicans, Democrats, Independents, city dwellers, country folks, and Americans of all walks of life have helped establish and protect our open spaces and wilderness areas. As we cruise into the twenty-first century, we must see to it that those protections continue and that the last bits of wildlands are also preserved for the enjoyment of future generations.

If you enjoy these trails, get involved! Trails may wind through trees, but they don't grow on them. Your involvement can be as simple as picking up trash, attending a work party, joining a trail advocacy group, educating fellow citizens, or writing Congress or your state representatives a letter. All of these seemingly small acts can make a big difference. Introduce children to our trails. We need to continue a legacy of good trail stewards. At the end of this book you'll find a list of organizations working on behalf of our trails and wildlands in Washington. Consider getting involved with a few of them.

Happy Hiking!

A NOTE ABOUT SAFETY

Safety is an important concern in all outdoor activities. No guidebook can alert you to every hazard or anticipate the limitations of every reader. Therefore, the descriptions of roads, trails, routes, and natural features in this book are not representations that a particular place or excursion will be safe for your party. When you follow any of the routes described in this book, you assume responsibility for your own safety. Under normal conditions, such excursions require the usual attention to traffic, road and trail conditions, weather, terrain, the capabilities of your party, and other factors. Because many of the lands in this book are subject to development and/or change of ownership, conditions may have changed since this book was written that make your use of some of these routes unwise. Always check for current conditions, obey posted private property signs, and avoid confrontations with property owners or managers. Keeping informed on current conditions and exercising common sense are the keys to a safe, enjoyable outing.

The Mountaineers Books

Opposite: Happy Lake Ridge, Olympic National Park (Trip 5)

Olympic Peninsula

Olympic Coast North: The Shipwreck Coast

1

RATING/ DIFFICULTY	ONE-WAY	ELEV GAIN/ HIGH POINT	SEASON
****/4	20.2 miles	260 feet/ 150 feet	Year-round

Maps: Green Trails Ozette No. 130S, Custom Correct North Olympic Coast; **Contact:** Olympic National Park, Wilderness Information Center, Port Angeles, (360) 565-3100, www.nps.gov/olym; **Permits/regulations:** National park entrance fee at Ozette Lake. Olympic NP wilderness camping permit required. Bear canister required, can be borrowed from Wilderness Information Center or Forks Outfitters. No fires from Yellow Banks to Cape Alava. Dogs prohibited north of Ellen Creek; **Special features:** Wilderness coast, secluded beaches; **Special concerns:** Car shuttle needed to do one-way. Some headlands can be rounded only at low tides, carry tide chart. Miles of slippery, rocky terrain; **GPS:** Rialto Beach N 47 55.242 W 124 38.282. Ozette Lake N 48 09.275 W 124 40.132

🏠 *Seventeen contiguous miles of some of the prettiest and wildest coastline and beaches in North America await you on this adventure. Pass sea stacks, natural arches, caves and coves, reefs, tide pools, cliffs, and silver strands of spectacular sandy beaches. Watch seals, scout for whales, listen to pool-probing oystercatchers and snag-sitting eagles add their own notes to the pounding surf. And visit two shipwreck memorials where voices in the wind speak of those who perished along this remarkable stretch of sea.*

GETTING THERE

For southern access at Rialto Beach: From Port Angeles, follow US 101 west for 55 miles to the junction with State Route 110 (signed "Mora–La Push"), located 2 miles north of Forks. Drive west on SR 110. In 7.7 miles, at Quillayute Prairie, SR 110 splits. Take the right fork (Mora Road) and proceed 5 miles to road's end and trailhead. Privy available. For northern access at Ozette: From Port Angeles, follow US 101 west for 5 miles to SR 112. Follow SR 112 west for 48.5 miles, turning left (2.5 miles beyond Seiku) onto Hoko-Ozette Road. Continue for 21 miles to the Ozette Ranger Station, car campground, and trailhead (elev. 100 ft). Privy available.

ON THE TRAIL

Beginning at popular Rialto Beach, share this classic coastline with beachcombers, dog walkers (allowed on-leash to Ellen Creek), and scores of Twihards from across the country. Like most of the sandy stretches on this hike, the going is easy during low tide and slow and cumbersome during high. Admire the huge driftwood logs lining the beach, but never climb upon them during high tides. A wave can easily jostle them loose, trapping and endangering you.

At 1 mile, come to Ellen Creek, where campsites can be found. The creek, like most along the coast, has a rusty appearance due to tannins in it—it is perfectly safe for drinking (provided you filter or treat it). Pass a couple of "shark teeth" sea stacks before coming to Hole-in-the-Wall, a natural arch at 1.7 miles. During low tides, strut right through it—otherwise take the steep and short trail over a bluff (elev. 70 ft) around it.

Pass a small cove and beach, with busy campsites tucked among salty spruces. Plenty of deer (cute) and raccoons (pesky) provide company. The going gets rockier as the way rounds two small headlands only negotiable during low and medium tides. High-top boots and trekking poles help keep you from slipping. Offshore reefs, sea stacks, and Dahdayla Island provide a dramatic backdrop.

Deserted Kayostla Beach

Enter a quiet, protected, island-dotted cove with good views north to prominent Cape Johnson. Clamber over or around a tangled mess of logs and rocks, compliments of a recent slide, before, at 4.2 miles, passing the small Chilean Memorial tucked on a bluff in the trees. In November 1920, the Schooner *WJ Pirrie*, while being towed, was cast aside in a storm. The vessel broke in half and all but two of the crew of twenty perished. The storm victims were buried in a common grave near the memorial. Campsites are nearby—sleep peacefully if you can!

Next, round Cape Johnson along ledges and rock and beneath cliffs—doable only during a low tide. Immediately offshore is a mini

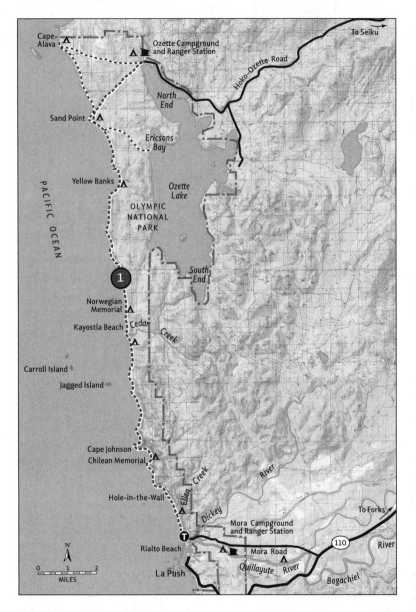

To Seiku

Cape
Alava

Ozette Campground
and Ranger Station

Hoko-Ozette Road

North
End

Sand Point

Ericsons
Bay

Ozette
Lake

Yellow Banks

PACIFIC OCEAN

OLYMPIC
NATIONAL
PARK

South
End

1

Norwegian
Memorial

Cedar Creek

Kayostla Beach

Carroll Island

Jagged Island

Cape Johnson
Chilean Memorial

River

Hole-in-the-Wall

Ellen Creek

To Forks

Dickey

Mora Campground
and Ranger Station

N

Rialto Beach

Mora Road

110

River

0   1   2

MILES

La Push

Quillayute River

Bogachiel

Hole-in-the-Wall, a flattop island and a sea stack shaped like praying hands. In a receding tide, oystercatchers probe for delicious morsels, piercing the air with their high-pitched calls.

Pass a small cobbled stone beach before rounding yet another headland (only passable at low and medium tides), and then come to a tough, slow-going section of rocks and jumbled boulders. Finally, at 6 miles, reach a section of smooth and easy beach. Pass good creeks for drinking water, buoy-filled trees, but no camps.

At 7 miles, climb steeply (use the rope) over a small "pass" (elev. 40 ft) near a prominent headland that can't be rounded. Survey a spectacular beach now spread out below. On hard-packed sand, enjoy the walk, passing "mountainous" headlands and flowerpot sea stacks along the way—creeks and campsites too.

At 8 miles is another headland that can't be rounded during high tides. A trail (with a sand ladder) leads up and over this bluff that was used during World War II as a lookout.

The view is amazing. Continue on more good beaches interspersed with rocky sections, coming to a creek at 8.5 miles. Snoop around the creek's north bank for rusting debris left behind from the old Starbuch Mining operation. Just beyond is Cedar Creek (decent water) and good camps.

Continue north, rounding a headland at low tide (using the overland trail at high), and arrive at the wide, attractive sandy expanse of Kayostla Beach at 10 miles. There are excellent camps from just north of a small creek to the Norwegian Memorial, site of the *Prince Arthur* shipwreck in 1903 in which eighteen mostly young Norwegian apprentices perished. They were buried in a mass grave at the memorial.

The Norwegian Memorial makes for a good out-and-back trip from Rialto if a car shuttle couldn't be arranged—or, if you don't care to hike the next section north, which is one of the roughest stretches of the Olympic Coast.

If continuing, take note: There are no places to camp between Kayostla and Yellow

COASTING TO THE COAST: WILDERNESS THROUGH THE BACKDOOR

You're standing on a gorgeous remote Olympic Coast beach after trudging over 10 miles of slippery rocks, soft sand, and rugged headlands—you waited patiently for low tides to safely proceed, and now you have this wilderness beach all to yourself. Well, not exactly. Suddenly some folks appear out of nowhere, sweat-free and looking like they didn't expend much energy to get here. Because they didn't! They took a secret shortcut trail (thanks to the Internet, not that secret). By driving a maze of logging roads and then following a bootleg path a mere mile or so, they attained what you worked all day for.

I prefer my wilderness beach to feel like a wilderness beach. Shortcut trails diminish its wilderness characteristics and make it easier for less than environmentally friendly things to occur—such as large groups and partying. I understand that many folks can no longer backpack great distances, so getting to this beach would have been impossible for them the "right" way. And I have friends and acquaintances living in coastal communities who cherish these secret trails, and they respect these beaches and treat them well. These trails allow them quick access to the natural beauty in their backyards. But national parks belong to all Americans, and there are plenty of easily reached beaches within Olympic National Park. Olympic National Park's wilderness coast is the wildest in the continental United States. But shortcut trails seem to somewhat diminish that wildness.

Banks, nor are there any water sources; and from Yellow Banks northward to Cape Alava, campsite reservations are required and fires are not permitted. The initial 4 miles beyond the Norwegian Memorial are extremely rough, with wet, slippery kelp-draped and barnacle-encrusted rocks and ledges and slimy downed trees that can only be negotiated during low tides. Hiking here is tiring and cumbersome and requires your full attention, lest you slip.

Tide pools are abundant and so are crabs, millions of them that seem to appear from every exposed rock and pile of kelp. Offshore rocks and sea stacks are missing from this section, making the ocean feel that much closer. At about 12 miles, pass an arch hidden in the cliffs. At about 14 miles, the walking gets easier as cobbles and then sand begin to replace jumbled rocks.

At 14.6 miles, reach a creek emptying into a crescent-shaped sandy beach flanked by big Sitka spruce beneath the Yellow Banks bluffs. Popular camps can be found 0.2 mile farther, just north of the creek.

Continuing north, clamber over a headland negotiable only during low and medium tides. Look to the right for a small tunnel passage, or round ledges on your left. Then emerge on one of the longest, widest, sandiest stretches of beach on the Olympic Coast. Farther north along the beach, where the bluffs subside, find plenty of campsites—water is plentiful, and so are campers, most of whom come in from Ozette Lake.

At 16.7 miles, pass the Ericsons Bay Trail, which leads 2 miles east to Ozette Lake. At 17.3 miles, come to the Sand Point Trail just shy of prominent Sand Point, where busy campsites and a backcountry privy can be found among salty windblown spruce and shoulder-high salal.

Leave the surf for turf and take the Sand Point Trail across boardwalks, through saturated cedar groves. Gain 150 feet and arrive at the Ozette Lake trailhead, ranger station, and car campground in 2.9 miles.

TRIP PLANNER	
4.2 miles	Chilean Memorial camps
8.7 miles	Cedar Creek camps
10 miles	Kayostla Beach camps
14.8 miles	Yellow Banks camps
17.3 miles	Sand Point camps
20.2 miles	Ozette Lake trailhead

EXTENDING YOUR TRIP

Continue north along the coast 3 more miles to Cape Alava and return via the Cape Alava Trail. There are plenty of campsites at the cape (reservations required). Good beaches and easy walking can be enjoyed for another 1.5 miles north. Beyond that, to Shi Shi Beach, the way gets rough again, headlands passable at low tide only, rough overland trails, and a potentially difficult ford of the Ozette River. And you'll need to pay to park at a private residence if you plan on leaving a vehicle at the Shi Shi end of the trip.

2 Olympic Coast South: The Wildcatter Coast

RATING/ DIFFICULTY	ONE-WAY	ELEV GAIN/ HIGH POINT	SEASON
****/5	17.5 miles	1900 feet/ 360 feet	Year-round

Maps: Green Trails La Push No. 163S, Custom Correct South Olympic Coast; **Contact:** Olympic National Park, Wilderness Information Center, Port Angeles, (360) 565-3100, www.nps.gov/olym; **Permits/regulations:** Olympic NP wilderness camping permit required. Bear canister required, can be borrowed from Wilderness Information Center or Forks Outfitters. Dogs prohibited; **Special features:** Wilderness coast, secluded beaches; **Special concerns:** Car shuttle required. Car break-ins are a problem at the northern

Hoh Head in the distance

trailhead. Some headlands can be rounded only at low tides, carry tide chart. Steep sand ladders up and down headlands. Potentially dangerous creek fords; **GPS:** Oil City N 47 44.956 W 124 25.140. Third Beach N 47 53.436 W 124 35.950

🏠 *Shorter but rougher than the northern coast route, the Wildcatter Coast consists of daunting headlands, saturated forest, secluded coves, sprawling tide pools, magical beaches, and the shattered dreams of oil men and realtors who had hoped to exploit this rugged beauty. But now you can extol it! Marvel at roving shorebirds harvesting the surf, and investigate crusty rocks decorated in purple and orange by colonies of starfish. Not least, experience amazing sunsets— a fire-red sun extinguished by a furious ocean and glowing amid jagged sea stacks and bulky guano-stained bird-incubating islands.*

GETTING THERE

For the southern trailhead: From Forks, travel south on US 101 for 15 miles, turning right onto Oil City Road (the turnoff is 1.3 miles south of the Upper Hoh Road junction). Proceed for 10.6 miles (the pavement ends at 5.2 miles) to the road's end and trailhead. Privy available. For the northern trailhead: From Port Angeles, follow US 101 west for 55 miles to the junction with State Route 110 (signed "Mora–La Push"), located 2 miles north of Forks. Proceed west on SR 110, bearing left at 7.7 miles onto La Push Road at Quillayute Prairie. Continue 3.8 miles to the Third Beach trailhead. Privy available.

ON THE TRAIL

It's best to do this route from south to north, timing your route around the initial headland with the tide, getting the hardest part of the hike—the trudge over Hoh Head—done first. If a car shuttle can't be arranged, a nice option is to start from the north and hike to Toleak Point and back.

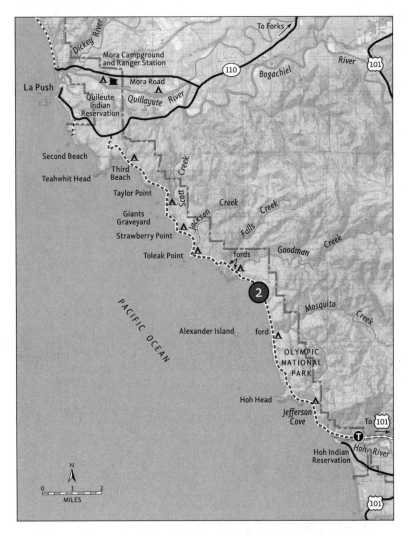

From the south, start in a forest of big cedars and hemlocks and follow the remnants of an old road, leaving Oil City, which was platted, with parcels sold to speculators, but never developed. Soon come along the Hoh River, and after 0.6 mile the trail ends on its rocky banks. Now walk toward the coast under the watchful eye of eagles perched above in riverside snags. Except for an abandoned house across the river, the surroundings are wild and ethereal. Abbey Island floats above the mist to the south, while

Destruction Island hovers above the surf farther out to sea.

Now turn north and immediately round imposing cliffs littered with jumbled rocks at their base—passable only at low tides. After clambering over some big boulders and stopping to admire the symmetry of scattered sea stacks, reach Jefferson Cove and its nice beach (with camps and a water source). At 2.7 miles, the *fun* begins with an insanely steep climb via muddy, slippery, and unnerving cables and sand ladders up over massive bulky Hoh Head. Consider bringing work gloves for gripping the cruddy ropes and cables. Take your time and concentrate; the going is tough and in rain can be downright hazardous.

At 2.9 miles, pass a wooded waterless campsite (elev. 175 ft) high above the pounding surf. Continue climbing through a lush forest of spruce and hemlock. Wren song replaces surf ballads. The way is muddy and slippery in places and can be slow going. At 3 miles, pass more good campsites, but these are waterless (elev. 315 ft). Continue on sometimes good tread, sometimes brushy walking to a 350-foot high point. Then descend, passing window views out to the sea and reaching a creek (elev. 180 ft) at about 3.8 miles. Shortly beyond, a very rough trail used to branch off left, dropping steeply for an extreme-low-tide-only sea level route. The path washed out—so continue on the main muddy thoroughfare, climbing again (elev. 225 ft) and dropping again to another creek crossing (elev. 150 ft).

Once again climb (elev. 360 ft), passing some decent viewpoints out to the crashing sea and Hoh Head. At 4.9 miles, cross another creek (elev. 190 ft) on a slick bridge and negotiate a mud hole capable of swallowing entire civilizations. Then it's up again, passing big trees (elev. 260 ft), slides, and more views—a lot more ups and downs follow, too numerous to record.

At 6.3 miles, come to good camps (with a privy) on a wooded bluff with fine views out to the ocean. Mosquito Creek lies just below, providing drinking water and a terrifying ford in high tides (don't) and rainy periods (use caution)—sometimes not fordable at all. During low tides in the warmer months, however, it is often just an ankle wetter.

North of Mosquito (which harbors no more of the pest than other coastal creeks) is one of the nicest stretches of sandy beach—often deserted—on the Olympic Coast. Savor it— after what you just walked, your feet deserve this soft, sandy stretch. Pass "shark fin" sea stacks and semisubmerged rocks, starfish clinging to them. Watch pool-probing black oystercatchers and surf-riding guillemots and scoters. Admire, too, Alexander Island off in the distance—a safeguarded sanctuary for pelagic birds.

At 8.8 miles, near a huge beach-protruding rock, locate a headland trail. Feel free to still explore the coast a short distance north (at low tide), but you can't round the next headland. Following the trail off the beach, steeply climb 150 feet before dropping steeply to Goodman Creek. In winter and high tides, it may be impossible to ford—otherwise, Goodman ranges from knee-deep to an ankle splasher. Kingfishers will watch over you while you wade. Campsites can be found just upriver.

Continue on trail through spruce forest, soon coming to Falls Creek and yet another ford that may be impossible during periods of heavy rain. A pretty cascade (hence the name) tumbles just upstream. Now climb once again, passing a huge cedar (and one of the shortcut trails that diminish the wilderness experience—see "Coasting to the Coast" in this section), reaching an elevation of 270 feet before steeply descending by way of rope and a precarious sand ladder—in 2010, this ladder was missing several lower rungs, making for a very difficult and potentially injury-causing rappel.

Jostled nerves will soon be relieved at the beautiful sandy beach now spread out before you. At 11 miles, come to Toleak Point, with its showy sea stacks and offshore natural arch making it a favorite destination for many an Olympic Coast traveler. Native peoples relished the area (and still do), and astute hikers may find a midden and other evidence of their past activities here.

Busy camps on the beach can be found by Jackson Creek. Better, more private, and less exposed sites can be found on a soothing cove just north of the point and the ranger's tent site. There are good camps all the way to Strawberry Point 1 mile farther. Beyond, it's steep bluffs, fabulous tide pools, lounging seals, and spectacular views of the Giants Graveyard, a flotilla of sea stacks and islands just off the coast. Try to time this section for low tide. And a low-to-medium tide is needed to get by two small headlands just beyond (there's no overland trail).

At 13.5 miles, come to Scott Creek beneath Scott Bluff, an imposing headland with a jumble of boulders at its base. Find good camps here among tall timber. While Scott Bluff can be rounded at low tide, doing so is too rough and not advisable—take the steep overland trail instead (there's rope, but it's not an easy route either). Continue across deep sand, rounding a small headland (passable only at low tide) to a cove flanked with flowerpot-shaped stacks reminiscent of the Bay of Fundy's famed flower-pot rocks.

Now at 15.2 miles, locate the overland trail to make the long (but not nearly as bad as Hoh Head) climb over Taylor Point, which can't be rounded at all. Ascend on steps and good tread, passing several campsites before leveling off at about 270 feet. Drop steeply to cross a creek (elev. 165 ft), and consider taking the short side trip left to the top of the tall,

showy waterfall seen and admired from Third Beach (use caution).

Steeply climb once more, topping out at 275 feet before dropping steeply with the aid of sand ladders to reach Third Beach at 16.2 miles. Walk an easy 0.5 mile on this gorgeous beach along Strawberry Bay to a trail located near a stream and campsite.

You can continue beach-hiking another 0.5 mile toward Teahwhit Head if you like, looking for abandoned equipment once used by wildcatters—or head home, following the trail for 1.3 miles and climbing 300 feet in the process to the trailhead, completing your adventure.

TRIP PLANNER	
2.5 miles	Jefferson Cove camps
6.3 miles	Mosquito Creek camps
11 miles	Toleak Point camps
13.5 miles	Scott Creek camps
16.2 miles	Third Beach camps
17.5 miles	Third Beach trailhead

3 Enchanted Valley

RATING/ DIFFICULTY	ROUND-TRIP	ELEV GAIN/ HIGH POINT	SEASON
****/1	26.4 miles	1900 feet/ 2000 feet	Mar–Nov

Maps: Green Trails Mt Christie, WA–No. 166, Mt Steele WA–No. 167, Custom Correct Enchanted Valley–Skokomish; **Contact:** Olympic National Park, Wilderness Information Center, Port Angeles, (360) 565-3100, www.nps.gov /olym; **Permits/regulations:** Olympic NP wilderness camping permit required. Dogs prohibited; **Special features:** Magnificent old growth. Wilderness valley flanked by steep cliffs and waterfalls. Bears and elk. Early and late-season backpacking; **Special concerns:** Bears abundant in valley. Graves Creek Road subject to temporary closure during winter months, call the park before setting out; **GPS:** N 47 34.368 W 123 34.193

🚶 ⚙ 🏠 *Enchanting? Dearly! Follow the East Fork Quinault River through ancient and towering cathedral rain forest to a deep open valley in the heart of the Olympics, where waterfalls plunge down sheer walls and turn to hanging ice in winter. Watch for harlequin ducks riding river rapids and elk and bears foraging the forest floor. Explore cascades, river flats, maple glades, spruce groves, a thundering chasm, and a historical chalet. This trip is an Olympics classic—the Enchanted Valley's low elevation allows exploring late and early season, adding to its popularity.*

GETTING THERE

From Hoquiam, travel north on US 101 for 38 miles, turning right (1 mile south of Amanda Park) onto South Shore Lake Quinault Road. Pass the ranger station (permits available) in 2.2 miles, the pavement ends at 7.9 miles, and come to a junction at the Quinault River Bridge at 13 miles. Continue to the right, now on Graves Creek Road, for 6.2 miles to the road's end and trailhead (elev. 600 ft). Privy available.

ON THE TRAIL

Start by crossing Graves Creek on a large wood-plank bridge and come to a junction in 0.2 mile. The trail right leads 7.3 miles to Lake Sundown, a quieter but more difficult to reach destination. Head straight on a wide and well-graded trail that once served as a road. Under big timber, the trail steadily climbs a small rise (elev. 1150 ft). At 2 miles, the way descends and the old road transitions to bona fide trail. At 2.5 miles, come to the Pony Bridge (elev. 900 ft) spanning the East Fork Quinault, which roars through a fern-ringed

Historical chalet in Enchanted Valley

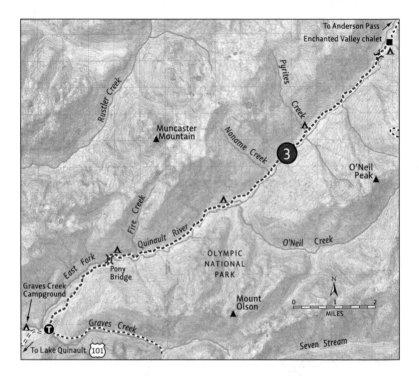

tight chasm. A couple of nice campsites can be found just past the bridge.

Day hikers usually call it quits here. The trail climbs again and then drops, a pattern repeated frequently along the way. Skirting high above the thundering chasm, cross several cascading tributaries. Water runs over and down the trail almost the entire distance. Well over 120 inches of rain saturate this valley. The air is heavy with moisture. Mosses cling to and drape everything—keep moving or you may begin to sport a green beard!

Imagine how difficult this terrain must have been to traverse in 1890 when Lieutenant O'Neil and his men came this way after starting from the Skokomish Valley near Hood Canal. O'Neil was one of the first people to call

for an Olympic National Park. He got to see his dream come true when President Franklin D. Roosevelt established the park in 1938, just weeks before O'Neil passed away.

Pass a nice riverside camp in a maple flat along the river before coming to Fire Creek, crossed by a foot log. Just beyond, more good riverside camps can be found among big Sitka spruce trees. Negotiate lots of wet and muddy sections of trail as you progress farther up the valley. Beyond some monster hemlocks is a nice gravel bar—perfect for watching dippers and embracing sunshine when it's available.

At 6.7 miles, reach a junction with a spur leading 0.25 mile to campsites across from O'Neil Creek (the creek flows into the East Fork Quinault from the opposite bank). Set in a flat along the river, the camp is equipped with bear wire and a privy.

Now halfway to the Enchanted Valley, carry on traversing gorgeous maple flats. Negotiate a crossing of Noname Creek on a steady foot log and then return to the riverside (and more camps) under a canopy of giant trees. The way then winds through a pasturelike environment, where there's a good possibility of sighting bear and elk.

At 9.8 miles, arrive at Pyrites Creek (elev. 1450 ft) with its excellent dispersed campsites (bear wire, no privy). Less crowded than the Enchanted Valley and offering more protection from the weather, Pyrites makes for a nice base camp from which to explore the valley.

From here the trail gains elevation more steadily, passing a humongous toppled cedar, maple glades, Lamata Creek and its gravel outwashes, and more open, pasturelike forest where you're almost guaranteed to see bears. After passing through an old fence, you'll crest, in essence, a small terminal moraine left by a long-ago receded glacier. Then at 12.7 miles come to a high, narrow bridge—unnerving to some—that replaced the old suspension model, spanning the East Fork Quinault in yet another chasm.

Now, cross some outwash areas and emerge at 13.2 miles at an old chalet at the head of the Enchanted Valley (elev. 2000 ft). The scenery is stunning, dominated by a channeled river flowing through meadows and cottonwood groves beneath sheer cliffs 3000 feet high streaked with waterfalls and, in winter, hanging snow and ice. This gem is also known as the Valley of 1000 Waterfalls, and the hyperbole is justified.

The chalet was opened in 1930 and provided shelter and meals to hikers and horseback riders until 1943. It was used during World War II by Aircraft Warning Service personnel and then became a hiker shelter

until 1980. Today it's used by backcountry rangers and for emergency shelter.

For your overnight options, there are excellent campsites (with privy and bear wire) in the surrounding meadows and several more about 0.5 mile upvalley near the stock camp. These camps can get busy, so you may end up camping on the river gravel bed—not a bad option on a clear evening, with moonlight shimmering on the stark canyon walls and dancing on the plummeting waterfalls.

TRIP PLANNER	
2.5 miles	Pony Bridge camps
6.7 miles	O'Neil Creek camps
9.8 miles	Pyrites Creek camps
13.2 miles	Enchanted Valley camps

EXTENDING YOUR TRIP
Continue up the Enchanted Valley for 2 more miles to a spur to the world's largest recorded western hemlock. Then head 1.2 miles farther to a junction, where it's 1.7 miles left to Anderson Pass (Trip 8) or 8.6 miles right to O'Neil Pass and Marmot Lake (Trip 10).

4 High Divide

RATING/ DIFFICULTY	LOOP	ELEV GAIN/ HIGH POINT	SEASON
*****/3	20.5 miles	4175 feet/ 5474 feet	late July–Oct

Maps: Green Trails Seven Lakes Basin/Mt Olympus Climbing, WA–No. 133S, Custom Correct Seven Lakes Basin–Hoh; **Contact:** Olympic National Park, Wilderness Information Center, Port Angeles, (360) 565-3100, www.nps.gov/olym; **Permits/regulations:** National park entrance fee. Olympic NP wilderness camping permit required. Permits limited, reservations recommended. Bear canister required, can be borrowed from Wilderness Information Center. No fires above 3500 feet. Dogs prohibited; **Special features:** Stunning

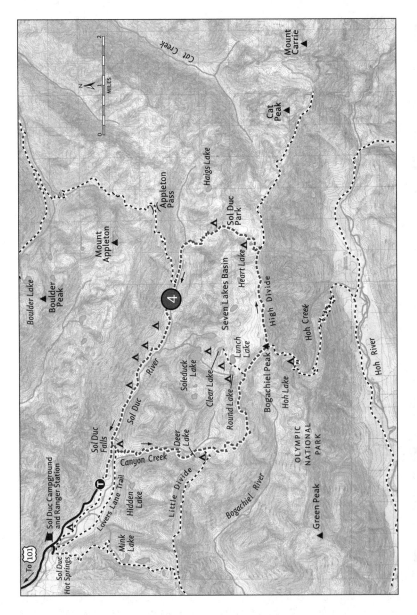

views of Mount Olympus and Hoh River valley from a lofty ridge exploding with wildflowers. Magnificent old growth. Wildlife-rich sub-alpine lake basin; **Special concerns:** Bears abundant. Snowfields can linger well into August, making travel potentially difficult and dangerous; **GPS:** N 47 57.310 W 123 50.103

👫 ⚙ *A classic loop to one of the most famed places within the nearly one-million-acre Olympic National Park—this hike has it all. Sparkling alpine lakes, resplendent alpine meadows, breathtaking views, abundant wildlife, primeval forest, inspiring waterfalls—and crowds. Backpackers come from near and far to experience this lofty ridge teetering high above the lush emerald Hoh Rain Forest and within the shadows of glacier-cloaked Mount Olympus, the highest and snowiest summit on the Olympic Peninsula.*

GETTING THERE
From Port Angeles, follow US 101 west for 29 miles, turning left onto Sol Duc Hot Springs Road (the turnoff is about 2 miles past the Fairholm Store). (From Forks, head east 28 miles, turning right onto Sol Duc Hot Springs Road.) Drive 14 miles, passing the entrance station early on, to the road's end at a large trailhead parking lot (elev. 2000 ft). Privy available.

ON THE TRAIL
Start on the Sol Duc Trail. At 0.2 mile bear left with a trail coming in from the Sol Duc car campground. After another 0.6 mile of nearly level hiking through spectacular old-growth forest, come to a junction. You'll be returning on the trail straight ahead. So head right here, and cross the Sol Duc River on a bridge spanning a chasm above gorgeous Sol Duc Falls. One of the most photographed cascades in the state, enjoy its

two- or four-segmented plunge (depending on the water level).

Nearby is a backcountry camping area, a good option if starting late. Just beyond the campsites, the trail bears left at a junction with the Lovers Lane Trail, where most day hikers lovelorn or not will probably depart. Now on a steep, sometimes rocky path, work your way up a dark ravine housing Canyon Creek. At 1.7 miles, cross high above the tumbling waterway on a wide and sturdy bridge. After another 0.5 mile the grade eases somewhat. En route pass three backcountry campsites offering respite if daylight or energy runs out.

After another upward push, cross Canyon Creek once more and emerge at placid Deer Lake (elev. 3550 ft) at 3.7 miles. Nestled in a forested and grassy bowl, the lake's waters reflect a soft green. Surrounded by yellow cedar, mountain hemlock, silver fir, and a thick understory of huckleberries, it's a pretty and serene spot. Deer, frogs, and mosquitoes are all common here. Good camps and a backcountry ranger station can also be found at the lake.

Near the lake's inlet, bear left at a junction for the High Divide; right goes to the Little Divide. Winding through heather fields, subalpine forest, and by a dozen pothole tarns (a.k.a. mosquito incubators), the trail works its way up to a high ridge dividing the Sol Duc and Bogachiel watersheds. Undulating between groves of mountain hemlock and open meadows, the trail continues to climb. Far-reaching views across rainforest valleys all the way to the Pacific can now be had.

The trail soon rounds the ridge crest working its way around a high isolated basin, headwaters of the Bogachiel River. Mount Olympus peeks its icy head over the next ridge. In September, bugling elk from down below can often be heard. And it's not rare to run into berry-munching bears from here on, so be aware.

Mount Olympus above the Hoh River Valley

At 7 miles, drop slightly into a big rocky depression and reach a junction (elev. 4900 ft) with a 1-mile trail that descends 500 feet to Seven Lakes Basin. A mandatory side trip, the Seven Lakes Basin is one of the most stunning places within the Olympic Mountains. A high basin recently scoured by glaciers, its meadows and rocky knolls surround a series of sparkling tarns. Good campsites can be found near Round, Lunch, and Clear lakes. Way paths lead to all the other lakes, where more camping options can be had. You can easily spend a week exploring the area.

For the High Divide, continue to the right across steep open slopes, angling beneath Bogachiel Peak. Snow often persists here well into summer, making it potentially dangerous to proceed. After a series of tight switchbacks, reach the ridge crest (elev. 5100 ft) and a junction at 7.9 miles from the trailhead (9.9 miles with out and back to Seven Lakes Basin). Right leads 1.2 miles to a big basin cradling Hoh Lake (elev. 4700 ft), where excellent camping and views can be had. Your loop leads left, soon coming to a short side trail to Bogachiel Peak.

From this 5474-foot former lookout site as well as from much of the High Divide that lies ahead, soak up views that are beyond breathtaking. The alpine jewels of the Seven Lakes Basin shimmer below. The snow-capped Bailey Range marches off into the eastern horizon. The emerald swath of the Hoh Rain Forest spreads out nearly one vertical mile below. And rising above it all, staring you right in the face, is Mount Olympus. Its glaciers and snowfields are blinding on a sunny summer day.

Continue east on the divide, with steep timbered slopes to the south and gentle meadowed slopes to the north. The way drops a couple hundred feet, regains them, and then loses them again. You probably won't notice it, though, being focused on the dazzling flowers (summer) or bountiful berries (fall) before

you. Watch for elk and bear too, especially in late summer—their numbers are often profuse here.

At 10 miles from the trailhead (12 miles with basin side trip), reach a junction (elev. 5050 ft). The Cat Basin Primitive Trail goes straight, the Sol Duc River Trail left. Head left, descending into a beautiful open basin harboring Heart Lake (elev. 4700 ft) and excellent camps. The way continues through glorious meadows, gently descending 1.2 miles to the flower gardens, berry patches, and good camps of Sol Duc Park (elev. 4200 ft) nestled in a hanging valley with excellent views to Mount Appleton north.

Now following Bridge Creek, the trail drops into the forested Sol Duc Valley, crossing the river on a sturdy bridge and reaching a junction (elev. 3100 ft) at 13.7 miles (15.7 miles with basin). The trail right climbs steeply to Appleton Pass. You want to continue left along the Sol Duc River through grove upon grove of magnificent old and towering Doug-firs and hemlocks. Four distinct camping areas along the way entice you to spend one more night out. At 17.7 miles (19.7 with basin), return to a familiar junction at Sol Duc Falls (elev. 2000 ft). Your vehicle waits for you 0.8 mile straight ahead.

TRIP PLANNER	
1 mile	Sol Duc Falls camps
3.7 miles	Deer Lake
8 miles	Lunch Lake camps
12.5 miles	Heart Lake camps
16.5 miles	Sol Duc River camps
20.5 miles	Trailhead

EXTENDING YOUR TRIP

From a base at Heart Lake, set off on the Cat Basin Primitive Trail, a ridge-running, view-granting route to the Bailey Range. The trail can easily and safely be followed for nearly 3 miles before it becomes a climbers track.

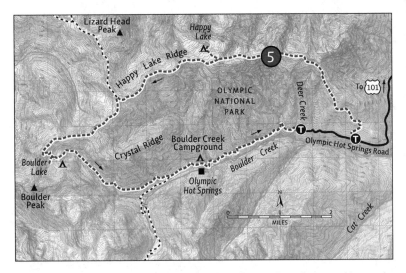

RATING/ DIFFICULTY	LOOP	ELEV GAIN/ HIGH POINT	SEASON
***/3	18 miles	4400 feet/ 5280 feet	late June– Oct

Maps: Green Trails Seven Lakes Basin/Mt Olympus No. 133S, Custom Correct Lake Crescent–Happy Lake Ridge; **Contact:** Olympic National Park, Wilderness Information Center, Port Angeles, (360) 565-3100, www.nps.gov /olym; **Permits/regulations:** National park entrance fee. Olympic NP wilderness camping permit required. Bear canister required at Happy Lake, can be borrowed from Wilderness Information Center. No fires above 3500 feet. Dogs prohibited; **Special features:** Alpine lakes, hot springs, solitude; **Special concerns:** Short road walk; **GPS:** N 47 59.005 W 123 37.540

This loop ties together two backcountry lakes: one popular, one quiet and remote. En route you'll travel through a popular valley graced by a rushing creek, cool plunge pools, hot springs, and big trees. And you'll traverse a lonesome high ridge that weaves through heather parklands and sun-kissed meadows offering spectacular views of peaks near and far. This trip offers a lot of contrasts, tying together one of the busiest and one of the quietest trails within Olympic National Park.

GETTING THERE

From Port Angeles, follow US 101 west for 9 miles. At milepost 240, before the Elwha River Bridge, turn left onto Olympic Hot Springs Road (signed "Elwha Valley"). Follow this paved road for 10 miles, passing the park entrance station and the Elwha Ranger Station, reaching the trailhead at the road's end (elev. 1800 ft). Privy available.

ON THE TRAIL

This loop can be done in either direction. I prefer counterclockwise for the following advantages: the road walk gets done first, the steep section is ascended (saving your knees), you get to camp at Happy Lake (for solitude), and the hot springs are on the way out (for an end-of-trip soak). Start your trip by walking back down the Olympic Hot Springs Road for an easy 1.3 shaded miles to the trailhead for Happy Lake Ridge (elev. 1700 ft).

Waste no time gaining elevation, and a lot of it too. In 0.25 mile you'll near a small creek, the last reliable water until the lake. Be sure water bottles are full. The trail winds its way up Happy Lake Ridge for almost 3 miles of unrelenting climbing. Relief is in sight upon reaching the ridge crest (elev. 4500 ft)—the way eases, the hard part over. At 4.8 miles, come upon a stunning viewpoint looking out to Mount Appleton, Hurricane Ridge, Mount Angeles, and the deep Elwha Valley.

Continue west, traversing subalpine forest and heather parkland, and reach the loop's high point (elev. 5280 ft) and the side trail for Happy Lake at 5.8 miles. Consider walking up one of the adjacent knolls for excellent views, otherwise head down the Happy Lake Trail, which takes off right.

Descend 400 feet and 0.5 mile through lovely subalpine country to the jovial tarn (supposedly named by three pioneer bachelors). Situated in a small cirque, the grassy-shored lake is a happy sight. But hungry mosquitoes may take some of the bliss away. Set up camp in one of the established sites, or hike a 0.5 mile back to the ridge to continue the loop. Fill water bottles, for after snowmelt the next 5 miles are dry.

The ridge trail continues west, gently descending through heavenly huckleberry flats, cool mountain hemlock groves, and delightful flower-dotted meadows. Views are excellent—north to Pyramid Mountain, Mount Muller, and all the way out to Pillar Point on the Strait of Juan de Fuca; south to Mount Olympus, the Elwha Valley, and the majestic Bailey Range.

Happy Lake

After reaching a 4600-foot low point, the trail makes a steep climb up a small knoll and reaches a junction with the Aurora Divide Trail (elev. 4950 ft), about 2.5 miles west of the Happy Lake Trail junction. This lightly used path travels north to Aurora Ridge and Barnes Creek and guarantees solitude for all who take to it.

For Boulder Lake, continue left, gaining and losing little elevation along the high ridge. Enjoy more delightful meadows and excellent viewing. About 1 mile from the previous junction, locate faint tread—the abandoned Crystal Ridge Trail heading left. The main trail passes a shallow tarn before making a short climb to a small knoll (elev. 4900 ft) offering a commanding view of Boulder Peak, with Boulder Lake shimmering below.

Now steeply drop 500 feet, reaching the short spur to Boulder Lake. Cross marshy meadows and reach the lake, perched in a

semi-open bowl at the base of 5600-foot Boulder Peak. Inviting shoreline ledges make perfect napping and lunch spots. Excellent developed campsites grace the basin. Don't expect to be alone, though.

From Boulder Lake, follow the Boulder Lake Trail downhill through gorgeous old-growth timber, reaching a junction with the Boulder Creek Trail at 2.9 miles from the lake (elev. 2300 ft). Head left, soon coming to busy Boulder Creek Campground (along the trail, not a car campground) and the spur trail to the even busier Olympic Hot Springs. Find a soaker pool for your aching legs, or continue hiking down the Boulder Creek Trail 2.3 miles back to the trailhead to close the loop. This final section is on recently converted road-to-trail. Enjoy a nice walk back to the trailhead on what used to be a pavement pounder.

TRIP PLANNER	
6.3 miles	Happy Lake camps
12 miles	Boulder Lake camps
15.7 miles	Boulder Creek Campground
18 miles	Trailhead

6 Press Expedition Traverse: Elwha to North Fork Quinault

RATING/ DIFFICULTY	ONE-WAY	ELEV GAIN/ HIGH POINT	SEASON
***/3	44.5 miles	3500 feet/ 3660 feet	June–Oct

Maps: Green Trails Hurricane Ridge/Elwha North No. 133S, Mount Steel No. 167, Mount Christie No. 166, Custom Correct Elwha Valley, Custom Correct Quinault–Colonel Bob; **Contact:** Olympic National Park, Wilderness Information Center, Port Angeles, (360) 565-3100, www.nps.gov/olym; **Permits/regulations:** National park entrance fee. Olympic NP wilderness camping permit required.

Dogs prohibited; **Special features:** Historic Press Party route across Olympics from Elwha River to the North Fork Quinault. Fly fishing in early spring and late fall; **Special concerns:** Long car shuttle required. River fords can be difficult and dangerous in high water; **GPS:** Northern trailhead N 47 58.055 W 123 34.941. Southern trailhead N 47 34.542 W 123 38.889

Hike across the Olympic Peninsula into the heart of the park, retracing the route of the famed 1889–90 Press Expedition, a group of hardy souls commissioned by the Seattle Press newspaper who became the first humans to cross the Olympic Mountains. The Press Party— with their four dogs, two mules, and 1500 pounds of gear—took six months to make the journey, but you should be able to comfortably traverse the Olympics in four to six days. Enjoy splendid river scenery, lush rain forest, historical cabins and relics, and perhaps a side trip or two to some hidden wonders.

GETTING THERE

For the northern trailhead (Elwha): From Port Angeles, follow US 101 west for 9 miles, turning left at milepost 240 (before the Elwha River Bridge), onto Olympic Hot Springs Road (signed "Elwha Valley"). Continue for 4 miles, passing the park entrance booth and Elwha Ranger Station, and turn left onto Whiskey Bend Road. Follow this narrow, gravel road 4.5 miles to its end at the trailhead (elev. 1200 ft). Privy available. For the southern trailhead (North Fork Quinault): From Hoquiam, travel north on US 101 for 38 miles, turning right (1 mile south of Amanda Park) onto South Shore Lake Quinault Road. Pass the ranger station (permits available) in 2.2 miles, the pavement ends at 7.9 miles, and come to a junction at the Quinault River Bridge at 13 miles. Turn left and cross the bridge and

Historical Remanns cabin along the Elwha River

then immediately turn right onto the North Fork Road, proceeding 3.5 miles to the road's end and trailhead (elev. 520 ft). Privy available.

ON THE TRAIL

While the complete Press Party traverse is long and requires a car shuttle, any distance out and back from either direction makes for a good shorter trip. And the northern 15 miles or so can often be hiked year-round.

The trail starts high above the Elwha River, bypassing narrow Rica Canyon. Pass the Elk Overlook, with its grand view over river bottoms sporting wintering elk. At 1.2 miles pass the Goblin's Gate Trail, which drops steeply to Geyser Valley—a good side trip. At 1.7 miles, pass the Krause Bottom Trail, which also drops to Geyser Valley. Continue left, coming to Michaels Cabin (elev. 1200 ft), a 1906 homestead at 2.3 miles, once occupied by a

predator hunter nicknamed Cougar Mike. The resident wildcats have rebounded nicely since Michael's departure.

Here a trail departs to the right for camps and the prepark Humes Ranch and then beyond to Dodger Point and its historical lookout. You want to continue left, climbing well away from the river, now flowing through its Grand Canyon. Between Antelope and Idaho Creeks, look for a handful of old trees bearing original ax blazes from the Press Expedition. Through stands of second-growth forest teeming with an understory of salal, reach a junction with the Lillian River Trail (elev. 1600 ft) at 4.4 miles.

That lonely trail heads left and dead-ends in 3 miles (good side strip for solitude). You want to continue right, steeply dropping 300 feet to dark forested camps along the Lillian River at 4.9 miles. The way then climbs

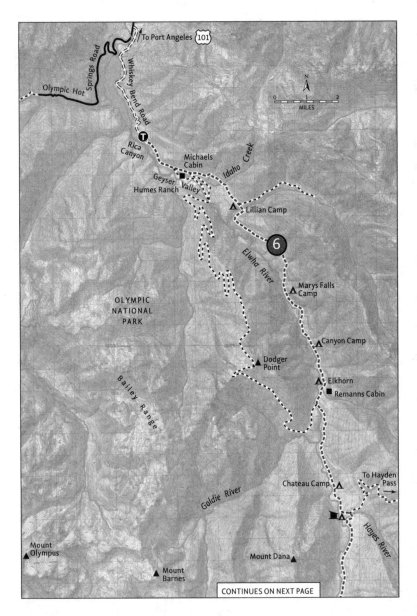

To Port Angeles 101

Olympic Hot Springs Road

Whiskey Bend Road

Rica Canyon

T

Michaels Cabin

Idaho Creek

Geyser Valley

Humes Ranch

Lillian Camp

6

Elwha River

Marys Falls Camp

OLYMPIC NATIONAL PARK

Canyon Camp

Dodger Point

Elkhorn

Remanns Cabin

Bailey Range

Goldie River

Chateau Camp

To Hayden Pass

Hayes River

Mount Olympus

Mount Dana

Mount Barnes

N

0   1   2
MILES

CONTINUES ON NEXT PAGE

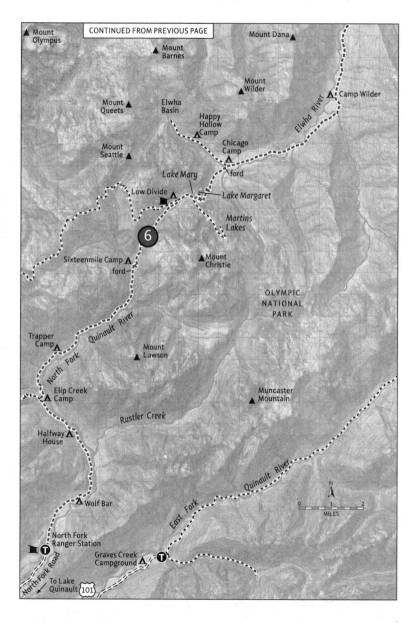

once again along forested slopes away from the Elwha to an elevation of 2000 feet. Then slowly descending, it reaches the river and Marys Falls Camp (elev. 1300 ft) at 8.9 miles. The waterfall is across the Elwha on a tributary stream.

Now finally hugging the river, the trail embraces the Elwha, the fourth-longest river on the Olympic Peninsula, draining over 300 square miles of surrounding wilderness. At 10.5 miles a short spur leads to the right to riverside Canyon Camp (elev. 1400 ft). At 11.5 miles reach a ranger station and the popular campsites at Elkhorn (elev. 1450 ft), located on a grassy bend on the Elwha.

Continue upvalley through groves of old-growth timber and across lush river bottom-lands, reaching Remanns Cabin (elev. 1500 ft), yet another prepark structure, at 13 miles. Here, during late summer, it's possible to ford the Elwha (look for harlequin ducks while in the middle of the river) and follow a primitive trail to the Semple Plateau and then steeply to Dodger Point.

The Elwha River Trail continues deeper into the wilderness, occasionally pulling away from the river. While overall elevation gain is slight, the way makes plenty of small climbs and dips to help keep your legs loose. At 16.1 miles, reach Chateau Camp (elev. 1700 ft) on a bend in the river. At 16.7 miles, a short spur leads to the ranger station and camps at the confluence of the Hayes and Elwha rivers.

The main trail bends left to meet the Hayden Pass Trail (which heads to the Dosewallips River valley) at 17 miles. Cross the Hayes River and continue deeper into the heart of the park. At 20.7 miles, find riverside Camp Wilder (elev. 1900 ft). After crossing several large tributaries and traversing luxuriant groves of old growth, cross the Elwha (elev. 2000 ft) on a bridge at 23.7 miles, and get a feeling for its west bank for a while.

At 25.7 miles, come to Chicago Camp (elev. 2200 ft) and a junction. The Elwha River Trail continues right for 3 lonely and lightly traveled miles to the meadows of Elwha Basin (elev. 2700 ft) beneath a wall of snow-capped peaks, including Mount Barnes, whose melting snows are the source of the 45-mile-long river. Set up a base at Chicago Camp and explore this trail—otherwise, continue left on the Low Divide Trail, negotiating an oft-challenging (and sometimes downright dangerous) ford of the Elwha.

Once across, begin the trip's only real climb, gaining 1400 feet in just over 2 miles to reach 3660-foot Low Divide at 28.2 miles. Here, among heather parklands, pass two small pools, Lakes Mary and Margaret wedged beneath steep emerald giants, 6246-foot Mount Seattle and 6177-foot Mount Christie.

Camps lie 0.3 mile ahead near a back-country ranger station. Camp here and consider exploring a 2.3-mile trail that takes off south from Lake Margaret for Martins Lakes (elev. 4700 ft), which are nestled in Martins Park beneath the glaciers of the peak named for the leader of the Press Expedition, Mount Christie.

To complete the Press Expedition traverse, continue southwest, now following the headwaters of the Quinault River. At 28.7 miles, the rough and spectacularly scenic Skyline Trail veers right. Continue left, dropping deep into luxuriant temperate rain forest and reaching Sixteenmile Camp (elev. 2000 ft) along the North Fork Quinault River at 32.3 miles.

Ford the river and come to Trapper Camp (elev. 1200 ft) at 36.3 miles. Continue across this saturated landscape, where the North Fork Quinault continues to collect water and the surrounding trees grow wider and larger. At 38 miles, just past a junction with the Elip Creek Trail (which climbs steeply to the Skyline Trail), reach Elip Creek Camp.

Ford Elip Creek (like all fords on this side of the divide, very tricky in periods of high water), and at 39.4 miles come to camps at Halfway House (elev. 800 ft) near a chasm on the river. Once the site of a lodge providing warmth and hospitality to visitors during the 1920s and '30s, the site is now quite dank.

Just beyond, negotiate a tricky ford of Wild Rose Creek and then proceed on an up and down course away from but within earshot of the North Fork Quinault. Massive Sitka spruce, gargantuan western hemlocks, and corridors of mossy maples and speckled alders grace the way. At 41.9 miles, arrive at Wolf Bar (elev. 630 ft), with its inviting camps and broad gravel bar perfect for soaking up views and sun (when it's not raining!).

The way continues for 2.6 miles on an old roadbed and over outwashes, through mossy maple flats and spruce groves, and across several side creeks and channels that during wet periods will leave your boots—well, wet! At 44.5 miles, arrive at the old North Fork Ranger Station and trail's end (elev. 520 ft). With your journey across the Olympics, now complete, breathe a sigh of relief,—back in 1890, the Press Party still had a ways to go.

TRIP PLANNER	
4.9 miles	Lillian Camp
8.9 miles	Marys Falls Camp
10.5 miles	Spur to Canyon Camp
11.5 miles	Elkhorn camps and ranger station
16.1 miles	Chateau Camp
16.7 miles	Hayes River camps and ranger station
20.7 miles	Camp Wilder
25.7 miles	Chicago Camp
28.5 miles	Low Divide camps and ranger station
32.3 miles	Sixteenmile Camp
36.3 miles	Trapper Camp
38 miles	Elip Creek Camp
39.4 miles	Halfway House camps
41.9 miles	Wolf Bar camps
44.5 miles	North Fork Quinault trailhead

7 Home Lake and Constance Pass

RATING/ DIFFICULTY	ROUND-TRIP	ELEV GAIN/ HIGH POINT	SEASON
****/4	22 miles	6300 feet/ 5950 feet	mid-July– Oct

Maps: Green Trails Tyler Peak, WA–No. 136, Custom Correct Buckhorn Wilderness; **Contact:** Olympic National Forest, Hood Canal District, Quilcene, (360) 765-2200, or Olympic National Park, Wilderness Information Center, Port Angeles, (360) 565-3100, www.nps.gov/olym; **Permits/regulations:** NW Forest Pass required. Unless in Buckhorn Wilderness, Olympic NP wilderness camping permit required. No fires above 3500 feet. Dogs permitted in Buckhorn Wilderness, prohibited in Olympic NP; **Special features:** Olympic rainshadow environment. Alpine meadows with spectacular views and remote lake beneath sheer east face of 7756-foot Mount Constance, highest summit on the Olympic eastern front; **Special concerns:** Potentially dangerous steep snowfield can linger well into summer; **GPS:** N 47 49.669, W 123 02.445

Hike to Marmot Pass, a high portal into the Olympic rain shadow, where sunbeams often kiss the flowered ground while nearby ridges swirl with clouds. Towering old-growth forest, a tumbling pristine river, resplendent alpine meadows, and a fortress of majestic snow-clad craggy spires greet you along the way. Then leave all that behind to venture into a jumbled boulder field beneath hulking Mount Constance and to a sparkling remote lake—and another high pass, this one offering jaw-dropping views into the heart of the Olympic wilderness.

GETTING THERE
From Quilcene, drive US 101 south for 1.5 miles and turn right onto Penny Creek Road.

A hiker stares out at Home Lake with Warrior Peak in the background.

(From Shelton, follow US 101 north for 48 miles and turn left.) After 1.5 miles, bear left onto Big Quilcene River Road (Forest Road 27) and follow this road for 9.3 miles, turning left onto FR 2750. Continue 4.7 miles to the trailhead (elev. 2450 ft). Privy available.

ON THE TRAIL

Following the popular Upper Big Quilcene River Trail, enter the 44,258-acre Buckhorn Wilderness, the largest roadless area within the Olympic National Forest. The trail starts off fairly easy, meandering through magnificent stands of primeval forest along the churning waters of the Big Quilcene River.

Cross several side creeks that cascade into the valley. Lack of water is not a concern along this trail—keeping your feet dry, however, might be. At 2.7 miles, reach wooded Shelter Rock Camp (elev. 3800 ft) along the river. From here the trail steeply climbs away from the river to begin traversing open avalanche chutes and scree slopes that radiate with flowers and offer good views of the rugged surroundings. At 4.8 miles, reach inviting but busy Camp Mystery (elev. 5400 ft) set in a grove of Alaska yellow cedar and subalpine fir. Take advantage of its dual springs, as water becomes scarce for the next several miles in the high country.

Beyond, the way breaks out into a meadow corridor streaked red, white, and purple and pockmarked with marmot and ground-squirrel burrows. After skirting beneath some cliffs, the trail attains a small hanging valley just below Marmot Pass. At 5.4 miles, crest the 5950-foot pass and savor one of the supreme views in the Olympics. Gaze east to Hood Canal, Puget Sound, and the Cascades. The Dungeness Valley spreads out below to the west, flanked by Mounts Mystery, Deception, and Walkinshaw—some of the highest summits in the Olympics.

From the pass, the Tubal Cain Trail veers right to climb a windswept ridge, skirting 6988-foot Buckhorn Mountain before descending into the Copper Creek valley. You want to head left instead, across wide-open slopes bursting with flowers—soak in the spectacular views south and west to a wall of craggy summits. Because of a rainshadow effect, the terrain here is dry and open, favoring lodgepole and whitebark pines. Quite different from the rest of the Olympics, the Buckhorn country resembles the east slopes of the Cascades. Look for Clark's nutcracker, a jaylike bird that feeds on pine nuts. Listen for its raucous call, a rare sound in the Olympics.

Despite the rain shadow, two steep snowfields often linger here well into summer, warranting an ice ax or a return trip later in

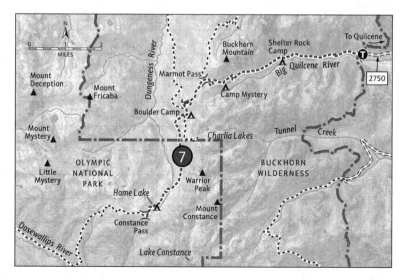

the year. Through open pine forest, the trail rapidly descends, reaching a junction with the Dungeness River Trail (elev. 4900 ft) at 7.1 miles. Continue left a short distance into an open basin of stunted trees and jumbled boulders, crossing a good creek and reaching Boulder Camp with its restored historical shelter.

For Home Lake, continue south, climbing to a forested swale and soon reaching an unmarked junction (elev. 5000 ft). The trail left leads 1 mile to a 6300-foot gap from where a steep scramble path drops 800 feet to the tiny Charlia Lakes tucked in a rugged cirque.

Continue right instead, traversing steep slopes sporting stunted trees. At 8 miles, enter Olympic National Park. If you're hiking with a dog, this is the end of the trip. From here, the lightly used path skirts steep and brushy-at-times avalanche-swept slopes and crosses several creeks, including one just beneath a cascade.

Traveling beneath the awesome towering and stark walls of 7300-foot Warrior Peak and 7756-foot Mount Constance, third-highest peak in the Olympics, the way descends and traverses a sprawling boulder and talus field. The walking is slow over the jumbled mess, not least because you'll be inclined to cock your head upward, pausing in amazement.

Upon leaving the rocky mess (elev. 4575 ft), the trail climbs again—up a forested rib bypassing permanent snowfields at the base of Constance. At 10.5 miles, reach Home Lake (elev. 5300 ft) in a small basin beneath steep flowered slopes. From its south shore, enjoy home-sweet-home views of Warrior Peak. Lightly used camps can be found on the wooded bluff above its western shore. A privy without privacy, on the verge of collapse, will pique interest if not the inspiration to use it.

Be sure to continue beyond the lake 0.5 mile, climbing steeply up heather and flower fields to 5800-foot Constance Pass. From here take in a magnificent view that includes the Brothers, Mount Anderson, Mount La Crosse, and a good portion of the wild Olympic interior.

TRIP PLANNER	
2.7 miles	Shelter Rock Camp
4.8 miles	Camp Mystery
7.2 miles	Boulder Camp
10.5 miles	Home Lake camps
11 miles	Constance Pass

EXTENDING YOUR TRIP

If transportation can be arranged, continue from the pass to Sunnybrook Meadows, climbing over 6500-foot Del Monte Ridge. Then follow the Dosewallips River Trail and currently closed-to-traffic road out. Home Lake can also be hiked via the Tubal Cain and Dungeness River trails.

8 Anderson Glacier

RATING/ DIFFICULTY	ROUND-TRIP	ELEV GAIN/ HIGH POINT	SEASON
****/3	33.2 miles	4800 feet/ 5100 feet	July–Oct

Maps: Green Trails The Brothers, WA–No. 168, Mount Steel No. 167, Custom Correct The Brothers–Mount Anderson; **Contact:** Olympic National Park, Wilderness Information Center, Port Angeles, (360) 565-3100, www.nps .gov/olym; **Permits/regulations:** Olympic NP wilderness camping permit required. No fires above 3500 feet. Dogs prohibited; **Special features:** Sprawling glacier, sparkling tarn, and alpine meadows bursting with flowers at a high pass dividing the Dosewallips and Quinault rivers; **Special concerns:** Dosewallips River Road is washed out 5.3 miles from trailhead, requiring a long road hike to reach the trail. It is possible to mountain bike to trailhead. Whether road will be repaired is yet to be determined, check with park service before setting out; **GPS:** N 47 44.190 W 123 10.130

This delightful hike takes you to the base of one of the largest glaciers in the Olympics, where you can explore moraine heaps being colonized by pioneer plants and a large sparkling lake fed by glacier meltwater. Follow alongside a chattering river through old-growth groves graced with an understory of showy Pacific rhododendrons, and traverse lush meadows donned in brilliant wildflowers on your way to the rock and ice below 7321-foot Mount Anderson.

GETTING THERE

From Quilcene, follow US 101 south 11 miles to Brinnon, turning right onto Dosewallips River Road. (From Shelton, follow US 101 north for 40 miles and turn left.) Proceed for 9.7 miles to the major road washout and temporary parking area (elev. 500 ft). Note that a smaller washout 1 mile before the parking area warrants a high-clearance vehicle to get around it.

ON THE TRAIL

The Dosewallips River flexed some serious muscle here in 2002, removing a huge section of roadway and putting the future of this popular Olympic National Park access road in doubt. Contact national park and forest officials as well as your elected representatives and let them know how you feel about the closed road.

In the meantime, follow a trail built by the Washington Trails Association that climbs around the huge washout. Then trudge 5 miles along the old roadbed, passing the once-popular U.S. Forest Service Elkhorn Campground, entering Olympic National Park, passing the climbers trail to Lake Constance (damaged by wildfire in 2009), and finally arriving at

A hiker explores the basin below the Anderson Glacier.

the shuttered Dosewallips Ranger Station (elev. 1600 ft). This is also the site of the now-deserted Dosewallips car campground, which can be used as a backpacking camp. If you've biked this far, secure your bike here.

Locate the Dosewallips River Trail and take it, immediately crossing Station Creek

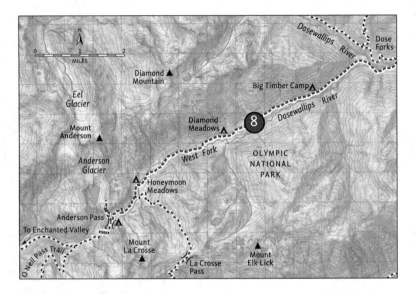

that rushes down from Constance Pass. Stay to the right at a Nature Trail junction, and at 6.7 miles (1.4 miles from the trailhead proper) come to a junction (elev. 1800 ft). Right leads to Hayden Pass and Constance Pass. Left leads to Anderson Pass, your route.

Descending 100 feet, soon come to campsites at Dose Forks, perched on the banks of the glacially clouded Dosewallips River. Cross the river on a sturdy bridge, and then briefly climb, contouring around a steep slope that offers a view of the confluence of the Dosewallips with its West Fork. In 7.7 miles, reach a bridge that stretches high above the West Fork Dosewallips, thundering below through a deep slot canyon.

Now high above the west bank of the West Fork, the trail ascends slopes of dry Douglas-fir forests decked out with rhododendrons that brighten the understory in purple and pink in early summer. After reaching a bench (elev. 2400 ft) several hundred feet above the river, the trail slowly descends to Big Timber

Camp (elev. 2300 ft), set amid big boulders and, yes, big timber, alongside the West Fork at 9.5 miles.

The trail continues upvalley through much bigger (and older) timber, traveling slightly above and away from the river. Note the abundance of elk trails along the way. It was the importance of the Olympics as elk habitat that first led President Theodore Roosevelt to protect this magnificent area.

At 11.9 miles, come to camps at Diamond Meadows (elev. 2700 ft), set in big trees near a small avalanche-swept opening. Beyond, the trail crosses the West Fork Dosewallips on a log bridge and climbs more steadily. Then it recrosses the creek and reaches Honeymoon Meadows (elev. 3500 ft) at 14.2 miles. Named by a climber who spent his honeymoon here with his new wife, this is an engaging place. Established campsites can be found at the edge of the meadows.

Just beyond Honeymoon Meadows, the La Crosse Pass Trail branches left for a grueling

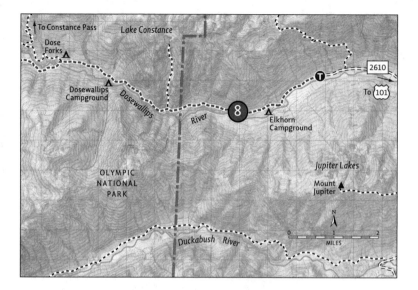

and scenic route to the Duckabush Valley by way of a high gap between 6417-foot Mount La Crosse and 6517-foot Mount Elk Lick.

The West Fork Dose Trail continues upvalley, climbing steadily through subalpine forest and reaching inviting campsites just below Anderson Pass (elev. 4100 ft) at 15.2 miles. In addition to the good camps at the edge of alpine meadows, there's an emergency shelter. Like in most of Olympic National Park, bears frequent the area, so make sure your food is hanging high.

For the glacier, continue on the trail another 0.6 mile to 4464-foot Anderson Pass. A pretty spot graced by a tarn and a wonderful view of Mount La Crosse, it gets even better. Locate the Anderson Glacier Trail branching right and take it, climbing into more open territory. Enjoy spectacular views, including down to the Enchanted Valley.

After 0.8 mile, come to the open moraine (elev. 5100 ft) left by Anderson Glacier—and a beautiful alpine lake set in a stark basin,

compliments of the glacier cradled above in craggy Mount Anderson. While the glacier is still of good size, it has been receding steadily over the decades. Be careful when exploring not to stomp on the fragile vegetation colonizing the basin.

TRIP PLANNER	
5.3 miles	Old Dosewallips car campground
6.9 miles	Dose Forks camps
9.5 miles	Big Timber Camp
11.9 miles	Diamond Meadows camps
14.2 miles	Honeymoon Meadows camps
15.2 miles	Camps below Anderson Pass
16.6 miles	Anderson Glacier

EXTENDING YOUR TRIP

Turn your trip into a cross-Olympic trek by exiting through the Enchanted Valley (Trip 3), or follow the O'Neil Pass Trail to the Lake La Crosse basin (Trip 10) and return via La Crosse Pass.

9 Flapjack and Black and White Lakes

RATING/ DIFFICULTY	LOOP	ELEV GAIN/ HIGH POINT	SEASON
***/3	18.3 miles	4200 feet/ 4475 feet	late June– Oct

Maps: Green Trails Mount Steel No. 167, Custom Correct Mount Skokomish–Lake Cushman; **Contact:** Olympic National Park, Wilderness Information Center, Port Angeles, (360) 565-3100, www.nps.gov/olym; **Permits/regulations:** National park entrance fee. Olympic NP wilderness camping permit required. Permits limited, reservations recommended. Bear canister required at Black and White Lakes, can be borrowed from Wilderness Information Center. No fires above 3500 feet. Dogs prohibited; **Special features:** Excellent alpine views from several subalpine lakes, particularly gorgeous in autumn; **Special concerns:** Flapjack Lakes can be crowded. **GPS:** N 47 30.968 W 123 19.691

This set of subalpine lakes is perched along a high divide separating Olympic National Park and the Mount Skokomish Wilderness. The Flapjacks are served with a good heaping of old-growth timber set beneath the craggy spires of Sawtooth Ridge, while Black and White sit cradled in an old burn zone carpeted in berry bushes and mountain ash that transform the area into living color come autumn.

GETTING THERE

From Shelton, travel north on US 101 for 15 miles to Hoodsport. Turn left onto State Route 119 and drive 9.3 miles to a T intersection with Forest Road 24. Turn left, continuing on SR 119 until it ends in 1.7 miles, and then continue on a pothole-prone gravel road. In 3.7 miles, bear right, coming to the Staircase Ranger Station in 1.2 miles and the trailhead (elev. 850 ft). Privy and car camping available.

ON THE TRAIL

Starting on the North Fork Skokomish River Trail, follow this popular pathway alongside the North Fork Skokomish River. Before the flow was dammed by Tacoma Power in the 1920s, this was one of the largest salmon-rearing rivers on the peninsula.

On an old roadbed (decommissioned in the early 1970s), head upstream and round a washout, and then slightly descend. Cross a couple of side creeks (bridged) and travel through a luxuriant bottomland of big cedars, Doug-firs, and moss-cloaked big-leaf maples. Stay right at a junction with the Staircase Rapids Loop Trail at 1 mile.

At 1.6 miles, come to Slide Camp (elev. 950 ft), a perfect spot for taking young children on their first overnighter. The trail then traverses the Beaver Fire of 1985, caused by an illegal campfire during a drought and resulting in 1400 acres of old growth going up in flames. Through big snags and feisty undergrowth the trail gradually moves away from the river. At 3.7 miles, reach a junction (elev. 450 ft) just before Spike Camp.

Head right, slowly climbing out of the valley along the old burn line. After a few switchbacks, the trail turns northward on a fairly level course. After passing through a marshy area of big cedars, arrive at Madeline Creek (elev. 2100 ft), which cascades through a narrow ravine at 5.4 miles. Cross it via a new sturdy bridge.

The way then becomes steeper and rockier, rounding a ridge to a dank ravine housing Donahue Creek. Now paralleling the cascading creek, the trail climbs steeply, passing some campsites before reaching a junction (elev. 3400 ft) at 7.4 miles. The Black and White Lakes lie to the left. First head right on rocky tread for 0.6 mile through silver firs and

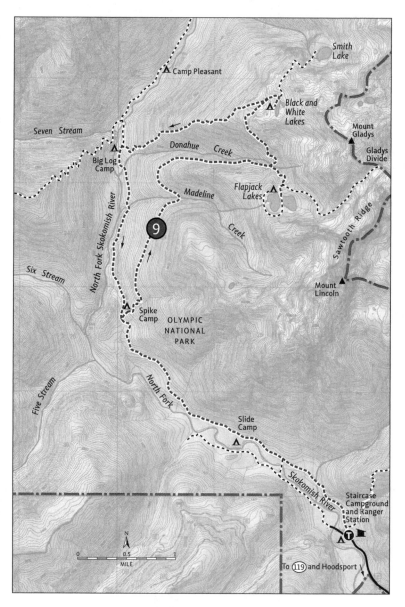

One of the Black and White Lakes in open basin

hemlocks, reaching the Flapjack Lakes and good camps (elev. 3900 ft).

Separated by a narrow isthmus, the two lakes are ringed by mature timber and flanked by the rugged spires of the Sawtooth Ridge and Mount Lincoln. A path leads 0.8 mile around the "lower" lake, granting excellent views of the jagged backdrop. Dippers and dragonflies flit about the placid waters.

Set up camp or continue, retreating 0.6 mile back to the previous junction. Head right, crossing two small creeks, and then steeply climb, rounding a ridge to emerge at an old burn, now blanketed in berry bushes and mountain ash. After passing the log foundation of an old cabin, come to a junction with the Black and White Way Trail (elev. 4350 ft) at 9.8 miles. Continue straight another 0.2 mile to an unmarked junction. Then turn right and in 0.1 mile reach the Black and White Lakes (elev. 4475 ft).

Starkly different from the forested Flapjack Lakes, these two lakes (the smaller one lies hidden behind a small knoll just to the east) sit in an open area providing sweeping views of the surrounding wilderness. Particularly striking is Wonder Mountain to the south, Six Ridge to the west, and Mount Steel to the north. In autumn, the basin transforms into dazzling reds, oranges, and yellows. A couple of camps are located near the outlet stream. Practice Leave No Trace principles and store food in a bear canister.

Once part of an old mining area, the lakes' names are believed to be derived from a brand of whiskey, but there are other theories. When ready to leave, retrace your steps 0.3 mile to the Black and White Way Trail and then follow it 2.3 incredibly steep miles down, first through burn and then through cool mature forest. While the way is knee-jarring (losing 2500 feet in 2 miles), the tread is smooth and not rocky. In any case, don't even think about hiking up this waterless trail.

The way trail ends at the North Fork Skokomish Trail (elev. 1550 ft), at the junction with the spur to Big Log Camp located on the river. Spend another night, or turn left and return 5.6 miles to the trailhead along the North Fork Trail (passing Spike Camp and then the Flapjack Lakes trail junction just beyond, in 1.9 miles).

TRIP PLANNER	
1.6 miles	Slide Camp
3.8 miles	Spike Camp
8 miles	Flapjack Lakes camps
10.1 miles	Black and White Lakes camps
12.8 miles	Big Log Camp
18.3 miles	Trailhead

EXTENDING YOUR TRIP

From Flapjack Lakes, follow good trail 1.4 miles to 5000-foot Gladys Divide beneath the impressive summit of 6104-foot Mount Cruiser. Then follow a way path west to the 5600-foot open summit of Mount Gladys, enjoying amazing views in every direction. Experienced off-trail travelers can follow the ridge west to the Black and White Lakes. From Black and White Lakes, the trail continues north for 0.8 mile to Smith Lake and camps. Set in deep forest, this lake is reached via a steep, rooty trail that drops 500 feet.

10 Lake La Crosse

RATING/ DIFFICULTY	ROUND-TRIP	ELEV GAIN/ HIGH POINT	SEASON
*****/5	41 miles	8100 feet/ 4900 feet	late July–Oct

Maps: Green Trails Mount Steel No. 167, Custom Correct Mount Skokomish–Lake Cushman, Custom Correct The Brothers–Mount Anderson; **Contact:** Olympic National Park, Wilderness Information Center, Port Angeles, (360) 565-3100, www.nps.gov /olym; **Permits/regulations:** National park entrance fee. Olympic NP wilderness camping permit required. No fires above 3500 feet. Dogs prohibited; **Special features:** Spectacular subalpine basin deep in the park, with large lakes, sprawling meadows, and copious bear and elk; **Special concerns:** Difficult river ford, dangerous in high water. Lingering snowfields. Lots of bears, store food properly; **GPS:** N 47 30.968 W 123 19.691

One of the wildest, most spectacular places within a park that overflows with incredible locations, the Lake La Crosse basin represents the very essence of Olympic National Park. Far from civilization, it's an untrammeled place of striking natural beauty, cradling sparkling pristine lakes amid sprawling alpine meadows set against a backdrop of cloud-catching, snow-clutching jagged summits. Relish the solitude—come here in autumn and count more bears than humans. There's no easy or short way here, making it all the more attractive and exceptional.

GETTING THERE

From Shelton, travel north on US 101 for 15 miles to Hoodsport. Turn left onto State Route 119 and drive 9.3 miles to a T intersection with Forest Road 24. Turn left, continuing on SR 119 until it ends in 1.7 miles, and then continue on a pothole-prone gravel road. In 3.7 miles, bear right, coming to the Staircase Ranger Station in 1.2 miles and the trailhead (elev. 850 ft). Privy and car camping available.

ON THE TRAIL

There are several ways to get to Lake La Crosse—none of them less than 20 miles. This way follows the historic O'Neil route and includes the beautiful meadows of Home Sweet Home.

Following the North Fork Skokomish River Trail, first on old roadbed, then on bona fide trail, retrace part of the O'Neil Expedition's 1890 exploratory route. One year after the famous Press Expedition (see Trip 6), which traversed the Olympic interior from north to south, Lieutenant O'Neil led a group of scientists and soldiers across the Olympics from east to west. Among the party's many findings was O'Neil's realization that the Olympic interior would serve admirably as a national park. In 1909, President Theodore Roosevelt established the Olympic National Monument, and in 1938 it became a park under President Franklin D. Roosevelt.

Head upriver, rounding a washout, and then slightly descend. Soon cross the first of many side creeks—there is no lack of water on this route and no crossing problems until the

Lake La Crosse with Mount Steel in background

Duckabush Valley. Stay right at a junction with the Staircase Rapids Loop Trail at 1 mile. Pass Slide Camp at 1.6 miles and traverse a large burn from the 1980s. The trail climbs slightly, moving away from the river. At 3.7 miles, reach a junction (elev. 1450 ft) with the Flapjack Lakes Trail (Trip 9). Continue straight and soon reach popular Spike Camp.

Now in impressive old growth, the trail gains little elevation. Cross Madeline and Donahue creeks in dank ravines before coming to a junction (elev. 1550 ft) at 5.7 miles. The trail right leads steeply to the Black and White Lakes; the spur trail left drops down to Big Log Camp along the North Fork Skokomish River.

Continue straight, crossing the North Fork Skokomish on a good bridge above an impressive chasm, and come to a junction at 6 miles with the lightly used Six Ridge Trail (elev. 1500 ft). Turn right and continue hiking along the river through maple glades. At 6.8 miles, reach riverside Camp Pleasant (elev. 1600 ft)—which really is pleasant, despite its popularity.

Continue easy walking along the river and through gorgeous old growth, arriving at Nine Stream Camp (elev. 2050 ft) at 9.7 miles. Up to this point the hiking has been easy and through low country that can be explored well into fall or early spring. But from here on, the mood changes—after negotiating a tumbling creek, the trail climbs steeply and with a purpose. Through beautiful groves of ancient timber, no time is wasted in gaining elevation. At 11.6 miles, come to Two Bear Camp (elev. 3650 ft) in a berry patch by the creek. Expect to see more than two bruins in the meadows and huckleberry patches that follow.

The way continues climbing, crossing pocket meadows with growing views to the south down the North Fork Skokomish. At 12.7 miles, bear left at the Mount Hopper Way Trail junction (elev. 4600 ft), skirting a pretty tarn before cresting First Divide (elev. 4700 ft). Then steeply descend (snow often lingers here well into July, use caution) into the sprawling meadows of Home Sweet Home (elev. 4200 ft), reaching a spur trail at 13.5 miles. The camps are located 0.2 mile to the east, set among the flowering meadow beneath a cascade that tumbles down from 6114-foot Mount Hopper. Views are excellent across the green carpet to 6223-foot Mount Steel.

Now following the Home Sweet Home Trail, rapidly lose elevation, first through a majestic forest of ancient yellow cedars and then magnificent hemlocks, silver fir, and Douglas-fir. At 15.6 miles, come to the Duckabush River Trail (elev. 2800 ft). Upper Duckabush Camp, located along the crashing

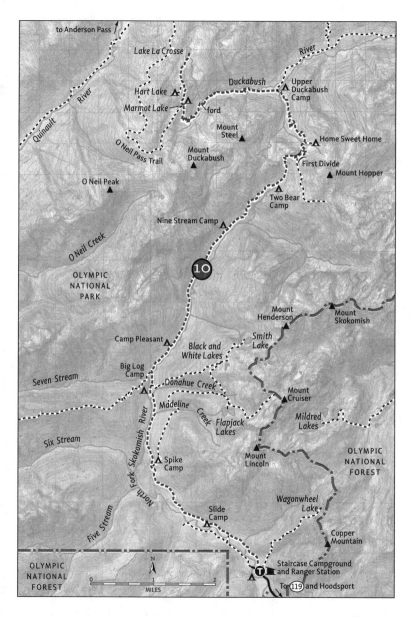

to Anderson Pass

Lake La Crosse

River

Duckabush

Upper
Duckabush
Camp

Hart Lake

Marmot Lake

ford

River

Quinault

Mount
Steel

Home Sweet Home

O Neil Pass Trail

Mount
Duckabush

First Divide

Mount Hopper

O Neil Peak

Two Bear
Camp

Nine Stream Camp

O Neil Creek

10

OLYMPIC
NATIONAL
PARK

Mount
Henderson

Mount
Skokomish

Camp Pleasant

*Black and
White Lakes*

*Smith
Lake*

Big Log
Camp

Donahue Creek

Mount
Cruiser

Seven Stream

Madeline

Creek

*Mildred
Lakes*

*Flapjack
Lakes*

Six Stream

North Fork Skokomish River

Spike
Camp

Mount
Lincoln

OLYMPIC
NATIONAL
FOREST

*Wagonwheel
Lake*

Five Stream

Slide
Camp

Copper
Mountain

OLYMPIC
NATIONAL
FOREST

N

Staircase Campground
and Ranger Station

T

To (119) and Hoodsport

0   1   2
MILES

river in big timber, lies just to the right. For Lake La Crosse, head left immediately and ford Home Sweet Home Creek, which may be tricky during periods of high rainfall.

The way now turns rough, traversing brushy avalanche chutes and crossing snow-melt creeks that cascade from steep, imposing cliffs. After a short, stiff climb, the trail skirts a steep slope high above the river, churning below through a tight canyon. At 17.6 miles, the trail approaches the crashing river (elev. 3350 ft), where it must be forded—it's usually knee-deep, but is much deeper and potentially dangerous in early season and during rainy periods.

Once across the Duckabush, the trail crosses yet another crashing creek and then swiftly climbs out of the valley, reaching a high bench cradling shallow Marmot Lake (elev. 4375 ft). Here, at 19 miles, find good camps and a junction. The trail left leads 1.2 miles to 5400-foot O'Neil Pass, a good side trip if camping in the vicinity.

For Lake La Crosse, take the right-hand trail, climbing 0.6 mile to an open knoll (elev. 4900 ft) where spectacular views can be had east down the Duckabush River valley, south to Mount Steel and Mount Duckabush's snowy slopes, and north to sparkling Lake La Crosse and its enveloping verdant meadows (often snow blotched until August). Here a side trail wraps 0.4 mile around a rocky outcropping to gorgeous Hart (or Heart) Lake (elev. 4825 ft), with its excellent private camps and breathtaking views of Mount Duckabush.

The main trail continues another 0.9 mile across shimmering creeks, flower-bursting meadows, and jaw-slacking alpine scenery to Lake La Crosse (elev. 4700 ft). The lake is surrounded by steep slopes rife with succulent grasses and berries coveted by bear, elk, and marmots—all abundant here in one of the most wild and untrammeled places in the Olympics.

TRIP PLANNER	
1.6 miles	Slide Camp
3.8 miles	Spike Camp
5.8 miles	Big Log Camp
6.8 miles	Camp Pleasant
9.7 miles	Nine Stream Camp
11.6 miles	Two Bear Camp
13.7 miles	Home Sweet Home camps
15.7 miles	Upper Duckabush Camp
19 miles	Marmot Lake camps
20.5 miles	Lake La Crosse

EXTENDING YOUR TRIP

With a car shuttle, exit via the long Duckabush River Trail or follow the O'Neil Pass Trail 8.6 miles to the North Fork Quinault River Trail. From there, either exit left via the Enchanted Valley (Trip 3) or right via Anderson Pass to the Dosewallips River valley (Trip 8).

11 Upper Lena Lake

RATING/ DIFFICULTY	ROUND-TRIP	ELEV GAIN/ HIGH POINT	SEASON
****/4	15 miles	4000 feet/ 4600 feet	late July– Oct

Maps: Green Trails The Brothers, WA–No. 168, Custom Correct The Brothers–Mount Anderson; **Contact:** Olympic National Park, Wilderness Information Center, Port Angeles, (360) 565-3100, www.nps.gov /olym; **Permits/regulations:** NW Forest Pass required. Olympic NP wilderness camping permit required. No fires above 3500 feet. Dogs prohibited in the park; **Special features:** Alpine lakes, scrambling opportunities, and beginning of a high-country route; **Special concerns:** A section of trail is extremely steep and on rough terrain, avoid in bad weather; **GPS:** N 47 35.984 W 123 09.055

Upper and Lower Lena lakes are night and day. Lower Lena is flanked by old-growth forest, easy to get to, accessible most

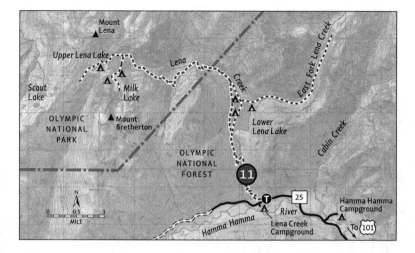

of the year, and is one of the most popular backpacking destinations in the Olympics, especially for families. Upper Lena sits in a stunning high basin surrounded by alpine meadows and steep rocky peaks. The trail to it is steep, eroded, and at times a root-tangled, rocky mess. But that hasn't dampened its appeal—it's one of the prettiest spots in the eastern reaches of the Olympics and is a launchpad for further high-country adventures.

GETTING THERE

From Hoodsport, travel US 101 north for 14 miles. At milepost 318, turn left (west) onto Hamma Hamma River Road (Forest Road 25). Continue for 7.6 paved miles to the trailhead (elev. 650 ft). Privy available.

ON THE TRAIL

The trail takes off climbing gently through second-growth timber. Lena Creek can be heard crashing in the distance. After about 1 mile, enter a forest of impressive old growth. As the trail nears a bridge (elev. 1500 ft) spanning Lena Creek, you may be surprised to find yourself standing over a dry rocky bed. The creek frequently flows through a subterranean passage here.

After 3 easy miles, reach a junction (elev. 1925 ft). Venture right, and within a few hundred feet reach an inviting sunny ledge overlooking Lower Lena Lake. The trail continues, descending to the shoreline and passing several well-established and well-used campsites (some with fire rings). Competition is fierce for these sites on most weekends. The trail continues to Lena Creek, where you can head left back to the Upper Lena Lake Trail or right to the Valley of Silent Men, a route primarily used by climbers on their way to the Brothers.

Back at the 3-mile junction, continue left for Upper Lena Lake, now on much lighter tread. After a short climb and drop, reach a junction (elev. 1975 ft) with the old trail (now a connector to the lower lake) at 3.5 miles. The way now turns westward, following along Lena Creek through a spectacular primeval forest. At 4.25 miles, enter Olympic National Park (elev. 2350 ft). Dogs are prohibited from this point on.

Mount Bretherton reflected in Upper Lena Lake

The elevation gain continues to be minimal as the way parallels Lena Creek through dark forest in an increasingly tight valley marred by avalanches on its north slopes. At 5 miles, cross a tributary on a log bridge (elev. 2650 ft), from whence the way gets downright nasty.

The way gets steep—insanely steep up a rocky, rooty, brushy course. With a full pack it can be arduous and quite taxing. In wet weather it can be treacherous. Carefully negotiate a ledge, pausing between maneuvers to look out at the valley below. After slowly clambering up a steep rocky bed of big rocks posing as trail, the climbing eases—somewhat.

At 6.5 miles, cross Lena Creek (elev. 3900 ft), which may be following a subterranean passage here as well. Continue through open forest and attractive old-growth groves before once again climbing steeply, this time across abrupt slopes above Lena Creek.

At 7.5 miles, crest a ridge (elev. 4600 ft) to see Upper Lena Lake below, and reach a junction. Enjoy an excellent view southeast to Mount Rainier before studying the campsite map posted at the junction. Reach day-use and good soaking spots by following the trail to the right. Here, too, you can enjoy a classic backdrop view of 5960-foot Mount Bretherton rising above and reflecting in the lake. Beyond, on the lake's eastern shore, are a handful of campsites.

The trail left traverses the backcountry camping area, dropping steeply to the lake's outlet and continuing along its southeastern shore to a couple of sites, including one lone attractive site pitched away from the lake at the edge of a meadow. The view of 5995-foot Mount Lena from the lake's southern shore is particularly soothing, especially in October when blueberry bushes set it ablaze in red. Set up camp and plan on spending some time exploring—you've worked too hard not to.

TRIP PLANNER	
3.2 miles	Lower Lena Lake camps
7.5 miles	Upper Lena Lake camps

EXTENDING YOUR TRIP

From the lone campsite at the lake's southern end, follow a well-defined trail 0.4 mile along a cascading creek and across glorious open meadows to Milk Lake (elev. 4725 ft), frozen most of the year. Wedged beneath steep rock walls and fed by glacial meltwater, its silty surface refracts light and color quite nicely. Adventurous and experienced off-trail travelers can follow the Scout Lake Way Trail west from Lena Lake. A good objective for most hikers is about 2 miles to a 5100-foot pass and series of small tarns below. And Mount Lena's open southern slopes invite scramblers to some excellent viewing.

Opposite: Mount Rainier and elk-frequented basin from Goat Mountain (Trip 16)

South Cascades

12 Trapper Creek and Observation Peak

RATING/ DIFFICULTY	LOOP	ELEV GAIN/ HIGH POINT	SEASON
****/3	13.8 miles	3400 feet/ 4207 feet	June–Nov

Maps: Green Trails Lookout Mtn No. 396, Wind River No. 397; **Contact:** Gifford Pinchot National Forest, Mount Adams Ranger District, Trout Lake, (509) 395-3400, www.fs.fed.us/gpnf; **Permits/regulations:** NW Forest Pass required. Free wilderness permit required, self-issued at trailhead. Wilderness rules apply; **Special features:** Rare South Cascades old growth, solitude; **Special concerns:** Difficult stream crossings in high water; **GPS:** N 45 52.886 W 121 58.813

A small but significantly important wilderness in the extreme southern reaches of Washington's Cascades, the 6050-acre Trapper Creek Wilderness protects an intact watershed and some of the region's largest and oldest trees. Surrounded by a sea of clear-cuts and managed forest, this wilderness area is biologically rich and home to endangered spotted owls. And despite the dense forest, Observation Peak, a former fire lookout, offers stunning views. Trapper Creek itself is a cascading delight, and seekers of solitude will delight in setting up camp along its banks.

GETTING THERE

From Stevenson, head east 3 miles on State Route 14. Turn left (north) onto Wind River Road (Forest Road 30) and proceed 14.4 miles on this good paved road and turn left onto Mineral Springs Road (FR 3065). Continue for 0.4 mile and turn right onto FR 5401. In 0.5 mile, come to the road's end and trailhead (elev. 1200 ft). Privy available.

ON THE TRAIL

Enter thick, dark forest and immediately come to a junction. The trail to the right travels along Dry Creek and Big Hollow Creek, offering an alternative return route that's longer by about 2.5 miles. While it's not within the wilderness, the roadless Big Hollow Creek area contains monstrous old trees and *should* be included within the Trapper Creek Wilderness.

Head left on the wide and well-graded Trapper Creek Trail. In 0.8 mile, enter wilderness and come to a major junction shortly afterward. The trail on the right will be your return. The trail left heads to a handful of cabins. Continue straight up the Trapper Creek Trail. After an easy 0.7 mile, reach a junction (elev. 1400 ft) with the Soda Peaks Lake Trail, a rewarding but strenuous side trip. Continue right.

Now climbing, with Trapper Creek nowhere in sight, pass showy Pacific dogwoods, fire-scarred big firs, and cedar snags. Even in this saturated valley, fire still plays a role in forest succession. At 2.5 miles, come to a junction with the Big Slide Trail (elev. 1900 ft). This side trail, along with others in the valley, was constructed by the Portland-based Mazama mountaineering club. The trails tend to be primitive and challenging.

Head left, ignore the Deer Cutoff Trail soon afterward, and drop 300 feet into a spectacular grove of old-growth giants along the creek. Good campsites can be found here among the yews and firs. Continue deeper into the valley, passing more good campsites, mineral springs, and impressive cedars, firs, and hemlocks.

At 3.3 miles, reach the second junction with the Deer Cutoff Trail and soon afterward the Sunshine Trail (elev. 1900 ft). The trail, now rougher, continues to climb, crossing several side creeks and passing by waterfalls and snug campsites. At about 4.5 miles, cross

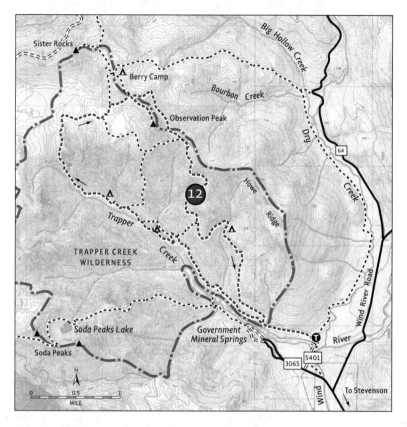

Trapper Creek on a big bridge. The trail now steeply climbs out of the valley. En route be sure to pause at a large ledge overlooking breathtaking Trapper Creek Falls plunging 100 feet.

In about another 1 mile, the climb eases and the trail reaches brushy huckleberry flats frequented by elk. Cross Trapper Creek once more, tricky here with no bridge, and then resume climbing. Pass a junction with the Rim Trail and reach a junction with the Shortcut Trail (elev. 3600 ft) at 6.1 miles.

Take the Shortcut Trail and, after 0.3 mile, intersect the Observation Peak Trail.

Berry Camp, with its spring, can be found by hiking left 0.4 mile to a junction and then 0.1 mile right. For the loop, turn right on Observation Peak Trail, immediately passing a trail to the left (your return) and continuing for 0.8 mile to the 4207-foot summit of Observation Peak. A former fire lookout site, the summit still provides excellent views, particularly south across the uncut Trapper Creek valley out to Mount Hood in Oregon.

Once content with your observation, return 0.8 mile to the Observation Peak Trail, turning right for a 5-mile gentle descent along Howe

Trapper Creek flows through majestic old-growth forest.

Ridge back to the Trapper Creek Trail (or, for a longer return, continue straight 0.4 mile to Berry Camp and follow the Big Hollow Creek Trail). Ignore all side trails along the well-maintained path back to Trapper Creek. But do stop to admire giant firs and good views out to Soda Peaks and other nearby ridges. The way passes a couple of attractive side creeks, including one with a nice campsite east of the Big Slide Trail junction. From the Trapper Creek Trail junction, it's 0.8 mile back to your vehicle.

TRIP PLANNER	
3 miles	Camps in old-growth forest
4 miles	Creekside camps
6.9 miles	Berry Camp
7.2 miles	Observation Peak
10.6 miles	Creekside camp
13.8 miles	Trailhead

PACIFIC CREST TRAIL: MEXICO TO CANADA

Completing a two- or three-day backpacking trip can certainly be challenging. Imagine spending three, four, or five months on the trail. A small but growing group of hikers from coast-to-coast do just that each year on one of America's eight long-distance National Scenic Trails. The granddaddy of them all, the 2175-mile Appalachian Trail (AT) is the most popular. Completed in 1937, it winds its way from Georgia to Maine.

Here in Washington, 500 miles of the Mexico-to-Canada 2650-mile Pacific Crest Trail winds its way along the Cascade crest. Officially completed in 1993, the Pacific Crest Trail, or PCT as it is lovingly known, joined the AT as one of America's first national trails (though both were designated as such in 1968). Administered by the National Park Service, the National Trails System consists of congressionally designated trails. Inclusion in the system is based on a trail's cultural, historic, and scenic attributes as well as its draw for outdoor recreation. The PCT, like most of the national trails, actually consists of many trails woven together to form one continuous corridor. The trail is well-maintained and cared for and looked after by several citizen groups, including the Pacific Crest Trail Association.

While only a handful of through-hikers complete the entire PCT each year, plenty of backpackers hike sections at a time, for instance, the popular 70-mile Snoqualmie Pass to Stevens Pass section. In this book, these trips include portions of the PCT: Indian Heaven Wilderness Lakes (Trip 13), Mount Adams (Trip 14), Cispus Basin (Trip 17), Fryingpan Lake (Trip 18), Big Crow Basín (Trip 21), Cougar Lakes and Three Lakes (Trip 28), Spectacle Lake (Trip 33), Deep Lake (Trip 35), Dishpan Gap (Trip 38), Chain and Doelle Lakes (Trip 40), Lyman Lakes (Trip 46), Image Lake (Trip 47), Glacier Peak Meadows (Trip 53), Snowy Lakes (Trip 59), and Twisp Pass–South Pass (Trip 60).

13 Indian Heaven Wilderness Lakes

RATING/ DIFFICULTY	LOOP	ELEV GAIN/ HIGH POINT	SEASON
****/1	14 miles	2150 feet/ 5225 feet	July–late Oct

Map: Green Trails Indian Heaven, WA–No. 365S; **Contact:** Gifford Pinchot National Forest, Mount Adams Ranger District, Trout Lake, (509) 395-3400, www.fs.fed.us/gpnf; **Permits/regulations:** NW Forest Pass required. Free wilderness permit required, self-issued at trailhead. Use established sites at Blue Lake. Wilderness rules apply. Fires permitted but discouraged; **Special features:** High plateau of alpine lakes and meadows. Historic Native American berry-gathering ground; **Special concerns:** Mosquitoes are brutal early to midsummer. Heavy equestrian use. Many lakes are quite popular on autumn weekends; **GPS:** N 46 02.795 W 121 45.384

A magical land of extinct volcanic craters and pastoral lawns along a high plateau dotted by over a hundred subalpine lakes, the 20,600-acre Indian Heaven Wilderness is indeed a heavenly place. Long a gathering ground for area tribes who came to gather huckleberries and fish, to tan hides, dry meats, race horses, and play games, the area still retains its significance to these First Peoples. Today the land has become a popular gathering place for hikers, with its many trails, gentle topography, and enticing lakes and berry fields. But be warned that this heaven can be a mosquito hell for much of the hiking season.

GETTING THERE

From Trout Lake, follow State Route 141 west to its terminus at Gifford Pinchot National Forest (4.7 miles beyond the ranger station), where it becomes Forest Road 24. Continue 2.5 miles to a junction with FR 60 at the Peterson Prairie Camp. Bear right, continuing on FR 24 and reaching Cultus Creek Campground after 9 miles. (Cultus Creek can also be reached from Carson by following the Wind River Road, FR 30, north for 38 miles, turning right onto FR 24, and continuing 4.2 miles to the campground.) Turn into the campground and proceed 0.2 mile to the Indian Heaven trailhead parking area (elev. 4000 ft). Privy available.

ON THE TRAIL

Most of the Indian Heaven Wilderness is easily accessible to day hikers. Road access is never far from the periphery and trails approach from all directions. The area is well loved and well hiked. However, it is still possible to find solitude in this small wilderness area by heading to the smaller, remoter lakes. Hikers with good compass skills and old maps can follow old abandoned trails leading to some of the quietest lakes. The loop described here leads to some of the prettiest lakes in the wilderness, with opportunities for side trips to more lakes and some great viewpoints.

From the trailhead, head out on the wide and well-beaten Indian Heaven Trail No. 33, soon entering the wilderness area and climbing in short order—steeply at times. The trail parallels a tributary of Cultus Creek for a ways. The tributary usually runs dry (actually, underground), and cultus means "worthless" in Chinook Jargon. At just over 1 mile, reach a ledge

(elev. 4800 ft) with an excellent view of Mount Adams, Sleeping Beauty, Mount Rainier, Goat Rocks, and the Dark Divide.

Continue, now on a gentle grade, through huckleberry meadows and reach Cultus Lake (elev. 5075 ft) at 2.4 miles. There are good campsites near meadows along the creek below the lake, about 0.1 mile farther. There's also good camping at Deep Lake, reached by a 0.2-mile side trail. The top of Mount Adams can be seen rising above this pretty lake.

In another 0.2 mile from Cultus Lake, come to Lemei Trail No. 34 (elev. 5100 ft), which leads to Lake Wapiki, tucked within the crater of an ancient volcano, 5925-foot Lemei Rock—the highest summit in the wilderness. Continue south on Trail No. 33, entering old-growth forest and reaching a junction with the Lemei Lake Trail No. 179 in 0.4 mile. Trail No. 33 continues right, passing pretty Clear Lake to reach the Pacific Crest Trail (PCT) in 0.4 mile, offering a shorter loop option. For the recommended trip, continue left on Trail No. 179, slightly descending and reaching expansive meadows and grassy shored Lemei Lake (elev. 4850 ft) in 0.8 mile (3.8 miles from the trailhead). *Lemei*, which is Chinook Jargon for old women, offers good camping to people of both sexes and all ages.

Beyond, the trail (with much needed recent improvements from the Forest Service) climbs a meadowed bluff (elev. 4975 ft), providing good views of Lemei Rock. The way then meanders through old-growth forest, descending to meet the PCT at pretty Junction Lake (elev. 4730 ft) set at the base of the East Crater, another extinct volcanic cone. There are good albeit busy campsites here.

From Junction Lake, 5 miles from the trailhead, return to the right (north) via the PCT if you prefer a shorter trip; or continue left (south) along the PCT, bearing right at a junction with the East Crater Trail No. 48. Skirt the crater, climbing a bit (elev. 4900 ft),

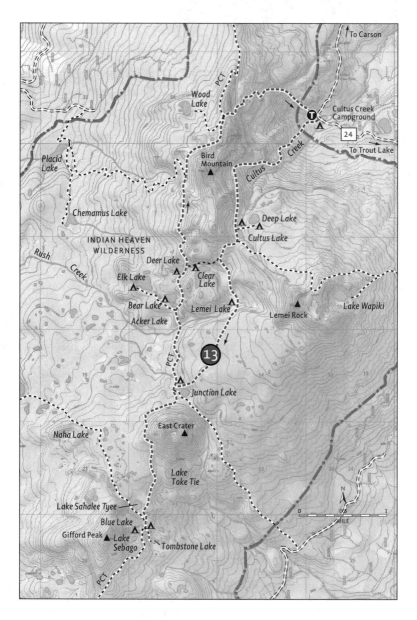

A pair of hikers at Junction Lake

and then make a gentle, forested descent to reach the Thomas Lake Trail No. 111 at Blue Lake (elev. 4640 ft), 2 miles from Junction Lake (and 7 miles from the trailhead). Set beneath the cliffs of Gifford Peak, Blue Lake is one of the deeper and larger lakes in the wilderness. And it's popular—use only established campsites here. Somewhat quieter sites can be found at the macabre-named

Tombstone Lake (elev. 4560 ft), reached by a 0.2-mile spur.

The PCT continues south through the wilderness for another 4 miles, but gone are the lakes. Return north instead, following the PCT past Junction Lake and continuing for another 1 mile to the junction with the Elk Lake Trail No. 176 (elev. 4775 ft), just above Bear Lake. Both Bear and Elk lakes, located 0.6 mile away, offer excellent camping and a chance to perhaps see their namesakes.

Continue on the PCT north for another 0.6 mile, passing an unnamed lake with good campsites before reaching a junction with Indian Heaven Trail No. 33 (elev. 4900 ft). Stay on the PCT, passing the Placid Lake Trail No. 29 in 1 mile. Then skirt below the craggy summit of Bird Mountain before reaching a fourway junction (elev. 5150 ft) after another 0.9 mile. The trail left leads 0.5 mile to Wood Lake, an often quiet spot. The trail right leads back to the Cultus Creek campground—take it, and crest a 5225-foot shoulder of Bird Mountain, where excellent views of Mount Adams can be had by heading out to the ledges on the left. The way then steeply descends, reaching the campground in 1.5 miles. Follow the campground loop road to the right back to your vehicle.

TRIP PLANNER	
2.5 miles	Cultus Lake camps
3.8 miles	Lemei Lake camps
5 miles	Junction Lake camps
7 miles	Blue Lake camps
10 miles	Elk Lake Trail junction to camps
10.4 miles	Unnamed lake camps
14 miles	Trailhead

14 Mount Adams: Devils Gardens

RATING/ DIFFICULTY	ROUND-TRIP	ELEV GAIN/ HIGH POINT	SEASON
*****/4	18.6 miles	3300 feet/ 7700 feet	late July– Oct

Map: Green Trails Mount Adams No. 367S;
Contact: Gifford Pinchot National Forest, Mount Adams Ranger District, Trout Lake, (509) 395-3400, www.fs.fed.us/gpnf;
Permits/regulations: NW Forest Pass required. Free wilderness permit required, self-issued at trailhead. Wilderness rules

apply. Fires prohibited; **Special features:** Alpine tundra, lava field, wildlife, sweeping views; **Special concerns:** Glacier-fed, extremely difficult creek crossings, especially in warm weather; **GPS:** N 46 18.479 W 121 32.366

 Hike along the loftiest and loneliest stretch of the Mount Adams Highline Trail to the hinterlands of Washington's second-highest and second-grandest mountain. While this massive volcano's southern slopes bustle with hikers, horseback riders, and climbers, its northern reaches remain wild and lightly traveled. This trip traverses glacial moraine and ancient lava flows to Devils Gardens, a heavenly alpine tundra wallowing with mountain goats and one hell of a view.

GETTING THERE

From Trout Lake, leave State Route 141 and follow the Mount Adams Recreational Highway north. At 1.3 miles, bear left onto Forest Road 23 and drive 19.3 miles to a junction with FR 90, coming in from Cougar (an alternative western approach). Continue to the right (north) on FR 23 for 4.3 miles and bear right onto FR 2329. (If coming from the north, follow FR 23 south from Randle for 32 miles and turn left onto FR 2329.) At 0.8 mile, bear right. At 1.6 miles, pass Takhlakh Lake Campground. At 7.6 miles, turn right onto FR Spur 086 and continue 0.4 mile to the Muddy Meadows trailhead (elev. 4400 ft). Privy and primitive campsites available.

ON THE TRAIL

Mount Adams welcomes you immediately at the trailhead, rising above the large green expanse spread out before you known as Muddy Meadows. A great place to look for wildlife, particularly in the morning and evening hours, unfortunately these wet meadows

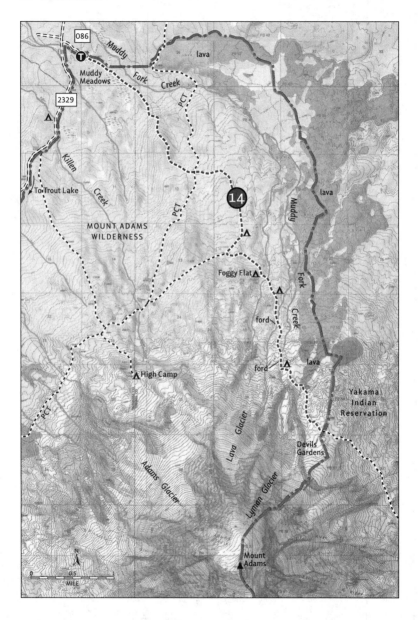

Reaching Devils Gardens

harbor a healthy population of biting insects as well.

On good, wide trail, immediately enter the Mount Adams Wilderness, staying in forest and skirting the meadowy expanse. The first few miles of this trip are also popular with equestrians, and chewed-up tread attests to this. After about 1.25 miles, cross a branch of the Muddy Fork Creek and start climbing, moderately, reaching a junction with the Pacific Crest Trail (elev. 5200 ft) at 3 miles.

Continue straight, gently climbing through forest. At 4.5 miles, pass a nice creekside camp beside a meadow. Just beyond are more meadows and blueberry patches and emerging views of Adams. At 5 miles, in subalpine meadows, come to a junction with the Highline Trail (elev. 5850 ft). The real fun is about to begin.

Head left (east) to start exploring the least-hiked section of the nearly-all-the-way-around-the-mountain Highline Trail. At 6 miles, after very little climbing, reach Foggy Flat (elev. 5950 ft), an excellent camping area at the edge of a meadow complete with a cascading creek and a view of Mount Adams.

The trail continues southeast, crossing the creek (expect wet feet). Steeply climb for a small stretch before emerging at an old lava flow punctuated with stunted trees. There are a few campsites near a small creek at the edge of the tree line. Beyond, the surroundings grow stark—and strikingly beautiful, a dusty lunarlike surface of glacial till and loose rock. The way is fairly defined but it's easy to go off course. Keep an eye on cairns for guidance and an eye on the weather too, for you are now fully exposed to wind and sun. Mount Adams' looming presence before you is entrancing, and an expanding view northward to Mount Rainier is equally captivating.

At 6.8 miles, reach the first (elev. 6300 ft) of two difficult creek crossings, this one originating from the Lava Glacier. In early season and warm weather (which hastens glacial melt), it may be impossible to cross safely. In which case, be content with what you've already seen and consider altering your plans to points westward along the Highline Trail. If the creek is safe to cross, continue climbing and traversing this harsh environment.

At 7.4 miles, the trail marches a short ways up the steep rocky embankment of glacier-fed Muddy Fork Creek (elev. 6850 ft) before crossing it. Scout carefully for a safe place to hop across this torrent of a creek. Then continue across a plateau of stunted trees and the last area to set up camp (and the last reliable water) before Devils Gardens.

Next it's up pumice fields, golden lawns, shale slopes, lava flows, and a big grove of whitebark pine tenaciously clinging to the slopes. Traverse a patch of krummholz before reaching the Devils Gardens in the alpine tundra zone at 9.3 miles. Here, at 7700 feet, on a crest radiating north to Red Butte, the Highline Trail attains its highest elevation. Explorations are in order. Being careful not to tramp delicate ground-hugging plants, roam south toward the looming mountain. Admire tiny blossoms in early summer. Scan cliffs and ridges for mountain goats. They're profuse here. Look too for their wallows. You'll smell them when close! Enjoy breathtaking views north to Rainier and the Goat Rocks and east over the forbidding Avalanche Valley and the sprawling, forested Yakama Indian Reservation.

TRIP PLANNER	
4.5 miles	Creekside camp
6 miles	Foggy Flat camps
6.5	Creekside camps near tree line
7.4 miles	Muddy Fork Creek camps
9.3 miles	Devils Gardens

EXTENDING YOUR TRIP

The Highline Trail continues onto the Yakama Reservation for 2 miles, dropping 1000 feet to a ridge just below Goat Butte. A spring and campsites invite an overnight stay, but you'll need to secure a permit from the Yakamas beforehand. Beyond, to Bird Creek Meadows, the trail only exists on paper, the way being one of the most arduous and dangerous cross-country treks in the South Cascades.

15 Mount Margaret Backcountry Lakes

RATING/ DIFFICULTY	ROUND-TRIP	ELEV GAIN/ HIGH POINT	SEASON
****/4	16.4 miles	3825 feet/ 5150 feet	late July– Oct

Map: Green Trails Spirit Lake No. 332; **Contact:** Mount Saint Helens National Volcanic Monument, (360) 449-7800, www.fs.fed.us /gpnf/mshnvm, or Gifford Pinchot National Forest, Cowlitz Valley Ranger District, Randle, (360) 497-1100 www.fs.fed.us/gpnf; **Permits/regulations:** NW Forest Pass required. Backcountry permit required, available by mail, fax, or in person from monument headquarters or Cowlitz Valley Ranger District. Permits limited. Camp in designated sites only. Fires and dogs prohibited; **Special features:** Alpine lakes within the Saint Helens blast zone; **Special concerns:** Shade is at a premium and snow lingers late into July. Take sunscreen all seasons and ice ax early in season; **GPS:** N 46 18.307 W 122 04.959

Shovel Lake with Mount Adams in the background

⚙ *Travel through Mount Saint Helens's famous 1980 blast zone to a series of alpine lakes tucked within rugged ridges denuded of their forest cover. Though the area took a full hit from the eruption that leveled ancient forests and blanketed the region in pumice, the Mount Margaret Backcountry is no barren wasteland. Nature has been busy recolonizing the region. Wildlife and wildflowers are prolific. The topography, however, is harsh, and the trails tough, with tread that frequently washes out. But this rugged landscape is also simply awe inspiring.*

GETTING THERE

From Randle on US 12, follow State Route 131 south for 2 miles to where it becomes Forest Road 25. Continue for 17.6 miles and turn right onto FR 99. After 9 miles, turn right onto FR 26, reaching the Norway Pass trailhead in 1 mile (elev. 3675 ft). Privy available. (The trailhead can also be reached by following FR 26 north for 16 miles from FR 25 near the Cispus River Bridge.)

ON THE TRAIL

Begin on the Boundary Trail (so named because it marked the old boundary between the Columbia and Rainier national forests,

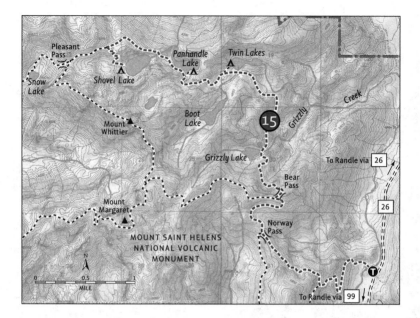

long since amalgamated into the Gifford Pinchot National Forest), and moderately climb across slopes laid waste on May 18, 1980. If this is your first time here, the denuded slopes will impress you, a testament to the raw force of Saint Helens' famous eruption. And if you've come here over the years, you'll be impressed by how much greener the area has become in the last two decades. Subalpine firs now reach over 20 feet tall. Wildflowers paint the pumiced slopes in an array of dazzling colors. The hills are alive, too, with furry fury—from colonies of ground squirrels to herds of elk.

At 1.2 miles, reach the Independence Ridge Trail (elev. 4300 ft). Turn right, continuing on the Boundary Trail and enjoying good views of blasted Meta Lake and blast-in waiting Mount Adams. After descending slightly into a gully, resume moderate climbing to reach the Independence Pass Trail at Norway Pass (elev. 4500 ft) at 2.2 miles. From here, enjoy the classic view of log-filled Spirit Lake with Saint Helens behind, crater in full view.

Stay on the Boundary Trail, making a long sweeping traverse up open slopes. Be careful not to go astray on one of the numerous elk-built paths. At 3.1 miles, reach a junction (elev. 4900 ft) with the Lakes Trail, your portal into the Mount Margaret lake country. Follow the Lakes Trail a mere 0.1 mile to Bear Pass (elev. 4950 ft), where stunning views of Mounts Adams, Rainier, and Saint Helens await you.

Now begin a steep descent (if snow is present, potentially treacherous), losing 700 feet in 1 mile to Grizzly Lake. No grizzlies here, but the surroundings *are* bare and not conducive to camping (which isn't permitted anyway). Rock hop across Grizzly Creek, following the trail through a tight draw and across slopes prone to washing out. The tread improves as the trail rounds a ridge, entering a basin that welcomes you with a waterfall. At 5.4 miles, reach Obscurity Lake (also known as Twin Lakes, elev. 4400 ft), with its campsite and composting toilet.

Cross a trout-filled creek on a log bridge and, after passing a waterfall emanating from hidden Boot Lake, climb to a 4700-foot gap. Drop 250 feet, reaching beautiful Panhandle Lake at 6.2 miles, with its attractive lakeside campsite. Beyond, the trail skirts a lakeside cliff, crosses an attractive creek, and then steeply ascends a ridge granting superb views of the lake, the Green River valley, Goat Mountain (Trip 16), and Mount Rainier in the distance.

Emerge on a rocky crest high above Shovel Lake, where you can dig into some awesome views of the lake twinkling beneath austere Mount Whittier. The way continues climbing, traversing steep slopes that often harbor dangerous snowfields well into summer. At 7.7 miles, reach a junction with the Shovel Lake Trail (elev. 5150 ft). If the Shovel Lake campsite is your objective, follow this trail 0.5 mile, losing a couple of hundred feet to a spot above the lake (water is available from a nearby creek). Enjoy the view and solitude.

TRIP PLANNER	
5.4 miles	Twin Lakes camp
6.2 miles	Panhandle Lake camp
8.2 miles	Shovel Lake camp

EXTENDING YOUR TRIP

Continue west on the Lakes Trail for 0.4 mile to 5200-foot Pleasant Pass. From here you can proceed another 0.5 mile to secluded Snow Lake (elev. 4700 ft), with its backcountry campsite; or, if transportation can be arranged, follow the trail another 8 miles to the Coldwater Lake trailhead on SR 504. The Whittier Ridge Trail can be followed back, to make a loop, but it's not recommended; this trail follows an exposed ridge, is prone to slides and slumping, and can be extremely dangerous to travel, especially for inexperienced hikers and hikers schlepping heavy packs.

16 Green River and Goat Mountain

RATING/ DIFFICULTY	LOOP	ELEV GAIN/ HIGH POINT	SEASON
***/3	20 miles	3500 feet/ 5050 feet	July–Oct

Map: Green Trails Spirit Lake No. 332; **Contact:** Mount Saint Helens National Volcanic Monument, (360) 449-7800; www.fs.fed.us /gpnf/mshnvm, or Gifford Pinchot National Forest, Cowlitz Valley Ranger District, Randle, (360) 497-1100, www.fs.fed.us/gpnf; **Permits/ regulations:** None; **Special features:** Saint Helens blast zone; **Special concerns:** None. **GPS:** N 46 20.946 W 122 05.095

Quiet and often lonely, this loop partially within the Mount Saint Helens National Volcanic Monument travels through a deep glacier-carved valley draped in spectacular old-growth forest and over a high ridge at the edge of the 1980 blast zone that now bursts with wildflowers and views. Add a couple of placid high-country lakes, an old fire lookout site, and a resident elk herd and you have all the makings of a wonderful adventure. And best of all, there are no complicated or limited permits to vie for—just head out when your little heart desires!

GETTING THERE

From Randle on US 12, follow State Route 131 south for 2 miles to where it becomes Forest Road 25, and continue for 6.7 miles. Upon crossing the Cispus River bear right onto FR 26 and follow it for 12.3 miles. (Alternatively, approach from the south via FR 99, turning

Rainier from Vanson Peak

north onto FR 26.) Turn right onto gravel FR 2612 and proceed for 1.7 miles, turning left on FR Spur 027 to the Green River Horse Camp. Continue 0.5 mile to trailhead parking in the campground (elev. 2850 ft). Privy available.

ON THE TRAIL

Do this loop clockwise, allowing for a downhill return and getting the least appealing section out of the way first. Follow the Green River Trail west, downriver through scrappy forest that has been intensively logged in the past. Numerous creeks cascade down from the Mount Margaret Backcountry lakes above (see Trip 15). Trail tread is good but has been relocated in many spots, as the Green River has jumped its banks on numerous occasions.

At 1.7 miles, just beyond crossing FR 2612, pass an impressive waterfall on the Green River. Continue downstream, passing old logging yards and an abandoned mine. The way is

brushy in spots, but good views up both sides of the valley should compensate for any hiking discomfort. At about 3.5 miles, enter the Mount Saint Helens National Volcanic Monument and magnificent old growth, one of the finest remaining ancient forests in the vicinity of Saint Helens.

The way continues downriver, weaving through groves of behemoth Doug-firs, western hemlocks, and western red cedars. At 4 miles, come to a bridged crossing of a side creek. Just beyond, find good riverside camps. Continue down the glacially carved U-shaped valley through magnificent primeval forest groves and across sparkling creeks. If Sasquatch exists, he may very well call this valley home.

At 5.3 miles, reach a junction (elev. 2200 ft). The Green River Trail continues downstream for 2.5 miles to private industrial forest. Turn right instead on the Vanson Ridge Trail to begin climbing out of the valley. At 6 miles, reach a ledge (elev. 2750 ft) that grants excellent viewing of the verdant valley. Reenter forest and continue to steadily climb, crossing numerous side creeks en route. Eventually the grade eases as the trail crests a broad shoulder, reaching a junction at 8.6 miles (elev. 4100 ft). Decision time—Vanson Peak or Vanson Lake?

To reach the lake, continue right, ignoring a side trail that immediately takes off right for boggy Vanson Meadow. After 0.25 mile, turn right again, and in another 0.25 mile reach the shallow, grassy-shored but attractive lake (elev. 4150 ft). Camping possibilities exist along its northwest shore.

To reach Vanson Peak, you have two options. The easier way is to hike past the lake spur for 0.5 mile to a four-way junction (elev. 4750 ft); then turn left and hike 0.5 mile to the old lookout site. The other option follows the trip's main loop: Instead of heading to the

lake, head left and reach another junction in about 0.2 mile. The trail straight heads to a remote trailhead used primarily by local day hikers and illegal motorcycle and ATV riders (report any motorized use you see to the Forest Service). Head right on the light tread, and after a steep 0.5-mile climb reach a ridge crest and trail junction. Head left for 0.2 mile to Vanson's 4948-foot open summit. Feast on excellent views of Rainier, Adams, Goat Rocks, Riffe Lake, and the obscure peaks known as the Rockies. Enjoy, too, a spectacular view of Tumwater Mountain towering over the loneliest and remotest part of the volcanic monument.

Then head back east from Vanson's summit, going straight at the junction in 0.2 mile and dropping 200 feet in a 0.3 mile to a saddle and another junction. The trail right heads to Vanson Lake. The trail left drops to Goat Creek. Continue straight on the Goat

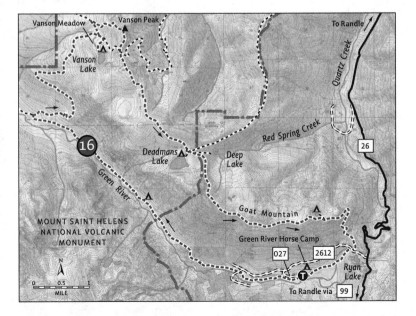

Mountain Trail, through open forest and bear grass, climbing over several knolls with good views north. After 2.3 miles, drop into a saddle (elev. 4450 ft) where the long, dry Tumwater Mountain Trail takes off left and a short spur for Deadmans Lake veers right. Find good camps and good swimming at this sandy-shored shallow lake. Lots of newts too, and unfortunately ... mosquitoes.

The Goat Mountain Trail continues east, passing a 0.3-mile fishermen's path that leads to Deep Lake, deep in mosquito terrain, before leaving the volcanic monument to steeply and steadily climb 1.5 miles to a 4950-foot saddle on Goat Mountain. Here, enjoy exceptional views north to Mount Rainier and down to a basin frequented by elk.

The way continues along the demarcation of the 1980 blast zone, traversing Goat's steep, open southern slopes. Wildflowers and hummingbirds proliferate here, as do good views too to Saint Helens, Adams, and Hood. Staying high along Goat Mountain for 1.5 miles, skirt beneath its 5500-foot summit (an easy scramble) before cresting beneath a knoll at 5050 feet. Then begin a steep and rapid descent. Look for an unmarked side trail to a small tarn and good campsites tucked in a hidden basin (elev. 4750 ft).

After about 2.5 miles of relentless descent, reach a trailhead (elev. 3300 ft) at FR 2612. Cross the road and continue another 0.5 mile to a junction (elev. 3050 ft). The trail left heads to Strawberry Mountain. You want to go right to close the loop, reaching your vehicle in another 0.5 mile.

TRIP PLANNER	
4 miles	Green River camps
9.1 miles	Vanson Lake
9.5 miles	Vanson Peak
13.5 miles	Deadman Lake camps
16 miles	Small tarn and camps
20 miles	Trailhead

17 Goat Rocks: Cispus Basin

RATING/ DIFFICULTY	ROUND-TRIP	ELEV GAIN/ HIGH POINT	SEASON
*****/2	14.4 miles	1950 feet/ 6470 feet	mid-July– Oct

Maps: Green Trails Blue Lake No. 334, Walupt Lake No. 335; **Contact:** Gifford Pinchot National Forest, Cowlitz Valley Ranger Station, Randle, (360) 497-1100, www.fs.fed.us /gpnf; **Permits/regulations:** Free wilderness permit required, self-issued at trailhead. Wilderness rules apply; **Special features:** Sprawling alpine meadows, spectacular wildflower display; **Special concerns:** Heavy hiker and equestrian use, especially around Snowgrass Flat; **GPS:** N 46 27.819 W 122 31.130

One of the most spectacular wild areas in the South Cascades, the Goat Rocks Wilderness encompasses over 100,000 acres of glacier-clad craggy peaks draped with alpine lawns dazzling with wildflowers, punctuated with sparkling tarns, and cut by cool cascading creeks. The remnants of a large ancient volcano, the Goat Rocks explode with stunning alpine splendor, luring legions of admirers from near and far. Supreme Court Justice William O. Douglas was among them—he immortalized the Goat Rocks in his writings. Cispus Basin is one of the area's most enchanting places. And yes, there are plenty of goats here too!

GETTING THERE

From Randle, follow US 12 east for 13 miles, turning right (south) onto Forest Road 21 (signed for Walupt and Chamber lakes). (From Packwood, follow US 12 west for 2.7 miles to FR 21.) Continue on FR 21 for 13 miles and turn left on FR 2150. Proceed for 3.3 miles on this bumpy road—bearing left at 1 mile, right at

Ives Peak hovers over the Cispus Basin.

2.9 miles, and right again at 3 miles—to reach the trailhead (elev. 4650 ft).

ON THE TRAIL

Don't be dismayed if the trailhead parking lot is overflowing with vehicles. The overwhelming majority of the occupants of those vehicles have Snowgrass Flat or Goat Lake as their objective. The equally magnificent Cispus Basin sees a fraction of the visitors, usually just through-hikers along the Pacific Crest Trail.

Start on the trail and immediately enter wilderness. One of the original areas designated in the 1964 Wilderness Act areas, this special place was recognized by the Forest Service as far back as the 1930s. Pass the horse trail coming in from the left and continue right on Snowgrass Trail No. 96. The trail is wide and well manicured. Swarms of mosquitoes will hasten your pace early in the season, while late in the season scads of huckleberries will tarry it.

After fairly level going, the trail descends slightly, crossing Goat Creek on a good bridge. It then swings around a bog graced with orchids and cursed with mosquitoes.

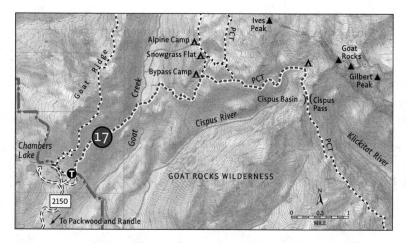

Traversing a slope decked with old-growth trees, the trail begins to climb. Upon approaching a cascading tributary of the Cispus River, the climb steepens. At 4.1 miles, come to a junction with Bypass Trail No. 97 (elev. 5650 ft), where there's a good but waterless camp. The Snowgrass Trail continues left to crowded Snowgrass Flat. You're heading right, on the trail less traveled.

Follow the Bypass Trail through parkland meadows and fields of lupine. Enjoy views of snowy Mount Adams looming in the southern sky. In 0.25 mile, come to a Cispus River tributary (elev. 5550 ft), with excellent campsites nearby. At 1 mile from the Snowgrass Trail (5.1 miles from the trailhead), the Bypass Trail terminates at the Pacific Crest Trail (elev. 6000 ft).

Now head south (right) on the PCT on a near-level jaunt across scree slopes and through beautiful groves of mountain hemlocks. Pass a small ledge offering a jaw-dropping view of the Cispus Basin before you. At 6 miles, enter the glorious basin, a sprawling verdant bowl speckled with a multitude of floral hues beneath the craggy crest of the Goat Rocks.

Continue deeper into the open basin, passing beneath a waterfall. Cherish the refreshing spray—especially if passing by on a hot summer's day. Flowers! Columbine, aster, bear grass, anemone, bistort, paintbrush, lupine, marigold, shooting star, lousewort, buttercup, daisy, and lace—simply stunning. And marmots—enjoy watching them munching on the floral arrangements and lounging in the warming sunlight.

At 6.5 miles, cross the Cispus River (elev. 6100 ft). Here in the heart of the basin, snowfields linger and you may too. Several small camps can be found on a small bench just above the river crossing. If the weather is good, seize one—otherwise, consider camping back in the more sheltered areas along the Bypass Trail.

After the tent is up, continue south along the PCT for another 0.7 mile, climbing out of the basin to 6470-foot Cispus Pass. Here, stare straight down into the headwaters of the Klickitat River draining the Yakama Indian Reservation. Follow a short way path right to a small knoll (elev. 6735 ft) for a blockbuster view of the Goat Rocks. The highest summit, 8184-foot Gilbert Peak, is right before you. Craggy, pointy Ives Peak and Old Snowy Mountain lie to the north. Stay for the sunset.

TRIP PLANNER	
4.1 miles	Bypass Camp
4.3 miles	Creekside camps
6.5 miles	Cispus Basin camps
7.2 miles	Cispus Pass

EXTENDING YOUR TRIP

On your return, bypass the Bypass Trail and continue on the PCT north for 1 mile to Snowgrass Flat (elev. 6400 ft). The lupine fields are legendary, the views of Mount Adams delectable. Return on the Snowgrass Trail, passing numerous well-used campsites and reaching the Bypass Trail junction after 1.5 miles. It's 4.1 miles from here to the trailhead.

18 Fryingpan Lake

RATING/ DIFFICULTY	LOOP	ELEV GAIN/ HIGH POINT	SEASON
***/1	14.6 miles	2200 feet/ 5170 feet	July–Oct

Map: Green Trails White Pass No. 303; **Contact:** Okanogan-Wenatchee National Forest, Naches Ranger District, (509) 653-1401, www.fs.fed.us/r6/wenatchee; **Permits/ regulations:** NW Forest Pass required. Free William O. Douglas Wilderness permit required, self-issued at trailhead. Wilderness rules apply. No camping within 100 feet of lakes; **Special features:** High plateau littered with small lakes and meadows; **Special concerns:** Mosquitoes are brutal throughout summer. Heavy equestrian and hunter use. Lots of social trails that can make

UNTRAMMELED WASHINGTON

While many of Washington's best hiking areas lie within national forests, that doesn't necessarily mean they're protected. National forests are managed for "multiple use." While some uses—like hiking—are fairly compatible with land preservation, other uses—like mining, logging, and off-road-vehicle use—are not.

Recognizing that parts of our natural heritage should be altered as little as possible, Congress passed the Wilderness Act in 1964, with bipartisan support (the House approved passage 373–1). One of the strongest and most important pieces of environmental legislation in our nation's history, the Wilderness Act afforded some of our most precious wild landscapes a reprieve from exploitation, development, and other harmful activities. Even bicycles are banned from federal wilderness areas. The legislation defined wilderness as "an area where the earth and its community of life are untrammeled by man, where man himself is a visitor who does not remain."

While Washington had no shortage of qualifying lands for inclusion in the wilderness system back in 1964, only two areas, Glacier Peak and Goat Rocks, were included. By 1976, however, the Alpine Lakes was added. The federal wilderness system would eventually include wilderness areas in national parks as well as wildlife refuges and other federal lands. In 1984, a sweeping statewide wilderness bill was passed and signed into law, creating several new wildernesses. And in 2008, the Wild Sky became Washington's newest wilderness area. Currently a movement spearheaded by Conservation Northwest is trying to establish several new wilderness areas in northeastern Washington's Colville National Forest, where at present only 3 percent of that forest is protected as wilderness. Most of the hikes in this book travel through one of the state's thirty-one wilderness areas.

Sedge-lined Fryingpan Lake

routefinding confusing; **GPS:** N 46 42.245 W 121 28.861

🏔️ 🔧 ⚙️ 🏠 The William O. Douglas Wilderness consists of countless small lakes among pumice flats and ancient cinder-cone volcanoes. A gentle landscape of bear grass meadows, small peaks, and plenty of sunshine, its hundreds of bodies of water also incubate millions of mosquitoes. Autumn is ideal, but be aware that the region's abundant

elk attract plenty of hunters. Wear orange or come in summer when, despite prolific insects, a multitude of flowers streaks the countryside in a wide array of dazzling colors. This loop to Fryingpan Lake will allow you to cook up plenty of additional wanderings to other delectable lakes within this wilderness.

GETTING THERE

From Enumclaw, head east on State Route 410 for 41 miles to Cayuse Pass, bearing right onto SR 123. Continue 16 miles to US 12 and turn left (east). Proceed for 1.3 miles, and turn left at milepost 140 onto Forest Road 45. (From Yakima, follow US 12 west for approximately 63 miles to the FR 45 turnoff.) After 0.4 mile, bear left onto FR 4510 and continue 4.2 miles to the Soda Springs Campground turnoff. Turn right, and after 0.7 mile reach the trailhead in the campground (elev. 3250 ft). Privy available.

ON THE TRAIL

This trip begins on Cowlitz Trail No. 44, following a historic route across the Cascades used by the Yakama and Cowlitz peoples. Immediately enter the William O. Douglas Wilderness, its 160,000-plus acres named for Yakima son, William O. Douglas, who served on the U.S. Supreme Court for over thirty-six years—the longest-serving justice in history. A champion of the environment, Douglas also spent many days roaming this high country now named in his honor.

In beautiful old-growth forest, cross a couple of creeks before coming to a junction in 0.5 mile with a horse access trail (elev. 3500 ft). Notice the state of the tread, and prepare for dusty and rocky sections of trail. Prepare, too, to pay attention to junctions and to have a map with you, for there are many old trails and social trails that can easily disorient you.

The way gently climbs, following along Summit Creek through nice forest and crossing many side creeks (often dry). At 2.2 miles, reach a junction with the Jug Lake Trail (elev. 3950 ft). Continue right; you'll be returning on the left-hand trail. Catch glimpses of nearby ridges as you continue to ascend, traversing slopes adorned in showy bear grass. The forest soon transitions to mountain hemlock and yellow cedar. Shortly after passing by a small cascade, reach a junction (elev. 4750 ft) at 3.7 miles. The Cowlitz Trail continues right for 1.5 miles to the Pacific Crest Trail and can be followed to make this loop longer. The trail left leads 1.7 miles to Jug Lake and can be followed to make this loop shorter. Take the trail straight—the Pothole Trail—for the recommended loop.

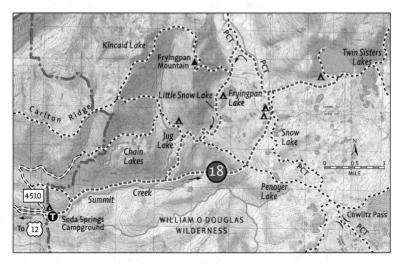

Now on decent tread, enjoy near-level wandering across huckleberry patches and fields of heather and lupine, skirting numerous pothole ponds. Campsites dot and game trails streak the gentle terrain. At about 4.5 miles, come to a long, shallow, nameless lake (elev. 4950 ft) with good camps just to the north. More small lakes lie left, and paths leading to them diverge along the way.

At 5 miles, reach the Pacific Crest Trail (elev. 4875 ft). The recommended loop continues north along the PCT, but includes first a mandatory side trip to the right, to the largest lakes of the bunch. Walk the PCT right for 0.1 mile and then head left on the Twin Sisters Trail. After 1.2 miles, past many small potholes, reach the larger of the gorgeous Twin Sisters Lakes (elev. 5170 ft). A side path heads left to excellent campsites, lakeside ledges, and inviting beaches. The smaller lake can be reached by continuing right for 0.6 mile. Fiercely buggy in summer, the Twin Sisters are quite conciliatory in the fall.

After a night out or leisurely afternoon at the Twin Sisters, retrace your steps 1.2 miles back to the PCT and continue north for 1.1 miles to the Jug Lake Trail (elev. 4700 ft). Now head south, passing through groves of old-growth forest and coming to a junction after 0.6 mile (elev. 4800 ft). The trail right climbs steeply for 1 mile, up 5700-plus foot Fryingpan Mountain, before heading to tiny Kincaid Lake. There are excellent views of the William O. country from the peak, making it a good side trip. The suggested loop proceeds straight for 0.2 mile to sprawling, inviting meadows surrounding Fryingpan Lake, where many good camping spots can be found.

Continuing south, the trail skirts forest-bound Little Snow Lake on the right and an unnamed lake (elev. 4850 ft) on the left. The way then descends via long switchbacks engineered for horses, coming to a junction (elev. 4600 ft) 1.4 miles from Fryingpan Lake. Left leads back to a familiar junction—go right instead, and in 0.4 mile come to another junction. Jug Lake (elev. 4400 ft) is 0.1 mile to the right, where good camps can be found in shoreline old-growth groves.

To finish the loop, stay to the left, climbing about 50 feet before losing elevation on rocky, chewed-up tread and reaching the Cowlitz Trail (elev. 3900 ft) in 1 mile. Turn right from there, retracing 2.2 familiar miles back to your vehicle.

TRIP PLANNER	
4.5 miles	Lakeside camp
6.5 miles	Camp at the bigger Twin Sisters Lake
9.4 miles	Fryingpan Lake camps
11.4 miles	Jug Lake camps
14.6 miles	Trailhead

19 American Ridge

RATING/ DIFFICULTY	LOOP	ELEV GAIN/ HIGH POINT	SEASON
***/5	18.3 miles	4900 feet/ 6946 feet	July–Oct

Map: Green Trails Bumping Lake No. 271; **Contact:** Okanogan-Wenatchee National Forest, Naches Ranger District, (509) 653-1401, www.fs.fed.us/r6/wenatchee; **Permits/ regulations:** NW Forest Pass required at Mesatchee Trailhead. Free William O. Douglas Wilderness permit required, self-issued at trailhead. Wilderness rules apply; **Special features:** Rugged backcountry ridge practically devoid of people and home to large elk herds; **Special concerns:** Extremely rough trail with fading and nonexistent tread. Potentially tough creek crossings. Mosquitoes. Heavy equestrian use on Mesatchee Creek Trail. Car shuttle needed to avoid road walk; **GPS:** N 46 56.628 W 121 19.672

Named for the American River in California that prompted a gold rush and made millionaires overnight, Washington's American River never provided a mother lode, but its lofty ridge is rich in wildlife and sought by those who value solitude. This is a tough hike through the heart of lonely, cloud-catching country to deep hidden basins, steep craggy knobs, sunny windswept meadows, and dark forested nooks, where just a few hikers have ever laid bootprint.

GETTING THERE

From Enumclaw, head east on State Route 410 for 40 miles, bearing left at Cayuse Pass. Continue east on SR 410 for another 14.5 miles, passing Chinook Pass, and turn right into the Pleasant Valley Campground. Park at the day-use area before the campground (elev. 3400 ft). (From Yakima, follow SR 410 from Naches west for 36 miles to the campground.)

ON THE TRAIL

This trip starts with a ford of the American River. From the day-use area, walk 0.3 mile through the campground and bear right to reach the river. Near the outhouse, ford the river—a log jam may be present—and immediately enter the William O. Douglas Wilderness. Once across, crash through brush for a bit to find the Kettle Creek Trail, located near some big larches and firs. Once you find it, follow good tread south for 0.2 mile to a junction with the Pleasant Valley Loop Trail. (It's possible to avoid the river ford and shorten the road walk at the end by starting the loop on this trail, which begins 2.7 miles west on SR 410; the trailhead is 2.3 miles west of the campground on SR 410.)

In another 0.1 mile, bear right at a second junction with the Pleasant Valley Loop Trail. Now climb through dry forest. At 1.1 miles, the trail steepens. Catch views of Fifes Peaks

Descending the American Ridge high point for Big Basin

through the trees. Mostly away from Kettle Creek, but crossing several side creeks, the trail heads up the heavily forested valley on an at times steep route, occasionally dropping 50 or 100 feet to frustrate you.

At about 5 miles, reach good camps at Kettle Creek (elev. 4950 ft), where a shin-deep (knee-deep in early season) ford awaits. Continue across open flats, and soon ford the creek once more before beginning a very steep climb. The way eases considerably before reaching a junction with the American Ridge Trail (elev. 5600 ft) at 6.5 miles. Most people who have ventured this far will continue east along the ridge to Goat Peak.

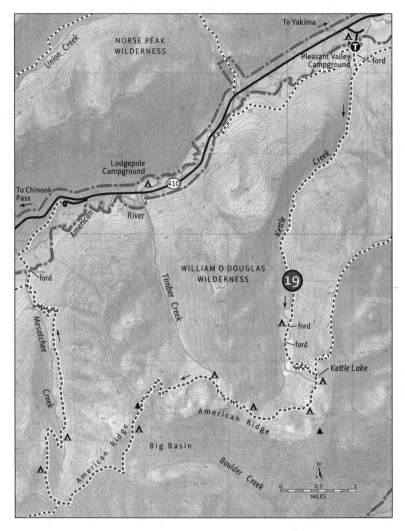

You'll be heading west, immediately coming to Kettle Lake, a shallow, grassy, mosquito-incubating pool. Camps are nearby, but better ones are in a grassy basin 0.7 mile west, so keep hiking, steeply climbing a draw alongside a creek. At 7.2 miles, reach the basin (elev. 6100 ft) flanked by granite ledges and dotted with small tarns, which may be dry late in the season.

Beyond, the tread grows faint—watch for cairns and notches in trees, being careful not to lose the way. Now descending steeply, cross a creek before coming to a beautiful old-growth Alaska yellow cedar grove (elev. 5900 ft). Then it's up again to another tarn-dotted basin with good camps and disappearing tread. Continuing upward, cross numerous elk paths leading to side basins (with exploration and camping possibilities), cresting a ridge (elev. 6350 ft) at 8.4 miles.

The way then makes a brutal descent, where the tread vanishes at a talus slope. Veer right and follow a creek through flowering meadows. At 8.9 miles, reach a small tarn (elev. 5850 ft) at the headwaters of Timber Creek in a basin sprinkled with elk droppings. There's good camping here, and elk watching.

Beyond, enter old growth and continue descending, crossing several Timber Creek tributaries and skirting boulder fields to reach another small tarn (elev. 5700 ft). The way then climbs, crossing more creeks, a rocky basin, and heather meadows, working your way up a steep shoulder, avoiding rocky and impressive knolls and crags.

Views increase as the tread once again vanishes. Now in gorgeous wildflower-dotted meadows, look for cairns and blazes in bordering trees. After tough climbing and routefinding, crest American Ridge (elev. 6900 ft) just below its high point at 10.8 miles. By all means drop your pack and hoof the short distance to the 6946-foot summit. You've earned the breathtaking views east to Bumping Lake and Mount Aix; south to Mount Adams, the Goat Rocks, and the craggy Cascade crest; west to Rainier crowding the horizon; and north to the Norse Peak high country.

Once visually satisfied, steeply descend into the appropriately named Big Basin (elev. 6250 ft), where elk sign are everywhere. I once caused an elk stampede here, when my presence was noted by a bugling sentinel bull. Good camps and springs can be found along the basin edge. Continuing on sketchy tread, leave the basin, rounding a shoulder

(elev. 6325 ft) and crossing steep gullies while admiring fantastic views of Mount Rainer and the Bumping River valley.

Continue steeply dropping along the ridge crest to reach a 5800-foot saddle. Then briefly climb again to reach the Mesatchee Creek Trail (elev. 5925 ft) at 13 miles. Turn right, gently descending, first through lupine parkland meadows and then forest. At 13.8 miles, come to a nice creekside camp. At 14.5 miles, come upon Mesatchee Creek and good camps. *Mesatchee* is Chinook Jargon for "evil" or "wicked." The creek is beautiful but the dusty, rocky, horse-churned trail fits the description well.

At 16.2 miles, reach the trail's highlight, an overlook (elev. 4000 ft) of a beautiful waterfall. From there the trail continues descending, now on short switchbacks, reaching the Dewey Lake Trail at 16.8 miles (elev. 3600 ft). Veer right, soon coming to a waist-deep ford—or a dry-boot detour on an adjacent log jam across the American River. Soon afterward, cross Morse Creek on a bridge and then follow old roads through open woods, arriving at the Mesatchee Creek trailhead (elev. 3700 ft) at 18.3 miles. Unless you've left a car or bike here, walk SR 410 east for 2.2 miles to the Pleasant Valley Loop Trail, which you can follow another 2.7 miles back to the Pleasant Valley Campground and your car. Or you can bike 4.5 miles along SR 410 to the campground.

TRIP PLANNER	
5 miles	Kettle Creek camps
6.5 miles	Kettle Lake camps
7.2 miles	Camps in grassy basin
8.9 miles	Timber Creek basin camp
10.8 miles	American Ridge high point
11.5 miles	Big Basin camps
13.8 miles	Creekside camp
14.5 miles	Mesatchee Creek camps
18.3 miles	Mesatchee Creek trailhead

EXTENDING YOUR TRIP

Skip Mesatchee Creek and continue 5 miles west on American Ridge to combine this trip with Cougar Lakes (Trip 28). Return via the PCT and Dewey Lake Trail.

20 Crow Creek Lake

RATING/ DIFFICULTY	ROUND-TRIP	ELEV GAIN/ HIGH POINT	SEASON
***/3	16 miles	4000 feet/ 5850 feet	mid-June– Nov

Map: Green Trails Bumping Lake No. 271; **Contact:** Okanogan-Wenatchee National Forest, Naches Ranger District, (509) 653-1401, www.fs.fed.us/r6/wenatchee; **Permits/ regulations:** NW Forest Pass required. Free Norse Peak Wilderness permit required, self-issued at trailhead. Wilderness rules apply. No camping within 100 feet of Crow Creek Lake and Sheepherder Lake; **Special features:** Alpine meadows, abundant wildlife; **Special concerns:** Crow Creek ford may be difficult/ dangerous in early season and during heavy rainfall; **GPS:** N 46 57.142 W 121 18.375

A sprawling, shallow, grass-ringed lake better suited for waterfowl and sipping quadrupeds than feet-soaking hikers, Crow Creek Lake is a wildlife lover's paradise. And a hunter's paradise too—so if it's solitude you seek, best stick to summer. The way is long and steep, and so is the return. But the views of the multispire Fifes Peaks, the deep glacier-carved American River valley, sun-dried Nelson Ridge, and snow-coned Mount Rainier are marvelous. And so are the high-country elk that browse flower-popping meadows along the way.

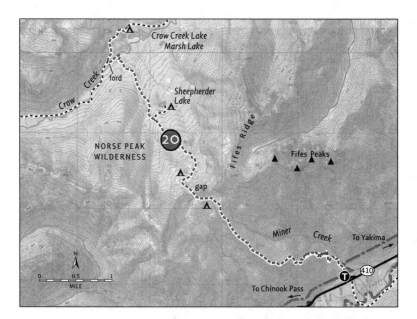

Fifes Peaks rise behind the grassy shores of Crow Creek Lake.

GETTING THERE

From Enumclaw, head east on State Route 410 for 40 miles, bearing left at Cayuse Pass. Continue east on SR 410 for another 17 miles, passing Chinook Pass, and reach the trailhead located in the Fifes Peaks lookout parking area (elev. 3400 ft). (From Yakima, follow US 12 west for 17 miles to SR 410 and follow it 35 more miles to trailhead. Privy available.)

ON THE TRAIL

From the horse camp, locate the trail taking off north. Immediately enter the Norse Peak Wilderness, a sprawling landscape of high ridges and meadows that provide excellent habitat for elk, deer, cougar, bear, and mountain goats.

After 0.25 mile, begin to climb. Despite getting a fair amount of equestrian use, the trail isn't as chewed up or dusty as other horseways. With Miner Creek below and the awesome remnant volcano of Fifes Peaks towering above, the trail steadily climbs up a steep ridge.

You'll wind past a handful of big ponderosa pines and Doug-firs, and then the forest eventually transitions to lodgepole pine and western larch. Water is at a premium along the way, and sunshine can be plentiful—carry plenty of water. At about 1.7 miles, come to a ledge (elev. 4750 ft) that provides excellent views of American River below and American Ridge across the valley. Contorted pines and firs along the ledge look straight out of a

Japanese landscape painting. Keep climbing—the views get better. Soon, Rainier reveals its snowy mass. Exercise caution, as the way teeters above a sheer cliff face. The dry, sandy trail and surrounding rocky spires and ridges help give the area a southwestern feel.

The grade once again steepens, reaching a 5850-foot shoulder on Fifes Peaks at about 3.5 miles. The way then steeply drops to a small spring (which may be dry) in an area that burned decades ago. After a few ups and downs, the way brushes up alongside a gorgeous meadow in a quiet basin (elev. 5575 ft), where camping, exploring, and wildlife observing can all be enjoyed.

Climb once more, reaching a small gap (elev. 5650 ft) at 4 miles. From here, the trail descends, first through glorious parkland meadows and then through cool old-growth forest. At about 0.25 mile beyond the gap, there are good campsites next to a small pond and creek.

At 5 miles, come to a junction (elev. 5100 ft). The right-hand trail leads 0.3 mile and drops 200 feet to tiny green-tinted Sheepherder Lake. This spot is overfished and overcamped, so carry on for Crow Creek Lake. The main trail continues its descent, crossing a creek and then passing the barely discernable path to a speck of a pond, Marsh Lake.

The trail then rounds a basalt bluff above Crow Creek and comes to a small meadow beside the creek (elev. 4650 ft) at 7.2 miles. Find a good place to ford the creek, usually just ankle-deep by late summer but possibly difficult in early season, reaching a junction with the Cougar Valley Trail.

Head to the right, downstream, traveling beneath cliffs and crossing a couple of creeks before emerging at 8 miles at the grassy expanse housing Crow Creek Lake (elev. 4550 ft). Plenty of excellent campsites are tucked in evergreen groves at meadow's edge. Watch for waterfowl, warblers, and wapiti at this

wetland wonderland. Slather on the DEET or wait until September. And enjoy watching the evening light dance off of Fifes Peaks.

TRIP PLANNER	
3.8 miles	Camps in quiet basin
4.25 miles	Camps beyond gap
5.3 miles	Sheepherder Lake
8 miles	Crow Creek Lake camps

EXTENDING YOUR TRIP

Hike 5.2 miles up Crow Creek to Big Crow Basin (Trip 21), or make a big 24.5-mile loop by following the Lake Basin Trail to Union Creek and taking the Pleasant Valley Lake Trail back to your vehicle. Or continue on the Cougar Valley Trail for 5 miles, climbing 1400 feet to the Raven Roost trailhead and views.

21 Big Crow Basin

RATING/ DIFFICULTY	LOOP	ELEV GAIN/ HIGH POINT	SEASON
****/3	20.7 miles	4125 feet/ 6400 feet	mid-June– Nov

Map: Green Trails Bumping Lake No. 271; **Contact:** Mount Baker–Snoqualmie National Forest, Snoqualmie Ranger District, Enumclaw, (360) 825-6585, www.fs.fed.us/r6 /mbs; **Permits/regulations:** Free Norse Peak Wilderness permit required, self-issued at trailhead. Wilderness rules apply. No camping within 100 feet of Goat Lake and Basin Lake; **Special features:** Alpine meadows and abundant wildlife, especially elk and mountain goats; **Special concerns:** Heavy equestrian use and popular hunting area; **GPS:** N 46 57.864 W 121 29.009

Here's a grand loop in the Norse Peak Wilderness, long on splendid scenery and alpine meadows—and short on crowds. Most visitors to these parts congregate on

Basin Lake

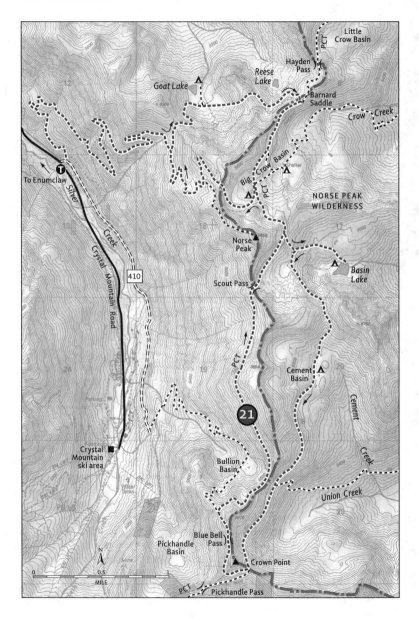

the 6856-foot peak that lends its name to this 52,000-acre wilderness, leaving the Big Crow Basin below it teeming with goats, elk, deer, and bear. Explore nearby Lake Basin, Cement Basin, and Bullion Basin and look for relics of the area's mining past. And, not least, stand on Crown Point, reeling in a royal in-your-face view of Mount Rainier.

GETTING THERE

From Enumclaw, head east on State Route 410 for 32 miles and turn left onto Crystal Mountain Road (just before the Mount Rainier National Park entrance). Continue for 4.2 miles to the parking area for the Norse Peak Trail, on your right (elev. 3850 ft).

ON THE TRAIL

Start by crossing the road and walking gravel Forest Road 410 for 0.2 mile to the Norse Peak trailhead (elev. 4025 ft). Start climbing via a series of long dusty switchbacks. Avoid wandering onto old sections of this trail and be careful not to step in any trail apples along the way. Through scrappy forest lined with lupine, window views grow. Much of this area succumbed to forest fire around 1900, leaving a much more open landscape favoring brilliant wildflowers.

Ascending higher, traverse resplendent meadows—all under the ever watchful icy eye of Rainier. At 3.8 miles, come to a junction (elev. 5900 ft). You'll be returning on the right, so head left, climbing steeply for 0.3 mile to a 6100-foot gap with good views of Castle Mountain and Goat Lake, tucked below in a secluded basin. Drop and traverse the lake basin (snow may linger here, use caution), crossing meadow and talus and reaching an unmarked but obvious trail junction (elev. 5900 ft) at 4.7 miles. The path left drops to Goat Lake, where you'll find good camps and a lot of elk activity.

The main trail continues, traversing talus (and perhaps snow) and climbing to another gap. Then, after crossing more meadows, reach the Pacific Crest Trail at 5.7 miles at Barnard Saddle (elev. 6150 ft), entering the Norse Peak Wilderness. Turn right and walk south along the PCT, across a meadowed ridge rife with rock gardens and excellent views east to craggy Fifes Peaks and the verdant Crow Creek valley.

Pass a side trail that drops into Big Crow Basin and leads to an old shelter and good camps. Look and listen for elk—they're prolific here. At 6.7 miles, at the head of Big Crow Basin, near the headwaters of Crow Creek, reach a junction (elev. 6200 ft)— the Crow Lake Trail heads left for 6 miles to Crow Creek Lake (Trip 20), and the right-hand trail heads to Norse Peak (your return route).

Continue straight through the lush basin, passing springs and creeks and many camping spots, coming to another junction (elev. 6400 ft) at 7.4 miles. You'll be returning on the right on the PCT. Here, head left on the Basin Trail, taking in gorgeous views of American and Nelson ridges. After 0.3 mile, reach a side trail (elev. 6150 ft)—a mandatory detour. Follow this eroded path 0.5 mile to lovely Basin Lake (elev. 5825 ft) beneath towering slopes of basalt and surrounded by meadow. There are good camps here, good wildlife viewing too— look for elk in the fields, mountain goats in the crags, and ground squirrels all over the basin.

After a good night's rest, retrace your steps back to the Basin Trail. A lot of game trails and user paths offer alternative routes—carry a good map. Now follow the Basin Trail south up a knoll for excellent views over Basin Lake, and then steeply climb up a gully to a 6400-foot gap to views of Mount Adams and Goat Rocks.

Drop steeply into Cement Basin (elev. 5950 ft), passing tarns and mud holes (and good camps after the bugs are gone), enjoying a lightly used trail that sports hoof marks as opposed to boot tracks. At 2.2 miles from Basin Lake (10.4 miles from your start), reach a junction with the Union Creek Trail (elev. 5900 ft). Continue to the right, and after 0.8 mile reach the PCT on an open ridge crest (elev. 6150 ft). Turn right, and after 0.2 mile round Crown Point. It's an easy 0.25-mile off-trail scramble to the 6470-foot summit. But even from the 6300-foot high point along the trail, the views of Rainier, Adams, Goat Rocks, and American Ridge are outstanding.

After soaking in the scenery, continue north on the PCT for a ridgeline viewing fest all the way back to Big Crow Basin. At 11.8 miles from your start, stay to the right at the junction with the Bullion Basin Trail. An alternative route back to the trailhead (via 2 miles on FR 410), this trail to an old gold-mining area gets heavy equestrian use and is quite rocky and dusty.

At 13.8 miles, reach Scout Pass (elev. 6200 ft)—you can make an easy off-trail scramble to Norse Peak from here. Otherwise,

continue 0.4 mile back to the Basin Trail (elev. 6400 ft). Then head north another 0.4 mile to a familiar junction (elev. 6200 ft), taking the Norse Peak Trail left, climbing out of the basin, and reaching a junction at a 6400-foot shoulder after about 1 mile. The 6856-foot summit can be reached by following the trail left for 0.7 mile. Otherwise, head right, reaching your vehicle in another 5.1 miles and completing this wonderful 20.7-mile loop.

TRIP PLANNER	
5 miles	Goat Lake camps
6.7 miles	Big Crow Basin camps
6.7–7.4 miles	Camps in lush meadow
8.2 miles	Basin Lake camps
9.2 miles	Cement Basin camps
11.4 miles	Crown Point
13.8 miles	Scout Pass
20.7 miles	Trailhead

EXTENDING YOUR TRIP

If you can arrange a car shuttle, combine this trip with Crow Creek Lake (Trip 20), using the Crow Lake Trail.

Opposite: Spray Park (Trip 22)

Mount Rainier

Mount Rainier reflected in tarn in Spray Park

22 | Ipsut Creek and Seattle Park

RATING/ DIFFICULTY	LOOP	ELEV GAIN/ HIGH POINT	SEASON
*****/3	16.2 miles	4375 feet/ 6350 feet	mid-July– Oct

Map: Green Trails Mount Rainier Wonderland Trail No. 269S; **Contact:** Mount Rainier National Park, Carbon River Ranger Station, (360) 829-9639, www.nps.gov/mora; **Permits/regulations:** National park entrance fee. Camping permit required, available from Carbon River Ranger Station (during open hours), or call park for alternatives. Backcountry reservations not required, but recommended. Fires prohibited. Dogs prohibited; **Special features:** Carbon Glacier close up, stunning wildflower displays, Mount Rainier views; **Special concerns:** Permanent snowfields at Seattle Park may make travel difficult; **GPS:** N 46 55.977 W 121 51.844

🚶 📷 *Cathedral forests, silver strands of cascading waters, the snout of a massive snaking glacier, fields of dazzling wildflowers, parklands teeming with deer, bear, and marmots, and stunning in-your-face views of the Mountain reflected in pretty alpine pools—this loop captures the very essence of Mount Rainier National Park and what makes it so special.*

GETTING THERE

From Buckley, follow State Route 165 (off of SR 410, from either Enumclaw or Sumner) south for 10.3 miles, bearing right on the road to Mowich Lake. Continue another 11 sometimes dusty and bumpy miles (the pavement ends at 1.6 miles) to the national park boundary. Proceed 5.8 miles farther, passing the entrance station, to the road's end at Mowich Lake (elev. 4950 ft). Privy available.

ON THE TRAIL

Don't be surprised by the number of vehicles parked at Mowich Lake. Spray Park (part of loop) and Tolmie Peak (a side-trip option) are extremely popular day-hiking destinations. But beyond these locales, the crowds thin, allowing you to enjoy this spectacular trip without being elbow-to-elbow with fellow hikers. Many hikers do this loop counterclockwise so as to approach Rainier, but I recommend clockwise—that way, you won't finish with a grueling climb, and you'll exit Spray Park later in the day when lighting for photography is optimal.

Head north on the Wonderland Trail, skirting lovely Mowich Lake (in Chinook Jargon, *mowich* means "deer"). Then in cool forest, gently climb and reach Ipsut Pass (elev. 5150 ft) at 1.5 miles (in Chinook Jargon, *ipsut* means "hidden"). Here a trail leads left for 1.7 miles to Eunice Lake and the Tolmie Peak lookout (elev. 5939 ft), a scenic and worthwhile side excursion.

The Wonderland Trail drops steeply on rocky tread through brushy avalanche slopes to follow Ipsut Creek on its way to the Carbon River. At about 2.8 miles, locate a massive Alaska yellow cedar, one of the largest in the state. Closer to the Carbon, traverse dank groves of magnificent old-growth hemlocks. At 5.1 miles, reach a junction (elev. 2500 ft) near the roaring, milky, glacier-fed Carbon River. The trail left leads 0.3 mile to Ipsut Falls and the Ipsut Creek Campground, once a car-accessed area (before the floods of 2006 washed out the Carbon River Road), now a backcountry campground (permits needed).

The Wonderland Trail turns right here and follows the wide, channeled river beneath an interior-rainforest canopy comprised of hemlock, cedar, and Doug-fir. At 6.8 miles, stay right at a junction (unless you want to head off on the Northern Loop, Trip 26), continuing to follow the Carbon upriver. Carbon River Camp is at 7.8 miles, just before the bridged crossing

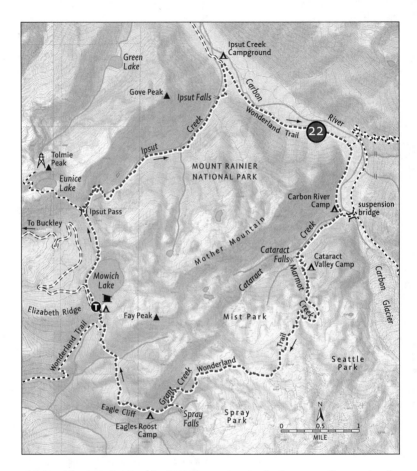

of Cataract Creek at a junction (elev. 3200 ft). Spend the night here, letting the roar of the Carbon lull you to sleep. Before carrying on to the right, be sure to wander left a short ways to a suspension bridge, offering great viewing of the Carbon Glacier, the lowest (and one of the largest) glaciers in the Lower 48.

Now on the Spray Park Trail, begin a long climb out of the deep valley. At 9.4 miles find the Cataract Valley Camp (elev. 4450 ft), which is dark, wooded, and away from the

cataracts. Continue ascending, passing the cascade of Marmot Creek before breaking out of forest into heather meadows. Crossing numerous creeks (no water shortage here), keep gaining elevation and enter beautiful Seattle Park. Mount Rainier reveals itself above while lesser-known peaks—Tyee, Old Desolate, Crescent—can be seen to the north.

After you skirt a couple of tarns, heather meadows soon yield to tundra and rock. Routefinding might be tough in bad weather.

Look for cairns and painted blazes in this rocky alpine "wasteland." Permanent snowfields are encountered next, making trekking poles a necessary item for this trip. In early season, an ice ax is a must.

At 12 miles, climbing ceases on a high shoulder (elev. 6350 ft). Relish sweeping views that extend from the Olympics to Mount Baker, before descending into spectacular Spray Park. Here, pass boulder gardens and fields flush in wildflowers—tarns, too, that reflect Mount Rainier in all its glory.

As you descend farther, the tread widens, attesting to the millions of boots that have plodded to this subalpine heaven over the years. After crossing Grant Creek, the way steeply descends via a series of short switchbacks, coming to a junction (elev. 4900 ft) at 14.1 miles. The way left is a mandatory 0.1-mile side trip to spectacular Spray Falls, a 300-foot cataract tumbling down an open andesite cliff.

Continuing the loop, reach Eagle's Roost Camp in a wooded nook 0.1 mile west. The way then climbs 100 feet to Eagle Cliff, where you can take in a breathtaking view of the Mountain. Then drop to skirt a talus slope (elev. 4725 ft) before climbing again. At 15.9 miles, come to the Wonderland Trail. Bear right and reach your start at Mowich Lake in 0.3 mile.

TRIP PLANNER	
5.4 miles	Old Ipsut Creek Campground
7.8 miles	Carbon River Camp
9.4 miles	Cataract Valley Camp
12.5 miles	Spray Park
14.2 miles	Eagle's Roost Camp
16.2 miles	Trailhead

THE WONDERLAND TRAIL: HIKING 22,000 VERTICAL FEET AROUND THE MOUNTAIN

More than a few backpackers have Mount Rainier National Park's Wonderland Trail on their bucket list. In fact, adventurers from all over America and the world come each year to Rainier to hike this amazing trail. Built in 1915, along with the Eagle Creek Trail in the Columbia River Gorge, it's one of the oldest trails in the Pacific Northwest. And like Eagle Creek, it's one of the most popular too. Thousands upon thousands of hikers from all walks of life each season take to parts of this trail, which completely circumnavigates Washington's highest and most famous peak.

Traversing old-growth forests, subalpine parklands, alpine meadows, and alpine tundra, the Wonderland Trail travels for 93 miles through all of the mountain's major life zones. Views are continuous, extensive, and beyond comparison. While parts of the trail are well built and pass through developed areas of the park, completing the entire trail can be a challenge, with its over 22,000 cumulative vertical feet of elevation gain, lingering snowfields, raging creeks, and often inclement weather. Competition is fierce, too, for campsites along the way, with the Park Service limiting permits to assure that the backcountry won't be overrun and visitors will have a positive experience. During the busy summer months, it is imperative to reserve sites for any long-distance trips on the Wonderland Trail.

There are plenty of good resources for backpackers wishing to hike the Wonderland Trail in its entirety (see Appendix I: Recommended Reading). The following trips in this guidebook offer a taste of this spectacular trail: Ipsut Creek and Seattle Park (Trip 22), Sunset Park and Golden Lakes (Trip 23), Klapatche Park (Trip 24), Emerald Ridge (Trip 25), and the Northern Loop (Trip 26).

23 Sunset Park and Golden Lakes

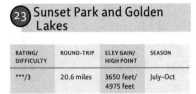

RATING/ DIFFICULTY	ROUND-TRIP	ELEV GAIN/ HIGH POINT	SEASON
***/3	20.6 miles	3650 feet/ 4975 feet	July–Oct

Map: Green Trails Mount Rainier Wonderland Trail No. 269S; **Contact:** Mount Rainier National Park, Carbon River Ranger Station, (360) 829-9639; www.nps.gov/mora; **Permits/regulations:** National park entrance fee. Camping permit required, available from Carbon River Ranger Station (during open hours), or call park for alternatives. Backcountry reservations not required, but recommended. Fires prohibited. Dogs prohibited; **Special features:** Old growth, solitude, subalpine lakes; **Special concerns:** Abundant mosquitoes. **GPS:** N 46 56.088 W 121 54.439

Though one of the more sedate sections of the Wonderland Trail, what Sunset Park lacks in jaw-dropping scenery it more than makes up for in solitude. One of the least visited areas of the park, Sunset Park and Golden Lakes lack day hikers, favored instead by Wonderland through-hikers. Enjoy tranquil old-growth forests, a ridgeline shrouded in bear grass, and one of the nicest backcountry camps in the park. Then watch a setting sun brush the surrounding small lakes golden. It's a softer, less experienced side of Rainier.

GETTING THERE

From Buckley, follow State Route 165 (off of SR 410, from either Enumclaw or Sumner) south for 10.3 miles, bearing right on the road to Mowich Lake. Continue another 11 sometimes dusty and bumpy miles (the pavement ends at 1.6 miles) to the national park boundary. Proceed 0.7 mile farther to the entrance station and the Paul Peak trailhead (elev. 3700 ft). Privy available.

ON THE TRAIL

Start your adventure on the Paul Peak Trail, one of the least hiked trails in the park. But despite its lack of notoriety, the trail is well maintained and in excellent shape. Immediately drop to cross Meadow Creek (elev. 3300 ft) on a bridge in a cool, dark draw. Then angle around heavily wooded Paul Peak, traversing gorgeous stands of old-growth timber. Savor the serenity. After gradually gaining elevation (to 3500 ft), begin losing it—first slowly, then more rapidly, passing through a semi-open area of windblown forest with good views of the Mountain en route.

At 3.3 miles, reach the Wonderland Trail (elev. 2850 ft). Turn right and continue losing elevation, remembering that this must all be gained on the way out! At 3.9 miles, cross the rushing and silty glacier-fed North Mowich River (elev. 2650 ft) on a solid log bridge, coming to the South Mowich River backcountry camp area shortly afterward. Located in open forest on a bank above the roaring South Mowich River, this area offers quite an audible contrast to the quiet lakes ahead.

Beyond this alluring camping area, continue south on the Wonderland Trail to the multichanneled crossing of the South Mowich River (log bridges are in place during summer and fall). Marvel upriver at the churning gray waters roiling down from glaciers that are wedged between steep stark ridges. Look north, too, to Paul Peak draped in an emerald robe of ancient conifers.

Once across the river, begin a long and arduous climb. There are no water sources until Sunset Park, so be sure your water bottles are full. Take comfort in the fact that the climb is entirely shaded. Steadily gain elevation by way

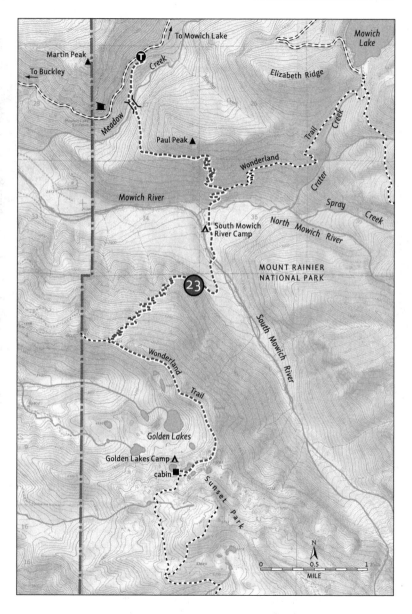

Channeled glacier-fed South Mowich River

of long switchbacks, ascending a steep ridge and transitioning from big old cedars to hemlocks to firs. The trail is generally in good shape but is slumping in places, needing some rehabilitation. At 8 miles, break out of forest cover and attain a small gap (elev. 4700 ft). To the right is an old trail leading to a jeep track outside of the park into adjacent mega tree farms. Follow it a short way if you'd like, to an open knoll with excellent views of the Mountain.

Otherwise continue—the way now easy, traversing fairly open slopes with good views west and south but only limited views of

Rainier, semihidden behind the long ridge known as the Colonnades. Much of the surrounding forest went up in flames in 1930 when a contractor commissioned to extend the Westside Road accidentally caused the ignition. The road plan was eventually extinguished (thankfully), and the forest is slowly recovering, offering nice flower and bear grass displays in the process. The way passes high above the largest of the Golden Lakes, a series of a dozen-plus subalpine bodies of water tucked on the high divide between the Mowich and Puyallup watersheds.

After attaining an elevation of 4975 feet, the way slightly descends to skirt a couple of lakes, finally arriving at the Golden Lakes Camp and ranger cabin (elev. 4900 ft) at 10.3 miles. Cozy campsites are tucked on a small bluff beside a good-sized lake, which warms nicely by late summer, enough for a swim. Sunset views out to the western horizon can be had from the camps, and Mount Rainier can be seen from along the lake's western shoreline. Savor the solitude and tranquility.

TRIP PLANNER	
4.2 miles	South Mowich River Camp
10.3 miles	Golden Lakes Camp

EXTENDING YOUR TRIP
For excellent views and wildflowers, continue south on the Wonderland Trail deep into Sunset Park. Locate an old trail approximately 2 miles south of the ranger cabin—it leads left for a little more than 1 mile to a 5700-foot knoll that once housed a fire lookout. The Golden Lakes can also be reached from the south by hiking or mountain biking the Westside Road for 9 miles; then follow the North Puyallup Trail (an old roadbed) 2.9 miles to the Wonderland Trail and hike it for 5 more miles.

24 Klapatche Park

RATING/ DIFFICULTY	ROUND-TRIP	ELEV GAIN/ HIGH POINT	SEASON
*****/4	21.4 miles	4600 feet/ 5950 feet	mid-July– Oct

Map: Green Trails Mount Rainier Wonderland Trail No. 269S; **Contact:** Mount Rainier National Park, Longmire Wilderness Information Center, (360) 569-4453, www.nps.gov /mora; **Permits/regulations:** National park entrance fee. Camping permit required, available from Longmire. Backcountry reservations not required, but recommended,

permits are limited. Fires prohibited. Dogs prohibited; **Special features:** Solitude, alpine lakes, spectacular sunsets; **Special concerns:** None. **GPS:** N 46 46.798 W 121 53.108

While Indian Bar and Summerland are often cited as the most beautiful places in Mount Rainier National Park, they are also among the most crowded. It's a different story on the west side. Here you won't find any day hikers, and overnighters are limited. Bear, mountain goats, and deer freely frolic in this high parkland's meadows. Reflections at sunset of Mount Rainier in Aurora Lake rival those of Glacier Peak's Image Lake. And the campsite? Legendary guidebook author Harvey Manning called it the most beautiful on the entire Wonderland Trail. I concur!

GETTING THERE
From Tacoma, follow State Route 7 south for 40 miles to Elbe. Continue east on SR 706, past Ashford, reaching Mount Rainier National Park in 6 miles. At 1 mile past the entrance station, turn left on Westside Road and reach the trailhead (elev. 2900 ft) in 3.3 miles.

ON THE TRAIL
Start by walking the gravel Westside Road (closed to traffic). Originally planned to run all the way to Mowich Lake, the road's last segment to Klapatche Point was constructed in the 1930s. After washing out numerous times along Tahoma Creek, the road was permanently closed in the late 1980s. The road makes for a quiet walk—or you can mountain bike it, stashing your bike at several former trailheads.

With Mount Wow on your left (look up for mountain goats) and Tahoma Creek on your right (admire the glacier-fed torrents), slowly ascend. At 1.8 miles, pass the Tahoma Creek Trail (Trip 25). A short distance later,

Anemones line the Wonderland Trail on the way to Klapatche Park.

pass the old Tahoma Vista picnic area. At 3.8 miles, come to Round Pass (elev. 3900 ft). There are bike racks here if you need to secure your mountain bike. A trail to the left leads 0.8 mile to Lake George and camping and then continues to Gobblers Knob and the Glacier View Wilderness. The road continues north. Your trail heads right. But first, check out the partially grown-in Marine Memorial commemorating a 1946 plane crash.

Head to the right onto the Round Pass Trail into cool old growth, descending 0.6 mile to a junction (elev. 3550 ft) with the South Puyallup

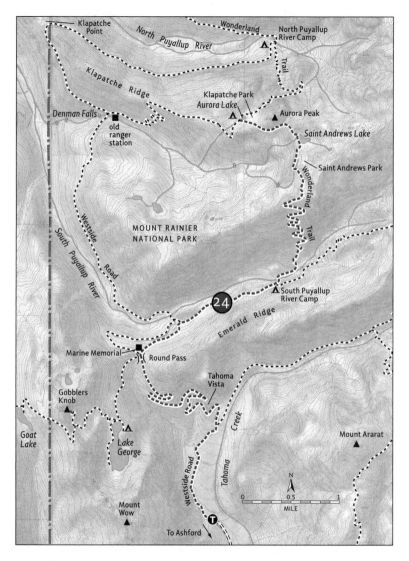

River Trail. Go right, paralleling the South Puyallup River and eventually passing a cliffside of beautiful columnar andesite. At 6 miles, come to the South Puyallup River Camp—and shortly afterward, the Wonderland Trail (elev. 4200 ft).

Right leads to Emerald Ridge (Trip 25). Go left to the emerald parklands of Saint Andrews and Klapatche. After dropping slightly to cross the silted river on a high bridge, begin climbing and enjoy good views to peaks and valleys west and Emerald Ridge east. As the trail marches up the spine of a ridge, meadow replaces forest, views expand, and huckleberries grow in profusion. Keep your eyes peeled for foraging critters.

At 8.7 miles, reach a high notch (elev. 5950 ft) and then slowly descend into a rocky basin. Here, in one of the wildest, quietest corners of Mount Rainer National Park, you can stare out at industrial forestland and Pugetopolis in the distance. After crossing a small creek (elev. 5700 ft), climb once more to soon reach gorgeous Saint Andrews Park (elev. 5850 ft), where sparkling Saint Andrews Lake invites lingering. Glistening Mount Rainier, above, will make you reach for your sunglasses, and the impressive Tokaloo Spire elicits wonderment. Near the lake's outlet, an unmarked trail heads right to a smaller, higher lake tucked in a remote basin.

The Wonderland Trail continues north, climbing 50 feet or so before reaching a small saddle beneath Aurora Peak. An unmarked and very steep scramble trail takes off for 0.3 mile to the peak's 6076-foot summit. Klapatche Park lies just ahead. Gently descending through flowering meadows, at 10.7 miles reach a junction (elev. 5500 ft) with the Saint Andrews Creek Trail at shallow, meadow-flanked Aurora Lake in gorgeous Klapatche Park.

The beautifully situated camp is on a small wooded knoll just above the lake. A spring just to the east of the lake (sometimes dry by late season) provides good drinking water. *Aurora* means "dawn" in Latin—and watching reflections in the lake of dawn's early light dancing upon the glaciers of Rainier is stunning. But the evenings are even grander. Indeed, this one of the most enchanting spots along the Wonderland Trail.

TRIP PLANNER	
6 miles	South Puyallup River Camp
10.7 miles	Klapatche Park Camp

EXTENDING YOUR TRIP

With a base camp at Klapatche Park, make a 9.5-mile loop to the North Puyallup River, Klapatche Point, and Klapatche Ridge via the Wonderland Trail, North Puyallup Trail, Westside Road, and Saint Andrews Creek Trail. Be sure to visit the historical ranger station and Denman Falls in the process. Or do this loop as your main hike, combined with an 18-mile round-trip mountain bike ride on the Westside Road.

25 Emerald Ridge

RATING/ DIFFICULTY	LOOP	ELEV GAIN/ HIGH POINT	SEASON
****/3	13.6 miles	3150 feet/ 5600 feet	July–Oct

Map: Green Trails Mount Rainier Wonderland Trail No. 269S; **Contact:** Mount Rainier National Park, Longmire Wilderness Information Center (360) 569-4453, www.nps.gov /mora; **Permits/regulations:** National park entrance fee. Camping permit required, available from Longmire. Backcountry reservations not required, but recommended. Fires prohibited. Dogs prohibited; **Special features:** Close-up glacier viewing, mountain goats, columnar basalt, and a cool suspension bridge; **Special concerns:** Tahoma Creek Trail is prone to washouts and may be difficult to follow; **GPS:** N 46 46.798 W 121 53.108

Hike around and along an emerald wedge lodged beneath the massive Tahoma Glacier and set between two deep canyons of glacier-fed, cloudy, milky, and turbulent creeks. Flowers sway above the moraine and dislodging ice, while herds of mountain goats graze on succulent tubers on precarious ledges. This short loop encompasses a diverse array of forest, mountain, and meadow and takes you to two of the least hiked trails in Mount Rainier National Park.

GETTING THERE

From Tacoma, follow State Route 7 south for 40 miles to Elbe. Continue east on SR 706, past Ashford, reaching Mount Rainier National Park in 6 miles. At 1 mile past the entrance station, turn left on Westside Road and reach the trailhead (elev. 2900 ft) in 3.3 miles.

ON THE TRAIL

There is only one camping option on this loop—the South Puyallup River campsites, roughly halfway around the loop. Be sure to reserve a site well in advance, or be prepared to alter your plans if campsites are not available. Begin by walking the gravel Westside Road (closed to traffic). After washing out numerous times over the years, the road was permanently closed in the late 1980s. Walking along Tahoma Creek, you immediately see evidence of the creek's past fury.

Crossing creek channels and walking up a rocky roadbed, reach the possibly unmarked Tahoma Creek Trail (elev. 3200 ft) at 1.8 miles, at a bend in the road. This trail is also prone to numerous washouts and receives sporadic and minimal maintenance. Pay attention to cairns and flagging, and watch your footing around and under uprooted trees.

After passing a small wetland area, emerge onto Tahoma Creek's rocky and sandy outwash. Take time to inspect the roaring creek—powerful enough to move boulders and topple centuries-old trees. Look carefully for where the trail leaves the riverbank to climb a steep bluff blanketed in old growth.

The rough-at-times trail climbs steeply above the roaring boulder-bound creek. At one point, you must detour around a large

The Colonnades, a wall of columnar andesite

washout area, which requires a 100-foot drop. Shortly after crossing a side creek beneath a small cascade, reach the Wonderland Trail (elev. 4300 ft) at 3.9 miles.

Before heading left for the loop, be sure to hike right a short distance to check out the huge suspension bridge high above Tahoma Creek. Then head north, immediately climbing and enjoying views of the bridge and creek gorge. After a couple of switchbacks, the way leaves forest and marches up the lateral moraine of the receding Tahoma Glacier. Enjoy excellent views of Pyramid Peak to the right, the Tokaloo Spire to the left, and Glacier Island straight ahead and up—a barren wedge of a ridge that not too long ago was

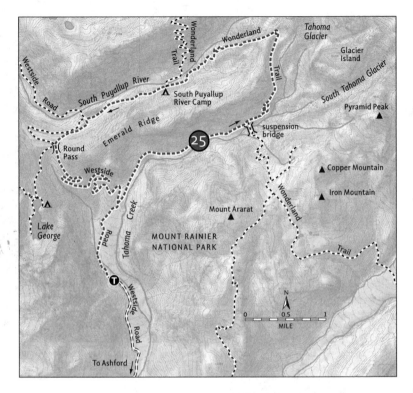

surrounded by snow and ice. Recent climate change is evident here at Mount Rainier's receding glaciers.

Across rock and glacial till, the trail crests a gap on Emerald Ridge (elev. 5600 ft) at 6.1 miles. Now standing just above the snout of the Tahoma Glacier, enjoy fascinating views of blue ice, dirty moraine, and deep crevasses. Be sure to scan Glacier Island too for moving clumps of white—mountain goats are often easily spotted along this ridge.

Then continue hiking along the ridge across flowered slopes on the edge of a deep canyon carved by the glacier. Reentering forest, the trail drops to reach the South Puyallup Trail (elev. 4200 ft) at 7.6 miles. Campsites

and good non-glacier-fed water are located just down this trail. One of the least hiked trails in the park, this pleasurable path gently descends through deep old growth, following alongside the roaring South Puyallup River. But the real treat is the Colonnades—a wall of columnar andesite (old lava flows) that tower above just past the campsites. To this writer of Italian descent, it appears as if giant strands of pasta are pushing out of the ridge!

At 9.2 miles, reach a junction (elev. 3550 ft). Veer left onto the Round Pass Trail and ascend through more primeval forest to reach the Westside Road at Round Pass (elev. 3900 ft) at 9.8 miles. Return to your vehicle via the old road, completing the 13.6-mile loop.

TRIP PLANNER	
6.1 miles	Emerald Ridge
7.6 miles	South Puyallup River Camp
9.8 miles	Round Pass
13.6 miles	Trailhead

EXTENDING YOUR TRIP

Spend another night out by hiking from Round Pass 0.8 mile to Lake George. Be sure to have a camping permit. Or combine this hike with Klapatche Park (Trip 24) for an even longer adventure.

26 Northern Loop

RATING/ DIFFICULTY	LOOP	ELEV GAIN/ HIGH POINT	SEASON
*****/5	36.3 miles	9000 feet/ 6750 feet	mid-July– Oct

Map: Green Trails Mount Rainier Wonderland Trail No. 269S; **Contact:** Mount Rainier National Park, White River Wilderness Information Center, (360) 569-2211 ext. 6030, www.nps.gov/mora; **Permits/regulations:** National park entrance fee. Camping permit required, available from White River Wilderness Information Center. Fires prohibited. Dogs prohibited; **Special features:** Rugged multiday loop in little-visited section of Mount Rainier NP. Excellent wildlife viewing opportunities, spectacular alpine scenery; **Special concerns:** Cumulative elevation gain makes loop arduous. Mosquitoes can be fearsome at Lake James; **GPS:** N 46 54.849 W 121 38.514

A spectacularly rugged and wild loop through the northern hinterlands of Mount Rainier National Park, this trip packs a wilderness wallop! Traverse parkland meadows, alpine tundra, old-growth forest, glacial moraine, high passes, and low valleys. Witness raging creeks, placid lakes, massive glaciers, and unsurpassed natural beauty. And experience much of it without the crowds that usually populate the Wonderland Trail.

GETTING THERE

From Enumclaw, follow State Route 410 east for 37.5 miles to Mount Rainier National Park, and turn right onto White River Road (signed for Sunrise). Continue for 1.4 miles to the entrance station and the White River Wilderness Information Center. Follow White River Road another 14 miles to its terminus at Sunrise (elev. 6400 ft). Privy and water available.

ON THE TRAIL

You have three choices: Take the Sunrise Nature Trail to the highly scenic Sourdough Ridge Trail to reach the Wonderland Trail in 1.5 miles at a five-way trail junction at Frozen Lake (elev. 6750 ft). Alternatively, you can follow the old Sunrise Camp Road to the Wonderland Trail to this junction (1.5 miles). Or take the meandering Sunrise Rim Trail to the Wonderland Trail, passing Shadow Lake en route (2.3 miles).

From this barren, windswept gap continue west on the Wonderland Trail, leaving the casual hiker brigades behind. Traversing alpine tundra under the icy watchful eye of the Mountain, descend slightly for 0.8 mile to reach a junction with the Northern Loop Trail (elev. 6400 ft). This loop trip is tough going in either direction—I prefer clockwise, so continue left on the Wonderland Trail, enjoying sweeping views of emerald Berkeley Park below.

After descending 100 more feet the way climbs steadily, reaching a 6700-foot pass beneath 7078-foot Skyscraper Mountain. Views of Rainier are excellent here (and even better from the summit, reached by way of scramble path), also of Old Desolate and Sluiskin Mountain. Next begin a long gentle descent, soon entering forest and reaching Granite Creek Camp (elev. 5850 ft) at 5 miles

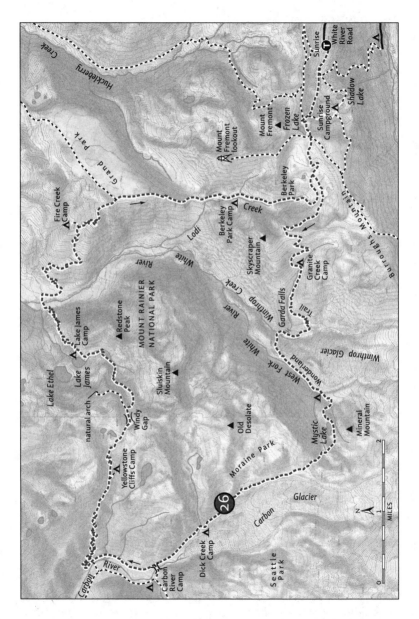

(from Sunrise). The wooded sites are close to water and fairly protected.

The Wonderland Trail continues descending, soon emerging on lateral moraine beneath the massive Winthrop Glacier. Winthrop Creek streams from the glacier—on a hot day it thunders! After passing Garda Falls on your right, cross the milky, silty, splashing creek on a foot log (elev. 4600 ft) before beginning a long ascent to Mystic Lake. Climb first along glacial moraine and then through hemlock forest beside the West Fork White River (here more of a stream). Cross it and arrive at Mystic Lake Camp (elev. 5550 ft) in thick forest at 9.3 miles (from Sunrise).

Attractive and inviting Mystic Lake (elev. 5700 ft) lies 0.2 mile farther. Enjoy soaking in its sparkling waters (warm in late summer), or just enjoy Mineral Mountain and Old Desolate reflecting from its surface. Continue on the Wonderland Trail along the lakeshore and across flowering bogs before steeply climbing to a 6060-foot gap. Views are splendid here of Rainier above and Moraine Park and the Carbon Glacier below.

The way now makes a long descent through Moraine Park. Mount Rainier majestically hovers above while gregarious marmots frolic and flitter in a mosaic of blossoming beauties. Continuing a downward journey, enter forest much wetter and danker than the whitebark pine and subalpine fir forests of Sunrise. The sound of crashing water grows louder as the trail parallels the Carbon Glacier, largest of the radiating ice packs emanating from the Mountain.

At 14.1 miles, after passing beneath a small waterfall, come to small Dick Creek Camp (elev. 4140 ft) just above cascading Dick Creek. Continue descending and, after another 1 mile, below the snout of the Carbon Glacier, reach a junction with the Northern Loop Trail (elev. 3325 ft). Your journey continues straight, but feel free to venture left across

the suspension bridge for a thrill. The nearby Carbon River Camp is a good choice for calling it a day.

The Northern Loop heads downstream, crossing cascading creeks through magnificent old-growth forest. At 1.2 miles from the last junction (16.3 miles from Sunrise), come to another junction (elev. 2950 ft). The trail left heads back to the Wonderland Trail, crossing over the Carbon River. Your route continues right, commencing one of the longer and steeper climbs on this loop. Arduously switchback up a steep hillside cloaked in ancient giants. After gaining 1800 feet in just over 2 miles, the way eases. The forest canopy soon retreats, revealing flowered meadows beneath the stark wall of the Yellowstone Cliffs. You have earned what comes next—one of the loneliest and loveliest stretches of trail in Mount Rainier National Park.

At 3.4 miles from the Carbon River (19.7 miles from Sunrise), come to the 0.2-mile spur leading to Yellowstone Cliffs Camp (elev. 5100 ft). Nestled along a cascading creek at the edge of alpine meadows, it is one of the most scenic and inspiring backcountry camps in the park.

Beyond, the Northern Loop makes its way 1.4 jaw-dropping miles to strikingly beautiful and wild Windy Gap (elev. 5800 ft). Open ridges and sparkling tarns invite wandering and lingering. Five hundred feet farther, a 0.9-mile side trail branches left, swinging around Independence Ridge to a viewpoint (elev. 5475 ft) of an intriguing natural arch.

The Northern Loop descends through parkland meadows, following alongside a picturesque creek beneath a jagged flank of peaks. After passing a side trail to a backcountry ranger cabin, come to shallow, forest-ringed Lake James (elev. 4500 ft). The Lake James Camp is 0.1 mile farther (23.5 miles from Sunrise), on a forested bluff above the lake. The setting is tranquil in autumn but in

Sluiskin Mountain from Windy Gap

summer is abuzz with clouds of ravenous mosquitoes.

The trail continues through primeval forest, gently descending 2 miles to the West Fork White River (elev. 3250 ft). Cross the numerous channels and reenter thick old growth. The trail makes a sharp turn right (where the long-abandoned West Fork White River Trail once diverged) and then begins another arduously long and steep (and dry) climb. After nearly 3 miles of climbing (28.6 miles from Sunrise), come to a junction (elev. 4900 ft) with the spur trail to Fire Creek Camp, a peaceful wooded camp with a water source (maybe dry in late season)—reach it by following the spur for 0.5 mile, losing 300 vertical feet.

Back on the Northern Loop, still upward bound, you'll eventually break out of the forest to find a series of stunning viewpoints of Mount Rainier. About 1.4 miles from the Fire Creek Camp junction, come to the Lake Eleanor Trail junction (elev. 5650 ft) at the edge of Grand Park, a near-level, nearly 2-mile-long expanse of meadow.

The Northern Loop, now heading south, crests a small knoll (elev. 5750 ft) before dropping to Lodi Creek (elev. 5300 ft). Following the creek through marshy meadows, the way once again climbs to reach heavily used Berkeley Park Camp (elev. 5600 ft), 3.8 miles from the Fire Creek Camp junction (32.4 miles from Sunrise). The way then makes its final climb, traversing Berkeley Park's boulder fields and tumbling-water-fed gardens to reach a familiar junction with the Wonderland Trail (elev. 6400 ft) in 1.6 miles (34 miles from Sunrise). Head left 2.3 miles back to Sunrise, greeting many a fresh-faced hiker along the way.

TRIP PLANNER	
5 miles	Granite Creek Camp
9.3 miles	Mystic Lake Camp
14.1 miles	Dick Creek Camp
15.4 miles	Carbon River Camp
19.9 miles	Yellowstone Cliffs Camp
23.5 miles	Lake James Camp
29.1 miles	Fire Creek Camp
32.4 miles	Berkeley Park Camp
36.3 miles	Sunrise

27 Huckleberry Creek

RATING/ DIFFICULTY	ROUND-TRIP	ELEV GAIN/ HIGH POINT	SEASON
***/3	15 miles	2750 feet/ 5700 feet	July–Oct

Maps: Green Trails Greenwater No. 238, Mount Rainier Wonderland Trail No. 2695, **Contact:** Mount Rainier National Park, White

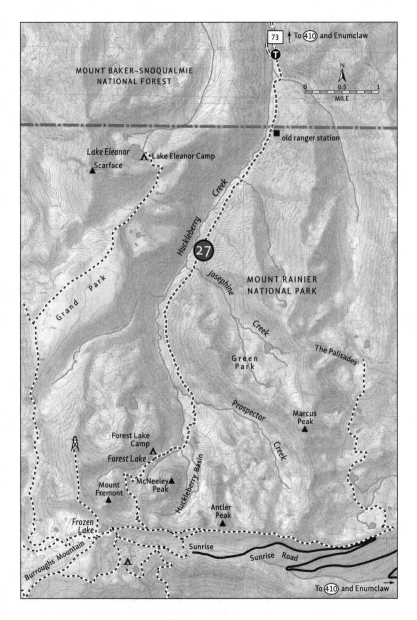

73 ↑ To (410) and Enumclaw

MOUNT BAKER–SNOQUALMIE
NATIONAL FOREST

N

0   0.5   1
MILE

■ old ranger station

Lake Eleanor
Lake Eleanor Camp
Scarface

Huckleberry

Creek

27

Grand

Park

Josephine

MOUNT RAINIER
NATIONAL PARK

Creek

The Palisades

Green
Park

Prospector

Marcus
Peak

Creek

Forest Lake
Camp
Forest Lake

Huckleberry Basin

McNeeley
Peak

Mount
Fremont

*Frozen
Lake*

Antler
Peak

Burroughs Mountain

Sunrise

Sunrise   Road

To (410) and Enumclaw →

River Wilderness Information Center, (360) 569-2211 ext. 6030, www.nps.gov/mora; **Permits/regulations:** National park day-use pass required if starting from Sunrise. Camping permit required, available from White River Wilderness Information Center. Fires prohibited. Dogs prohibited; **Special features:** Sprawling alpine meadows, spectacular wildflower display; **Special concerns:** High-clearance vehicle recommended; **GPS:** N 47 00.551 W 121 37.024

🏃🏔️⚙️🏠 *On this rarely hiked trail in Mount Rainier National Park, wander through ancient trees as magnificent as the Mountain and as old as the nation. This historical route into the park predates the park's roads and passes an old guard station. Then it follows lovely Huckleberry Creek up a deep valley of primeval forest to a placid little lake set in a remote high basin beneath the rocky cliffs of Mount Fremont. Set up camp and savor a quiet night all alone in one of America's grandest parks.*

GETTING THERE

From Enumclaw, follow State Route 410 east for 25 miles, turning right onto Forest Road 73 (just after milepost 49 and just before The Dalles Campground). Continue on FR 73 (high clearance recommended) for 6 miles to where the road sharply turns and crosses Huckleberry Creek. Park here in a pullout and locate the unsigned trailhead on the east side of the creek (elev. 2950 ft).

ON THE TRAIL

Starting at a makeshift campsite along Huckleberry Creek, locate the trail heading alongside the tumbling waterway. After about 0.4 mile, the trail turns left to follow Lost Creek to the terminus of an old logging road and the previous trailhead. Cross Lost Creek (elev.

3050 ft) and continue in national forest land, eventually coming alongside Huckleberry Creek once more.

At 1.4 miles, enter the national park. Locate boundary post no. 71, which was placed in 1908, the year that Snoqualmie National Forest was carved out from the greater Washington Forest Reserve. Mount Rainier National Park was established nine years earlier as the nation's fifth national park. Just south of the park boundary is an old ranger station (elev. 3150 ft). Long gone are the days when it was staffed—the historical structure is still intact but is in desperate need of rehabilitation. It would be a shame to lose this piece of our cultural history.

The trail continues south through spectacular groves of primeval forest, passing monstrous Douglas-firs. Traversing lush creek flats, the way lazily heads upvalley. Eventually the grade increases, gently at first, moderately soon afterward. At about 4 miles, cross Josephine Creek on a bridge (elev. 3700 ft). Continuing through stand after stand of ancient forest, the trail begins to climb more steadily and away from Huckleberry Creek, now tumbling in a ravine below.

At about 6 miles, cross Prospector Creek (elev. 4800 ft), without aid of a bridge. Soon afterward come to a tributary of Huckleberry Creek (elev. 5200 ft). Carefully cross it on a damaged bridge. The way now steepens, heading up a ridge draped in huckleberries and shaded by arboreal giants. Cross a couple more cascading tributaries before making a final steep climb to Forest Lake (elev. 5700 ft) and its one and only prized lakeside campsite (be sure to plan ahead to secure a permit for this spot).

The lake is flanked by yellow cedars in a semi-open forested bowl beneath the rocky and meadowed slopes of Mount Fremont's northeast ridge. Set up camp, enjoying the solitude and tranquility while hundreds of your fellow hikers head to Fremont's lookout tower above. Sleep well.

Huckleberry Basin above Forest Lake

TRIP PLANNER	
1.5 miles	Old ranger station and park boundary
7.5 miles	Forest Lake Camp

EXTENDING YOUR TRIP

If you're itching for some alpine action and perhaps a view of the Mountain, continue south on the trail, first climbing through parkland meadows, then subalpine forest, and then finally alpine meadows and rocky tundra. The trail snakes around a gorgeous open basin (where snows linger well into summer) and above emerald Huckleberry Basin climbing for 1.9 miles to a 6900-foot notch along the Sourdough Mountains. The view of Mount Rainier, Yakima Park, and the valley you just came up from is spectacular. Sunrise is 0.8 mile away. If you can arrange a car shuttle, turn this trip into a one-way 10.2-mile downhill hike starting from Sunrise.

28 Cougar Lakes and Three Lakes

RATING/ DIFFICULTY	ONE-WAY	ELEV GAIN/ HIGH POINT	SEASON
****/3	23.4 miles	2600 feet/ 5950 feet	mid-July– Oct

Map: Green Trails Mount Rainier Wonderland Trail No. 269S; **Contact:** Okanogan-Wenatchee National Forest, Naches Ranger District, (509) 653-1401, www.fs.fed.us/r6/wenatchee, or Mount Rainier National Park, White River Wilderness Information Center, (360) 569-2211 ext. 6030, www.nps.gov/mora; **Permits/regulations:** NW Forest Pass required at Chinook Pass. Free William O. Douglas Wilderness permit required, self-issued at trailhead. Camping permit required for Three Lakes in Mount Rainier NP, available from White River Wilderness Information Center. Wilderness rules apply. No camping within 100 feet of lakes. Fires prohibited. Dogs

prohibited at Three Lakes and on Laughingwater Creek Trail in the national park; **Special features:** One-way ridgeline hike to a half-dozen lakes and spectacular old growth in one of the quietest corners of Mount Rainier NP; **Special concerns:** Car shuttle required. Mosquitoes fearsome in early season. Cougar Lakes are popular during hunting season; **GPS:** Chinook Pass trailhead N 46 52.492 W 121 31.063. Laughingwater Creek trailhead N 46 45.103 W 121 33.441

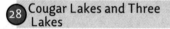 *Hike the Pacific Crest Trail along Mount Rainer National Park's eastern border to lakes and viewpoints seldom visited by the park's millions of annual visitors. Explore quiet meadows and high basins flush with wildflowers and wildlife. Explore old trails and ancient forests and a historical ranger station. Come in summer for the blossoms or in fall for boundless berries and bugling elk.*

GETTING THERE

For the Chinook Pass trailhead: From Enumclaw, head east on State Route 410 for 40 miles, bearing left at Cayuse Pass. Continue east on SR 410 for another 4 miles to large parking lot at Chinook Pass (elev. 5400 ft). For the Laughingwater Creek trailhead: Bear right at Cayuse Pass and follow SR 123 south for 11.2 miles to a small parking area (elev. 2200 ft) on the right (0.3 mile south of Mount Rainier National Park's Stevens Canyon entrance).

ON THE TRAIL

The recommended trip described here starts at Chinook Pass and comes out the Laughingwater Creek Trail, for minimal elevation gain. Hikers who prefer an out-and-back trip or who want to take their dogs may want to go to Cougar Lakes and back or return via the American Ridge Trail to the Mesatchee Creek Trail (see

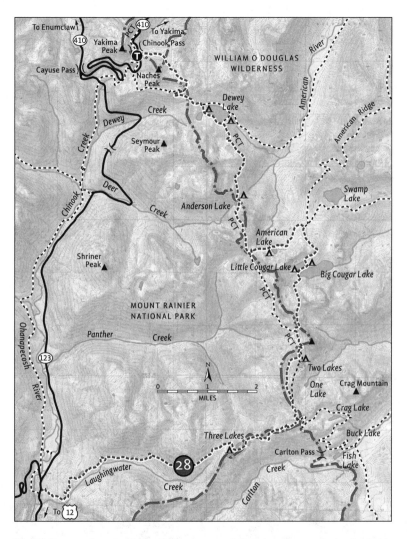

Trip 19). Dogs are allowed on the Pacific Crest Trail in the national park, but not on any of the other park trails.

Following the PCT south, cross SR 410 on a park gateway bridge and soon enter the William O. Douglas Wilderness. Traversing

meadows and crossing creeks—and probably snow patches too—pass a lovely tarn beneath craggy Naches Peak. Views are excellent east down the American River valley. At 1.5 miles, reach a junction with the Naches Loop Trail (an alternative approach, dogs prohibited)

Meadows along the Pacific Crest Trail near American Lake

and a splendid viewpoint (elev. 5850 ft) overlooking large and shimmering Dewey Lake.

Briefly enter Mount Rainier National Park and then reenter the William O., dropping down to a junction at Dewey Lake (elev. 5150 ft) at 2.7 miles. The lake is a popular (and crowded) camping destination, with good camps along the lake's north shore and outlet. There are good swimming spots on the lake's southeast shore. Expect a lot of mosquitoes in summer.

Continue right, hiking along Dewey Lake and reaching another junction at 3.6 miles. The trail left follows the American River to the Mesatchee Creek trailhead. Stay right on the PCT, gently climbing and traversing old-growth groves, huckleberry patches, pocket meadows, and skirting small tarns. After cresting a 5450-foot ridge, slowly descend and enter Mount Rainier National Park once again, reaching tiny and remote Anderson Lake (elev. 5350 ft) at 5.7 miles, where there's a small campsite by a meadow.

The way then climbs out of the lake basin, rounding a knoll with views out to Rainier. After cresting a ridge (elev. 5650 ft), reenter the William O. in a marshy, meadowy draw and reach a junction (elev. 5350 ft) at 7.2 miles. If you want to skip Cougar Lakes (why?), keep hiking south on the PCT. Otherwise, turn left on the American Ridge Trail, reaching pretty American Lake (elev. 5250 ft) tucked in a small cirque on House Rock in 0.6 mile. There are good camps here.

The trail continues east, reaching a junction (elev. 5050 ft) at 8.6 miles. The American Ridge Trail veers left, shortly coming to the Swamp Lake Trail, which provides quicker and easier access from the east to Cougar Lakes. Despite its name, Swamp Lake (elev. 4765 ft), 1 mile away, is actually a fairly nice lake with good camps.

For the Cougs, go right, cresting a ridge (elev. 5400 ft) and then descending over rocky terrain reaching Little Cougar Lake (elev. 5000 ft) at 10 miles. There are good camps near the lake's eastern shore, complete with viewing out to impressive House Rock. Elk frequent this basin—and not surprisingly, cougars too. For more private camps, follow a trail 0.5 mile west along the small rise (do not camp here) separating the two lakes to developed sites near Big Cougar's inlet.

To continue the trip, either retrace your way back to the PCT, or follow a rougher, shorter, highly scenic, more adventurous route back to the PCT. This route climbs steeply out of the lake basin, following a brushy but generally decent trail along cascading creeks, heather meadows, and up flowering slopes to a high draw (elev. 5950 ft) on the Cascade crest. Enjoy excellent views east over the Cougs and south along the craggy crest.

At 11.8 miles, this unmaintained trail reaches the well-groomed and graded PCT (elev. 5650 ft), 2 miles south of the American Ridge junction. Continue south through meadows and Christmas trees, reaching a junction (elev. 5600 ft) at 12.3 miles. The trail on the left is the old PCT, paralleling the current PCT for 1.3 miles and traveling through a basin and by Two Lakes (where there's camping). The official PCT stays high on the crest, traversing meadows and lingering snowfields, meeting up with the Two Lakes Trail at 13.8 miles. Now back in Mount Rainier National Park, reach the Laughingwater Creek Trail (elev. 5700 ft) in 0.2 mile.

Enjoy wonderful views of the snowy volcanic giant as you meander along the park's southern boundary, dropping into small basins that harbor tiny tarns feeding Panther Creek. Cougars, panthers—there seems to be a theme here! At 16.1 miles, reach an old ranger station (still used) and nice campsites at the shallow and grassy-shored Three Lakes (elev. 4700 ft). This tranquil spot set in deep timber far away from Rainier's busy centers is nonetheless abuzz with mosquitoes for most of the summer.

From the lakes, the trail climbs to a small gap (elev. 4850 ft), where the long-abandoned and near-impossible-to-find trail to Sheep Lake takes off. The Laughingwater Creek Trail, one of the few open to stock in the park, languidly descends, meandering through spectacular groves of ancient and giant yellow cedars.

At 19.8 miles, the trail comes upon Laughingwater Creek (elev. 3700 ft) at the head of a hanging valley, after which it drops more rapidly. Creek and trail soon diverge. The trail makes a brief 100-foot climb up a knoll before dropping in earnest again to reach SR 123 (elev. 2200 ft) at 23.4 miles.

TRIP PLANNER	
3.5 miles	Dewey Lake camps at outlet, north shore
5.7 miles	Anderson Lake camps
7.8 miles	American Lake camps
10 miles	Little Cougar Lake camps
10.5 miles	Big Cougar Lake camps
16.1 miles	Three Lakes camps
23.4 miles	Trailhead on SR 123

EXTENDING YOUR TRIP

Make a 35-mile loop out of this adventure by following the Eastside Trail back to Chinook Pass (there are camps at Deer Creek at 7.2 miles).

Opposite: Kaleetan Lake (Trip 31)

Snoqualmie Region

29 Snoqualmie Lake

RATING/ DIFFICULTY	ROUND-TRIP	ELEV GAIN/ HIGH POINT	SEASON
***/2	17 miles	2100 feet/ 3200 feet	June–Nov

Maps: Green Trails Mount Si No. 174, Skykomish No. 175; **Contact:** Mount Baker–Snoqualmie National Forest, Snoqualmie Ranger District, North Bend, (425) 888-1421, www.fs.fed.us/r6/mbs; **Permits/regulations:** NW Forest Pass required. Free Alpine Lakes Wilderness permit required May 15–Oct 31, self-issued at trailhead. Wilderness rules apply. Dogs must be leashed; **Special features:** Waterfalls, large backcountry lake, old growth; **Special concerns:** Middle Fork Road can be rough and bumpy; **GPS:** N 47 33.656 W 121 31.912

In an area of abundant alpine lakes, Snoqualmie Lake might not be the biggest, remotest, or perched in the most beautiful setting. But this large lake set in old timber and surrounded by rocky, rugged terrain boasts an attribute that many of the nearby lakes can't—a good chance for solitude. The hike to the lake also passes by several quite stunning waterfalls, and the low elevation means that snows come late and leave early, making this trip a good choice for the first or final overnighter of the season.

GETTING THERE

From Seattle, drive I-90 east to exit 34, just east of North Bend, and turn left (north) onto SE Edgewick Road (468th Avenue SE). Proceed for 0.6 mile, turning right onto Middle Fork Road (Forest Road 56). At 2.5 miles, the pavement ends. Continue for 9.6 agonizingly slow and bumpy miles to a junction (just after the Middle Fork Campground and Taylor River Bridge). Turn left and reach the trailhead (elev. 1100 ft) in 0.4 mile (12.5 miles from Edgewick Road).

ON THE TRAIL

Much of this trip follows an old road long since converted to trail. At one time the Forest Service was intent on punching this road all the way through to the Miller River valley near Skykomish. Such a road would have had devastating effects on Snoqualmie, Deer, Bear, and Dorothy lakes. Fortunately, the road idea failed and Snoqualmie and company won protection in 1976 within the Alpine Lakes Wilderness. Then in the 1980s, 6-plus miles of the old road was converted to trail, placing Snoqualmie Lake into deeper wilderness. While the converted road-to-trail up the Taylor River to Snoqualmie Lake sees a fair amount of visitation (and is open to mountain bikes), use dramatically peters out within a few miles of the trailhead.

Immediately cross the Taylor River on a solid bridge and pass inviting campsites (useful in a pinch for a late-evening start), a registration box, and then a junction at 0.4 mile. The trail left follows Quartz Creek on another road that's been converted to trail, leading 4-plus miles to Lake Blethen, recently added to the Mount Si Natural Resources Conservation Area.

Head right instead, following the Taylor River through mossy forest. Peek through the dense foliage for views of cliffy Garfield Mountain guarding the waterway. The grade is gentle, with only an occasional incline here and there. The river stays close by, always within earshot if not eyeshot. At 2.8 miles, come to a bridged crossing of Marten Creek (elev. 1750 ft), which plunges into a deep, boulder-ringed pool. An unmarked rough path follows the cascading creek's west bank for

Opposite: Thundering cascade on Taylor River below Snoqualmie Lake

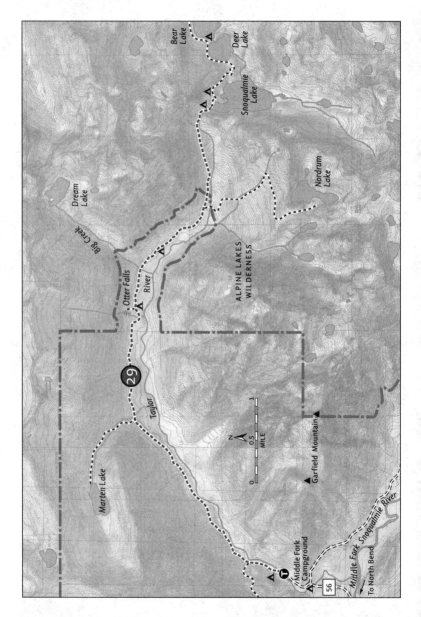

1.3 miles and 1200 vertical feet through giant cedars to Marten Lake.

Continue deeper up the Taylor River valley, crossing small creeks and old rock slides. At 4.5 miles, come to a signed junction for Otter Falls. The 0.2-mile side trip is a must-see. The falls languidly slide several hundred feet over a steep polished glacial slab into little Lipsy Lake, a deep pool at its base. Good campsites can be found along the Taylor River Trail near the side-trail junction.

Continue upriver, passing a giant split boulder, the converted road-trail now resembling trail more than road. At 5 miles, come to a big bridge (a remnant of the past road-building scheme) that spans Big Creek at the base of a big, beautiful waterfall bordered by big trees. Take a break, gaping at the creek plummeting over smooth granite ledges. The accompanying cool mist is most welcome on a hot day.

Good campsites line the way for the next 0.5 mile. Then at 6.6 miles, come to a junction (elev. 1800 ft). The trail right fords the river (difficult in high water) and continues 2.5 rough miles to Nordrum Lake (elev. 3670 ft), where solitude is almost guaranteed. Snoqualmie Lake, however, is a better (and thankfully easier) objective, so take the trail left, immediately enter the Alpine Lakes Wilderness, and begin climbing steeply.

The way gets rough and rocky. The trees get old and massive. Another waterfall appears—this one tiered within a tight chasm. Continue climbing, weaving through groves of giant cedars and firs. After crossing a couple of talus slopes, catch glimpses of yet another gorgeous waterfall—this one a harbinger, sitting at the lake's outlet.

At 8.5 miles, reach the big, beautiful backcountry lake (elev. 3200 ft). Good camps are nestled among yellow cedars on a small bluff above Snoqualmie's outlet. More campsites can be found on another bluff just past a

grassy, sunny, shoreline soaking spot. Savor the solitude. If it's September, savor the huckleberries.

TRIP PLANNER	
0.1 mile	Camps near trailhead
4.5 miles	Camps near Otter Falls junction
5–5.5 miles	Trailside camps
8.5 miles	Snoqualmie Lake camps

EXTENDING YOUR TRIP

Day hike from your base camp to Deer Lake and Bear Lake, reached by continuing up the trail another 1.5 miles and 400 vertical feet.

30 Williams Lake

RATING/ DIFFICULTY	ROUND-TRIP	ELEV GAIN/ HIGH POINT	SEASON
****/4	30 miles	3600 feet/ 4650 feet	July–Oct

Maps: Green Trails Skykomish No. 175, Stevens Pass No. 176, Snoqualmie Pass No. 207; **Contact:** Mount Baker–Snoqualmie National Forest, Snoqualmie Ranger District, North Bend, (425) 888-1421, www.fs.fed.us/r6/mbs; **Permits/regulations:** NW Forest Pass required. Free Alpine Lakes Wilderness permit required May 15–Oct 31, self-issued at trailhead. Wilderness rules apply. No fires above 4000 feet. Dogs must be leashed; **Special features:** Deep valley flanked by jagged peaks. Historical mining area. Fairly remote lake; **Special concerns:** Middle Fork Road can be rough and bumpy, with parts impassable to many vehicles; **GPS:** Trailhead N 47 31.050 W 121 27.193

Follow the rugged and remote Middle Fork Snoqualmie River through a deep canyon to its sustaining sources, in a notch of a pass guarded by gigantic granitic peaks glistening with snow and ice. Set up camp at a sparkling lake that captures the reflections of cloud-probing peaks and echoes with the fading voices of long-gone hardscrabble prospectors. The approach to this wild valley in the west end of the Alpine Lakes Wilderness is long, but chances are good for lonely wandering.

GETTING THERE

From Seattle, drive I-90 east to exit 34, just east of North Bend, and turn left (north) onto SE Edgewick Road (468th Avenue SE). Proceed for 0.6 mile, turning right onto Middle Fork Road (Forest Road 56). At 2.5 miles, the pavement ends. Continue for 9.6 agonizingly slow and bumpy miles to a junction (just after the Middle Fork Campground and Taylor River Bridge). Turn right, continuing on FR 56 for 5.7 miles on an extremely rough road, now passable to high-clearance vehicles only. Reach a gate and the trailhead (elev. 1300 ft). If the road from Taylor River is impassable, start the hike from the Middle Fork trailhead near the Middle Fork Campground, adding 12 miles round-trip.

ON THE TRAIL

You have two choices to begin: Either take the Middle Fork Snoqualmie River Trail, snaking along the river through nice groves of timber for 8.7 miles (longer but prettier); or hike, or better yet mountain bike, the closed Middle Fork Road for 7.7 miles to the old trailhead (shorter and quicker). Advantages of the Middle Fork Trail include options to camp along the river; while advantages of taking the road are quick mountain bike access, getting you to the good stuff faster, and passing Dingford Creek Falls. Both approaches allow for the possibility (preferably on the return) to visit Goldmyer Hot Springs (www.goldmyer.org) for a soak and camping. Reached by following the closed road for 4.8 miles or the trail for

5.3 miles, Goldmyer is owned by a nonprofit corporation and requires reservations and a nominal fee. Dogs are not allowed.

Beyond the hot springs (elev. 1800 ft) both road and trail steeply climb, meeting up just shy of a former car-accessible horse camp at the original road end and trailhead (elev. 2850 ft). Now a quiet spot, the riverside campground complete with fire rings makes a perfectly acceptable place to bed down.

From here, take the Dutch Miller Gap Trail and immediately come to a bridge across Hardscrabble Creek, which tumbles down from lakes of same name beneath Big Snow Mountain. Through groves of old growth and open brushy areas, the trail marches up a wide valley surrounded by lofty granite peaks that make it feel like you're in Yosemite.

After crossing a rocky, washed-out creekbed, enter the Alpine Lake Wilderness (elev. 3200 ft) at 1.2 miles from the old trailhead (OTH). The way then drops about 50 feet, passing a riverside camp before gradually ascending again and crossing a large brush-choked opening. Don't despair—the trail gets much better. At 2.5 miles (from OTH), drop about 150 feet along a talus slope before crossing one more unpleasant brushy section.

Soon, old forest is entered on good tread. At 2.9 miles (from OTH), rock hop across Crawford Creek, where there's a good camp. Continue upvalley, crossing more creeks and coming to an excellent creekside camp (elev. 3600 ft) at about 4.2 miles (from OTH).

The way now steepens, passing a thundering waterfall and entering a hanging valley. Forest yields to marshes (with plenty of mosquitoes in early summer) as the way angles beneath shiny cliffs and big talus slopes. Pass a beautiful, tiered slab waterfall before entering a broad meadow dotted with pools. Then at 5.6 miles (from OTH), reach

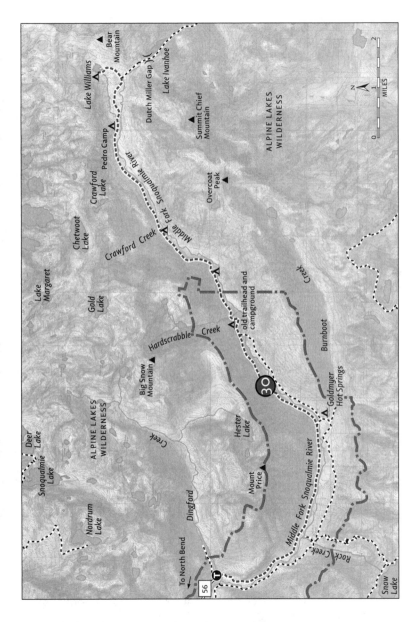

Williams Lake is set beneath a wall of granite.

the good but buggy sites at Pedro Camp, next to a big bridge spanning a refreshing tributary creek (elev. 4100 ft).

The trail continues, weaving through heather and mountain hemlock groves, reaching a junction 1 mile farther (elev. 4350 ft). Head left 0.7 mile, crossing a creek, and then climb briskly to cross snowmelt streams and heather meadows, cresting a small rise (elev. 4650 ft) and dropping to gorgeous Williams Lake (elev.

4600 ft), tucked in a dramatic bowl beneath imposing 7197-foot Bears Breast Mountain. There are excellent camps on the bluff just beyond the lake outlet, complete with dramatic views south to the icy imposing wall formed by 7225-foot Little Big Chief, 7120-foot Middle Chief, and 7464-foot Summit Chief mountains.

TRIP PLANNER VIA CLOSED ROAD	
4.8 miles	Goldmyer Hot Springs and camps
7.7 miles	Old trailhead and campground
9.2 miles	Riverside camp
10.6 miles	Crawford Creek camp
11.9 miles	Creekside camp
13.3 miles	Pedro Camp
15 miles	Williams Lake and camps

EXTENDING YOUR TRIP

Sure-footed hikers can follow sketchy tread beyond Williams Lake to cabin ruins, old mines, and the Chain Lakes, a group of tarns tucked in a cirque beneath 5850-foot La Bohn Gap. All hikers can hike the 1 mile of trail to 5000-foot Dutch Miller Gap, taking in a spectacular view of Waptus Lake and gorgeous Lake Ivanhoe just below. There are good camps at Ivanhoe if you're compelled to explore.

31 Kaleetan Lake

RATING/ DIFFICULTY	ROUND-TRIP	ELEV GAIN/ HIGH POINT	SEASON
***/4	22.2 miles	5185 feet/ 4500 feet	July–Oct

Map: Green Trails Snoqualmie Pass Gateway, WA–No. 207S; **Contact:** Mount Baker–Snoqualmie National Forest, Snoqualmie Ranger District, North Bend, (425) 888-1421, www.fs.fed.us/r6/mbs; **Permits/regulations:** NW Forest Pass required. Free Alpine Lakes Wilderness permit required May 15–Oct 31, self-issued at trailhead. Wilderness rules apply. No fires above 4000 feet. Dogs must be leashed; **Special features:** Good-size

alpine lake in remote valley beneath striking Kaleetan Peak in popular I-90 corridor; **Special concerns:** Pratt River ford may be difficult in early season; **GPS:** N 47 23.862 W 121 29.202

Tucked behind the high serrated wall formed by Mount Roosevelt and Kaleetan Peak is one of the loneliest, trail-accessible lakes in the Snoqualmie Pass region. It's a long approach, with lots of elevation gained and lost, and a few other lakes along the way siphon hikers away from Kaleetan Lake. But those who persevere will find a large lake reflecting a jagged backdrop, some good campsites, abundant huckleberries in season—and a good chance they'll be all alone.

GETTING THERE

From Seattle, drive I-90 east to exit 47. Turn left and, after passing under the highway, turn left again and reach the trailhead in 0.3 mile (elev. 1900 ft). Privy available.

ON THE TRAIL

While Kaleetan Lake is one of the least visited lakes along the I-90 corridor, getting there involves passing some of the area's busiest bodies of water. Expect plenty of company for the first several miles—you'll slowly lose your fellow trail users the farther into wilderness you venture.

Start on the well-beaten path to Pratt Lake, wasting no time heading up. At 1 mile, stay left at the Granite Mountain Trail junction (elev. 2500 ft). Steadily gaining elevation, traverse steep slopes and cross several creeks high above Talapus Creek. At 2.9 miles, cross the wilderness boundary. At 3.3 miles, come to the Talapus Lake junction (elev. 3750 ft), an alternative approach.

Stay right, crossing more creeks and angling high above a snug valley cradling

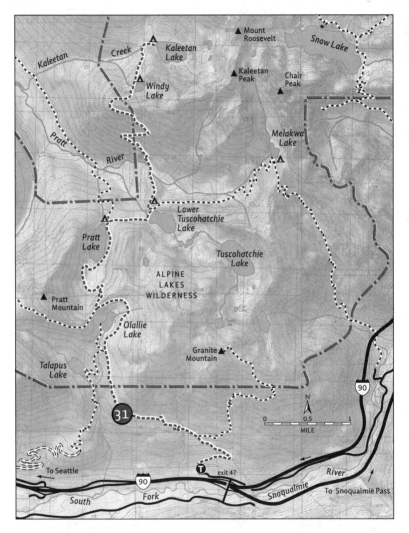

Olallie Lake, visible below. Mount Rainier is now visible too, peeking above the moth-eaten (logged, actually) forested ridges to the south. At 4.4 miles, reach a junction with the Mount Defiance Trail (elev. 4175 ft) on a ridge crest.

Head to the right into nice old-growth forest, switchbacking down off the ridge. Cross open talus slopes, enjoying views north to Kaleetan Peak piercing the sky above the Pratt River valley. Continue descending into a boggy area before coming to pretty Pratt

Lake, set in a semi-open basin. Enjoy morning and evening reflections of Pratt Mountain and September huckleberry harvesting. Follow the trail along the lake's rocky eastern shore to reach a good camping area at its outlet near the junction with the Pratt River Trail (elev. 3425 ft) at 6.5 miles.

The trail left is in the process of being rehabilitated through a large unprotected parcel that will hopefully soon become an addition to the Alpine Lakes Wilderness. Once this trail is rebuilt, it will make for a nice alternative approach from the Middle Fork Snoqualmie River Trail.

Head to the right instead, crossing open avalanche slopes that provide excellent views down the Pratt River valley to Middle Fork peaks. Enjoy views upvalley too to Kaleetan

A pair of hikers admires Kaleetan Peak from Kaleetan Lake.

and Chair peaks. Soon come to forested, pretty Lower Tuscohatchie Lake, crossing its outlet on a log bridge and coming to a junction at 7.2 miles (elev. 3450 ft). There are good campsites here—set up camp and day hike to Kaleetan Lake, or continue in full backpacking mode.

Head left on lightly used but discernable tread through towering old-growth firs and hemlocks, dropping to a cool ravine housing Pratt River (elev. 3075 ft). The crossing may be difficult in high water; otherwise, hop across smooth rock ledges or dare to use a precarious log. The way then steeply climbs out of the valley onto a high ridge (elev. 4500 ft) before descending to little Windy Lake (elev. 4185 ft) at 10.4 miles, where there's limited camping.

In deep timber, the trail continues descending to reach Kaleetan Lake (elev. 3850 ft) in a big cirque beneath Kaleetan Peak at 11.1 miles. Find good campsites in forest near the outlet. Enjoy good fishing in the lake and good huckleberry harvesting all around it. Find a good sitting log along the marshy shoreline and watch the lake surface for breathtaking reflections of Kaleetan Peak. The peak's name is Chinook Jargon for "arrow"—the mountain's sharp summit is blunted from this angle but still pierces the sky. Savor the sharp stillness of the solitude here as well.

KLAHOWYA TILLICUM

Many place names in Washington come from the Chinook Jargon. Not an actual language, Chinook is a collection of several hundred words drawn from various Native American tribal languages, particularly Coast Salish, as well as English and French. It was used as a trade language among Native peoples, Europeans, and American settlers and explorers in the Pacific Northwest throughout the nineteenth century. A unique part of our Pacific Northwest cultural heritage, Chinook names are sprinkled across our landscape. Below are some Chinook Jargon words you may encounter while backpacking in Washington, with their meanings in English.

chuck	water, river, stream	moolock	elk
cultus	bad, worthless	muckamuck	food
elip	first, in front of	ollalie	berries
hyas	big, powerful, mighty	pil	red; therefore Pilchuck means "red stream"
ipsoot	hidden		
kimtah	behind, after	saghalie	above, high, on top, sacred
klahowya	hello, greetings, how are you?	sitkum	half of something, part of something
klip	deep, sunken	skookum	big, strong, mighty
lemolo	wild, crazy	tenas	small, weak, children
melakwa	mosquito	tillicum	friend, people
memaloose	dead	tupso	pasture, grass
mesachie	bad, evil, dangerous	tyee	chief, leader

TRIP PLANNER	
6.5 miles	Pratt Lake camps
7.2 miles	Lower Tuscohatchie Lake camps
10.4 miles	Windy Lake camp
11.1 miles	Kaleetan Lake camps

EXTENDING YOUR TRIP

For a variation on the return, and if you can arrange a car shuttle, head east from Lower Tuscohatchie Lake for 2.9 miles to striking Melakwa Lake (elev. 4500 ft), set in a tight rocky basin between Kaleetan's starker south face and rugged Chair Peak. Camping available, but expect plenty of company (of the tiny variety as well: *melakwa* is Chinook Jargon for "mosquito"). Then follow the Denny Creek Trail 4.5 miles to its trailhead off of FR 58 to complete the journey.

32 Wildcat Lakes

RATING/ DIFFICULTY	ROUND-TRIP	ELEV GAIN/ HIGH POINT	SEASON
****/3	17 miles	4020 feet/ 4920 feet	mid-July– Oct

Map: Green Trails Snoqualmie Pass Gateway, WA–No. 207S; **Contact:** Mount Baker–Snoqualmie National Forest, Snoqualmie Ranger District, North Bend, (425) 888-1421, www.fs.fed.us/r6/mbs; **Permits/regulations:** NW Forest Pass required. Free Alpine Lakes Wilderness permit required May 15–Oct 31, self-issued at trailhead. Wilderness rules apply. No fires above 4000 feet. Dogs must be leashed; **Special features:** Little-visited pair of lakes in one of the most popular hiking regions in the state; **Special concerns:** First 4 miles of trail can be extremely crowded, especially on weekends; **GPS:** N 47 26.706 W 121 25.414

⚙ *Who would believe that solitude and peace and quiet can be found just beyond Snow Lake? Yeah, that Snow Lake— one of the busiest hiking destinations in the*

state. But believe it. Just keep hiking past Snow and Gem lakes and then drop 1000 feet out-of-sight-and-mind from the frenzy into a remote basin harboring two good-sized lakes. Lower Wildcat is ringed by forest, but the Upper Wildcat is a real beauty, surrounded by steep walls and shiny talus.

GETTING THERE

From Seattle, drive I-90 east to exit 52 at Snoqualmie Pass. Turn left and, after passing under the highway, turn right onto Alpental Road. Continue 1.1 miles to the large ski area parking lot and trailhead (elev. 3100 ft). Privy available.

ON THE TRAIL

Snow Lake is truly a gorgeous place—over 1 mile long and reflecting stunning stark walls, spiraling summits, and perpetual snowfields. It's also a mere 3.3 miles from a trailhead, located just off an interstate, only one hour away from a metropolitan area of over three million people. No wonder this trail is so darn popular! But rather than lament its notoriety, appreciate it as the type of trail that gets newbies hooked on hiking and helps folks young and old to "green bond."

The lake and its surroundings have taken a beating in the past, but new restrictions (dogs on-leash, areas closed for rehabilitation, camping only in designated sites) have allowed this heavily used area to recover fairly well. Continued enlightenment on the part of all trail users must continue lest we love this place to death.

Start out on some of the best tread and trail construction in the Cascades, and gradually gain elevation as the way undulates between old-growth groves and brushy avalanche slopes. At 1.7 miles, reach a junction (elev. 3800 ft). The short trail left goes 0.4 mile to an overlook at the headwaters of the South Fork Snoqualmie River. You want to go

Upper Wildcat Lake

right, climbing more steeply now up rocky, warm-in-the-sun slopes to reach a small gap on a high ridge (elev. 4400 ft), where you'll cross into the Alpine Lakes Wilderness. The wilderness regulation of no more than twelve to a party doesn't seem to mean much here.

The trail now descends, passing spectacular viewing spots of Snow Lake along the way. At 3.1 miles, reach a junction (elev. 4050 ft). Left heads to a day-use area on the lake's shore. Right continues, passing a side trail to legal (and extremely busy) campsites and angling over ledges along the lake's eastern shore. Pause frequently to marvel at Chair Peak reflecting in Snow Lake's sparkling waters.

Climb a small rise, passing another legal camping area, and come to a junction (elev. 4125 ft) at 3.5 miles. Right drops into the Middle Fork Snoqualmie River valley, which is a beautiful view from this spot. Head left

instead, dropping to cross Snow Lake's outlet creek (elev. 4025 ft). Then, leaving the masses behind, begin a winding and exceptionally beautiful climb out of the lake basin.

Pass reflecting tarns, shiny granite shards, heather meadows, and talus slopes and come to Gem Lake (elev. 4875 ft), set in a high open divide at 5.2 miles. Find well-beaten camps to the left, a privy with panoramic views to the right. The way to the Wildcat Lakes also heads right. The trail rounds Gem Lake, passing through heather meadows and talus and by a scramble path up 5430-foot Wright Mountain. The jagged summits of Kaleetan Peak and Mount Roosevelt across the lake are breathtaking.

At 5.6 miles, crest the lake-cradling ridge (elev. 4920 ft). Ignore a climbers path on the left, and begin descending—1000 feet's worth into a remote valley dotted with tarns and littered with rockfall from sky-piercing

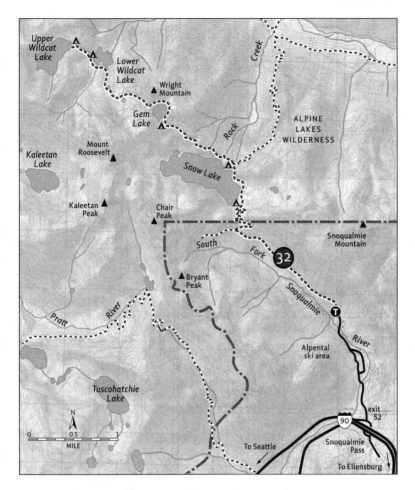

peaks. The tread, much narrower now, switchbacks and plummets rapidly. After passing a marshy area above a tarn, cross a cascading creek and then traverse a huge talus slope, staying left of the creek. Reenter forest and swing around another small tarn (note: maps show the trail route incorrectly), which reflects tall timber beautifully and incubates pesky mosquitoes annoyingly.

The way then makes a final steep drop, crossing a braided creek (use caution hopping the slimy rocks) and swinging by another tarn to abruptly end at a campsite on the forested shores of Lower Wildcat Lake (elev. 3920 ft) at 8 miles. Fishing is good here—but it's the upper lake you want to head to.

Cross the creek on the left and locate an indistinct path. Head west on good tread choked with brush (mostly huckleberries, though, so eat your way through). The way then parallels a cascading creek, steeply at times. Eventually cross the creek (there's a log in place), and continue hiking along its opposite side.

At 8.5 miles, reach an excellent campsite near the outlet of pretty Upper Wildcat Lake (elev. 4220 ft). Set in a large bowl beneath cliffs and talus, the upper lake is more rugged and breathtaking than the lower one. The lake warms up nicely by late summer, for soaking, and more campsites can be found along the forested north shore. More lakes lie beyond, too, for those long on time and experienced in off-trail travel.

TRIP PLANNER	
3.3 miles	Snow Lake and camps
5.2 miles	Gem Lake and camps
8 miles	Lower Wildcat Lake camp
8.5 miles	Upper Wildcat Lake camp

33 Spectacle Lake

RATING/ DIFFICULTY	ROUND-TRIP	ELEV GAIN/ HIGH POINT	SEASON
****/2	19.8 miles	1760 feet/ 4400 feet	July–Oct

Maps: Green Trails Snoqualmie Pass No. 207, Kachess Lake No. 208; **Contact:** Okanogan-Wenatchee National Forest, Cle Elum Ranger District, (509) 852-1100, www.fs.fed.us/r6/wenatchee; **Permits/regulations:** NW Forest Pass required. Free Alpine Lakes Wilderness permit required May 15–Oct 31, self-issued at trailhead. Wilderness rules apply. No fires at Spectacle Lake; **Special features:** Beautiful ledge-lined lake in the heart of the Alpine Lakes Wilderness, considered by many hikers to be the prettiest of the Snoqualmie area lakes; **Special concerns:** Long detour may be necessary if Lemah Creek can't be safely forded. A 2009 forest fire closed a section of the Pete Lake Trail, so call the ranger

district to check status; **GPS:** N 47 26.028 W 121 06.421

A sprawling lake with myriad inlets and fingers of polished granite, Spectacle Lake is indeed a spectacle, especially when reflecting the shiny granite turrets of Chikamin Peak and Lemah Mountain. En route pass Pete Lake, a popular watering hole, and also rushing Lemah Creek, groves of old growth, and a beautiful waterfall—all on good tread and at a gentle grade. Spectacle is popular, especially with Pacific Crest Trail hikers, so shoot for a quiet week in fall if you can.

GETTING THERE
From Seattle, drive I-90 east to exit 80 (signed "Roslyn/Salmon la Sac"). Turn left onto Bull Frog Road and follow it 2.8 miles to State Route 903. (From Ellensburg, take I-90 west to exit 84, turn right onto N Oakes Avenue, and follow it to SR 903). Turn left on SR 903 (which eventually becomes Salmon la Sac Road) and drive 15.5 miles, turning left onto Forest Road 46 (signed for Cooper Lake, the turnoff 1.1 mile before the Salmon La Sac guard station). After 4.6 miles, turn right onto FR 4616 and proceed 1.9 miles to the road's end and trailhead for Pete Lake Trail (elev. 2800 ft). Privy available.

ON THE TRAIL
Starting on the Pete Lake Trail, expect a lot of company—and not just hikers, but plenty of horses and bikes too. Heading up the valley of the lazy Cooper River, the way gains little elevation. Although well shaded by old-growth conifers, the tread is dusty and rocky thanks to the heavy traffic. At 1.4 miles, reach a junction with the Tired Creek Trail (elev. 2900 ft). Climbing steeply up Pollalie Ridge, this trail will definitely leave you tired. Stay on the Pete Lake Trail instead, and after another

Chikamin Ridge provides a dramatic backdrop for Spectacle Lake.

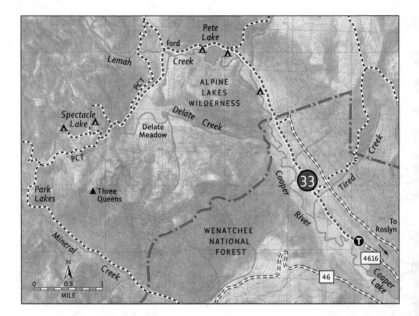

1.2 miles reach another junction, this one with a spur leading to a closed logging road. Mountain bikes depart here, since they aren't allowed in the Alpine Lakes Wilderness and the boundary is straight ahead.

At about 3 miles, pass some creekside campsites—nearby marshy meadows harbor many mosquitoes waiting for your arrival. Continue upvalley, crossing many side creeks—some capable of washing your boots early in the season. At 4.4 miles, reach a junction (elev. 3000 ft) at Pete Lake. The trail right leads to Waptus Lake via Waptus Pass and can be used to combine this route with a trip to that large lake (see Trip 34). Well-used campsites along Pete Lake's outlet are to the left. While the shallow lake provides some good lounging rocks and some nice viewing west toward Snoqualmie Pass' high peaks, its appeal for swimming, wading, and fishing is limited.

Continue west for the spectacle of this hike, passing better Pete Lake campsites (with privy) near lakeshore meadows. Then enter attractive mature forest, coming to another junction (elev. 3100 ft) at 5.7 miles. The quickest preferred route to Spectacle Lake is left, requiring a ford of Lemah Creek, which often runs fast, deep, and cold early in the season. If it's safe to ford, take this route, and after 0.8 mile skirt marshy meadows and reach the Pacific Crest Trail (elev. 3300 ft). If the ford is too dangerous to negotiate, head right for 0.8 mile to the PCT; then head left, crossing Lemah Creek on a bridge and reaching the terminus of the Pete Lake Trail after 1.9 miles.

This area sustained considerable fire damage in the summer of 2009. I was caught in it while researching this trail—making this hike one of my hottest memories. In all seriousness, though, it was quite terrifying to be caught in such an awesome act of nature.

Humbling too, as there are things that man just can't control.

Follow the PCT left (south) and, staying above buggy Delate Meadow, finally start gaining elevation. After a series of switchbacks, reach cascading Delate Creek (elev. 3900 ft) at 8.5 miles. Here, an obscure, brushy, steep, and rocky shortcut trail leads to the right to Spectacle Lake. Don't bother with it, as it's a very difficult route. Instead, cross Delate Creek on a good bridge and continue climbing, taking in views north along the way and reaching the Spectacle Lake spur trail (elev. 4400 ft) after another mile.

Follow this trail 0.4 mile, descending over ledges and through parkland meadows to reach spectacular Spectacle Lake (elev. 4240 ft) and a maze of social trails leading to campsites, protruding glacier-polished ledges, and quiet coves. The best soaking is north, in a small and somewhat protected cove. The best camps (and the privy) lie along a rib south of the lake. Be careful to not trample the flower and heather meadows in your explorations. And enjoy breathtaking views of the jagged array of Cascade crest peaks rising to the west. Chikamin Peak and Lemah Mountain donned in snowy apparel reflect beautifully off of Spectacle's waters when the evening calm sets in.

TRIP PLANNER	
3 miles	Creekside camps
4.4 miles	Pete Lake and camps
9.9 miles	Spectacle Lake and camps

EXTENDING YOUR TRIP

An alternative, lightly traveled, and somewhat shorter approach can be made via the 5.5-mile Mineral Creek Trail and then by following the PCT north for 3 miles. Arrange a car shuttle for a one-way hike and either exit via Mineral Creek or continue 16.5 miles south on the PCT to Snoqualmie Pass. Campsites can be found at Gravel and Ridge lakes as well as Park Lakes on Mineral Creek.

34 Waptus Lake

RATING/ DIFFICULTY	ROUND-TRIP	ELEV GAIN/ HIGH POINT	SEASON
***/1	18 miles	900 feet/ 3100 feet	late June– Nov

Maps: Green Trails Kachess Lake No. 208, Stevens Pass No. 176; **Contact:** Okanogan-Wenatchee National Forest, Cle Elum Ranger District, (509) 852-1100, www.fs.fed.us/r6/wenatchee; **Permits/regulations:** NW Forest Pass required. Free Alpine Lakes Wilderness permit required May 15–Oct 31, self-issued at trailhead. Wilderness rules apply; **Special features:** Spectacular river valley. Largest lake in the Alpine Lakes Wilderness; **Special concerns:** Required ford of Waptus River is dangerous to impossible in early season; **GPS:** N 47 24.562 W 121 06.421

Nearly 2 miles long and situated in one of the largest glacial troughs in the Central Cascades, Waptus is the largest lake in the 394,000-acre Alpine Lakes Wilderness. There are campsites aplenty and many side-trip opportunities. But don't feel compelled to move on. You won't tire of staring across Waptus' sparkling waters at a towering flank of granite peaks that shimmer in the light of both sun and moon.

GETTING THERE

From Seattle, drive I-90 east to exit 80 (signed "Roslyn/Salmon la Sac"). Turn left onto Bull Frog Road and follow it 2.8 miles to State Route 903. (From Ellensburg, take I-90 west to exit 84, turn right onto N Oakes Avenue, and follow it to SR 903). Turn left on SR 903 (which eventually becomes Salmon la Sac Road) and drive 16.6 miles to the old guard station and

Summit Chief and Bears Breast mountains from Waptus Lake

pavement's end. Bear left, crossing Cle Elum River to the Salmon la Sac Campground, and at the campground entrance bear right, continuing 0.6 mile to the Salmon la Sac trailhead (elev. 2500 ft). Privy available.

ON THE TRAIL

The approach is long but easy, following alongside the delightful Waptus River for most of the way. Presenting many moods, from languid slithering to furious frothing, the wild waterway helps keep your mind off the grind. But first you need to reach it. From the trailhead, follow the tempting Cooper River for a short distance before veering right at a junction. A couple of hundred feet farther, at another junction, bear right again, now on the Waptus River Trail.

In dry forest, wind up and around a series of low knolls, gaining and losing a couple of hundred feet. At about 0.8 mile, just after entering the Alpine Lakes Wilderness, pass an unmarked horse trail on your right. Continue left, past mosquito pools and a recently burnt area, before finally coming to the Waptus River. At about 2.5 miles, cross Hour Creek—a ford early in the summer, a rock hop later— and reach a big camping area on a bank above the Waptus shortly afterward.

The way then follows along Hour Creek and turns up a cool draw of old-growth giants before reuniting with the Waptus River where it churns and tumbles through a spectacular rocky chasm. Cone Mountain, which looks like it belongs in Yosemite, rises above. Find plenty of riverside campsites along this

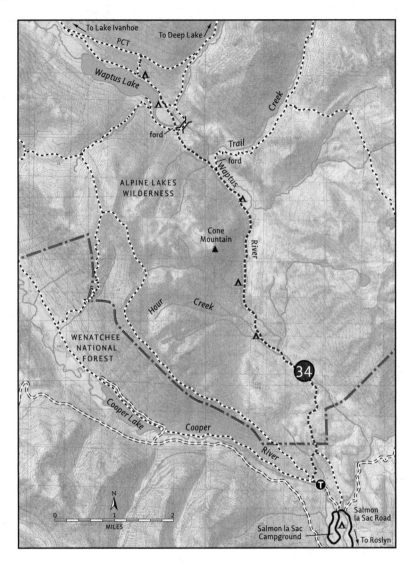

scenic stretch of trail. Continue upvalley, darting between some big boulders before making a short climb to a ledge overlooking the river.

Then drop back down to river level to traverse a small meadow and big spruce flats, and swing by a good camp near a big log jam. At 7.3 miles, reach a junction (at a ford) for the lightly used Trail Creek Trail (elev. 2900 ft). The main trail climbs once again before dropping a little and reaching a junction with the Waptus Horse Ford Spur, which is your route because the hiker bridge across the river is long gone. Do not cross at the old bridge site where the river careens through a rocky gorge. The horse ford is usually knee-deep and not too swift.

Once across, continue through an open lodgepole pine flat, reaching the Spinola Creek Trail after 0.4 mile. Waptus Lake (elev. 2963 ft) and plenty of campsites lie 0.1 mile to your left. While these sites at the lake's east end tend to get busy, it's easy to see why. They come with a shoreline suitable for wading (the lake actually warms up fairly well) and a knockout view of 7197-foot Bears Breast Mountain and 7464-foot Summit Chief Mountain guarding Dutch Miller Gap (see Trip 30). But if you prefer more privacy, continue up the trail along the lake for another 0.5 mile to more secluded sites set amid old-growth giants.

TRIP PLANNER	
2.5 miles	Camps near Hour Creek ford
6–7 miles	Riverside camps
9 miles	Waptus Lake and camps

EXTENDING YOUR TRIP
Waptus Lake makes a great base for exploring other Alpine Lakes Wilderness gems. Breathtaking Spade Lake (elev. 5210 ft) set in a high cirque beneath 7899-foot Mount Daniel can be reached by a 4.2-mile trail. Lake Ivanhoe (elev. 4682 ft) can be reached by following good trail west for 6.8 miles. And Deep Lake (Trip 35) can be reached by following the Pacific Crest Trail north for 5 miles. A longer, harder, and more scenic return can be made by following the Quick Creek Trail for 3.7 miles to Waptus Pass and then following the Pollalie Ridge Trail 8.8 miles back to Salmon la Sac.

35 Deep Lake

RATING/ DIFFICULTY	ROUND-TRIP	ELEV GAIN/ HIGH POINT	SEASON
****/3	16 miles	3400 feet/ 5600 feet	late July– Oct

Map: Green Trails Stevens Pass No. 176; **Contact:** Okanogan-Wenatchee National Forest, Cle Elum Ranger District, (509) 852-1100, www.fs.fed.us/r6/wenatchee; **Permits/ regulations:** NW Forest Pass required. Free Alpine Lakes Wilderness permit required May 15–Oct 31, self-issued at trailhead. Wilderness rules apply. Fires prohibited; **Special features:** Waterfall-fed lake in big cirque beneath glacier-clad peak; **Special concerns:** Return hike involves a long climb. Unbridged Scatter Creek, 3 miles before the trailhead, requires a high-clearance vehicle to cross in early season; **GPS:** N 47 32.609 W 121 05.803

Waterfall-fed and tucked in a deep cirque on the snow-clad giant, Mount Daniel, Deep Lake may not be that deep in the Alpine Lakes Wilderness, but the depth of its beautiful setting will touch you deeply. Just be aware that reaching this lake requires a deep drop of over 1200 feet, all which must be regained on the way out.

GETTING THERE
From Seattle, drive I-90 east to exit 80 (signed "Roslyn/Salmon la Sac"). Turn left onto Bull Frog Road and follow it 2.8 miles to State Route 903. (From Ellensburg, take I-90 west to exit 84, turn right onto N Oakes Avenue, and follow it to SR 903). Turn left on SR 903 (which eventually becomes Salmon la Sac Road) and drive 16.6 miles to the old guard station and pavement's end. Continue north on Forest Road 4330 for 12.3 rough and slow miles to the trailhead (elev. 3400 ft). Privy available.

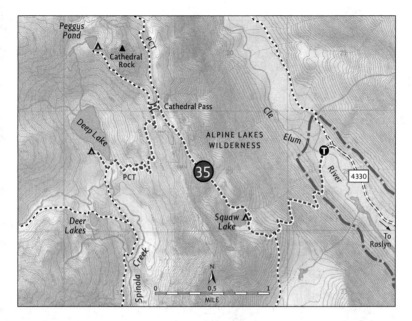

ON THE TRAIL

Don't despair if the parking lot is bursting with vehicles upon your arrival. Chances are that the majority of the occupants are day hiking to Cathedral Rock, scrambling up Mount Daniel, or out on an easy overnighter to Squaw Lake.

Immediately cross the Cle Elum River on a hardy bridge, entering gorgeous old-growth forest. Enter the Alpine Lakes Wilderness at 0.4 mile, shortly after hopping across a small creek. Now on good tread and by way of long switchbacks, gently climb. At 1.8 miles, reach a junction (elev. 4400 foot) with the lightly used Trail Creek Trail, which takes off for the Waptus River (Trip 34).

Continue to the right on the Cathedral Rock Trail, through thinning forest along a high bench, and reach Squaw Lake (elev. 4850 ft) set in a forest basin beneath a rocky ridge. Good but busy campsites can be

found here. Push on, crossing Squaw's outlet creek, and after a short, steep climb reach a tarn-blotched wonderland of parklands and heather meadows. Views too—to Cathedral Rock towering above, Granite Mountain shining across the Cle Elum River valley, and Mount Stuart majestically piercing clouds out on the horizon. Campsites can be found tucked behind hemlock knolls, but exercise care in this extremely fragile and overused environment.

At 4.5 miles, come to the Pacific Crest Trail (elev. 5500 ft). Turn left onto the PCT and follow it south to Cathedral Pass (elev. 5600 ft). Enjoy the views, especially of glistening with snow and ice 7899-foot Mount Daniel. Then begin the long descent to Deep Lake. At 4.8 miles, an exhilarating trail veers right for 0.7 mile to Peggys Pond and its busy campsites, perched in a basin beneath Cathedral Rock.

Your route continues downward across fields of phlox and other flowering beauties, always under Daniel's watchful eye. Deep blue Deep Lake twinkles below. To accommodate horses, the way saunters downward at a ridiculously gentle grade. At 7.8 miles, 3 miles from Cathedral Pass, emerge in a series of wet meadows that embrace Spinola Creek (elev. 4375 ft).

Easily wade across the refreshing creek and come to a junction. Campsites are to the right along Deep Lake's scenic western shoreline. Deep's eastern shores also harbor some nice sites—all with knockout views of tumbling waterfalls and Cathedral Rock hovering above. Let jumping fish and peeping spotted sandpipers serenade you to sleep. Rest well for the return climb.

Deep Lake beneath Mount Daniel

TRIP PLANNER	
2.2 miles	Squaw Lake and camps
4.8 miles	Trail to Peggys Pond and camps
8 miles	Deep Lake and camps

EXTENDING YOUR TRIP

Set up base camp at Deep Lake and explore the wildlife-rich Spinola Meadows and Deer Lakes 1 mile south. Or head 2.3 miles west, climbing 1100 vertical feet to secluded Lake Vincente. If you can arrange a car shuttle, consider hiking out via the Waptus River Trail (Trip 34) or making a long, quiet loop via the Trail Creek Trail.

36 Tuck and Robin Lakes

RATING/ DIFFICULTY	ROUND-TRIP	ELEV GAIN/ HIGH POINT	SEASON
*****/5	14.4 miles	3000 feet/ 6300 feet	late July– Oct

Map: Green Trails Stevens Pass No. 176; **Contact:** Okanogan-Wenatchee National Forest, Cle Elum Ranger District, (509) 852-1100, www.fs.fed.us/r6/wenatchee; **Permits/regulations:** NW Forest Pass required. Free Alpine Lakes Wilderness permit required May 15–Oct 31, self-issued at trailhead. Wilderness rules apply. Fires prohibited; **Special features:** Alpine lakes set in granite basins with outstanding views of Mount Daniel's glacial face; **Special concerns:** Trail is extremely steep and rocky, requiring use of hands in spots. Routefinding can be tricky, the way dangerous in bad weather. Not recommended for dogs. Can be crowded, especially on summer weekends. Unbridged Scatter Creek, 3 miles before the trailhead, requires a high-clearance vehicle to cross in early season; **GPS:** N 47 32.685 W 121 05.865

Set in a granite wonderland high in the Wenatchee Mountains, a handful of lakes rival the Enchantments when it comes to stunning scenery and pure alpine rapture. But unlike the Enchantments, there are no complicated permits or quotas for visiting Tuck and Robin Lakes. Consequently, they can be mobbed—so this is not a place to seek solitude. The trail is difficult too—never officially built, it clambers up and around ledges and shelves and rocky gullies and is not for the inexperienced. But views of the blinding glaciers of the Alpine Lakes Wilderness' highest peak, Mount Daniel, rising behind shimmering cobalt waters, themselves surrounded by polished granite—that'll forever be etched in your mind.

GETTING THERE

From Seattle, drive I-90 east to exit 80 (signed "Roslyn/Salmon la Sac"). Turn left onto Bull Frog Road and follow it 2.8 miles to State Route 903. (From Ellensburg, take I-90 west to exit 84, turn right onto N Oakes Avenue, and follow it to SR 903). Turn left on SR 903 (which eventually becomes Salmon la Sac Road) and drive 16.6 miles to the old guard station and pavement's end. Continue north on Forest Road 4330 for 12.3 rough and slow miles to the trailhead (elev. 3400 ft). Privy available.

ON THE TRAIL

From the very popular trailhead, set off north on the wide and well-traveled Deception Pass Trail. At 0.4 mile, cross Skeeter Creek (yes, there are lots of those throughout the area) and enter the Alpine Lakes Wilderness. Skirt a grassy wetland (mosquito roost) with views to Cathedral Rock. Then, after a few minor ups and downs but generally level walking, come to elongated Hyas Lake (elev. 3450 ft).

Chinook Jargon for "large" or "great," Hyas is a popular spot for fishing, swimming, beginning backpackers, and those who got a late start. The lake usually teems with human activity, and good camps can be found along its entire 1-mile length, with privies at 2.2 and

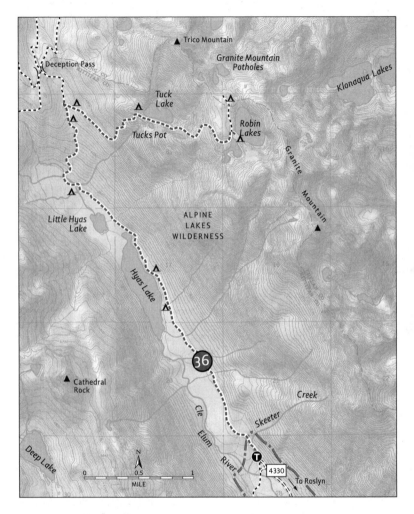

2.8 miles. Farther north, the trail hugs the lake's shoreline, winding past excellent views of Cathedral Rock. In early mornings and late evenings, reflections of that landmark on Hyas' cobalt waters are stunning.

The good trail crosses many creeks, including the outlet streams of Tuck and Robin Lakes high above. At about 3.5 miles, after passing Little Hyas Lake, the smooth and level trail becomes rockier and begins to climb. Switchbacking out of the valley, cross a nice creek (elev. 4000 ft) at 4.1 miles (and good camps) before coming to a junction at 4.5 miles (elev. 4275 ft). The way left continues

Upper Robin Lake embraced by Granite Mountain

to Deception Pass (Trip 37). Head right on the Robin Lakes Trail—a path never officially built but heavily traveled.

Immediately cross a creek with good camps, and then begin a steep, relentless, often rocky, and hazardous climb. Roots, ledges, and loose rocks require your constant attention. Trekking poles will come in handy—especially on the knee-jarring descent. Pack light—this is not the trail you want to be schlepping a burdensome rucksack up.

At about 5.5 miles, the way skirts some ledges, offering a grand view down to the Hyas lakes. A little farther, enter a cool forested nook and—lo and behold—Tuck Lake (elev. 5275 ft) at 5.7 miles. Flanked by granite ledges and walls, camping is at a premium here—and on weekends you'll be hard-pressed to find a spot. Better to skip camping here if you can and push on to the much prettier and roomier Robin Lakes.

The way is a bit confusing leaving Tuck—you'll need to hoof up a granite ledge and then work your way down to the outlet stream. Cross it on logs and then look for the most boot-beaten path heading up a granite and heather rib. It would do the Forest Service some good to mark the trail here for two reasons: one, social paths run everywhere, only further degrading the fragile lake basin; and two, it is really easy to get disoriented and wind up on a steep cliff.

Heading up the steep, increasingly open rib, admire little Tucks Pot directly below sparkling Tuck Lake and big, beautiful 7899-foot Mount Daniel dominating the backdrop. The way stays right of a gully and makes two small dips to avoid cliffs. The journey is arduous. At about 6.6 miles, the route heads up a heather draw, emerging onto slopes of granite ledges and slabs (elev. 6000 ft). Cairns mark the way, but even then it's easy to lose your way—especially in bad weather. Generally angling to the southeast, the way crests an open ridge (elev. 6300 ft), from where you can survey below you—the strikingly beautiful Robin Lakes sparkling in the sun and reflecting snow and rock from 7144-foot Granite Mountain.

Drop into the basin to follow a trail angling above the lower lake. At 7.2 miles, arrive at a ledgy rib (elev. 6200 ft) dotted with firs and larches separating the upper and lower lakes. Teeming with tents, it's a centrally located spot—but not very private. Better, secluded camps can be found near the lower lake's outlet and on a ledge north of the upper lake. Secure food and boots—mountain goats are prolific here.

TRIP PLANNER	
2 miles	Hyas Lake and camps
4.1 miles	Creekside camps
4.6 miles	Camps near trail junction
5.7 miles	Tuck Lake and camps
7.2 miles	Camps between upper and lower Robin Lakes

EXTENDING YOUR TRIP

While the terrain was rough getting here, exploring the high country around the Robin Lakes is inviting. Nontechnical scrambling ascents can be made to both 7144-foot Granite Mountain and 6600-plus foot Trico Mountain. Follow a good path along the upper lake's northern shoreline to goat wallows and hidden tarns; then drop down to the pretty Granite Mountain Potholes for solitude and spectacular sunrises over the Icicle Creek valley.

37 Marmot Lake

RATING/ DIFFICULTY	ROUND-TRIP	ELEV GAIN/ HIGH POINT	SEASON
***/3	18.8 miles	2975 feet/ 4950 feet	late July–Oct

Map: Green Trails Stevens Pass No. 176; **Contact:** Okanogan-Wenatchee National Forest, Cle Elum Ranger District, (509) 852-1100, www.fs.fed.us/r6/wenatchee; **Permits/ regulations:** NW Forest Pass required. Free Alpine Lakes Wilderness permit required May 15–Oct 31, self-issued at trailhead. Wilderness rules apply. Fires prohibited; **Special features:** Large alpine lake in a basin flanked by rocky knolls. One of the least-visited lakes in the popular Hyas–Deception Pass area, chance of solitude is good. Other quiet, remote lakes can be explored from Marmot Lake. **Special concerns:** Unbridged Scatter Creek, 3 miles before the trailhead, requires a high-clearance vehicle to cross in early season. Mosquitoes can be fierce in early and mid-summer; **GPS:** N 47 32.685 W 121 05.865

One of the larger lakes ringing the deep basins within the shadows of glacier-clad Mount Daniel, Marmot Lake is also one of the less popular. It's not because of its characteristics or any inherent flaws—it's an attractive lake with nice sunny ledges for lounging. Campsites are good—fishing too—and the trail leading to the lake is pleasant and well graded. So what gives? Nearby Tuck and Robin Lakes siphon away the masses, leaving Marmot and nearby Lake Clarice for those intent on not sharing backcountry campsites with half of Seattle.

GETTING THERE

From Seattle, drive I-90 east to exit 80 (signed "Roslyn/Salmon la Sac"). Turn left onto Bull Frog Road and follow it 2.8 miles to State Route 903. (From Ellensburg, take I-90 west to exit 84, turn right onto N Oakes Avenue, and follow it to SR 903). Turn left on SR 903 (which eventually becomes Salmon la Sac Road) and drive 16.6 miles to the old guard station and pavement's end. Continue north on Forest Road 4330 for 12.3 rough and slow miles to the trailhead (elev. 3400 ft). Privy available.

ON THE TRAIL

Head north on the well-trodden Deception Pass Trail, soon entering the Alpine Lakes Wilderness. After a few minor ups and downs, but generally level walking, come to elongated Hyas Lake (elev. 3450 ft) with its numerous good camps—a popular spot for beginning backpackers and those who got a late start.

The trail skirts the lake's mile-long shoreline, passing nice views of Cathedral Rock hovering high above it. At about 3.5 miles, after passing Little Hyas Lake, the trail's mood changes from smooth and level to rocky and up. Through a series of switchbacks, the trail leaves the valley, crossing a creek (elev. 4000 ft) at 4.1 miles (and good camps) and the junction with the Tuck and Robin Lakes Trail (Trip 36) at 4.5 miles (elev. 4275 ft). Continue left, winding through the three H's (hemlock, heather, and huckleberry), coming to a junction with the Pacific Crest Trail at forested Deception Pass (elev. 4475 ft) at 5.1 miles.

Use a stove and keep a clean camp.

Head right and immediately come to the Lake Clarice Trail junction, where you'll veer left immediately, passing a couple of campsites perched above sprawling mosquito-breeding grounds. The trail gently winds beneath talus slopes, traversing heather meadows and berry patches. At 5.8 miles, cross a creek—there's a good campsite just beyond. The trail passes several tarns before cresting a gap in Blue Ridge (elev. 4750 ft), where there's a pretty tarn.

The trail then begins to lose elevation, skirting an avalanche-prone valley that cradles small Hozzbizz Lake (camping possible) beneath waterfall-streaked walls at 6.4 miles. Rock hop across Hozzbizz Creek and continue to descend. Avoiding steep cliffs, the way traverses talus and old growth before bottoming out in an avalanche slope (elev. 4050 ft).

With lost elevation now needing to be regained, the trail steadily ascends, first

Marmot Lake's rocky shoreline with Terrace Mountain in the background

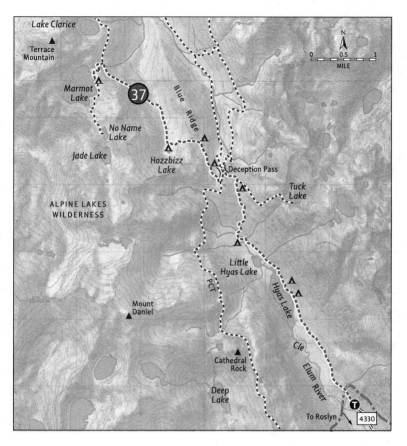

Lake Clarice

Terrace
Mountain

Marmot
Lake

37

Blue Ridge

No Name
Lake

Jade Lake

Hozzbizz
Lake

Deception Pass

Tuck
Lake

ALPINE LAKES
WILDERNESS

Little
Hyas Lake

PCT

Hyas Lake

Mount
Daniel

Cathedral
Rock

Deep
Lake

Cle
Elum River

To Roslyn

4330

N

0   0.5   1
MILE

steeply up brushy slopes and then gently through cool forested groves. A couple of talus slopes are crossed along the way too, providing nice views of the Deception Creek valley, Mac Peak, Surprise Mountain, and Glacier Peak in the distance.

Soon after crossing Marmot Lake's cascading outlet creek, come to a junction (elev. 4675 ft) at 8.7 miles. The trail right continues 0.8 mile to pretty Lake Clarice (elev. 4525 ft), tucked in a deep cirque on the north slopes of 6361-foot Terrace Mountain. Fishing is good—but the camping isn't, with the lake's rocky and brushy shoreline. Save it for an exploration from your base at Marmot Lake, reached by following the trail left for 0.7 mile, recrossing the cascading outlet creek, and climbing up a steep forested slope.

Just beyond a large shoreline ledge (elev. 4950 ft), the trail ends along Marmot Lake (elev. 4925 ft) in a large camping area complete with backcountry privy. If these lakeside camps aren't to your liking, there are more camps back by the outlet. In any case, you shouldn't have too much company—probably no marmots either. They're more likely to be found higher up the slopes toward Mount Daniel, hidden here behind a fortress of knolls.

TRIP PLANNER	
2 miles	Hyas Lake and camps
4.1 miles	Creekside camps
4.6 miles	Camps near Tuck and Robin trail junction
5.2 miles	Deception Pass
5.8 miles	Creekside camps
6.4 miles	Hozzbizz Lake
9.4 miles	Marmot Lake and camps

EXTENDING YOUR TRIP

Definitely make the easy side trip to Lake Clarice. Hardy souls may want to follow a rough and tumble path from Marmot's inlet creek to No Name Lake and glacier-fed Jade Lake just beyond. For a variation on the return, follow the PCT to the Cathedral Rock Trail back to the trailhead. This adds about 5 miles to the trip. The scenery is fantastic, but be mindful that two glacial melt creeks must be forded along the way—dangerous to downright impossible in early season and after wet periods. Marmot Lake can also be reached from the north following the lightly traveled Deception Creek Trail.

Opposite: Upper Florence Lake (Trip 41)

Central Cascades

38 Dishpan Gap

RATING/ DIFFICULTY	LOOP	ELEV GAIN/ HIGH POINT	SEASON
****/3	22 miles	3500 feet/ 5650 feet	mid-July–Oct

Maps: Green Trails Monte Cristo, WA–No. 143, Benchmark Mtn No. 144; **Contact:** Mount Baker–Snoqualmie National Forest, Skykomish Ranger District, (360) 677-2414, www .fs.fed.us/r6/mbs; **Permits/regulations:** NW Forest Pass required. Wilderness rules apply. No fires at Lake Sally Ann and along the PCT; **Special features:** Large tracts of old growth. Sprawling alpine meadows, brilliant with wildflowers in summer and dazzling colors in fall; **Special concerns:** Two unbridged creek crossings may be dangerous or impossible to negotiate in early season and periods of heavy rain. Popular equestrian and hunting area; **GPS:** N 47 55.608 W 121 16.601

Follow a tumbling waterway to the Cascade crest, where miles of mile-high alpine-meadow roaming await. Cross three passes, amble by one sparkling lake snug in its rocky cirque, and roam through boundless blossoming flowers—or walk this way in autumn and traverse ground ablaze in crimson. The views are breathtaking year-round—from radiating emerald ridges and stark sky-probing crags to Glacier Peak, the snowy-white sentinel of the Central Cascades.

GETTING THERE

North Fork Skykomish River Road from Index, the normal approach for this trip, is washed out. Until it's repaired, access the trail from Skykomish via Jack Pass. From Everett, head east on US 2 for 50 miles and turn left (just past Skykomish) onto Beckler River Road (Forest Road 65). Continue for 14.9 miles

(the pavement ends at 6.9 miles), coming to a junction just after crossing the North Fork Skykomish River. Turn right onto FR 63 and proceed 4.3 miles to the road's end and trailhead (elev. 2500 ft). Primitive camping and privy available.

ON THE TRAIL

While this loop follows a very popular section of the Pacific Crest Trail, chances are that most folks come here from the east via Cady Ridge and the Little Wenatchee River trails. By coming from the west, via trails less-traveled, you'll be able to savor some solitude along this spectacular loop.

Start by hiking the North Fork Skykomish River Trail—first on old road, then at 1.5 miles on bona fide trail. You immediately enter the Wild Sky Wilderness, Washington's latest wilderness addition, signed into law by President Bush in 2008. Wind through magnificent old-growth forest now fully protected from the ax. Bountiful huckleberry bushes thrive beneath the ancient canopy. Watch for berry-craving bears—especially during the autumn harvest.

At 2.1 miles, enter the Henry M. Jackson Wilderness, created in 1984 and honoring Everett native son and longtime Washington senator and conservationist, Henry "Scoop" Jackson. Continue through deep forest, occasionally on puncheon across pungent skunk-cabbage patches. At 3 miles, come to a junction (elev. 3300 ft). You'll be returning left, so proceed to the right on the Pass Creek Trail. Descend 0.4 mile to a gorgeous old-growth grove and campsites by the North Fork Skykomish River (elev. 3150 ft).

The river must be forded—fairly easy late in the year, downright dangerous early in the season. After traversing a spectacular bog (abuzz with mosquitoes) via a sturdy boardwalk, reenter forest and gradually climb. At 4.3 miles, ford Pass Creek (elev. 3300 ft), another tricky crossing early in the season.

The Pacific Crest Trail cuts through a carpet of blueberries.

The lightly traveled but well-built trail continues climbing along Pass Creek, crossing several tributaries along the way, and eventually reaches the Pacific Crest Trail (elev. 4200 ft) and good camps at 6.5 miles. Right heads to Bench Mark Mountain and Pear Lake, both excellent destinations. You want to head left, crossing Pass Creek (now a trickle) once more—take in the good views of 6368-foot Skykomish Peak, which you'll be hiking around.

At 7 miles, come to good but waterless camps and a junction with the Cady Creek Trail at 4300-foot Cady Pass. Once considered for railroad passage, this low pass remains wild while Stevens Pass to the south became the busy transportation portal. Continue north on the PCT, switchbacking through groves of mountain hemlock that soon give way to meadows—miles of meadows. And views, stunning views—to Poet Ridge and the Chiwaukum Mountains east; Mounts Stuart, Daniel, and Rainier south; Ten Peak, Clark (look for the "cat ears"), and many more north.

The way rounds a 5450-foot knoll before dipping into a small saddle, and then it climbs and dips again. Across sprawling meadows

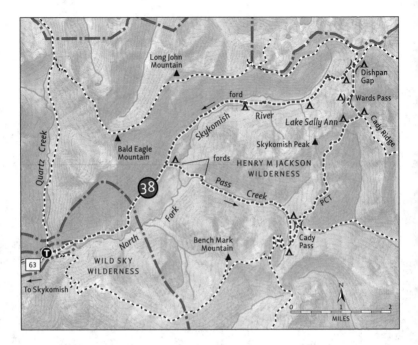

dancing with dazzling wildflowers in summer, and streaked in scarlet in autumn, the way continues around Skykomish Peak's fluted ridges. Reach an elevation of 5500 feet before descending into a small snow-retaining cirque cupping little Lake Sally Ann (elev. 5450 ft) at 11 miles, where you'll find good but well-used camps.

In another 0.5 mile, find more camps in a saddle (and water, just north on the PCT), just to the east of the Cady Ridge Trail junction (elev. 5350 ft). From here, continue north on the PCT, winding through more meadows and profuse berry patches. Views north to Glacier Peak are mesmerizing. At 12.3 miles, reach Wards Pass (elev. 5650 ft), with waterless camps but excellent views of the Monte Cristo peaks.

The way then gently descends, reaching a major trail intersection at Dishpan Gap (elev. 5550 ft) at 13 miles. There are outstanding

views and good camps here, though there may not be water late in the season. The PCT veers right to White Pass (Trip 53), while the Bald Eagle Trail heads northwest toward Blue Lake (Trip 52)—you want to head west on the North Fork Skykomish River Trail, losing elevation through gorgeous parkland meadows.

At 13.6 miles, pass an inviting creekside camp (elev. 5050 ft) before reentering forest and rapidly descending. After skirting some willow flats, reach more creekside camps (elev. 4300 ft) at 14.9 miles. Then enter a broad hanging valley, bordered by rushing creeks on both sides and graced with berry bushes galore. At 16.7 miles, pass a good camp at the creeks' confluence. Shortly afterward ford the North Fork Skykomish River (elev. 3700 ft), another potentially dangerous crossing in high water.

The way now gently continues down the valley, passing wetland pools, giant trees, and nice riverside lounging sites. At 19 miles, bear right at the familiar Pass Creek Trail junction, returning to the trailhead in 3 more miles.

TRIP PLANNER	
3.4 miles	North Fork Skykomish River camps
6.5 miles	Camps near PCT junction
7 miles	Cady Pass and camps
11 miles	Lake Sally Ann and camps
11.5 miles	Camps in saddle
12.3 miles	Wards Pass and camps
13 miles	Dishpan Gap and camps
13.6 miles	Creekside camp
14.9 miles	More creekside camps
16.7 miles	Camp at creek confluence
22 miles	Trailhead

EXTENDING YOUR TRIP
Consider a loop variation by following the Bald Eagle Trail (Trip 52) or West Cady Ridge Trail over Bench Mark Mountain.

39 Necklace Valley

RATING/ DIFFICULTY	ROUND-TRIP	ELEV GAIN/ HIGH POINT	SEASON
***/3	18 miles	3200 feet/ 4800 feet	mid-July– Oct

Maps: Green Trails Skykomish No. 175, Stevens Pass No. 176; **Contact:** Mount Baker–Snoqualmie National Forest, Skykomish Ranger District, (360) 677-2414, www.fs.fed.us/r6/mbs; **Permits/ regulations:** NW Forest Pass required. Free wilderness permit required, self-issued at trailhead. Wilderness rules apply. Fires prohibited. Dogs must be leashed; **Special features:** String of alpine lakes tucked in high valley beneath cliffs and glaciers of 7492-foot Mount Hinman; **Special concerns:** Abundant mosquitoes in summer; **GPS:** N 47 39.898 W 121 17.292

A strand of aquatic alpine gems strung together in a tight valley shadowed by lofty craggy summits and sheer rock faces, the Necklace Valley is indeed a backpacking jewel. The approach is long, steep at times, rocky, and taxing— all the better for crowd control. Compared to the nearby, much more easily accessible Foss Lakes, Necklace Valley's lakes are much smaller and not nearly as dramatic, further reducing their demand but by no means diminishing their value.

GETTING THERE
From Everett, drive US 2 east to the small city of Skykomish. Continue east for 2 miles (passing the ranger station), and turn right onto Foss River Road (Forest Road 68). Continue for 4.2 miles (the pavement ends at 1.1 miles) to the trailhead (elev. 1600 ft). Privy available.

ON THE TRAIL
On good tread, on an old logging railroad bed, begin hiking through a cool canopy of second growth interspersed with giant springboard-notched stumps. At 1.6 miles, enter the 394,000-acre Alpine Lakes Wilderness, among the state's larger and most popular wilderness areas. While the trail initially stays above and away from the East Fork Foss River, you'll cross numerous side creeks and plenty of swampy terrain, making lack of water a nonissue.

At about 3.2 miles, the East Fork Foss is finally encountered, along with a nice campsite (elev. 2150 ft). Cross a large rock slide, traverse several forest openings, and pass more riverside campsites. After walking through a bottomland of big cedars, at 5.2 miles reach good camps (with privy) and a log bridge (hopefully, as many wash away) across the East Fork Foss (elev. 2200 ft).

The way now radically changes gears, climbing steeply out of the valley. Cross talus,

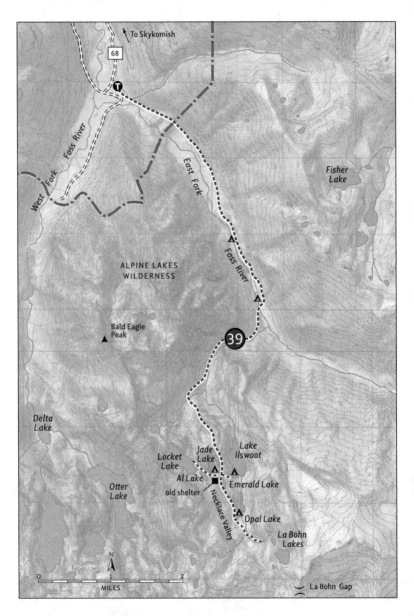

Opal Lake

hemlock and yellow cedar groves, rocky, rooty, and brushy slopes (hot in the sun), gaining over 2000 feet in less than 2 miles. At 7 miles, cross a raging side creek in a rocky cleft (elev. 3700 ft), which may be tricky, since the bridge got swept away. The grade eases somewhat before making one last steep drive to reach the first jewel in the Necklace, little Jade Lake (elev. 4600 ft) at 8 miles. Flanked on the east

and west by big slabs of talus, good-but-busy campsites can be found around the lake's inlet and outlet streams. Catch nice reflections in the lake's jade-colored waters.

The trail continues, crossing Jade's inlet stream and climbing through muddy heather meadows, arriving at 8.6 miles at a 1950-built shelter cabin (elev. 4750 ft) with a grammatically challenged plaque. Resident rodents welcome you to use it. From just north of the cabin, well-trodden but unmarked user trails take off west for Al Lake and good-sized Locket Lake (elev. 4600 ft); and east for shallow Emerald Lake, with its good camps and fine views, and for Lake Ilswoot (elev. 4590 ft), with its limited campsites in deep timber above its gorgeous turquoise waters.

The main trail continues south, skirting above shallow Opal Lake—there's camping near its outlet, complete with lovely views and reflections—then through parkland meadows of heather and blueberry beneath imposing sheer cliffs. A short distance beyond where a small creek tumbles across a rock slab at 9 miles, the trail fades in a small upper basin—with good camps (elev. 4800 ft)

TRIP PLANNER	
3.2 miles	East Fork Foss River camp
5.2 miles	East Fork Foss River camp at log bridge
8 miles	Jade Lake and camps
8.6 miles	Old shelter and trail junction to other lakes and camps
8.8 miles	Opal Lake camps
9 miles	Upper basin camps

EXTENDING YOUR TRIP

Hikers with good navigation and off-trail travel skills can continue 0.5 mile beyond the upper basin on sketchy tread to the base of a large talus slope. From there, a difficult but rewarding trip can be made to the La Bohn Lakes in a cirque beneath 4960-foot La Bohn Gap.

40 Chain and Doelle Lakes

RATING/ DIFFICULTY	ROUND-TRIP	ELEV GAIN/ HIGH POINT	SEASON
****/4	25 miles	6200 feet/ 6200 feet	mid-July– Oct

Map: Green Trails Stevens Pass No. 176; **Contact:** Okanogan-Wenatchee National Forest, Wenatchee River Ranger District, Leavenworth,

(509) 548-6977, www.fs.fed.us/r6/wenatchee; **Permits/regulations:** NW Forest Pass required. Free wilderness permit required, self-issued at trailhead. Wilderness rules apply. No fires at lakes; **Special features:** Some of the loneliest alpine lakes and most dramatic scenery within the popular Alpine Lakes Wilderness; **Special concerns:** Brushy trail due to lack of maintenance; **GPS:** N 47 44.775 W 121 05.205

🗡 👫 ⚙ ❌ *Trek to five remote sparkling lakes occupying two granite cirques within the shadows of the 6807-foot Bulls Tooth, one of the most distinct landmarks in the Alpine Lakes Wilderness. A long approach, a steep finish, and easier to get to lakes along the way help siphon off and discourage many hikers from this spectacular location. All the better to let you savor the solitude and revel in the wildness and ruggedness of these lakes.*

GETTING THERE

From Everett, head east on US 2 for 65 miles to Stevens Pass (From Leavenworth, travel west on US 2 for 35 miles.) Turn right (south) into the large parking area just east of the main Stevens Pass ski area buildings (elev. 4100 ft). Privy available.

ON THE TRAIL

Starting on the Pacific Crest Trail, head south into mature forest. Soon begin traversing ski slopes and lift lines from the Stevens Pass ski area—not the most aesthetic hiking terrain, but the open slopes do offer good viewing and, later in the season, good berry picking.

On an easy grade, ascend to a 5150-foot ridge crest at 2.1 miles, and then slowly descend on wide switchbacks across more ski slopes taking in excellent views east to the Chiwaukum Mountains and Bulls Tooth. After crossing a powerline swath and service

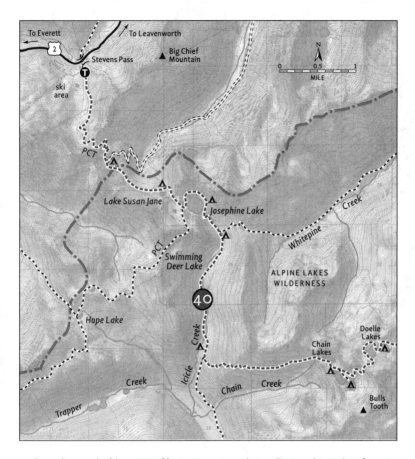

road, reach a swale (elev. 4600 ft) at 3.5 miles, where camps can be found alongside a creek. Soon afterward, enter the Alpine Lakes Wilderness and contour across a rocky ridge, coming to pretty little Lake Susan Jane (elev. 4600 ft) perched beneath talus at 4.3 miles. Find well-used camps here.

The PCT then climbs to a small gap, passing grassy tarns and coming to a junction with the Icicle Creek Trail (elev. 4900 ft) at 4.9 miles. Turn left here, traveling across heather knolls that harbor reflecting tarns and rounding the cirque that cradles Josephine Lake. After gaining 100 feet, the trail rapidly drops, coming to Josephine's outlet (elev. 4700 ft) and good camps at 5.6 miles.

Now leaving the crowds behind, continue on the Icicle Creek Trail, steeply descending in big timber beside a big talus slope and coming to a junction (elev. 4400 ft) at 6.1 miles with the Whitepine Creek Trail. Once a viable alternative approach to Chain and Doelle lakes, a good portion of this trail is now nearly lost in avalanche brush.

Upper Doelle Lake

Continuing right, through heather meadows, pass some good camps and slowly descend, following Icicle Creek. While the way is pretty gentle, the trail crosses the creek three times (expect wet boots) and through choking brush (expect wet clothing). Shortly after the third crossing, pass a good camp and come to the Chain Lakes Trail junction (elev. 3800 ft) at 8.1 miles.

Now on a trail that doesn't believe in switchbacks, arduously climb steep timbered slopes to reach the promised land of the Chain Lakes (elev. 5600 ft) at 10.5 miles. The first lake reflecting rocky pinnacles greets you in a lovely meadow. Cross its outlet and come to the second lake (elev. 5660 ft) set in parkland meadows surrounded by granite outcroppings, clusters of subalpine fir, and imposing rocky peaks looking down

upon it. Find excellent established camps here too.

Scenery keeps getting better, so continue. Cross the second lake's outlet and come to a junction at 10.8 miles. The right-hand trail heads into a wide-open basin housing the third Chain Lake (elev. 5680 ft), with more camps and exploring possibilities. The main trail heads left, climbing up shiny white talus slopes (admire the excellent work of past trail builders), with astounding views of the Chain Lakes sparkling below.

At 11.4 miles, the way turns steep before reaching a 6200-foot gap teetering between the two lake-embracing cirques. Catch your breath. Then lose it again staring out at upper Doelle Lake, shimmering below the waves of majestic peaks—Sloan, Pugh, Baker, Glacier, Jim Hill, Nason Ridge, and the Chiwaukums.

The trail veers right here (do not follow the path left, which leads into a steep, dangerous snowfield). Then steeply descend heather and granite to reach the grassy shore of the upper Doelle Lake (elev. 5775 ft) at 12 miles. Find good camps 0.5 mile farther at the second, smaller lake (elev. 5600 ft). There's no arguing that these lakes are among the most beautiful in the Cascades. There is debate, though, on how to pronounce *Doelle*. The lakes were named by Wenatchee National Forest Supervisor A. H. Sylvester for Bill Doelle, a fire warden who lost his life in a fire in 1929—and Doelle pronounced his name *dooley*.

TRIP PLANNER	
3.5 miles	Creekside camp
4.3 miles	Lake Susan Jane and camps
5.6 miles	Josephine Lake camps
6.1 miles	Meadow camps near trail junction
7.9 miles	Camp near third crossing of Icicle Creek
10.7 miles	Second Chain Lake camps
12 miles	Upper Doelle Lake
12.5 miles	Lower Doelle Lake and camps

EXTENDING YOUR TRIP
The Chain Lakes Trail can also be reached (with less elevation gain) from the Icicle Creek Road by hiking 9 miles up the Icicle Creek Trail. Hikers with good navigational skills can follow an abandoned (but still good in spots) trail for 3 miles from the Doelle Lakes across a fairly open ridge to Frosty Pass (Trip 41).

41 Ladies Pass and Chiwaukum Lakes

RATING/ DIFFICULTY	ROUND-TRIP	ELEV GAIN/ HIGH POINT	SEASON
****/4	25 miles	4500 feet/ 6900 feet	July–Oct

Maps: Green Trails Wenatchee Lake No. 145, Chiuwaukum Mts No. 177; **Contact:** Okanogan-Wenatchee National Forest, Wenatchee River Ranger District, Leavenworth, (509) 548-6977, www.fs.fed.us/r6/wenatchee; **Permits/regulations:** NW Forest Pass required. Free wilderness permit required, self-issued at trailhead. Wilderness rules apply. No fires at lakes; **Special features:** Ten alpine lakes tucked along high open slopes of Chiwaukum Mountains. Spectacular views, off-trail exploring; **Special concerns:** Brushy and eroded trail due to lack of maintenance. Fair amount of horse traffic. Limited lakeside campsites are often full; **GPS:** N 47 46.242 W 120 55.624

At the convergence of the lush and lofty Chiwaukum Mountains and the rough and tumble Icicle Ridge lie nearly a dozen sparkling alpine lakes. Often referred to as the Mormon Lakes (one's named for Brigham Young and two for two of his wives), this is definitely the place if you like sprawling wildflower meadows, showy rock gardens, inviting ridges and basins for exploring, breathtaking views—and of course, gorgeous sparkling backcountry lakes.

GETTING THERE
From Everett, head east on US 2 to Stevens Pass. Continue east for another 13.5 miles, turning right just after milepost 78 onto Whitepine Road (Forest Road 6950) (signed for Cascade Meadows). (From Leavenworth, the turnoff is 6.5 miles west of Coles Corner.) At 2.7 miles, bear left at a Y junction. Continue for just over a mile to the trailhead at road's end (elev. 2800 ft).

ON THE TRAIL
There are several ways to get to the high-country lakes of the Chiwaukum country. The most popular is via the Frosty Creek Trail from the Icicle Creek Road. But it's popular

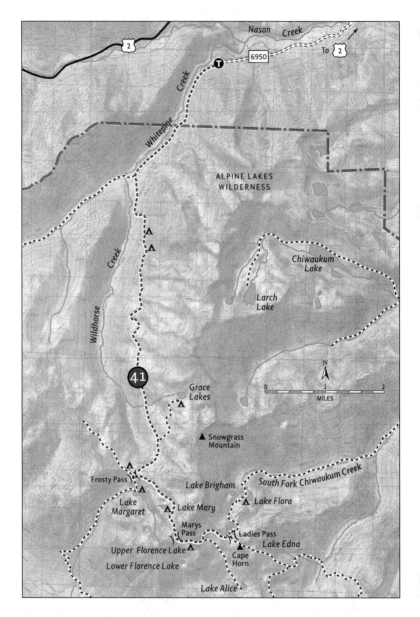

with horses and requires a longer approach until the road (washed out since 2008) is repaired. The Chatter Creek Trail is god-awful, deeply eroded, grown-over, and steep. The South Fork Chiwaukum Creek Trail is a good choice, but long. The recommended approach described here is via the Wildhorse Creek Trail. While it's brushy in spots, views are excellent, water is plentiful, and chances for solitude are good.

Starting on the Whitepine Creek Trail, head into a dark forest of big burnt snags and remnant giants. Cross numerous side creeks and brushy, shrub-choked avalanche chutes along the way. Shortly after entering the Alpine Lakes Wilderness, check out a sunny ledge above a small cascade on the chattering creek.

At 2.5 miles, come to a junction (elev. 3200 ft). The Whitepine Creek Trail continues right into a tangled cloak of vegetation. It has seen very little maintenance in the last two decades and is at risk of disappearing. Continue left on the Wildhorse Creek Trail, which receives a little more maintenance but is also choked with brush in spots. Climbing well above Wildhorse Creek, the trail at first wastes little time gaining elevation—then it eases up.

At 4.5 miles, in cedars, come to a small creekside camp (elev. 4500 ft). More camps near another creek lie 0.5 mile farther. At 5.4 miles, get your boots wet crossing yet another creek. Derived from the Wenatchee dialect, *chiwaukum* means "many little creeks running into one big one." And from the Chiwaukum Mountains' hidden nooks and massive cirques above, many creeks cascade down into frothing waterways.

At 5.9 miles, after a series of short, steep switchbacks, bear right at an unmarked trail (elev. 5300 ft), taking off for the high country. The way now gets much brushier, a result of past large fires. Berry bushes favoring acidic soils and colonizing mountain ash (not a true

ash but a member of the rose family) grow profusely here, offering pretty fall foliage and forage for area critters. Alders and willows choke creekbeds. The going can be excruciatingly frustrating.

After dropping 150 feet to cross a big creek, start climbing across a large avalanche chute and come to the Grace Lakes Trail (elev. 5400 ft) at 8.3 miles. An excellent side trip (or to camp), this lightly traveled path travels 1.5 miles to lower Lake Grace (elev. 6240 ft). The upper lake is for adventurous travelers only.

At 9.3 miles, reach the Icicle Ridge Trail at Frosty Pass (elev. 5800 ft). The way right leads 0.1 mile to good camps at a junction with the abandoned trail to Doelle Lakes (see Trip 40); and then it continues to forested Lake Margaret (where there are decent camps), ending in 4.7 miles at the Icicle Creek Trail.

You want to continue left, climbing past a ledge offering spectacular views north across the Wildhorse and Whitepine valleys, then past another ledge offering wonderful views over Lake Margaret and the Icicle Creek valley. Continue higher into glorious meadows, coming to a junction (elev. 6050 ft) at 9.9 miles with a spur to Lake Mary and its delightful camps. Lake Mary is an excellent place to call it quits—however, the best is yet to come.

The trail continues, rounding wide-open slopes screaming with flowers, climbing high above Lake Mary to windswept, krummholz-lined 6900-foot Marys Pass at 11.3 miles. The views are beyond breathtaking across the rugged Icicle Ridge to Mount Stuart—the Wenatchee Mountains and Bulls Tooth too!

Now descend, startling marmots along the way, coming to a junction (elev. 6675 ft) at 11.6 miles with a spur to Upper Florence Lake, an inspiring (and exposed) place to spend the evening. The main trail then climbs an open shoulder (elev. 6750 ft) before dropping into a beautiful spring-fed basin (elev. 6550 ft). From here, a faint 2.4-mile trail

A pair of backpackers approaches Ladies Pass.

leads right to isolated Lake Alice beneath the rocky behemoth, 7533-foot Grindstone Mountain.

Wherever you've chosen to camp, make sure you make the trip up the main trail to 6800-foot Ladies Pass at 12.5 miles, climbing across alpine tundra punctuated with white-bark pines. Sit in the sun and soak up satisfying views of the lofty craggy walls of the surrounding Icicle Ridge and Chiwaukum Mountains and the green, deep, glacier-carved valleys emanating from them.

TRIP PLANNER	
4.5–5 miles	Creekside camps
8.3 miles	Grace Lakes Trail to camps
9.4 miles	Frosty Pass camps
10 miles	Lake Mary camps
11.8 miles	Upper Florence Lake camps
12.5 miles	Ladies Pass

EXTENDING YOUR TRIP

You can spend a week exploring here. From Ladies Pass head east 1 mile up Cape Horn (if steep snowfields are absent) and to Lake Edna, set in an open basin of heather and tundra. Or head down the Chiwaukum Creek Trail 1.6 miles to beautiful Lake Brigham, set in a magnificent cirque—and 0.3 mile farther to Lake Flora (elev. 5800 ft), with its nice camps. If you can arrange a car shuttle, continue 12.5 miles down the Chiwaukum Creek Trail, passing a stunning waterfall and following the South Fork Chiwaukum Creek through Timothy Meadows (nice camps) to the Chiwaukum Creek Trail out to US 2.

42 Lake Augusta and the Badlands

RATING/ DIFFICULTY	LOOP	ELEV GAIN/ HIGH POINT	SEASON
***/4	21 miles	6400 feet/ 7300 feet	July–Oct

Map: Green Trails Chiwaukum Mts No. 177; **Contact:** Okanogan-Wenatchee National Forest, Wenatchee River Ranger District, Leavenworth, (509) 548-6977, www.fs.fed .us/r6/wenatchee; **Permits/regulations:** Free wilderness permit required, self-issued at trailhead. Wilderness rules apply; **Special features:** High alpine lake, alpine tundra, secluded wilderness valley; **Special concerns:** Painter Creek Trail is brushy and hard to follow in spots. Required fords may be difficult in early season and periods of heavy rain; **GPS:** N 47 40.273 W 120 45.320

One of the highest sizeable lakes in the sprawling Alpine Lakes Wilderness, Lake Augusta sits in a large cirque beneath 7763-foot Big Jim Mountain, one of the highest summits along Icicle Ridge. Far less visited than the nearby Mormon Lakes (Trip 41) and Scottish Lakes, Lake Augusta delivers just as much spectacular alpine scenery and wilderness roaming as those popular destinations. Enjoy wildflowers in summer, golden larches in fall, and excellent wildlife-watching in the Painter Creek valley anytime.

GETTING THERE

From Everett, head east on US 2, passing Stevens Pass to Coles Corner. Continue east on US 2 for 5.8 miles and turn right onto Hatchery Creek Road (Forest Road 7905), across from the Tumwater Campground entrance just before Tumwater Bridge. (From Leavenworth, follow US 2 west for 9 miles to the turnoff.) Follow Hatchery Creek Road for 2.5 rough miles to the trailhead (elev. 2800 ft).

ON THE TRAIL

Starting in scrappy forest, the Hatchery Creek Trail immediately sets out to gain altitude. In about 0.6 mile, enter wilderness, where bigger and better trees supplant the scrap. Continue climbing on tight switchbacks, reaching a small creek and campsite (elev. 4600 ft) at about 2.2 miles. The grade soon eases as the forest transitions from fir to pine. At 3 miles, in a pocket meadow, reach an easy-to-miss junction with the Badlands Trail (elev. 5350 ft), your return route.

Proceed straight, marching up a ridge and breaking out into meadows and cresting a small knoll (elev. 6100 ft) at about 4.5 miles. Enjoy good views down the Wenatchee River valley to the Columbia and out to the Entiat Mountains, Mount Stuart, and Icicle Ridge. Continue along a high ridge through parkland

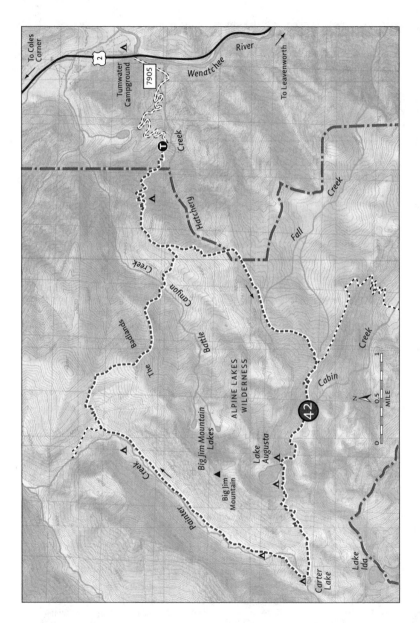

Setting up camp near Lake Augusta

meadows and old burns, twittering with woodpeckers and nutcrackers.

Pass through cool spruce and fir groves before traversing lush meadows, once more gaining elevation. Cross Fall Creek (which may be dry in late season) before steeply switch-backing up a meadowed ridge and reaching a junction with the Icicle Ridge Trail (elev. 6700 ft) at 6.5 miles. Views are excellent here of the long and lonely Icicle Ridge and Cash-mere Mountain rising behind it.

Turn right, following the Icicle Ridge Trail, and drop into a gorgeous basin (elev. 6350 ft) bursting with blossoms and bustling with bruin activity. Cross a tributary of Cabin Creek and begin climbing steeply across open slopes, reaching the spectacular basin housing Lake Augusta (elev. 6857 ft) at 8.2 miles. Good camps can be found along the bluff south of the lake and in the larch groves just north of the lake's outlet.

The loop continues west, climbing steeply 0.5 mile over alpine tundra to a gap (elev. 7300 ft) high on the southern reaches of Big Jim, where views are outstanding of the Chiwaukums, snowy Mount Daniel, golden Mission Ridge, and Augusta twinkling below. Scramble the ridge north for even better views extending all the way to Rainier, Baker, Glacier Peak, and the Olympics. If your objective is Big Jim's summit, however, it is more

easily attained from the south via the Big Jim Mountain Lakes.

The way now drops steeply into a remote flower-filled basin. Pay close attention to your route, as the tread is faint to nonexistent in places. At 10.4 miles (2.2 miles from Lake Augusta), reach the Painter Creek Trail junction. Head right—but first consider a short side trip left 0.1 mile to little, grassy-shored, larch-ringed Carter Lake (elev. 6150 ft), where camping is possible.

The Painter Creek Trail immediately crosses the creek, dropping rapidly through cool groves of spruce and fir. Cross the creek again and soon emerge in talus slopes and meadows beneath Big Jim. About 1.2 miles down the trail, tread disappears. Angle left toward the creek to relocate it. Pass good campsites. Cross the creek again and then once again lose tread in a broad meadow (elev. 5400 ft). Ford the creek for a fourth time and look for cairns to find the trail—it's extremely difficult to follow here.

Reenter forest and ford the creek for a fifth time at about 2.6 miles from Carter Lake. About 0.7 mile farther, in spruce bottomlands (elev. 5150 ft), ford the creek for a sixth and final time. Find good campsites on a bluff brushing up against Painter Creek. The trail and creek then diverge as Painter plummets into a deep gorge on its way to the South Fork Chiwaukum River. At 14 miles (3.6 miles from Carter Lake), reach the Badlands Trail.

Head right on it, climbing steeply and relentlessly out of forest to sprawling meadows. Admire views up the broad Painter Creek valley and of the Chiwaukum Mountains. At about 15.5 miles (1.5 miles from the last junction), crest the Badlands (elev. 6200 ft), not a Dakota-style eroded canyonland but a forested ridge.

Looking at Lake Augusta from ridge of Big Jim Mountain

On better tread, though it's brushy in spots, drop steeply to reach Battle Canyon Creek (elev. 4850 ft) in about 1.5 miles. One last climb awaits you. Then at 18 miles, reach the Hatchery Creek Trail (elev. 5350 ft) and turn left. Your vehicle can be retrieved in 3 miles, after dropping 2550 knee-knocking feet.

TRIP PLANNER	
2.2 miles	Creekside camp
8.2 miles	Lake Augusta and camps
10.5 miles	Carter Lake and camps
11.6 miles	Camps along Painter Creek
13.8 miles	Creekside camp near sixth ford
15.5 miles	Badlands
21 miles	Trailhead

EXTENDING YOUR TRIP

Experienced off-trail travelers may want to branch off from Carter Lake for Lake Ida, one of the crown jewels of Icicle Ridge.

43 Enchantment Lakes

RATING/ DIFFICULTY	ROUND-TRIP	ELEV GAIN/ HIGH POINT	SEASON
*****/5	26 miles	6500 feet/ 7800 feet	July–Oct

Map: Green Trails The Enchantments No. 209S; **Contact:** Okanogan-Wenatchee National Forest, Wenatchee River Ranger District, Leavenworth, (509) 548-6977, www.fs.fed.us /r6/wenatchee (general), www.fs.fed.us/r6 /wenatchee/passes/enchantments (permit process); **Permits/regulations:** NW Forest Pass required. Enchantment Permit required June 15–Oct 15, issued by lottery months in advance and a limited number first come, first served if there are cancellations. Group size limited to eight. Fires prohibited. Dogs prohibited; **Special features:** Scores of alpine lakes in a high, scoured-out glacier-carved valley, surrounded by towering granite spires; **Special concerns:** Beware of rattlesnakes at lower elevations. Aasgard Pass should only be attempted by experienced and strong hikers, dangerous in snow and bad weather; **GPS:** N 47 32.648 W 120 42.582

⚙ *One of the legendary nooks of Washington's Cascades, the Enchantment Lakes basin is a magical place of mystical names tucked in a high tiered valley within the craggy, cloud-piercing, glacier-topped Stuart Range. A land of shiny rock, sparkling waters, perpetual snowfields, prolific herds of mountain goats, and, in autumn, golden larches, the Enchantments attract legions of backpackers from near and far. While many hikers grumble about the complexities of the permit system, it has been fairly successful in maintaining ecosystem integrity and providing a wilderness experience in this extremely popular and fragile area. This Shangri-la will indeed inspire and soothe your soul, but getting here will try your lungs and punish your soles. The trail is long, dusty, hot, rocky, and steep— a grand price for this paradise—but worth every sore muscle gained along the way.*

GETTING THERE

From milepost 99 on US 2 on the western edge of Leavenworth, follow paved Icicle Creek Road (Forest Road 76) for 4.2 miles and turn left into a large parking lot at the trailhead. (elev. 1350 ft). Privy available.

ON THE TRAIL

The long approach starts by dropping fifty feet to cross Icicle Creek on a big bridge. Then, after crossing an irrigation canal, commence climbing, switchbacking up hot, dusty, rocky slopes denuded of shade thanks to a 1994 wildfire. At 1.2 miles, enter the Alpine Lakes Wilderness (elev. 2200 ft). Now at an easier grade, traverse the lower reaches of Wedge Mountain into a tight slot of a valley.

Snow Creek crashes below the impressive sheer face of the Snow Creek Wall.

At about 2.2 miles, enter a cool grove of old cedars and amble a ways along the creek before steeply climbing again, heading up rocky gullies and across slides to a hanging valley. At about 4.4 miles, after passing a showy cascade, cross Snow Creek on a reliable bridge (elev. 4100 ft). The way, now more agreeable and under forest canopy, passes a lot of nice spots along the creek for camping or napping. After traversing a talus slope, reach Nada Lake at 5.5 miles (elev. 4900 ft), which is quite a pleasant lake (when bugs aren't present), with a good number of campsites and pooped backpackers.

The trail resumes climbing, heading up a hot talus slope to a forested gap (elev. 5450 ft) before dropping a tad to the large Snow Lakes (elev. 5415 ft) at 6.5 miles, set in a wide-open basin beneath jagged and spiraling peaks and separated by a small irrigation dam. Views of the 8292-foot Temple and the large, rocky, snow-blotched cirque beneath 8364-foot McClellan Peak from the pine-studded shoreline of the upper Snow Lake are awesome. The lower lake, with its shoreline of granite ledges, looks like something right out of the Canadian Shield. Plenty of good campsites can be found at both lakes—the busiest near the dam.

Cross the dam (during high water you'll be walking on water as it spills over), and continue along the south shore of the upper lake, passing good camping areas. At about 7.8 miles, reach the lake's inlet and an abrupt trail transformation from good tread to an awful track of roots, dust, and rocks—it's steep too! Beside a tumbling creek, the trail arduously climbs a headwall. Parts of the trail have been blasted into granite ledges and there are iron handholds to help you along the way—take it easy and avoid in wet and snowy conditions.

At 9.4 miles, reach Lake Viviane (elev. 6800 ft) beneath spiraling walls of shiny granite adorned with jagged turrets—8000-plus-foot Prusik Peak, a quintessential Enchantments landmark, dominates the backdrop. The landscape now looks remarkably like the High Sierra. The trail continues deeper and higher into this mystifying terrain, hugging lakes and tarns, traversing ledges, and passing through pocket meadows and clusters of tenacious larches. Other lakes hide behind knolls and ledges—inviting hikers to better acquaint themselves with this remarkable backcountry. Campsites dot the Enchantment Basin. Use established sites and, when exploring cross-country, stick to rock whenever possible. Use the provided privies—and when urinating, do so on rock. The area's mountain goats crave the salty urine and will dig up vegetation to get it. You'll soon find out that the goats here know well the sound of urine splattering on a rock. Pee and they will come!

Continue hopping back and forth over pretty creeks, passing Leprechaun Lake, Sprite Lake, and Perfection Lake, with Little Annapurna (a popular scrambling destination) just to the southwest. At 11 miles, reach a junction (elev. 7100 ft). The trail right climbs 0.4 mile to larch-lined 7450-foot Prusik Pass, granting excellent views of shimmering lakes and glaciers to the southwest and lonely lakes and country to the northeast.

The main trail continues climbing to the upper Enchantments, a land of little forest cover and much rock and snow and ice—an area much exposed to the elements and best to avoid in bad weather. After passing Inspiration Lake, climb a rocky and snowy gulch to a broad bench dotted with sparkling tarns and an overlook of Crystal Lake, sitting on the edge of the Enchantment Basin.

Pass an old irrigation gate (elev. 7500 ft), pondering the fortitude of the early settlers.

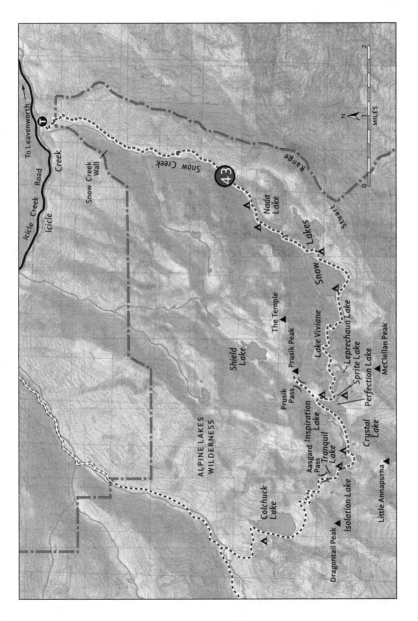

Mountain goat at Enchantment Lakes

Then traverse alpine tundra, keeping an eye out for ptarmigans. Continue higher, passing a beautiful waterfall and entering a basin that not too long ago was covered in glacial ice. The surroundings are stark, raw, and magnificent. At about 12.8 miles, come to Isolation Lake, flanked by a steep wall capped in hanging glaciers. At 7700 feet, it is one of the highest sizeable lakes in the Cascades. Little Tranquil Lake lies just ahead—last in the shimmering ring of icy enchanting lakes.

The trail continues across snow and rock, reaching 7800-foot Aasgard Pass beneath 8800-foot Dragontail Peak at 13 miles. Survey this heavenly kingdom from this stark, forbidding, rocky notch before retreating to your favorite lakes and spots on the long return.

TRIP PLANNER	
4.7 miles	Trailside camps
5.5 miles	Nada Lake and camps
6.5 miles	Snow Lakes and camps
9.4 miles	Lake Viviane and camps
10 miles	Sprite Lake and camps
11 miles	Prusik Pass trail junction and camps
12.8 miles	Isolation Lake and camps
13 miles	Aasgard Pass

EXTENDING YOUR TRIP

The trail—now more a route, but well defined (when not covered in snow)—continues from Aasgard Pass to Colchuck Lake, steeply plummeting over 2200 feet in 1.5 miles. The route is fully exposed, insanely steep, and more than a few hikers have died on it due to losing their way, slipping, or being caught in a storm. Only the most experienced backcountry travelers should consider it. If, like many backpackers (including this author), you'd like to make a classic 20-mile one-way traverse of the Enchantments, start at the Colchuck Lake trailhead and end at the Snow Lakes trailhead—it's better to ascend Aasgard than to descend it.

44 Napeequa Valley via Boulder Pass

RATING/ DIFFICULTY	ROUND-TRIP	ELEV GAIN/ HIGH POINT	SEASON
****/5	36 miles	6500 feet/ 6300 feet	late July– mid-Oct

Maps: Green Trails Holden No. 113, Wenatchee Lake No. 145; **Contact:** Okanogan-Wenatchee National Forest, Lake Wenatchee Ranger Station (summer), (509) 763-3103, or Wenatchee River Ranger District, Leavenworth, (509) 548-6977, www.fs.fed.us/r6/wenatchee; **Permits/regulations:** NW Forest Pass required. Wilderness rules apply; **Special features:** Secluded wilderness valley, spectacular alpine scenery, solitude; **Special concerns:** Required Boulder Creek ford can be dangerous and difficult in early season and periods of heavy rain; **GPS:** N 47 57.792 W 120 56.729

Quite possibly the wildest, most awe-inspiring, and revered valley in the whole state, the Napeequa is as magical as it sounds. Guarded by forbidding canyon walls, there are only three ways into this flower-bursting, meadow-draped, wide U-shaped valley. Via Boulder Pass is the easiest way—but easy it isn't. The route is long. The climb is tough. The drop is knee jarring. But to behold from the pass the view of the ice blue Napeequa River slithering through sprawling emerald carpets shadowed by towering walls of glistening rock and ice—is to behold one of nature's true masterpieces.

GETTING THERE

From Everett, head east for 85 miles on US 2 to Coles Corner. (From Leavenworth, travel west on US 2 for 15 miles.) Turn left onto State Route 207 (signed for Lake Wenatchee) and in 4 miles reach a Y intersection upon crossing

A pair of backpackers approaches Boulder Pass as Clark Mountain looks on.

the Wenatchee River. Bear left onto North Shore Road, pass the ranger station, and continue 6.2 miles, turning right onto White River Road (Forest Road 6400). Continue for 10.3 miles (the pavement ends at 6 miles) to the road's end at the trailhead (elev. 2300 ft). Privy available.

ON THE TRAIL

Before starting up the White River Trail, admire the lovely cascade at the trailhead. Then follow the glacier-fed White River along its east bank, undulating between brushy avalanche chutes and impressive groves of old-growth giants. The cedars are particularly impressive. At about 3.75 miles, encounter your first challenge: a ford of rushing Boulder Creek. If daunting, return another time and consider a trip up nearby Indian Creek instead. A quarter mile beyond, reach the junction with the Boulder Pass Trail (elev. 2550 ft) and good campsites scattered along the White River and among ancient towering evergreens. You've hardly gained any elevation thus far, but the next 7 miles quickly correct that vertical deficit.

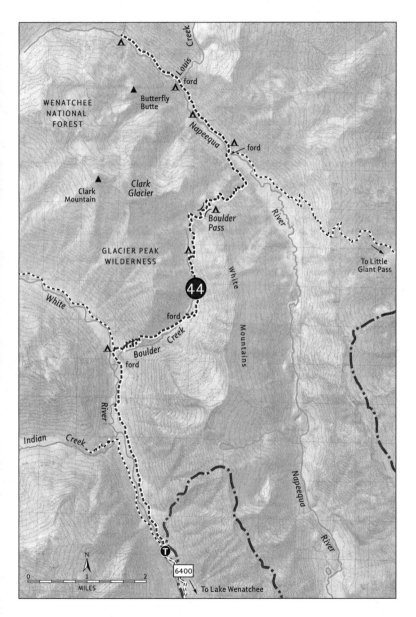

WENATCHEE
NATIONAL
FOREST

Butterfly
Butte

Louis

Creek

ford

Napeequa

ford

Clark
Glacier

Clark
Mountain

Boulder
Pass

GLACIER PEAK
WILDERNESS

River

To Little
Giant Pass

44

White

White

Mountains

ford

White

Boulder

Creek

ford

River

Indian

Creek

Napeequa

River

N

T

6400

To Lake Wenatchee

0   1   2

MILES

The Boulder Pass Trail commences to switchback, climbing rapidly out of the valley. While most of the way is under a cool forest canopy, occasional openings allow for warming rays of sunlight and nice valley views. After about 2.5 miles, the grade eases. At 7 miles from your start, reach the second crossing of Boulder Creek (elev. 4100 ft), another potentially difficult ford.

After another round of switchbacks, the trail turns northward. Vegetative cover retreats, leaving you to traverse open slopes and boulder fields. The views become excellent—of towering 8602-foot Clark Mountain before you and prominent 7420-foot Mount David across the White River valley. Continue climbing along and above Boulder Creek, through flower meadows and patches of old trees. At 8.5 miles, reach good camps at a meadow's edge (elev. 4950 ft).

Now in a wide-open basin beneath Clark Mountain, wind through flower gardens and tree islands and around ledges and cascades toward Boulder Pass. The tread is rough and rocky in places, but the grade is tame, catering to the horse parties that frequent these parts during high buck hunting season.

At 11 miles, in heather meadows and hemlock hummocks, reach Boulder Pass (elev. 6300 ft), a notch of a gap between the glacier-draped granite spires of Clark Mountain and the long craggy flank of the White Mountains. The view south and west is fine, but it's outstanding to the east, down to the Napeequa—a valley seen by few and hiked by fewer. Campsites can be found in sheltered spots around the pass, and snow patches remain all year, feeding lulling creeks. Flowers bloom until September. This is a good spot to stay, explore, or call it quits—but if the Napeequa calls, continue for another 3.5 miles, dropping rapidly and at times steeply 2000 vertical feet.

Note that a potentially dangerous snowfield may linger on the north side of the pass (bring an ice ax in early season), before the trail switchbacks endlessly through parkland meadows, across avalanche slopes, and then through cool old-growth firs and hemlocks. At 14.5 miles, at forest edge with very limited camping spots, reach the milky, silty Napeequa River (elev. 4300 ft). To go farther requires fording this river, named after a Native word meaning "white water." It's often impossible in early season and is difficult throughout the season late in the day.

If you can get safely across, reach a junction and options for extending your journey. To the left, the Napeequa River Trail, such as it is—it's kept open mainly through the work of volunteer horsemen and women—travels upvalley 3.5 miles (elev. 4900 ft) to glorious meadows, waterfalls, secluded campsites, and knock-your-smelly-hiking-socks-off views of Clark's glaciers.

TRIP PLANNER	
4 miles	Boulder Pass trail junction and camps
8.5 miles	Meadow camps
11 miles	Boulder Pass and camps
14.5 miles	Napeequa River ford and camps
15–18 miles	Trailside camps along Napeequa River

EXTENDING YOUR TRIP

The trail to the right heads downriver and climbs Little Giant Pass, a grueling, at times precarious 2000 feet in 3.5 miles, for one of the finest views in all of the Cascades. It then drops nearly 4000 feet in 5 miles to end at the Chiwawa River Road. If the Chiwawa River can be safely forded and a car shuttle arranged, it makes for an excellent alternative return. Either way, however, you're facing a steep and brutal climb out of this paradise valley.

45 Buck Creek Pass

RATING/ DIFFICULTY	ROUND-TRIP	ELEV GAIN/ HIGH POINT	SEASON
*****/3	19.2 miles	3150 feet/ 5950 feet	July–Oct

Map: Green Trails Holden No. 113; **Contact:** Okanogan-Wenatchee National Forest, Lake Wenatchee Ranger Station (summer), (509) 763-3103, or Wenatchee River Ranger District, Leavenworth, (509) 548-6977, www.fs.fed .us/r6/wenatchee; **Permits/regulations:** NW Forest Pass required. Wilderness rules apply; **Special features:** Portal to amazing Glacier Peak Wilderness backcountry, close-up views of Glacier Peak; **Special concerns:** Buck Creek Pass is popular on weekends; **GPS:** N 47 57.792 W 120 56.729

Make an easy and gentle climb to a high pass overlooking Washington's fourth-highest summit and most remote volcano, 10,541-foot Glacier Peak. Be mesmerized watching incredible sunsets over the glaciated massive mountain. Roam flowered ridges and explore hidden basins that harbor marmot colonies and bands of mountain goats. Set up camp in parkland meadows and forget that a civilized world exists beyond the

A pair of backpackers admires the spectacular view of Triad Lake.

serrated snow-capped peaks hugging the horizon.

GETTING THERE

From Everett, head east for 85 miles on US 2 to Coles Corner. (From Leavenworth, travel west on US 2 for 15 miles.) Turn left onto State Route 207 (signed for Lake Wenatchee) and in 4 miles reach a Y intersection upon crossing the Wenatchee River. Bear right onto Chiwawa Loop Road. After 1.3 miles, turn left onto Chiwawa River Road (Forest Road 62) and drive 22.6 miles (the pavement ends at 10.8 miles) to the road's end and trailhead (elev. 2800 ft).

ON THE TRAIL

On a good bridge, cross Phelps Creek, which comes down from Spider Meadow, and then skirt the old mining (now private) community of Trinity. Soon afterward, enter the Glacier Peak Wilderness and continue hiking on an old roadbed, coming to a junction (elev. 3100 ft) at 1.4 miles. The trail right leads to old mines and good wanderings high on Red Mountain. For this trip you want to continue left on a bench above Buck Creek.

Traverse open forest with views up to surrounding high peaks, and listen to the sound of cascading water as it tumbles down the valley walls. At about 2.7 miles, cross the Chiwawa River on a big bridge (elev. 3350 ft)—a fine spot for lunching and soaking dusty feet. Find a couple of campsites nearby, too: good if you got a late start.

Now avoiding a brushy valley bottom, the way switchbacks above Buck Creek before meeting up with it in wide avalanche slopes. After passing through a grove of old-growth fir, find good campsites near a small side creek. Continuing along Buck Creek in increasingly open terrain, enjoy good views up toward the pass and 8528-foot Buck Mountain.

At about 6.5 miles (elev. 4500 ft) pass another campsite as the trail makes a wide switchback away from Buck Creek to begin ascending out of the valley. Viewing is excellent of Buck Creek Pass flanked by sentinels, Liberty Cap and Helmet Butte. Angling higher across steep slopes, at 8.8 miles come to a nice creek and way path (elev. 5600 ft) that comes down from Pass No Pass. The tread heading right was once used by sheepherders and can still be followed by experienced off-trail travelers. The way to Buck Creek Pass is well defined and continues left, traversing high meadows. Soon reach the pass (elev. 5950 ft) at 9.6 miles, beneath the steep avy-streaked slopes of 7366-foot Helmet Butte. Immediately clutch your chest—the in-your-face view to the west of majestic Glacier Peak rising across the deep emerald chasm cut by the Suiattle River will take your breath away.

With plenty of exploring options from this outpost of wind-swaying flowers and frolicking marmots, waste no time setting up camp to begin. Find plenty of excellent sites to the left (follow the trail toward High Pass) around a small meadow and creek.

EXTENDING YOUR TRIP

From Buck Creek Pass, many fine explorations can be made. Continue west from the pass 0.3 mile on the Buck Creek Pass Trail to the Flower Dome Trail. Follow this wonderful path through floral heaven for 0.75 mile to the dome's 6332-feet summit. Feast on Glacier Peak views and a bevy of blossoms.

Or, instead of heading left to Flower Dome, continue north on the Middle Ridge Trail for 2.5 miles, dropping to cross Small Creek (elev. 5150 ft) before climbing to Middle Ridge (elev. 6150 ft) and reaching a junction. Then head right 0.9 mile on good trail into a remote and wide-open basin (elev. 6300 ft) beneath 8674-foot Fortress Mountain.

The High Pass route should be attempted only by experienced off-trail hikers.

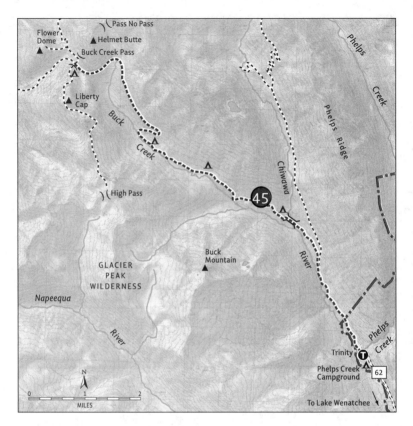

For the supreme adventure, from Buck Creek Pass continue south on the excellent trail (once slated to be part of the Pacific Crest Trail), past the camping area, and climb around Liberty Cap to a pumicey pass (elev. 6450 ft) at 1.6 miles. Good tread continues for another 1.3 miles across steep slopes and beneath craggy summits to a high ridge (elev. 6950 ft) with one of the finest views on planet Earth (en route, dangerous snowfields often linger late into the season, so stop when the going gets obscured). From here, gaze out at cobalt Triad Lake tucked in a barren, glaciated basin, against a backdrop of rock, ice, and snow. Beyond, the route is for experienced off-trail travelers and scramblers only, crossing perpetual and potentially dangerous snowfields to High Pass (elev. 7150 ft) before descending into the fabled Napeequa Valley (see Trip 44).

TRIP PLANNER	
2.7 miles	Camps near Chiwawa River
6 miles	Forested camps near switchback
9.6 miles	Buck Creek Pass and camps

46 Lyman Lakes via Spider Gap

RATING/ DIFFICULTY	LOOP	ELEV GAIN/ HIGH POINT	SEASON
*****/5	34.6 miles	7335 feet/ 7050 feet	late July– Oct

Map: Green Trails Holden No. 113; **Contact:** Okanogan-Wenatchee National Forest, Lake Wenatchee Ranger Station (summer), (509) 763-3103, or Wenatchee River Ranger District, Leavenworth, (509) 548-6977, www.fs.fed .us/r6/wenatchee; **Permits/regulations:** NW Forest Pass required. Wilderness rules apply. No fires at Lyman Lakes; **Special features:** Glacier-fed cobalt blue lakes, incredible alpine scenery, gorgeous meadows, glaciers; **Special concerns:** Potentially dangerous snow travel requiring ice ax. Swarming biting insects. Crowded camping areas. Car shuttle required, or add 3 miles and 600 vertical feet of road walking to trip; **GPS:** N 48 04.976 W 120 50.092

This is a Northwest classic: Walk up a broad valley once coveted by miners to one of the region's famed flower fields. Then travel up a small glacier to a high rocky notch in a formidable wall of craggy summits. From there, descend snow, talus, and meadow to a pair of shimmering lakes at the base of one of the most studied glaciers in America. Then return via several high passes that burst with radiant blossoms and mesmerize with horizon-spanning views. No wonder this trip is on many a backpacker's bucket list!

GETTING THERE

From Everett, head east for 85 miles on US 2 to Coles Corner. (From Leavenworth, travel west on US 2 for 15 miles.) Turn left onto State Route 207 (signed for Lake Wenatchee) and in 4 miles reach a Y intersection upon crossing the Wenatchee River. Bear right onto Chiwawa

Loop Road. After 1.3 miles, turn left onto Chiwawa River Road (Forest Road 62) and drive 22 miles (the pavement ends at 10.8 miles) to a junction. Bear right onto FR 6211 and continue for 2.3 very rough miles to the road's end and trailhead (elev. 3500 ft).

ON THE TRAIL

While this loop involves traveling over Spider Gap on a small glacier and then descending on fairly steep snowfields, in good conditions it poses only moderate difficulty for fit and experienced hikers. However, for inexperienced travelers, in bad weather, or when the snow is hard and icy, Spider Gap can be

Upper Lyman Lake's bare glaciated basin

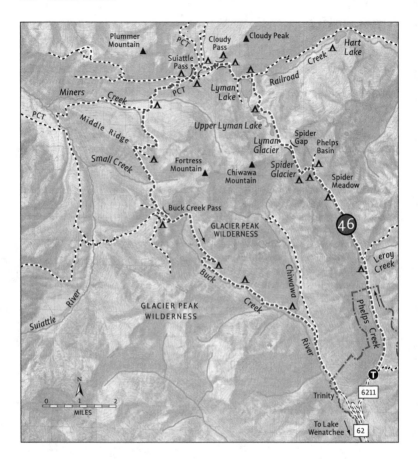

downright dangerous. Be sure that snow and weather conditions are favorable before leaving, and bring an ice ax if warranted. That said, this classic hike is successfully completed and enjoyed by hundreds of backpackers from all over the country every year.

Begin on the Phelps Creek Trail, a long-ago mining road. At 0.25 mile, after hopping across a refreshing creek, bear left at the Carne Mountain Trail junction. Traverse pleasant forest and cross several side creeks, entering

the Glacier Peak Wilderness at 2.5 miles. Look for evidence (mostly tailings) from past mining activities along the way. At 3.2 miles, pass some nice camps at a meadow's edge. At 3.4 miles, cross Leroy Creek (elev. 4100 ft), which may be tricky during periods of high runoff. The Leroy High Route takes off right for Mount Maude and the Ice Lakes (see Trip 49).

Continue along Phelps Creek, gently ascending. Come to wildflower-bursting Spider Meadow (elev. 4750 ft), sprawled out in a

U-shaped valley at 5.5 miles. There are plenty of camps here, but they're often crowded. The trail carries on, blazing up the middle of the meadow. After crossing a creek, bear right (the path left leads to more camps). Then, shortly after crossing Phelps Creek, come to good camps at a junction (elev. 5300 ft) at 6.7 miles. The trail right leads to Phelps Basin, a wide-open cirque offering additional private camps.

Continue left and steeply climb on an old miners path, angling above and around ledges and cliffs to reach spectacularly scenic camps (elev. 6200 ft) perched on a larch-ringed bluff above a cascade at 7.4 miles. Then reach the toe of the slender Spider Glacier and trudge up it (or scramble a bordering ledge if you prefer). The glacier heads through a tight fold of rock to 7050-foot Spider Gap at 8.5 miles. Welcome to mountain goat and pipit country!

Now behold a most amazing view down snow- and rock-covered slopes to the cobalt-blue, glacier-fed Lyman Lakes, with emerald Cloudy Pass hovering in the background. Getting to those lakes, however, requires descending a very steep snowfield that should not be attempted without an ice ax and when it's frozen over. And do not be led astray by a path taking off to the right of the snowfield—it leads to an old mine, not down to the lakes.

Once below the snowfield, reach a rocky shelf with a commanding view of the Lyman Glacier, clutched beneath 8459-foot Chiwawa Mountain's bulky, hulking north face—the glacier's crevassed snout protrudes into the sparkling upper lake. One of the most studied glaciers in the North Cascades, Lyman, like most of the region's glaciers, has been receding at an alarming rate.

Now veering northeast, descend on rocky slopes, picking up tread near a tumbling creek. Following the creek through glacial moraine, the way soon transforms into good trail. After

paralleling the lakeshore (elev. 5975 ft) the way veers to a bench of heather and larch, where there are campsites complete with awesome lake and glacier views.

Upon cresting a small ridge (elev. 6050 ft), the way meanders through boundless berry patches and rounds small tarns (that incubate millions of mosquitoes), dropping to cascading Railroad Creek. Cross it on a good bridge and reach a junction (elev. 5600 ft) at 12 miles. The trail right follows Railroad Creek for 8 miles to Hart Lake and Holden, a former mining town now religious retreat center (and alternative approach via Lake Chelan).

Head left immediately, coming to the lower Lyman Lake, with its well-established and well-used forested campsites that are often crowded and plagued by biting flies. Better camps can be found below and at Cloudy Pass. Continue west, passing a nice lakeshore day-use area and bearing right at a junction. The trail left leads 0.7 mile along lower Lyman's west shore to a beautiful waterfall—and makes for a good side trip if camping in the area.

Pass more camps and then gently climb through mature forest and parkland meadow, coming to a spur to the Cloudy Pass camps (elev. 6300 ft) at a refreshing creek at 13 miles. The spur leads 0.2 mile east to scattered camps at meadow's edge, offering spectacular views—and when a breeze is present, some relief from the area's swarming biting flies. An easy scramble of 7915-foot Cloudy Peak can be made from the camp area.

The trail continues through lovely meadows tromped by marmots, reaching 6450-foot Cloudy Pass at 13.3 miles. More camps, outstanding views, and your first glimpse of Glacier Peak await you. Now start descending, enjoying excellent views north down the Agnes Creek valley. At 14.1 miles, a shortcut leads left 0.7 mile to Suiattle Pass. While it saves elevation and distance, the way is rocky and often buried in snow. Better to continue

Lyman Lake spreads out beneath Cloudy Peak.

right on good trail, crossing a fountainlike cascading creek. At 14.8 miles, come to a junction (elev. 5550 ft) with the South Fork Agnes Creek Trail (the old Pacific Crest Trail) and camps at the creek's headwaters.

Then it's once again up, coming to the PCT (elev. 5700 ft) at 15 miles. Turn left, passing meadow and creekside camps (elev. 5800 ft) at 15.2 miles, cresting forested 5983-foot Suiattle Pass at 15.6 miles, with more camps, and coming to the western terminus of the previously mentioned shortcut at 15.7 miles.

Then through subalpine forest, gently descend to a junction with the Miners Ridge Trail (elev. 5500 ft) to Image Lake (Trip 47) at 16.7 miles. To complete the loop, continue south on the PCT, crossing Miners Creek (elev. 4525 ft). Then follow the Buck Creek Pass Trail up and over Middle Ridge (elev. 6150 ft), dropping down to Small Creek (elev. 5150 ft) and reaching Buck Creek Pass (elev. 5950 ft) at 25 miles (see Trip 47 to Image Lake for a more complete description of the Middle Ridge area). Finally, follow Buck Creek Trail 9.6 miles back to the trailhead at Trinity to complete loop.

TRIP PLANNER	
3.2 miles	Meadow camps
5.5 miles	Spider Meadow and camps
6.7 miles	Camps near junction to Phelps Basin
7.4 miles	Camps on bluff below Spider Glacier
8.5 miles	Spider Gap
11 miles	Camps near Upper Lyman Lake
12.2 miles	Lyman Lake and camps
13.2 miles	Camps below Cloudy Pass
13.3 miles	Camps at Cloudy Pass
14.8 miles	South Fork Agnes Creek camps
15.2 miles	PCT camps
15.7 miles	Camps near Suiattle Pass
16.7 miles	Miners Ridge Trail junction, camps nearby
19.1 miles	Miners Creek camps
22.2 miles	Middle Ridge and trail to basin camps
25 miles	Buck Creek Pass and camps
28.6 miles	Forested camps near switchback
34.6 miles	Trailhead

47 Image Lake

RATING/ DIFFICULTY	ROUND-TRIP	ELEV GAIN/ HIGH POINT	SEASON
*****/5	42.4 miles	7550 feet/ 6300 feet	mid-July– Oct

Maps: Green Trails Glacier Peak No. 112, Holden No. 113; **Contact:** Mount Baker–Snoqualmie National Forest, Darrington Ranger District, (360) 436-1155, www.fs.fed.us/r6/mbs, or Okanogan-Wenatchee National Forest, Lake Wenatchee Ranger Station (summer), (509) 763-3103, or Wenatchee River Ranger District, Leavenworth, (509) 548-6977, www.fs.fed.us/r6/wenatchee; **Permits/regulations:** NW Forest Pass required. No camping within 0.25 mile of Image Lake, use established campsites and respect revegetation areas. Lake closed to swimming when water is low. No fires at lake; **Special features:** Snow- and ice-covered Glacier Peak reflected in pretty alpine lake. Miles of mile-high flowering meadows; **Special concerns:** None; **GPS:** N 47 57.792 W 120 56.729

An iconic location in the Cascades, and a destination sought by photographers from around the world, there are few places on the planet prettier than Image Lake and the flower-bursting lofty slopes surrounding it. You haven't experienced the full grandeur and glory of the rugged and awesomely beautiful Cascade Range until you've watched morning's first rays—or the evening's fading light—waltzing across the snow and ice of Washington's most remote volcano, and perfectly reflected in the placid waters of Image Lake.

GETTING THERE
From Everett, head east for 85 miles on US 2 to Coles Corner. (From Leavenworth, travel west on US 2 for 15 miles.) Turn left onto State Route 207 (signed for Lake Wenatchee) and in 4 miles reach a Y intersection upon crossing the Wenatchee River. Bear right onto Chiwawa Loop Road. After 1.3 miles, turn left onto Chiwawa River Road (Forest Road 62) and drive 22.6 miles (the pavement ends at 10.8 miles) to the road's end and trailhead (elev. 2800 ft).

ON THE TRAIL
The shortest and most popular way to Image Lake is from the west via the Suiattle River Road. From there, it's an 11-mile journey through old growth along the Suiattle River, gaining a mere 1000 vertical feet. Then it's an arduous climb up Miners Ridge, gaining 3200 feet in 4.7 miles, and 1 final ridgeline mile to the lake. Hiker traffic on this route nearly evaporated after the Suiattle River Road sustained major washouts in 2003. The good news is that the road is finally being repaired—but it will still be some time before all the trails originating from it are maintained.

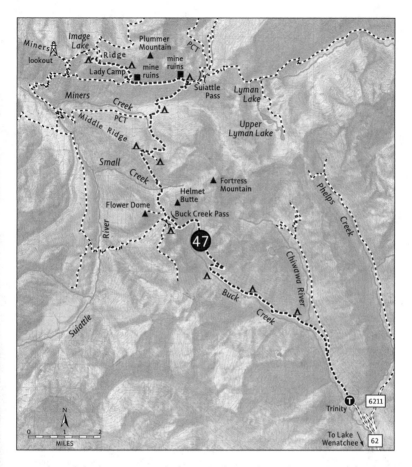

But the trails leading to Image Lake from the east are in good shape, allowing intrepid hikers to still get to this magnificent location. And what you'll soon discover is that, while this eastern approach is longer, it's more scenic, traversing miles of magnificent mile-high, wildflower-saturated meadows. Most hikers who visit Image Lake from this direction do so as an add-on to the Spider Gap–Lyman Lakes–Buck Creek Pass loop (see Trip 46). However, a direct hike from Trinity as described here isn't a bad idea. For one thing, you won't have to contend with the loop's potentially dangerous snowfields.

Follow the Buck Creek Trail for 9.6 miles to 5950-foot Buck Creek Pass (see Trip 45 for details). Here, beneath the steep flowered slopes of 7366-foot Helmet Butte, catch

Opposite: Early morning light cast on Image Lake and Glacier Peak

your first in-your-face wide-angle view of majestic 10,541-foot Glacier Peak rising above the deep Suiattle River valley. Buck Creek Pass has good camps and excellent side-trip options.

Continue north on the Middle Ridge Trail, passing the Flower Dome Trail at 9.9 miles and then dropping steeply to cross Small Creek (elev. 5150 ft), which might not be too small at all. Then climb to Middle Ridge (elev. 6150 ft) at 12.4 miles. Here find dry camps and a trail heading east 0.9 mile to a remote and wide open basin (elev. 6300 ft), where there are camps beneath 8674-foot Fortress Mountain.

Next, descend and cross heather meadows and marmot burrows, taking in excellent views north of Plummer Mountain and Miners Ridge, which cradles Image Lake. The way then steeply plummets through stunted trees and along avalanche gullies, entering beautiful old-growth forest. Following alongside a pretty creek, reach the Pacific Crest Trail (elev. 4575 ft) at 15.1 miles.

Veering right and continuing north through attractive old-growth forest, come to nice camps on a bluff above Miners Creek. Then cross the roiling creek on a good bridge (elev. 4525 ft) at 15.6 miles and begin climbing once more. At 17.4 miles, reach a junction (elev. 5500 ft). Turn left on the Miners Ridge Trail, immediately crossing a creek and coming to good camps scattered around an old mining building and some interesting relics. After crossing a raging creek, the trail makes a long traverse across avalanche chutes with good views south. The views get better.

At 19 miles, reach a junction (elev. 5550 ft), just after passing some more mine ruins—they call this Miners Ridge for a reason (and a good portion of the ridge almost became an open-pit copper mine in the 1960s, but for the actions of so many conservationist citizens). The trail straight descends to the Suiattle River valley (the western approach). You want to head right, steeply climbing through thinning forest to reach Lady Camp (elev. 6100 ft) at the edge of an alpine floral carpet at 19.9 miles. While primarily a horse camp, don't skip a visit to the see "the lady," a somewhat feminine figure carved in a tree by a lonely sheepherder a century ago.

Now brace yourself for one of the premier meadow walks in the Cascades. Traversing a steep emerald slope bursting with a kaleidoscope of color, stop and smell the flowers and stare in astonishment at Glacier Peak, Washington's most noble volcano. At 20.8 miles, come to a junction with the Canyon Lake Trail (elev. 6300 ft), and then begin descending into the open basin that houses Image Lake.

At 21 miles, come to a junction (elev. 6100 ft). The trail left leads 0.2 mile to camps (elev. 6000 ft). The trail straight leads 0.2 mile to the lake. The trail right swings around and above the lake, offering the coveted reflection views. Sunset is nice, but sunrise is supreme—plan on getting up early the next morning.

TRIP PLANNER	
2.7 miles	Camps near Chiwawa River
6 miles	Forested camps near switchback
9.6 miles	Buck Creek Pass and camps
12.4 miles	Middle Ridge and trail to basin camps
15.5 miles	Miners Creek camps
17.5 miles	Miners Ridge mining ruins and camps
19.9 miles	Lady Camp
21.2 miles	Image Lake and camps

EXTENDING YOUR TRIP

From a base camp at Image Lake, head west 1.5 miles to the staffed lookout (elev. 6200 ft) on Miners Ridge. Views are extensive and breathtaking. For a long and lonely journey, follow the 7-mile lightly used trail to Canyon Lake.

48 Mad Lake

RATING/ DIFFICULTY	ROUND-TRIP	ELEV GAIN/ HIGH POINT	SEASON
***/1	17 miles	1500 feet/ 5825 feet	late June– Oct

Maps: Green Trails Plain No. 146; **Contact:** Okanogan-Wenatchee National Forest, Entiat Ranger District, (509) 784-1511, www.fs .fed.us/r6/oka; **Permits/regulations:** None; **Special features:** Gentle high-country meadows. Pretty, placid lake; **Special concerns:** Trail open to motorcycles July 15–Oct 15. High-clearance vehicle recommended to access trailhead. Difficult river ford in early season; **GPS:** N 47 50.652 W 120 36.138

Enjoy miles of hiking through gentle high-country meadows and along a delightful river to a pretty lake ringed by pine forest and flourishing with wildlife. The Mad River country will leave you happy, but the Forest Service's decision to allow motorcycles here won't. However, you don't need to shun this inviting corner of the Entiat Mountains. Motorcycle use is moderate and practically absent during the week. And there's a window of motor-free (and horse-free) roaming from snowmelt until mid-July, when only hikers and wild critters are permitted to play in this enchanting backcountry.

GETTING THERE
From Everett, head east for 85 miles on US 2 to Coles Corner. (From Leavenworth, travel west on US 2 for 15 miles.) Turn left onto State Route 207 (signed for Lake Wenatchee) and in 4 miles reach a Y intersection upon crossing the Wenatchee River. Bear right onto Chiwawa Loop Road. Continue for 5 miles and turn left onto Forest Road 6100 just past a river crossing and the Thousand Trails Lodge. Drive 1.6 miles, turning right onto FR 6101, and after

0.6 mile bear right at an unsigned junction. Continue on FR 6101 for 2.5 miles, coming to a junction at Deer Camp. Turn left, continuing on FR 6101 for 2.7 extremely steep and rough miles (four-wheel-drive recommended) to Maverick Saddle and a junction. Park here or continue left on a rough spur another 0.3 mile to the trailhead (elev. 4350 ft).

ON THE TRAIL
Like my guidebook predecessors Harvey Manning and Ira Spring, I'm saddened that the lower Entiat Mountains—a huge roadless area—were left out of the 1984 Washington Wilderness Act, which opened the way for motorized recreation (actively promoted by the Forest Service). I'm not against motorized recreation; but it's ill-suited for this area. With its fragile pumice soils, large meadows, abundant wildlife, and unbroken forests, the upper Mad River country should be included in the adjacent Glacier Peak Wilderness.

Follow the wide Mad River Trail north through thick timber, soon meeting up with the river. In early summer the Mad River is truly enraged—crashing and frothing—but by autumn its disposition is mellow. After a couple of short dips and climbs to warm you up, come to a junction at 1.2 miles with the Hi Yu Trail (elev. 4650 ft) to little Lost Lake.

Continue straight, soon crossing the Mad River on a large bridge and coming to a junction, near the base of a large talus slope, with the Jimmy Creek Trail to Cougar Mountain. Stay straight on good trail and a gentle grade, traveling through pleasant forest alongside the tumbling river. At 3.2 miles, at the edge of a riverside meadow where excellent camps can be found, the Lost Lake Trail (elev. 5100 ft) takes off left.

At 3.9 miles, the trail crosses the Mad River. Absent a bridge, the river must be forded—sometimes near impossible in early season. At 4.6 miles, ford the Mad River again (slightly

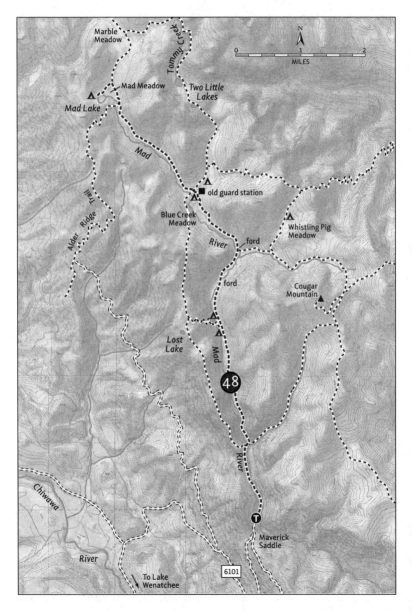

Serenity at Mad Lake

easier here), coming to a junction with the Tyee Ridge Trail (elev. 5250 ft). Veer left, following the river, and make a short steep climb before coming to the edge of sprawling, tranquil, flowering-in-summer Blue Creek Meadow.

The way skirts the fragile pumiced lawn, coming to Blue Creek and a junction at 5.8 miles near an old guard station (elev. 5425 ft); it once served as a dude ranch in the 1920s. The trail left leads to Lost Lake, an alternative return. The trail right leads to Two Little

Lakes, a nice side trip. Good camps, complete with picnic tables, can be found in the vicinity.

For Mad Lake, keep heading straight along the river—now a creek traversing an open forest of lodgepole pine and subalpine fir. Unlike terrain farther south, this area has not sustained any large fires in recent times. At 7.8 miles, the Alder Ridge Trail comes in from the left. Veer right, skirting Mad Meadow and reaching a junction (elev. 5825 ft) at 8.1 miles.

Turn left and, after 0.4 mile, come to placid Mad Lake (elev. 5800 ft), its greenish waters surrounded by golden grasses and small groves of fir and spruce. Find good camps here and good performances by flitting dragonflies, dabbling waterfowl, and jumping fish.

TRIP PLANNER	
3.2 miles	Meadow camps near Lost Lake junction
5.8 miles	Blue Creek Meadow and camps
8.5 miles	Mad Lake and camps

EXTENDING YOUR TRIP

Head north to beautiful Marble Meadow, and then return to Blue Creek Meadow via Two Little Lakes for an additional 6 miles or so. There are plenty of camping options along the way. Arrange for a car shuttle and hike out 10.5 miles downhill via Alder Ridge to the Chiwawa River Road.

49 Ice Lakes

RATING/ DIFFICULTY	ROUND-TRIP	ELEV GAIN/ HIGH POINT	SEASON
****/5	30.6 miles	4325 feet/ 7200 feet	late July– Oct

Maps: Green Trails Holden No. 113, Lucerne No. 114; **Contact:** Okanogan-Wenatchee National Forest, Entiat Ranger District, (509) 784-1511, www.fs.fed.us /r6/oka; **Permits/regulations:** NW Forest Pass required. Wilderness rules apply. No fires at Ice Lakes; **Special features:** Pair of sparkling lakes in a high glaciated basin beneath 9082-foot Mount Maude; **Special concerns:** First 4 miles of trail open to motorcycles. Trail traverses recent burn zones. Potentially treacherous river fords. Final 1.4 miles climb 1500+ feet up a steep headwall; **GPS:** N 48 01.459 W 120 39.012

This pair of snow-ringed shimmering lakes is tucked in a glacially scoured basin sprinkled with pumice and dotted with larches high in the stark, grey, towering Entiat Mountains. With perpetual snowfields and silver cascades crashing below and above, the Ice Lakes are a cool oasis in an area of abundant sunshine and frequent wildfires. The approach is long, dusty, hot, and buggy. Fierce waters must be forded, and an insanely steep climb is a final hurdle before you can explore this snowbound, intensely beautiful Shangri-la.

GETTING THERE

From Wenatchee, follow US 97/A north for 15 miles to Entiat. (From Chelan, travel south for 20 miles on US 97/A.) Turn left (west) onto Entiat River Road (Forest Road 51) and proceed for 37.2 miles to the road's end and trailhead (elev. 3150 ft). Privy available.

ON THE TRAIL

You'll share the first few miles of this hike with mountain bikers, motorcyclists, and plenty of day trippers and overnighters heading to Myrtle Lake. But the farther you head up the Entiat River Trail, the quieter it gets. Eventually deer and bear outnumber bipeds. The wide dusty path gains very little elevation in the beginning. A few dips thrown in for good measure break a near-level appearance.

After about 1.2 miles of trudging through thick forest, you'll see the wild Entiat River come into view. Openings in the forest canopy

Perpetual snowfields ring upper Ice Lake

provide views upward to the Rampart Mountains too. At 2.3 miles, pass the Anthem Creek Trail (elev. 3550 ft). Shortly afterward, cross the creek itself (which has an adjacent campsite) on a good bridge. At 3.8 miles, come to the Cow Creek Meadows Trail (elev. 3750 ft). The vast majority of people will head left here to Myrtle Lake and its busy camps—the better choice is to keep heading upriver.

At 4.4 miles, enter the Glacier Peak Wilderness, saying goodbye to motorcycles and mountain bikes. Notice how the trail instantly

becomes less dusty. Come to the Larch Lakes Trail junction (elev. 3800 ft) and camps after another 0.6 mile. The twin Larch Lakes make for a wonderful backpacking destination and, by way of the Pomas Creek Trail, can be combined with the Ice Lakes.

Head farther upvalley, reaching Snow-brushy Creek (elev. 3800 ft) at 5.5 miles. Cross it via a log or hop rocks. Then notice the fire-scarred terrain—most of the area to your right was recently scorched, but along the river on the left, much greenery managed to survive. In

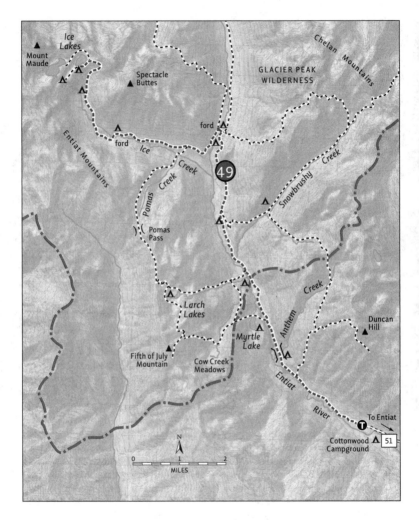

high summer at high noon it can be pretty hot hiking—plan accordingly.

At 6.5 miles, the Emerald Park Trail (elev. 3950 ft) heads right across the scorched landscape, traversing the lofty Chelan Mountains. A good campsite can be found near the Entiat River just before the trail junction.

The Entiat River Trail weaves through more charred forest, dipping and slightly climbing and gaining little overall elevation in the process. Through burnt snags, catch glimpses of the wide U-shaped, glacially carved Ice Creek valley—and begin anticipating the wild country ahead.

After passing some good trailside camps on the left, and the lightly used 45-mile Sheep Drive Trail up Borealis Ridge on the right, reach the Ice Creek Trail junction (elev. 4350 ft) at 8.5 miles. Drop 50 feet or so, coming to good camps and the Entiat River. Long gone is a bridge providing safe passage—the river must now be crossed by way of a potentially treacherous ford, not advised in early season. In 2010, a small log jam offered crossing for the nimble-footed. Otherwise ford at the wider and shallower stock crossing. Once across, come to a junction with the Cool Creek Trail coming from Entiat Meadows—there are several good campsites here on a bluff above the river.

Head left, climbing 200 feet across a scorched hillside before dropping 100 feet to meet up with the Pomas Creek Trail (elev. 4350 ft) at 9.7 miles, marked by a post in an eroded creekbed. Continue straight, eventually entering cool green forest again—and huckleberries, plenty for you and the resident bears. The way crosses pocket meadows and several avalanche chutes careening from Spectacle Buttes before coming to Ice Creek (elev. 4775 ft) and a good camp at 11.5 miles.

You'll get your feet wet here crossing—usually just boot-deep by late summer, much more fearsome in early season. Beyond, the valley opens up, the trail weaving through willow-choked bottomlands, old-growth groves, and flowered meadows. Expect stupendous views of an imposing wall of Entiat peaks casting shadows upon your humble being.

At 12.6 miles, cross Ice Creek again (elev. 5050 ft)—this time with the help of a large log. Just beyond, at 13.1 miles, is a wonderful campsite (elev. 5250 ft) at forest's edge, within sight and sound of a magnificent waterfall tumbling down from the high shelf housing the upper Ice Lake. The way from here gets interesting—and increasingly difficult.

The trail becomes a mere boot-beaten path, working its way up an avalanche slope and following the cascading creek that comes down from the lower Ice Lake. Cross the creek twice, and then angle across talus before finally heading straight up the last steep pitch of the valley headwall. Gaining 1650 feet in 1.4 miles, your heart will beat strong and your thighs will quiver—it's all worth it though, quickly confirmed as you crest a 6900-foot shelf and catch your first sight of the shimmering lower Ice Lake (elev. 6825 ft). Spread below you, it reflects mighty Mount Maude and its snowy craggy neighbors.

The terrain around the lake is barren yet fragile. A few whitebark pines and larches add greenery to pumiced plains. Somewhat exposed camps line the shelf above the lake. Blowing pumice dust can be a problem. More protected camps can be found by following a path 0.7 mile west across the lake's outlet over a ridge to a flat above two tarns, just below the shelf of the upper lake.

To reach the upper, more barren, and more stunning larger lake, walk along the north shore of the lower lake, following a path (sort of) 0.8 mile up a draw alongside a creek across steep heather, then rock, then snow to the lake (elev. 7200 ft). Camping is possible on surrounding ledges and nooks. Marmots and mountain goats frequent the basin, so don't be surprised if a visitor or two drop by camp.

TRIP PLANNER	
2.5 miles	Camp near Anthem Creek
3.8 miles	Trail to Myrtle Lake and camps
5 miles	Larch Lake junction
6.5 miles	Emerald Park Trail junction
8.3 miles	Trailside camps
8.5 miles	Entiat River ford and camps
11.5 miles	Ice Creek ford and camp
13.1 miles	Camp at basin edge
14.5 miles	Lower Ice Lake and camps
15.3 miles	Upper Ice Lake and camps

EXTENDING YOUR TRIP
Experienced scramblers can make the non-technical but still challenging climb up 9082-foot Mount Maude. For a longer return through lonely country, follow the lightly used but maintained Pomas Creek Trail to a high pass in the Entiat Mountains and to upper Larch Lake, where good camps can be found.

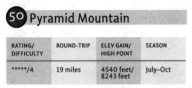

50 Pyramid Mountain

RATING/ DIFFICULTY	ROUND-TRIP	ELEV GAIN/ HIGH POINT	SEASON
*****/4	19 miles	4540 feet/ 8243 feet	July–Oct

Map: Green Trails Lucerne No. 114; **Contact:** Okanogan-Wenatchee National Forest, Entiat Ranger District, (509) 784-1511, www.fs.fed .us/r6/oka; **Permits/regulations:** NW Forest Pass required; **Special features:** Old lookout site 7000 feet above Lake Chelan. Incredible views, plenty of solitude; **Special concerns:** Extremely difficult creek fords in early season. Trail open to mountain bikes; **GPS:** N 48 00.673 W 120 34.338

Saunter (okay, grunt) to the top of an 8000-plus-foot peak that stands watch over the dramatic inland fjord of Lake Chelan and the lonely high country of the North Fork Entiat River basin. Flanked by the craggy, sky-piercing Chelan Mountains, and graced with miles of unbroken forest, inviting meadows, and soothing creeks, the North Fork Entiat country is de facto wilderness—and devoid of crowds.

GETTING THERE
From Wenatchee, follow US 97/A north for 15 miles to Entiat. (From Chelan, travel south for 20 miles on US 97/A.) Turn left (west) onto Entiat River Road (Forest Road 51) and proceed for 33 miles, turning right onto FR 5608

(2.9 miles beyond Silver Falls). Continue 4 miles to the road's end and trailhead (elev. 3950 ft). Privy available.

ON THE TRAIL
Starting on the North Fork Entiat River Trail, immediately confront Crow Creek. Easy to cross late in the season, in July it's a foot soaker. After dropping about 100 feet, maintain a fairly level disposition and come first to a bridged crossing of South Pyramid Creek (elev. 4000 ft) and then a junction shortly thereafter at 1.2 miles. Before turning right onto the Pyramid Creek Trail, admire the vintage signpost. The way is adorned with them!

Now through dry open forest, steadily gain elevation, climbing above and away from crashing South Pyramid Creek. Lightly traveled, the trail's soft pumiced tread is a delight to walk. But it surely would have become trenched if citizen activists hadn't halted the Forest Service from turning it into a motorcycle expressway.

The grade eases as you approach the first ford (difficult in early season) of South Pyramid Creek (elev. 4600 ft) at 2.6 miles. A little over 0.5 mile farther, negotiate a ford (difficult in early season) of Butte Creek. At 3.3 miles, continue straight at a junction (elev. 4850 ft) with the Butte Creek Trail. Then once again ford South Pyramid Creek.

The way then climbs through pocket meadows, where camping is possible. At 4 miles, come to a good camp (elev. 5075 ft) and ford South Pyramid Creek yet one more time. Now steadily climbing, reach Three Tree Camp (elev. 5750 ft) at 5.5 miles, at a junction with the Pyramid Mountain Trail—a good place to set up for the night, at the edge of a peaceful meadow.

Turn right and traverse meadows, rounding granite ledges and steeply ascending to the Pyramid Viewpoint Trail (elev. 6800 ft) at 6.7 miles, on a grassy shoulder. Head left

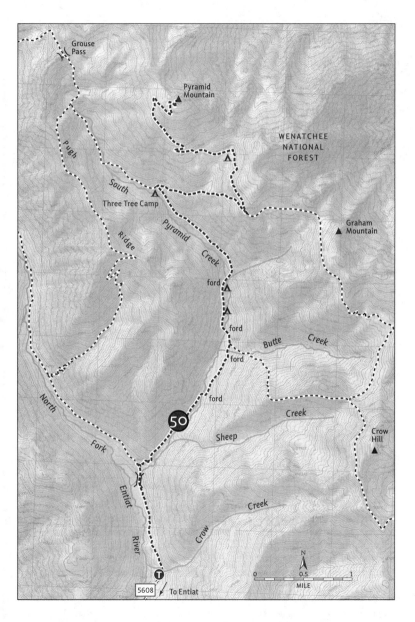

Grouse
Pass

Pyramid
Mountain

WENATCHEE
NATIONAL
FOREST

Pugh

South

Three Tree Camp

Ridge

Pyramid

Creek

Graham
Mountain

ford

ford

Butte Creek

ford

ford

North

50

Creek

Sheep

Crow
Hill

Fork

Entiat

Creek

Crow

River

N

0   0.5   1
MILE

T

5608 ↙ To Entiat

reaching the 8243-foot former lookout site at 9.5 miles. As you noticed on the way up, the views are far-reaching and breathtaking.

With map in hand, scan the horizons: East to the Columbia Plateau and fire-scarred Stormy Mountain. South across the Entiat Mountains to the Stewart Range, Chiwaukums, and Rainier. West to Glacier Peak, Clark, Maude, and the craggy cloud-catching Chelan Mountains dominated by 8590-foot Cardinal Peak, right in front of you. North it's the serrated Sawtooth Range and, 7000 feet directly below, Lake Chelan—its azure waters shimmering in the sun. See if you can find the old lookout privy directly below the summit. What a view from this precariously positioned loo!

TRIP PLANNER	
3.5 miles	Pocket meadows and camps
4 miles	Third ford of South Pyramid Creek and camp
5.5 miles	Three Tree Camp
7.5 miles	Small grassy basin camps
9.5 miles	Pyramid Mountain

Remnants of one of Washington's highest privies on 8243-foot Pyramid Mountain

through larch groves (beautiful in October), slightly descending to a small grassy basin (elev. 6650 ft) at 7.5 miles, where there are two creeks and some nice campsites.

The trail then gets down to business scaling Pyramid Mountain. First via short switchbacks, then a sweeping traverse, then switchbacking once again, you'll cross alpine tundra, krummholz, and rock gardens,

EXTENDING YOUR TRIP
Several loop options exist to extend your trip. Follow the Pyramid Mountain Trail east across Graham Mountain's alpine meadows and then return via the Butte Creek Trail. However, the latter trail is rarely maintained and difficult to follow in spots. A better choice is to follow the Pyramid Mountain Trail west and return via the Pugh Ridge Trail—or continue past Grouse Pass (good camps) and return via the North Fork Entiat River Trail, where there are several good camps. Consider, too, a side trip to Fern Lake.

Opposite: Looking south from Devils Dome to Crater Mountain (Trip 58)

North Cascades

51 Twin Lakes

RATING/ DIFFICULTY	ROUND-TRIP	ELEV GAIN/ HIGH POINT	SEASON
***/4	17 miles	3900 feet/ 5450 feet	late July– Oct

Maps: Green Trails Sloan Peak, WA–No. 111, Monte Cristo, WA–No. 143; **Contact:** Mount Baker–Snoqualmie National Forest, Darrington Ranger District, (360) 436-1155, or Verlot Public Service Center (summer weekends), (360) 691-7791, www.fs.fed.us/r6/mbs; **Permits/regulations:** NW Forest Pass required. Wilderness rules apply. Respect areas closed for restoration; **Special features:** Large backcountry lake, historical mining region and ghost town; **Special concerns:** Major washout at Twin Bridges requires ford of South Fork Sauk River, difficult and dangerous in early season and periods of heavy rain. Dangerous snowfields sometimes linger on ridge to lakes. Trailhead subject to frequent break-ins, leave no valuables in car; **GPS:** N 48 01.567 W 121 26.550

⚙ 🏠 *Set amid rock and heather gardens against a backdrop of towering snow-faced spires, and lined with gnarly hemlocks resembling bonsai trees, the Twin Lakes are tucked in a remote, rugged, and enchanting basin. Once the domain of hardscrabble prospectors, the twins are now claimed by backpackers seeking rewarding adventure and stunning scenery. Bountiful berry patches and abundant grasses and shrubbery help keep the resident marmot, mountain goat, and bear populations content.*

GETTING THERE

From Granite Falls, follow the Mountain Loop Highway east for 31 miles to the trailhead at Barlow Pass (elevation 2360 ft). Privy available. The trip begins on the gated Monte Cristo Road.

ON THE TRAIL

Start by hiking the 4-mile Monte Cristo Road. Closed since 1980 to vehicular traffic (except for a handful of permit owners), the road has become a popular hiking and biking destination for recreationists from all walks of life. For a variation on this trip, consider mountain biking the road to Monte Cristo. Lock your bike at the rack and then hoof to the lakes. On the return, look forward to an easy final 4 miles.

At 1 mile, pass the trail to Gothic Basin (a great backpacking destination) just before arriving at the Twin Bridges over the South Fork Sauk River. Locate a log crossing or safe place to ford, and then continue along the delightful road. Except for two short sections, the way is fairly level. At 2.1 miles, reach Haps Hill Camp. Dark and dank, it'll do in a pinch, but push on to Monte Cristo for much nicer campsites.

At 4 miles, reach the Monte Cristo campground (privy available) at the road's end. Cross the South Fork Sauk on a good bridge and enter the old mining town turned ghost town, Monte Cristo (elev. 2800 ft), where about a dozen structures still stand. Linger and explore or carry on. The trail to Twin Lakes starts at the east end of a grassy opening by a cabin.

Cross Sunday Creek, passing through a white picket fence welcoming you to the "76" building. Then begin working your way toward Sunday Flats, following an old water line and passing the ruins of an old concentrator. At 0.25 mile from the townsite, reach a junction at the Sunday Falls overlook. Continue right, soon entering the Henry M. Jackson Wilderness. Through groves of big old hemlocks and yellow cedars, steadily climb. After crossing Sunday Creek, the way steepens, twisting up a small gully to a heathered and huckleberried junction at Poodle Dog Pass (elev. 4350 ft), 1.75 miles from Monte Cristo.

Misty day at Twin Lakes

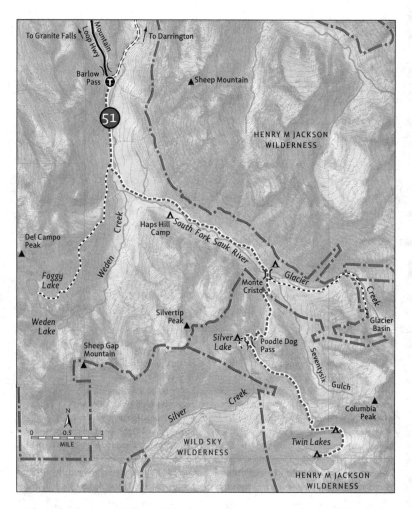

The trail right drops 100 feet in 0.25 mile to glistening Silver Lake, tucked in a cirque beneath Silvertip Peak. It's a worthy side trip for lunching or an extra night out. Good camps can be found on bluffs above the lake's outlet.

For Twin Lakes continue left, climbing a knoll with good views of Silver Lake before dropping into a small saddle. Skirting ledges and steep slopes, continue up a rugged ridge, views growing north and south. After dropping to avoid cliffs, the way regains the ridge crest, growing steeper and increasingly difficult as it heads up heather meadows and granite ledges. Expect to use your hands in spots, and consider turning around if there's steep snow or if bad weather threatens. Going astray here could lead to a fatal fall down Seventysix Gulch.

Continuing along the narrow ridge crest, the trail swings right to avoid a wall of rock and then traverses a steep flower field before emerging at a precarious notch of a pass (elev. 5450 ft). Behold the Twin Lakes twinkling 700 feet below! Using extreme caution, continue along a narrow cleft before steeply dropping across scree, heather, mountain hemlock groves, and rock gardens to a bench above the lakes.

Continue losing elevation to emerge at the larger Twin (elev. 4730 ft) in an open boulder-strewn basin beneath towering, glacier-capped 7172-foot Columbia Peak. There are good but exposed camps here. Better camping can be found on a hemlocked knoll at the large lake's outlet, between the Twins, reached by continuing on a rough and tumble 0.5-mile trail that climbs and drops 200 feet along the way. Set up here beside a waterfall crashing into the hard-to-access smaller Twin, enjoying views across the North Fork Skykomish River to Spire Mountain.

TRIP PLANNER	
2.1 miles	Haps Hill Camp
4 miles	Monte Cristo campground
6 miles	Silver Lake and camps
8.5 miles	Camps between Twin Lakes

52 Blue Lake

RATING/ DIFFICULTY	LOOP	ELEV GAIN/ HIGH POINT	SEASON
****/4	27.3 miles	5725 feet/ 6000 feet	late July–Oct

Maps: Green Trails Sloan Peak, WA–No. 111, Glacier Peak No. 112, Monte Cristo No. 143, Benchmark No. 144; **Contact:** Mount Baker–Snoqualmie National Forest, Darrington Ranger District, (360) 436-1155, or Verlot Public Service Center (summer weekends), (360) 691-7791, www.fs.fed.us/r6/mbs; **Permits/regulations:** NW Forest Pass required. Wilderness rules apply. No fires at Blue Lake; **Special features:** Spectacular alpine lake that harbors icebergs well into summer, some of the finest flower fields and ridge walking in the Cascades; **Special concerns:** Dangerous snowfields linger late in summer, long waterless stretch, potentially tough river ford, 2.5-mile road walk; **GPS:** N 48 03.488 W 121 17.298

Blue Lake viewed from the high ridge that cradles it

This amazing loop follows two long ridges exploding with wildflowers and teeming with jaw-dropping views, all centered on a deep blue lake set in a deep rocky cirque where summer comes late—if at all. Huge chunks of ice languidly bob on Blue Lake's alluring azure waters, sometimes well into September. But on nearby Pilot Ridge, blossoms take flight just after snowmelt and paint the hillside in dazzling colors while Blue is still white.

GETTING THERE

From Darrington, head south on the Mountain Loop Highway 16 miles (the pavement

ends at 9 miles), coming to a junction with Forest Road 49. Turn left and follow FR 49 for 6.4 miles, coming to a junction signed for Sloan Creek Trail. Bear left and reach the trailhead for the North Fork Sauk River Trail in 0.1 mile (elev. 2075 ft). Park here and backtrack to walk the road to the Bald Eagle trailhead. Privy and primitive camping available.

ON THE TRAIL

A drawback to this loop is the 2.5 miles of road walking required. The walk isn't difficult, but to lessen the drudgery you can always drive to the Bald Eagle trailhead first, drop packs, and then go back and park at the North Fork Sauk trailhead. From there, walk FR 49 south just over 2 miles to a junction. Then walk right on FR 4920 0.4 mile to the Bald Eagle trailhead (elev. 2400 ft).

Cross Sloan Creek on a good bridge and proceed about 2.5 miles on an old roadbed through old cuts, catching good views of Pride Basin and the rugged Monte Cristo peaks above it. The trail then briskly climbs before resuming a gradual grade across damp slopes, entering the Henry M. Jackson Wilderness. Soon afterward reach a junction at Curry Gap (elev. 3950 ft), a low-lying notch of meadow and mountain hemlock at 6.8 miles (4.3 miles from the trailhead). Camping is possible here—reliable water can be found following the Quartz Creek Trail straight a short distance.

The Bald Eagle Trail turns left here and begins a steep and rough climb up timbered slopes, skirting a knoll and large avalanche chute. Catch window views west of the massive Monte Cristo block while negotiating the rough terrain. At 9.5 miles, skirt a steep north-facing open slope (elev. 5200 ft)—often buried in hard-packed snow until

Johnson Mountain rises above Blue Lake.

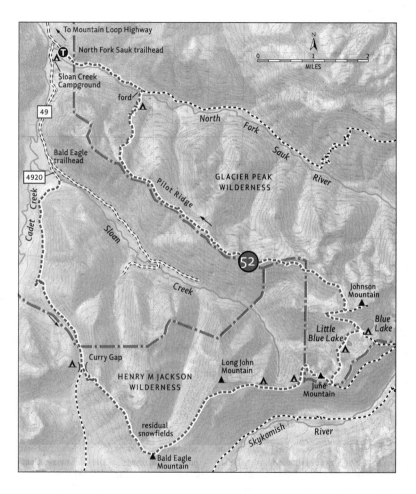

midsummer—below the summit of 5668-foot Bald Eagle Mountain. Without an ice ax, don't attempt to cross.

The way then follows along a high ridge, descending slightly to a small gap (elev. 4800 ft) before slowly climbing, rounding 5697-foot Long John Mountain, and coming to a good but maybe dry camp (elev. 5200 ft) at 11.5 miles. The trail then rounds another

knoll, coming to another good camp with more reliable water at 12.5 miles.

Then it's up again, climbing steeply to just beneath the summit of 5946-foot June Mountain, where excellent views can be had of emerald Pilot Ridge, Johnson Mountain, and snowy Glacier Peak. Continuing around the summit, you may encounter steep snowfields again, warranting an ice ax and caution.

The way then comes to a junction in a small gap (elev. 5700 ft) at 14 miles. The Bald Eagle Trail continues straight for 2.5 miles, traversing view-granting, flower-covered open slopes to 5550-foot Dishpan Gap (Trip 38). You want to head left, entering the Glacier Peak Wilderness and descending across a barren boulder field (and probably snowfields too), coming to Little Blue Lake (elev. 5150 ft) in about 1 mile. Then start climbing again, reaching a junction (elev. 5500 ft) at 15.5 miles. Just to the right, in 0.1 mile, tucked in a big, rocky, and snowy cirque, is Blue Lake (elev. 5600 ft). Good camps can be found among the treed knolls surrounding the lake's outlet. Cascades crash down the surrounding steep slopes while chunks of ice float on the lake's reflecting surface.

Before continuing the loop, fill water bottles, as Pilot Ridge is bone dry after snowmelt. Then head back to the last junction and begin a long sweeping traverse up the open slopes of Johnson Mountain. Views of the lake shimmering below are wonderful. At 16.7 miles, come to a junction (elev. 6000 ft). Taking off right is the old (but still good) 0.8-mile path to the old fire lookout site on Johnson Mountain's 6721-foot summit. Commanding views of Sloan Peak, Glacier Peak, and a plethora of other peaks up and down the Cascade crest make it a mandatory side trip on a clear day.

The main trail continues along Pilot Ridge, flying high through sprawling flower-filled meadows for nearly 4 miles. The far-reaching views are hard to beat. After cresting a 5700-foot knoll, the way retreats to forest, dropping steeply to a 4950-foot saddle. Then a good little climb follows to a 5400-foot knoll. Then it's back down to another 4950-foot knoll, up again 100 feet to skirt a meadowed knoll, then a rapid knee-jarring descent through old-growth timber to reach the North Fork Sauk

River (elev. 2400 ft) at 25.2 miles. Ford the river, difficult in high water—or look for a log crossing—and reach the North Fork Sauk River Trail. There are good campsites here, but your vehicle is only 2.1 miles away, to the left.

TRIP PLANNER	
6.8 miles	Curry Gap, camping possible
11.5 miles	Dry camp rounding Long John Mountain
12.5 miles	Camp with more reliable water
15.6 miles	Blue Lake and camps
25.2 miles	North Fork Sauk ford and camps
27.3 miles	Trailhead

EXTENDING YOUR TRIP
From Blue Lake, a steep, exhilarating, slightly exposed way trail for sure-footed hikers only heads 1.5 miles up and over the ridge behind Blue Lake, connecting with the Bald Eagle Trail. From that ridge crest scramble north to an open 6562-foot summit for spectacular views.

53 Glacier Peak Meadows

RATING/ DIFFICULTY	ROUND-TRIP	ELEV GAIN/ HIGH POINT	SEASON
****/4	25 miles	5325 feet/ 6450 feet	mid-July– Oct

Maps: Green Trails Sloan Peak, WA–No. 111, Glacier Peak No. 112; **Contact:** Mount Baker–Snoqualmie National Forest, Darrington Ranger District, (360) 436-1155, or Verlot Public Service Center (summer weekends), (360) 691-7791, www.fs.fed.us/r6/mbs; **Permits/regulations:** NW Forest Pass required. Wilderness rules apply. No fires beyond Mackinaw Shelter; **Special features:** High mountain passes, extensive meadows, spectacular views of Glacier Peak and Cascade crest; **Special concerns:** Snow lingers late at Red Pass. Area is popular with hunters; **GPS:** N 48 03.488 W 121 17.298

High meadows along the Pacific Crest Trail near Red Pass

Set up camp near the headwaters of the serenading White Chuck River, in tranquil parkland meadows in the shadow of snowy, showy 10,541-foot Glacier Peak. Reaching this idyllic setting requires an arduous journey—first through deep primeval forest, then up steep slopes bursting with wildflowers, and finally over a high barren pass through stark alpine tundra. But hey, getting here is half the fun!

GETTING THERE

From Darrington, head south on the Mountain Loop Highway 16 miles (the pavement ends at 9 miles), coming to a junction with Forest Road 49. Turn left and follow FR 49 for 6.4 miles, coming to a junction signed for Sloan Creek Trail. Bear left and reach the trailhead in 0.1 mile (elev. 2075 ft). Privy and primitive camping available.

ON THE TRAIL

When floodwaters ravaged the White Chuck River valley in 2003, it was *arrivederci* for the White Chuck Road (FR 23), the very popular trail to also-demolished Kennedy Hot Springs, and the beautiful high country around the upper White Chuck. But all is not lost—by way of the North Sauk River valley, the upper reaches of this spectacular valley are still attainable. And with the added mileage and elevation gain now required, there are a lot fewer people competing for campsites.

Immediately enter majestic primeval forest and reach a junction with the Red Mountain Trail. Continue straight and soon enter the sprawling Glacier Peak Wilderness. Through groves of gargantuan cedars (some measuring more than nine feet in diameter), head upvalley, trying not to stumble while you're looking up. The North Fork Sauk River, while audible, reveals itself only occasionally along the way.

At 2.1 miles, reach a junction with the Pilot Ridge Trail (Trip 52) and camps by the river (elev. 2400 ft). Continue upvalley under a centuries-old canopy, coming to good camps at Red Creek (elev. 2800 ft) at 4.5 miles. Cross the raging creek on a steady bridge. Then, after passing through a large brushy avalanche zone, reach the still-standing Mackinaw Shelter (elev. 3000 ft) in big timber at 5.8 miles. Forget about staying in the shelter unless you like hantavirus. There are plenty of good campsites around the shelter. And be sure to fill water bottles here, for it's in short supply for the next several miles.

The trail now changes gears, climbing steeply (gaining 3000 vertical feet) up hot southern-exposed slopes stripped of shade thanks to numerous avalanches. Switchbacks ease some of the pain, but the way is often brushy, further slowing your upward progress.

Stunted trees eventually give way to blueberry bushes, in turn yielding to magnificent meadows. The climb eases a bit in intensity as the trail makes a long sweep across flower-dancing open slopes.

At 8.3 miles, pass a small spring (elev. 5500 ft). At 9 miles, reach the Pacific Crest Trail (elev. 5975 ft). Right leads a few hundred feet to a good spring and, in another 0.5 mile, to 5900-foot White Pass. Good but popular camps are in a basin below, and an excellent high-country route takes off from the pass for the impressive White Chuck Glacier.

You want to head left (north) on the PCT, traversing high windswept meadows where the only thing more impressive than the floral show at your feet are the views in front of your face: Indian Head Peak, Johnson Mountain, the Monte Cristo range, Sloan, Stuart—the list goes on! At 10.7 miles, reach 6450-foot Red Pass beneath 6999-foot Portal Peak. Drop your pack and easily scramble the ridge to the right, to an impressive viewpoint across the alpine tundra.

From Red Pass, descend the PCT into a barren high basin where snows often linger. Meltwater cascades and alpine breezes break the stillness. At about 11.5 miles, a faint path leads left to a small tarn (elev. 5900 ft) beneath the White Chuck Cinder Cone (elev. 6080 ft). Good but exposed camps can be found on a knoll east of the tarn. The cinder cone can be scrambled from the west.

The PCT continues descending, leaving tundra for greenery. Glacier Peak soon reveals itself in all its glory. At about 12.5 miles, near the site of an old shelter (elev. 5500 ft), find wonderful camps scattered about the Glacier Peak Meadows parkland. Let the cascading White Chuck and its many tributaries soothe you to sleep. Except for late summer, when PCT through-hikers are marching by, this place is pretty deserted.

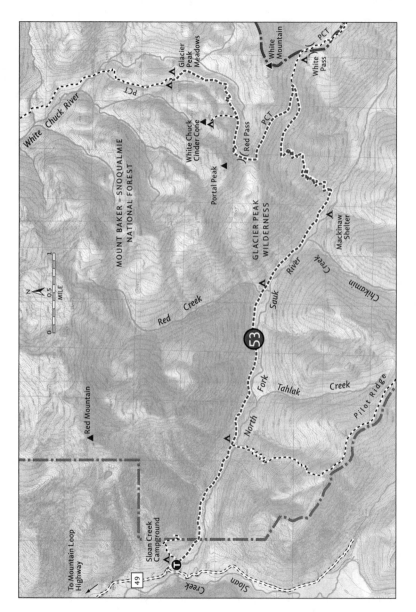

Glacier Peak Meadows

White Mountain

PCT

PCT

White Pass

PCT

White Chuck River

PCT

Red Pass

PCT

MOUNT BAKER – SNOQUALMIE
NATIONAL FOREST

White Chuck
Cinder Cone

Portal Peak

GLACIER PEAK
WILDERNESS

Mackinaw
Shelter

N

0   0.5   1
MILE

Red   Creek

Sauk   River

Chikamin   Creek

53

Red Mountain

North   Fork   Tahlak   Creek

Pilot Ridge

Sloan Creek
Campground

T

To Mountain Loop Highway

49

Sloan   Creek

TRIP PLANNER	
2.1 miles	Pilot Ridge Trail junction and camps
4.5 miles	Red Creek camps
5.8 miles	Mackinaw Shelter and camps
8.3 miles	Spring
9.5 miles	White Pass and camps
10.7 miles	Red Pass
11.5 miles	Small tarn beneath White Chuck Cinder Cone and camps
12.5 miles	Glacier Peak Meadows and camps

EXTENDING YOUR TRIP

Turn this trip into a spectacular loop—from White Pass, follow the PCT south for 7 miles to Dishpan Gap, and then return via the Bald Eagle and Pilot Ridge trails.

54 Copper Ridge

RATING/ DIFFICULTY	ROUND-TRIP	ELEV GAIN/ HIGH POINT	SEASON
*****/4	20.4 miles	5485 feet/ 6260 feet	late July– Oct

Maps: Green Trails Mount Shuksan No. 14, Mt Challenger No. 15; **Contact:** North Cascades National Park, (360) 854-7245, www.nps.gov /noca, and Mount Baker–Snoqualmie National Forest, Glacier Public Service Center, Glacier (360) 599-2714, www.fs.fed.us/r6/mbs; **Permits/regulations:** NW Forest Pass required. Free backcountry permit required for North Cascades NP, issued morning of or day before from Glacier Public Service Center, limited and difficult to secure on summer and autumn weekends. Fires prohibited. Dogs prohibited in national park; **Special features:** Spectacular ridgeline hike into North Cascades NP, one of the wildest, largest roadless areas in the country. Unsurpassed alpine scenery, glaciers, cloud-piercing summits; **Special concerns:** Lingering snowfields require ice ax in early season. Bears common, secure food well; **GPS:** N 48 54.616 W 121 35.523

Trek up a wide open valley of avalanche chutes awash in resplendent wildflowers, flanked by snowy crags, and pulsing with the sound of crashing water. Under the ever-watchful eye of snow-draped Ruth Mountain, make your way to Hannegan Pass—portal into the deep wilderness of North Cascades National Park. Then begin your alpine odyssey across Copper Ridge to a fire lookout perched on a 6260-foot knob, gazing along the way at more sky-touching rock and ice.

GETTING THERE

From Bellingham, follow the Mount Baker Highway (State Route 542) east for 34 miles to the Glacier Visitor Center. Then drive 13 miles and turn left onto Hannegan Pass Road (Forest Road 32) just before a bridge over the North Fork Nooksack River. Continue for 5.3 miles to the road's end and trailhead (elev. 3125 ft). Privy and primitive camping available.

ON THE TRAIL

This is a major departure area for points north and east into the North Cascades backcountry, so don't be surprised by the overflowing parking lot. But don't despair—crowds quickly disperse in this sprawling wilderness complex. Head up a wide glacier-carved valley swept clean of most of its trees thanks to countless avalanches. The scenery is dramatic from the get-go. Sparkling waters glide off towering polished walls. Tenacious snowfields cling to dark clefts in spiraling crags.

Traveling mainly in the open and through herbaceous greenery, it's best to get an early start to avoid the sun and voracious insects. At 0.6 mile, cross the first of many crashing creeks. Water is abundant to Boundary Camp. Snow-capped Ruth Mountain soon comes into view and will command your attention most of the trip. After crossing a creek beneath a

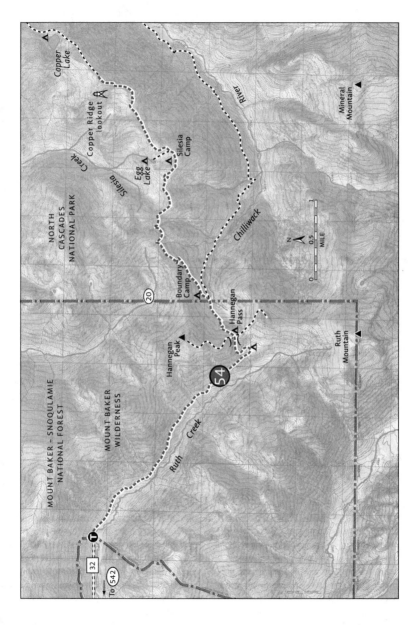

Mount Redoubt dominates the eastern horizon from Copper Ridge.

refreshing cascade, the way enters cool forests and begins to switchback toward Hannegan Pass.

At 3.5 miles, a spur trail leads to the right across Hannegan Creek to backcountry campsites set in a lovely meadow (elev. 4600 ft). No permit is necessary to camp here, but these sites often fill. Continue left, through forest and meadows, reaching 5050-foot Hannegan Pass at 4 miles. A side trail left leads a steep 1.2 miles to 6186-foot Hannegan Peak. Views are excellent. Camping is possible too at the pass, but after snowmelt there's no water.

Continue east from the pass, rapidly losing elevation. Cross scree and a cascading creek to an avalanche-ravaged basin (elev. 4450 ft), coming to the North Cascades National Park boundary and appropriately named Boundary Camp (permit required) at 5 miles. There's an important junction here too. The trail right descends deep into the unbroken ancient forests of the Chilliwack River valley. You want to head left, ascending above the valley on the Copper Ridge Trail. Be sure to fill water bottles—water is at a premium, particularly later in the season along the ridge.

Under cool forest canopy at first, then across parkland meadow, the trail moderately ascends. At 6.7 miles, reach a narrow, steep gully known as Hells Gorge (elev. 5400 ft). Snow often remains late here, making for a possibly dangerous crossing. Once beyond hell it's pure heaven—the way breaking out into the open to unsurpassed alpine views. Walking a mile-high divide between the deep Silesia Creek and Chilliwack River drainages (both emptying into British Columbia's Fraser River), gaze in astonishment at an endless sea of cloud-piercing peaks.

Now across heather and pockets of alpine tundra (look for ptarmigans), the way crests a 5550-foot knoll, drops to a 5350-foot swale, and then rounds a 5650-foot knoll before coming to Silesia Camp (elev. 5575 ft) at 8.2 miles, perched on a bluff 2500 feet above the valley below. This is an excellent camp for stargazing, but not so good in bad weather. Water can be attained from snowmelt pools for most of the summer.

Beyond, the trail descends 0.1 mile, traversing lingering snowfields (ice ax necessary in early season) to another swale (elev. 5475 ft). A spur trail leads left 0.3 mile, dropping a couple of hundred feet to a basin housing little Egg Lake and its fine camps. More protected than Silesia Camp, Egg is a better choice in less-than-ideal weather.

Beyond the two camps (the last camping spots before the lookout), the trail continues to descend, bottoming out at a 5250-foot forest-ringed gap. It then steeply ascends open slopes to the 6260-foot lookout knoll at 10.2 miles. The 1930s-built fire lookout is one of the last remaining in the North Cascades and is still staffed during the summer. From this high point on Copper Ridge, you can see why it was placed here. The views encompass most of the northern reaches of the national park.

Look north down the Silesia Creek valley to pointy Mount Larrabee in the United States, on the left, and pointier Slesse Mountain in Canada, on the right. Middle Peak and Copper Mountain dominate the northeast. To the east, massive 8956-foot Mount Redoubt fills the viewscape, and farther west snow and ice glisten in the sun thanks to Ruth Mountain, Icy Peak, Shuksan, and Baker. Easy Peak and Mineral Mountain lie directly to the south, and farther south is the deep cleft of Whatcom Pass, shadowed by 8236-foot Mount Challenger with its extensive glacial system and serrated surrounding summits known as the Pickets.

TRIP PLANNER	
3.5 miles	Hannegan Creek camps
4 miles	Hannegan Pass and camps
5 miles	Boundary Camp
8.2 miles	Silesia Camp
8.6 miles	Egg Lake camps
10.2 miles	Copper Ridge lookout

EXTENDING YOUR TRIP

Gorgeous Copper Lake and its camps lie snug in a basin 1.2 miles east of the lookout and 1000 vertical feet below. You can continue from there for a classic loop, descending 7.5 knee-jarring miles to the Chilliwack River (difficult ford in early season), where it's 10.4 forested miles (and a cable-car river crossing) and 2200 feet of climbing back to Boundary Camp.

55 Horseshoe Basin (Stehekin)

RATING/ DIFFICULTY	ROUND-TRIP	ELEV GAIN/ HIGH POINT	SEASON
*****/3	17.6 miles	4550 feet/ 5400 feet	mid-July– Oct

Map: Green Trails Cascade Pass No. 80; **Contact:** North Cascades National Park, Wilderness Information Center, Marblemount, (360) 854-7245, www.nps.gov /noca; **Permits/regulations:** Free backcountry permit required, limited number available, issued morning of or day before from Wilderness Information Center. Fires prohibited. Dogs prohibited; **Special features:** High pass awash with wildflowers, abundant wildlife, old mine, huge cirque streaked with cascading water; **Special concerns:** Crowds at Cascade Pass; **GPS:** N 48 28.535 W 121 04.543

👣 ⚙ 🏠 *A dramatic cirque at the head of the Stehekin Valley, Horseshoe Basin will enthrall you with its cavalcade of cascades, sprawling flowered meadows, and old mine burrowed in a steep and forbidding wall. Hike up and over popular and spectacular Cascade Pass, and then drop into Pelton Basin surrounded by towering peaks capped in snow and ice. While the way is popular with climbers and backpackers hiking through to Stehekin, the masses bypass Horseshoe Basin, making it a ringer for solitude.*

GETTING THERE
From Marblemount on the North Cascades Highway (State Route 20), head east on the Cascade River Road for 23 miles to its end at the trailhead (elev. 3600 ft). Privy available.

ON THE TRAIL
With the fierce face of Johannesburg Mountain peering down on you, amazing views begin right from the parking lot. The trail starts by switchbacking some thirty times on a forested rib to propel you high above an avalanche-debris-littered valley floor. After climbing 1400 feet in about 2 miles, the grade eases, making a long traverse toward Cascade Pass. Long used by Native Americans, explorers, prospectors, and surveyors, this relatively low pass was a wise choice for providing passage through the nearly impenetrable North Cascades. It was once considered by railroad and highway planners, but Cascade Pass is now protected within the North Cascades National Park, serving hikers, backpackers, and climbers as a magical portal into this wild corner of America.

After traversing meadow, talus, and perhaps a lingering snowfield or two, reach 5400-foot Cascade Pass at 3.7 miles. The surrounding heather parklands are fragile and have taken a beating from past visitors. Please stay on established paths—and there is no camping at the pass. Marvel at the views, especially the formidable wall to the south—Johannesburg, Pelton Peak, Cascade Peak, Mix-Up Peak, and the Triplets.

Now it's time to lose the majority of your fellow hikers. They're heading left for the Sahale Arm, while you'll continue straight, dropping into the Pelton Creek basin, a hanging valley of cascading waters tumbling down from spiraling icy walls. At 4.5 miles, shortly after crossing a tributary creek, reach a 0.2-mile spur (elev. 4900 ft) to Pelton Basin Camp (elev. 4750 ft). Set up camp here among tall firs and hemlocks at the edge of the open basin and day hike to Horseshoe Basin—or continue backpacking to your next legal camping option at Basin Creek Camp.

The way crests a small knoll and then teeters along a headwall. Mighty McGregor Mountain at 8122 feet stands watch east over the Stehekin Valley. Traverse huge avalanche slopes across brush and rock, and with

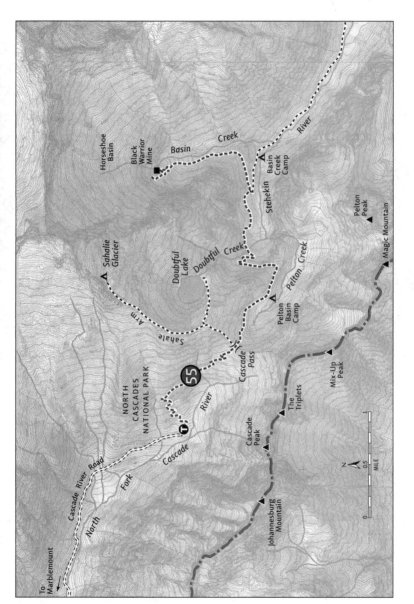

A hiker stares out at the Stehekin River valley from the Black Warrior Mine.

the help of a few switchbacks continue to descend.

At 6.3 miles, cross cascading Doubtful Creek across polished ledges, which may be challenging in high water. After traversing scree, reach a junction with the Horseshoe Basin Trail (elev. 3700 ft) at 7 miles. For the Basin Creek Camp, proceed right another 0.5 mile or so, dropping 500 feet to the camp, which was relocated here in 2008. You'll find a separate cooking area and a bear box.

For Horseshoe Basin, continue left on an old rocky road, now trail, lined with alders, following alongside Basin Creek into the large amphitheater-like basin. Within fields of swaying grasses and dancing flowers, and

beneath no less than a half dozen silvery cascades, the trail begins to fade after about 1.5 miles. Standing in the midst of this magnificent cirque, cock your head back and marvel at the sheer walls capped with hanging glaciers, one of the most impressive sights in the Cascades.

Old mining relics lie littered among the blossoms and boulders. They're part of the Black Warrior Mine, which operated until the late 1950s. Now on the national historic register, the mine can still be explored. Stay left of Basin Creek and a huge talus slope and follow road traces steeply for about 0.3 mile to the mine (elev. 4750 ft), bored deep into the face of the cirque. Snoop around, but don't venture beyond the shaft's entrance. The view from the shaft out over the Basin Creek valley to Trapper Mountain is just as impressive as the views of Horseshoe Basin from the valley floor.

TRIP PLANNER	
3.7 miles	Cascade Pass
4.7 miles	Pelton Basin Camp
7.5 miles	Basin Creek Camp
8.8 miles	Black Warrior Mine in Horseshoe Basin

EXTENDING YOUR TRIP

From a base at Pelton Basin Camp, explore Sahale Arm and Doubtful Lake. From a base at Basin Creek Camp, continue on trail east along the Stehekin River to Cottonwood Camp, where hardy off-trail travelers can carry on to Trapper Lake, one of the aquatic gems of the North Cascades.

56 Little Beaver and Big Beaver Creeks

RATING/ DIFFICULTY	LOOP	ELEV GAIN/ HIGH POINT	SEASON
***/3	37 miles	3100 feet/ 3650 feet	late June– Oct

Maps: Green Trails Mt Challenger No. 15, Ross Lake No. 16, Diablo Dam No. 48; **Contact:** North Cascades National Park, Wilderness Information Center, Marblemount, (360) 854-7245, www.nps.gov/noca; **Permits/ regulations:** Free backcountry permit required, limited number available, issued morning of or day before from Wilderness Information Center. Dogs prohibited; **Special features:** Wilderness valleys with ample wildlife. One of the finest old-growth forest hikes in the country; **Special concerns:** Water taxi required, visit http://rosslakeresort.com for schedule, reservations, and fares. Difficult creek crossings and hordes of mosquitoes in early season; **GPS:** SR 20 trailhead

N 48 43.672 W 121 03.746. Little Beaver landing N 48 54.916 W 121 04.499

Experience the vast wilderness and wildness of the North Cascades from below. Traipse through two remote valleys shadowed by jagged peaks and animated by thundering creeks. This classic North Cascades hike is all about the trees. They're huge here—and old! Wander through grove upon grove of western red cedars that have graced the planet for a millennium. And share this unbroken primeval forest with black bears, spotted owls, cougars, and other wild critters great and small.

GETTING THERE

From Burlington, follow the North Cascades Highway (State Route 20) east to Marblemount. Then continue another 29 miles east to the Ross Dam trailhead (elev. 2100 ft), located just beyond milepost 134. Privy available.

ON THE TRAIL

Starting on the Ross Dam Trail, descend through a thin veil of forest, crossing cascading Happy Creek along the way. At 0.6 mile, turn right on a dirt road (you'll be returning from the left), and after 0.4 mile (ignore the Happy-Panther Trail to the right) reach a dock. Catch your prearranged water taxi here, which will whisk you 15 miles north up Ross Lake (a fjordlike reservoir created in the 1930s by damming the Skagit River to power Seattle) to the landing at Little Beaver Camp (elev. 1625 ft).

Following the Little Beaver Trail, briskly climb about 500 feet skirting ledges high above Little Beaver Creek. Catch nice glimpses south of azure Ross Lake reflecting majestic North Cascades peaks. Drop about 200 feet and continue west up the Little Beaver Valley. Still well above the tumbling creek, traverse beautiful groves of old cedars, Doug-firs, and hemlocks—a scene repeated throughout this hike.

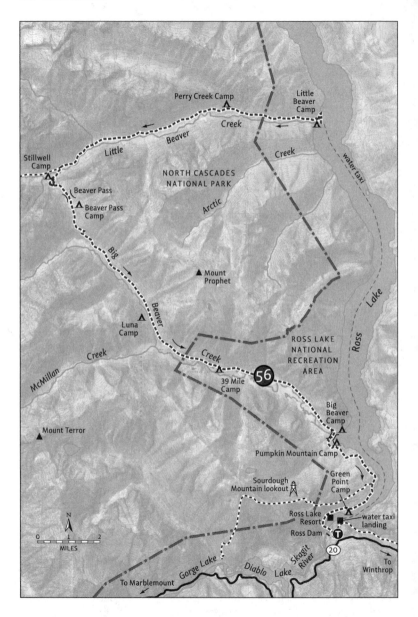

Perry Creek Camp

Little Beaver Camp

Beaver Creek

Little Beaver Creek

water taxi

Stillwell Camp

Beaver Pass

Beaver Pass Camp

NORTH CASCADES NATIONAL PARK

Arctic

Big

Beaver

▲ Mount Prophet

Luna Camp

Ross Lake

Creek

McMillan Creek

Creek

39 Mile Camp

56

ROSS LAKE NATIONAL RECREATION AREA

Big Beaver Camp

▲ Mount Terror

Pumpkin Mountain Camp

Sourdough Mountain lookout

Green Point Camp

Ross Lake Resort

Ross Dam

water taxi landing

20

N

0   1   2
MILES

To Marblemount

Gorge Lake

Diablo Lake

Skagit River

To Winthrop

At about 2.5 miles, enter North Cascades National Park. After crossing the base of a talus slope, arrive at Perry Creek Camp (elev. 2100 ft), set in thick timber at 5.6 miles (the cumulative mileage includes your walk to the water taxi dock). Then continue west, passing an emergency shelter before crossing Perry Creek on a precarious log. Heading farther upvalley, work your way across rocky outwashes and brushy avalanche openings (that'll soak you in wet weather) with nice views upward of the surrounding vertical walls. And follow along the clear cool waters of Little Beaver Creek, crossing numerous side creeks, weaving around giant boulders, and meandering through swampy skunk cabbage patches along the way. Finally, at 12.2 miles, reach the junction (elev. 2375 ft) with the Big Beaver Trail.

Turn left, soon coming to a big bridge spanning Little Beaver Creek. Then walk across a big talus slope before reaching Stillwell Camp (elev. 2525 ft) at 13.2 miles. From here, the trail steeply climbs, switchbacking underneath a cool canopy of hemlocks and firs to crest thickly forested Beaver Pass (elev. 3650 ft) in about 2 miles.

Shrouded in old growth, including fine stands of Alaska yellow cedar, the broad pass also bursts with huckleberries, making it a favorite feasting spot for bears. At 16 miles, reach attractive Beaver Pass Camp (elev. 3600 ft) among giant firs along Big Beaver Creek. Just down the trail is an emergency shelter and separate horse camp.

From Beaver Pass Camp the trail descends through ancient timber and brushy understory. Yellow diamonds mark the way, but the route is beyond obvious. Cross several avalanche chutes through tunnels of vine maple and dogwood. Catch mesmerizing glances into the deep Luna Creek valley, bounded by the forbidden and impressive Picket Range.

At about 19 miles, Big Beaver Creek—now truly *big*—loudly announces its nearby presence, although it'll remain mostly out of sight until it nears Ross Lake. At 20.4 miles come to Luna Camp (elev. 2500 ft), set in scrappy forest along a creek crashing down from Mount Prophet.

Still descending, pass through cool cedar groves and a sun-kissed bench of pine and mountain hemlock, where Big Beaver Creek thunders below in a narrow chasm. Pause for limited but impressive views up McMillan Creek to glacier-covered Mount Terror. Then drop some more, entering the Ross Lake National Recreation Area and a lush flat of giant cedars—survivors of many past forest fires. At 24.8 miles, reach popular 39 Mile Camp (elev. 1800 ft) on the creek of the same name.

Cross the nice waterway on a steady log, passing the horse camp and then oxbow ponds and bogs teeming with carnivorous sundew plants and more than enough mosquitoes to keep them nourished. Birds, frogs, and toads enjoy the buzzing buffet too. You'll savor the mountain reflections.

Now in lush bottomlands, pass through groves of some of the oldest (1000 years plus), largest (10 feet wide at chest height), and most impressive cedars left on the planet. Several decades ago, plans were on the table to raise Ross Lake, which would have flooded this valley and destroyed these cedars. Citizen outrage halted the desecration of this sacred natural shrine.

Continuing, the trail briefly leaves the river bottom before returning to it at a junction (elev. 1650 ft) at 29.9 miles. The trail left leads 0.4 mile to Big Beaver Camp and the landing where a water taxi pickup can shorten your loop. Otherwise, continue hiking right, crossing Big Beaver Creek on a big suspension bridge and coming to hiker-only Pumpkin Mountain Camp shortly afterward. Then in dry open forest, climb above a deep cleft where Pierce Creek tumbles over a spectacular

A backpacker crosses Perry Creek in the Little Beaver Creek Valley.

waterfall. A well-appreciated bridge (elev. 1900 ft) spans the fissure.

Now high above Ross Lake, the way continues through open forest and occasional ledges, providing nice views of the lake below and big peaks above. At 33.1 miles, pass the Pierce Mountain Trail (elev. 1950 ft) that leads right, to Sourdough Mountain. After climbing to about 2050 feet, gradually descend, passing some fine views of Ross Lake and its dam. At 35 miles, a spur (elev. 1925 ft) leads left, dropping to lakeside Green Point and its camps.

A little farther on, a spur leads left to the Ross Lake Resort and its floating cabins. At 36 miles, reach the Ross Dam (elev. 1625 ft). Hike across it to a dirt road, mustering up enough strength for 1 final mile and one more climb. Bear left at a junction, and then turn right on trail to complete the loop and retrieve your vehicle.

TRIP PLANNER	
1 mile	Water taxi dock near Ross Dam, Little Beaver Camp at water taxi landing
5.6 miles	Perry Creek Camp
13.2 miles	Stillwell Camp
16 miles	Beaver Pass Camp
20.4 miles	Luna Camp
24.8 miles	39 Mile Camp
30.3 miles	Big Beaver Camp and landing
30.3 miles	Pumpkin Mountain Camp
35 miles	Spur to Green Point and camps
36 miles	Ross Dam
37 miles	Trailhead

EXTENDING YOUR TRIP

From the Big Beaver–Little Beaver junction, continue up the Little Beaver Trail 6.5 miles to spectacular subalpine 5200-foot Whatcom Pass, where you'll find camping and chances to further explore.

PACIFIC NORTHWEST TRAIL: NORTH BY NORTHWEST

Back during the backpacking boom of the 1970s, transplanted New Englander Ron Strickland was struck with a novel idea. How about adding another classic long-distance hiking trail to our country's stock? One to accompany and rival the likes of the Appalachian, Pacific Crest, and Colorado Divide trails. Such began his quest to build the Pacific Northwest Trail (PNT), a 1200-mile path from Cape Alava on the Olympic Peninsula to Montana's Glacier National Park.

Soon forming the Pacific Northwest Trail Association, Strickland and a good number of tireless volunteers set out promoting, constructing, and maintaining the new trail. Utilizing existing trails along with new tread, the PNT weaves together a good portion of northern Washington. While parts of the trail still exist only on paper, much of the Pacific Northwest Trail is currently hikeable, and more than a handful of backpackers have through-hiked it. The trail should soon be seeing improvements, with new construction and better maintenance as the result of President Obama signing a bill in 2009 designating the Pacific Northwest Trail as our newest national scenic trail—a status that the PCT and AT hold.

The following trips in this guidebook include portions of the Pacific Northwest Trail: Shipwreck Coast (Trip 1), Wildcatter Coast (Trip 2), High Divide (Trip 4), Happy Lake Ridge (Trip 5), Copper Ridge (Trip 54), Little Beaver and Big Beaver Creeks (Trip 56), East Bank Trail and Desolation Peak (Trip 57), Devils Dome and Jackita Ridge (Trip 58), Horseshoe Basin and Windy Peak (Trip 64), Kettle Crest South (Trip 65), Kettle Crest North (Trip 66), and Little Snowy Top Mountain (Trip 67).

57 East Bank Trail and Desolation Peak

RATING/ DIFFICULTY	ROUND-TRIP	ELEV GAIN/ HIGH POINT	SEASON
*****/4	45.6 miles	6500 feet/ 6102 feet	late June– Oct

Maps: Green Trails Ross Lake No. 16, Diablo Dam No. 48, Mount Logan No. 49; **Contact:** North Cascades National Park, Ross Lake National Recreation Area, Wilderness Information Center, Marblemount, (360) 854-7245, www.nps.gov/noca; **Permits/regulations:** Free backcountry permit required, limited number available, issued morning of or day before from Wilderness Information Center. Dogs must be leashed; **Special features:** Lakeside hike to historic fire lookout once staffed by Beat poet Jack Kerouac. Sprawling wildflower meadows, spectacular views into wild, remote corners of North Cascades; **Special concerns:** Boat noise on lake. Shorten to one-way by arranging for a water taxi drop-off, visit http://rosslakeresort.com for schedule, reservations, and fares; **GPS:** N 48 42.484 W 120 58.686

📷 🏠 *There is nothing desolate about this peak or the long and winding lakeside trail leading to it. Au contraire mon frère (et ma soeur)! Desolation is alive with color—shrouded in dazzling alpine flowers during the summer bloom. And the view? C'est magnifique! Stand mouth agape, staring down at the cobalt waters of fjord-like Ross Lake cradled beneath glacier-covered peaks. It was inspirational to Franco-American poet Jack Kerouac and no doubt will be for you as well.*

GETTING THERE
From Burlington, follow the North Cascades Highway (State Route 20) east to Marblemount. Then continue another 33 miles east to just beyond milepost 138, to a large parking area on your left signed for the East Bank Trail (elev. 1800 ft). Privy available.

ON THE TRAIL
Beginning by a handsome log cabin privy, drop 100 feet or so in 0.3 mile to a sturdy bridge spanning Ruby Creek. Cross it and turn left at a junction onto the East Bank Trail. Now, gently rising above Ruby Arm (an inlet created on Ross Lake by the damming of the Skagit River in the 1930s), travel through mostly dry open forest, thanks to a rainshadow effect that cloud-catching peaks to the west have created. Farther along, notice the abundance of paper birch, a tree more common in Washington's northeastern Columbia Highlands than here in the North Cascades. The Ruby Creek and Ross Lake area are full of remnants from the area's mining past—look for relics and listen for voices from the past in the breezes.

At 3 miles, come to a junction (elev. 1900 ft). The trail left leads 0.5 mile through an old pasture and to Hidden Hand Camp on a ledge above Ruby Arm. Just ahead on the East Bank Trail is another junction, where a trail right climbs steeply to lonely country high on Little Jack Mountain. Continue straight, gradually climbing to Hidden Hand Pass (elev. 2500 ft) at about 4 miles. The way then slowly descends, still remaining a good distance from Ross Lake. At 6.7 miles, come to the hiker-only Roland Creek Camp on Roland Creek. Beyond, the trail finally makes contact with Ross Lake. Enjoy views of Pumpkin Mountain at the head of Big Beaver Creek and Little Jerusalem Island, the name an early homesteader gave to his nearby claim. At 8 miles, there are more camps along glacier-fed May Creek, and a spur leads to camps on a cove on Ross Lake.

At 8.9 miles, come to appealing Rainbow Point Camp (elev. 1620 ft) on Ross Lake—and the beginning of over 2 miles of lakeshore-hugging trail. Blasted into ledges at places,

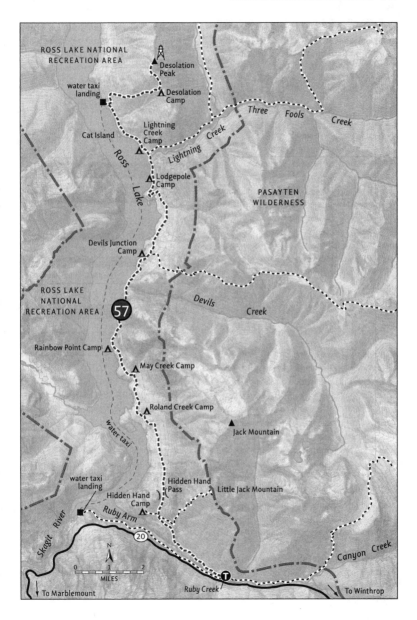

ROSS LAKE NATIONAL
RECREATION AREA

Desolation
Peak

water taxi
landing

Desolation
Camp

Three   Fools   Creek

Cat Island

Lightning
Creek
Camp

Ross   Lake

Lightning   Creek

Lodgepole
Camp

PASAYTEN
WILDERNESS

Devils Junction
Camp

ROSS LAKE
NATIONAL
RECREATION AREA

57

Devils   Creek

Rainbow Point Camp

May Creek Camp

Roland Creek Camp

Jack Mountain

water taxi

water taxi
landing

Hidden Hand
Pass

Little Jack Mountain

Hidden Hand
Camp

Ruby Arm

20

N

0   1   2
MILES

Skagit River

Canyon Creek

To Marblemount

Ruby Creek

To Winthrop

Jack Mountain hovers above fjord-like Ross Lake.

where the trail hovers just a few feet above water level, this is the nicest section of this long lowland trail. When Ross Lake's surface is calm, enjoy gorgeous mountain reflections.

After crossing Devils Creek at a narrow gorge on a suspension bridge, the trail leaves the lakeshore and once again gradually climbs, coming to a junction (elev. 1800 ft) with the Devils Dome Trail (Trip 58) at 12 miles. Continue north and soon pass a spur leading left to Devils Junction Camp on a bench above the lake. The trail then continues through forest above and away from the lake, crossing Dry Creek and swinging around a small peninsula before coming back to lake level at Lodgepole Camp and reaching Lightning Creek at 15.6 miles.

There are camps here, on both sides of the long suspension bridge. Although some

are hiker-only, the horse and boater camps are more attractive. Set your tent up here before pushing on to Desolation Peak, so you can make the steep summit climb with a light day pack. Or, camp high on the peak itself. You'll get solitude and outstanding views, but the camp is waterless after the last snowfields melt, usually by mid-July.

Just north of the bridge, the Lightning Creek Trail strikes out eastward, climbing ledges high above its namesake. Continue north along Ross Lake instead, on the Desolation Peak Trail, climbing 150 feet and traversing dry forest and grassy areas that burst in floral bloom in June and July. Enjoy nice views out to Cat Island, and then doggedly continue hiking north, crossing a cascading creek in a cedar grove before coming to a junction (elev. 1850 ft) at 17.8 miles. The trail left drops steeply 0.2 mile to a dock, where you can be dropped off or picked up by the Ross Lake water taxi. You'll want to continue right, gaining elevation, at times steeply.

Through dry forest with east-slope characteristics, ascend Desolation Peak. At 19.7 miles, pass a ledge (elev. 3350 ft) with a preview of the visual treats that await. At 20.1 miles, cross a creek (elev. 3750 ft)—the last reliable source of water. Steadily ascending, the way leaves forest for open slope about 1 mile farther. In 1926 a fire scorched this mountain, leaving it desolate. While much of the mountain's upper elevations are still bare of forest cover, they sport clusters of colonizing trees and blankets of brilliant wildflowers. But it's the view that'll captivate you the most—especially south along Ross Lake, Washington's glacier-fed, cobalt-blue, inland fjord (albeit manmade).

At 21.8 miles, reach Desolation Camp (elev. 5200 ft; no fires), perched on a semi-open ridge. While it lacks water, it overflows with views. The trail continues up open, southern-exposed slopes—downright hot in summer's afternoon sun. Buggy too. After cresting a 5850-foot knoll, the way slightly descends before making the final push to Desolation's 6102-foot summit.

The recently restored 1932 fire lookout perched atop the peak's open summit, surrounded by an ocean of peaks, makes it without a doubt one of the most beautiful lookouts in the nation. Hosting Jack Kerouac for sixty-three days in the summer of 1956 makes it one of the most famous. Fearsome 8066-foot Mount Hozomeen just to the north captivated and mesmerized the poet, as it will you too. "Hozomeen, Hozomeen, most beautiful mountain I've ever seen," waxed Kerouac. And from this glorious summit there are hundreds of other beautiful mountains to be seen as well. Baker, Redoubt, Spickard, and the Prophet west.

Snowfield, Colonial, Ruby, and Jack south. Skagit and Castle east—and BC's Silvertip north!

TRIP PLANNER	
3.5 miles	Hidden Hand Camp
6.7 miles	Roland Creek Camp
8.0 miles	May Creek Camp
8.9 miles	Rainbow Point Camp
12 miles	Spur to Devils Junction Camp
14.6 miles	Lodgepole Camp
15.6 miles	Lightning Creek Camp
17.8 miles	Spur to dock
21.8 miles	Desolation Camp
22.8 miles	Desolation Peak lookout

58 Devils Dome and Jackita Ridge

RATING/ DIFFICULTY	LOOP	ELEV GAIN/ HIGH POINT	SEASON
*****/5	28.1 miles	8150 feet/ 6982 feet	late July– Oct

Maps: Green Trails Ross Lake No. 16, Jack Mountain No. 17, Mount Logan No. 49; **Contact:** Okanogan-Wenatchee National Forest, Methow Valley Ranger District, Winthrop, (509) 996-4003, www.fs.fed.us/r6 /oka, or North Cascades National Park, Ross Lake National Recreation Area, Wilderness Information Center, Marblemount, (360) 854-7245, www.nps.gov/noca; **Permits/ regulations:** NW Forest Pass required at Canyon Creek trailhead. Free self-issued backcountry permit at Canyon Creek trailhead. For camps along East Bank Trail in Ross Lake NRA, national park backcountry permit required, issued morning of or day before from Wilderness Information Center. Wilderness rules apply; **Special features:** Parkland meadows, rugged and dramatic ridges; **Special concerns:** Car shuttle and water taxi required, visit http://rosslakeresort.com for schedule, reservations, and fares. Abundant mosquitoes, limited water sources, brushy sections, steep-gullied talus slope, dangerous lingering snowfields. Popular high-buck hunting area in September; **GPS:** Devils Junction landing N 48 50.126 W 121 01.428. Canyon Creek trailhead N 48 42.305 W 120 55.069

⚙️ ⊗ *Challenging but highly scenic, this is a classic ridgeline hike around 9066-foot Jack Mountain and 8128-foot Crater Mountain. Journey across windswept alpine tundra, wildlife-rich parkland meadows, and steep slopes bursting with dazzling wildflowers, taking in sweeping views spanning the North Cascades range, from its snowy western front to its sun-kissed eastern edge.*

GETTING THERE

From Burlington, follow the North Cascades Highway (State Route 20) east to Marblemount and continue for 29 more miles to the Ross Dam trailhead (elev. 2100 ft) located just beyond milepost 134. This is where you'll access the water taxi. Privy available. Leave your second vehicle 7.1 miles farther along SR 20, at the Canyon Creek trailhead (elev. 1900 ft) (or arrange a car shuttle). If you'll be walking the complete loop, start at the East Bank trailhead, 4.3 miles beyond the Ross Dam trailhead, just beyond milepost 138 (elev. 1800 ft).

ON THE TRAIL

Most guidebooks recommend doing this trip counterclockwise, starting at Canyon Creek. By going clockwise instead, you gain the advantages of arranging your water taxi first (instead of worrying about coordinating a pickup at the end) and ascending the steep scree section instead of descending it. Either direction, there's a lot of vertical to be gained and lost. If you want to skip the expense of the water taxi or want more mileage, you can do this trip as a 43-mile loop using the East Bank Trail (see Trip 57) and the Ruby Creek Trail.

Starting on the Ross Dam Trail, descend 0.6 mile to a dirt road. Turn right and after 0.4 mile reach a dock, where you'll catch your prearranged water taxi. It will whisk you north, up Ross Lake to the landing at Devils Junction Camp (elev. 1625 ft) (permit required for camping).

From the dock, head left, passing several camping areas and reaching a junction (elev. 1800 ft) in 0.3 mile, for a total trip mileage thus far of 1.3 miles (the cumulative mileages given include your walk to the water taxi dock from your car). The East Bank Trail leads left to Desolation Peak (Trip 57) and right to SR 20. You want to go straight on the Devils Dome Trail, beginning a climb of over 1 mile of vertical elevation gain. At 2.3 miles, in dry scrappy forest, enter the Pasayten Wilderness (elev. 2700 ft). At 3.5 miles, come to an opening (elev. 3400 ft) and your first view of massive Jack Mountain cradling the large Nohokomeen Glacier. You'll be treated to fine views of this prominent peak throughout this hike.

While the elevation gain is serious, the grade isn't bad, but sections of the trail are choked in brush—more evidence of a dwindling Forest Service budget for maintenance. At 4.5 miles, come to a creek (elev. 4100 ft), which may be your last reliable water for miles—fill up. The way continues across southern-exposed slopes, sporting deer brush and other vegetation more common farther east. The going is hot in the summer sun.

After crossing two more creeks (which may be dry), views open up south and west. The climb eases a bit before entering a grove of silver firs and steadily climbing once more. At 6.9 miles, reach forested Dry Creek Pass (elev. 5825 ft), with its waterless camp. The way then breaks out of forest, traversing berry patches and heather meadows, granting an excellent view northwest to Ross Lake, Desolation Peak, and British Columbia's Silvertip Mountain.

A pair of backpackers traverses Devils Dome's alpine tundra.

At 7.2 miles, reach an unmarked junction (elev. 6025 ft). The trail left leads a short way to the old Bear Skull Shelter, with camps and a spring. From there the path can be followed for another 0.5 mile or so along open ridge toward 7258-foot Spratt Mountain. Off-trail trekkers can keep going farther.

Bear right to traverse beautiful meadows alive with scurrying ground squirrels and swaying pasque flowers. Climbing higher, the trail traverses alpine tundra, rounding a rocky basin that harbors creeks and often snow, before making a final ascent to the broad summit of 6982-foot Devils Dome at 8.5 miles. The views are fiendishly delightful! To the west is a horizon of glistening snow, with Mounts Challenger and Baker stealing the show. North, Castle Mountain dominates the horizon, with Mount Frosty in Canada's

Manning Park just to its left. East lie Blizzard, Powder, Shull, and Three Fools along the Cascade crest. Finally, south finds Crater and Jack vying for your attention.

The way now drops, traversing steep open slopes before meandering through parkland meadows teeming with berries and bears. At 10 miles, reach delightful Skyline Camp (elev. 6350 ft)—find water in the basin below it to the east. From this camp, the trail rounds steep open slopes above that basin before reaching a forested saddle (elev. 5950 ft). The way then gently climbs, coming to a junction and good camps at Devils Pass (elev. 6100 ft) at 12.5 miles. For water, follow the trail north (which leads to the Pacific Crest Trail) for 0.1 mile; then bear right onto another path, shortly coming to a piped spring. If it's dry (which it often is late in the season), continue

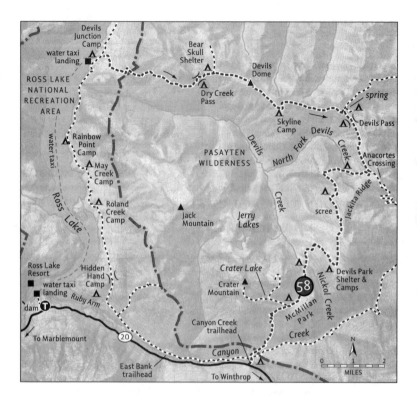

on the path for 0.3 mile, dropping to a basin with reliable water, more camps, and the now-collapsed Devils Pass Shelter. Here, as at other campsites along the way, deer can be bothersome—keep a clean camp.

From Devils Pass, climb 200 feet before engaging in 2 miles of pure splendid strolling across spectacular meadows bursting with wildflowers and bustling with marmots. At 14.5 miles, pass an unmaintained trail (elev. 6200 ft) that leads left to Anacortes Crossing high on Jackita Ridge. The way then enters an avalanche basin and steeply descends into forest along the base of towering rocky cliffs. At 15.1 miles, come to good camps along the

North Fork Devils Creek. At 15.8 miles, cross the creek (elev. 5150 ft), and then regain lost elevation on a brutally steep and brushy course. After traversing a lovely basin, crest a ridge (elev. 6200 ft) that radiates from rugged Jackita Ridge. Then drop again, coming to a nice campsite by a creek in a secluded basin (elev. 5800 ft) at 17.5 miles.

Then once again climb, gradually at first, to another ridge crest (elev. 6150 ft) before beginning a steep ascent up a larch-lined rib. The way then switchbacks up steep scree, where lingering snow and eroded gullies may make travel difficult and potentially dangerous. Use caution. Once out of the scree, crest yet another high ridge (elev. 6825 ft) with superb views to the Jerry Lakes teetering high on Jack Mountain.

Then begin a glorious and easy descent across open slopes to Devils Park, where there are good camps and ample opportunities for easy off-trail exploring. At 20.7 miles, come to the old shelter (elev. 5850 ft) and a reliable creek. Then descend through an old burn with plentiful berries, reaching Nickol Creek (which may be flowing underground) and a good camp (elev. 4950 ft) at 22.1 miles.

The way then gently climbs through McMillan Park (elev. 5300 ft), a gentle plateau of grassy wetlands pretty in fall and teeming with mosquitoes in summer. After passing a good camp, soon come to a junction (elev. 5200 ft) at 23.8 miles. The trail right leads to Crater Lake and Mountain—good side trips.

Your route continues straight on a rapid descent, reaching Canyon Creek and a junction (elev. 1900 ft) at 27.8 miles. If you're returning to the East Bank trailhead, continue straight for 3.5 miles on the Ruby Creek Trail. Otherwise, cross Canyon Creek on a sturdy bridge, pass a dilapidated cabin, camps, and the Chancellor Trail, and arrive at the Canyon Creek trailhead (elev. 1900 ft) at 28.1 miles.

TRIP PLANNER	
1 mile	Water taxi dock near Ross Dam, Devils Junction Camp at water taxi landing
6.9 miles	Dry Creek Pass
7.2 miles	Spur to Bear Skull Shelter and camps
8.5 miles	Devils Dome
10 miles	Skyline Camp
12.5 miles	Devils Pass and camps
15.1 miles	North Fork Devils Creek camp
17.5 miles	Basin camp
20.7 miles	Devils Park Shelter and camps
22.1 miles	Nickol Creek camp
23.8 miles	Camp at Crater Lake Trail junction
28.1 miles	Canyon Creek trailhead on SR 20

59 Snowy Lakes

RATING/ DIFFICULTY	ROUND-TRIP	ELEV GAIN/ HIGH POINT	SEASON
*****/3	20.2 miles	3550 feet/ 6900 feet	late July– Oct

Map: Green Trails Washington Pass, WA–No. 50; **Contact:** Okanogan-Wenatchee National Forest, Methow Valley Ranger District, Winthrop, (509) 996-4003, www.fs.fed.us/r6/oka; **Permits/regulations:** NW Forest Pass required; **Special features:** High alpine ridge along PCT, alpine lakes, autumn larches; **Special concerns:** Potentially dangerous snowfields may linger near Granite Pass, requiring ice ax; **GPS:** N 48 31.084 W 120 43.988

Meander up the Pacific Crest Trail to an alpine world flush in wildflowers, larches, and craggy mountains spiraling toward the heavens. Trek along a high ridge beneath pointy pinnacles watching for ravens and nutcrackers above and ground squirrels and mountain goats below. Then climb to a high hidden bench that holds the shallow, shimmering, summit-reflecting Snowy Lakes. Frozen in July, sparkling in August, and golden in September, the Snowy Lakes are showy lakes throughout the hiking season.

GETTING THERE
From Marblemount, follow the North Cascades Highway (State Route 20) east for 51 miles to Rainy Pass, near milepost 158, and turn left onto a spur road. (From Winthrop, drive 35 miles west on SR 20 and turn right.) Follow the spur 0.3 mile to the Pacific Crest Trail parking area (elev. 4800 ft). Privy available.

ON THE TRAIL
The first 5 miles to Cutthroat Pass are on one of the easiest stretches of high-country trail in the North Cascades. Engineered for horses,

Upper Snowy Lake

the Pacific Crest Trail here follows wide, gentle switchbacks to make the 2000-foot climb to 6800-foot Cutthroat Pass. En route, pass tumbling Porcupine Creek, a good source for filling water bottles—by late summer, the ridge may be dry.

A half mile before the pass is a nice developed camping area set amid an open forest of larches. It's popular with weekend backpackers, so don't expect to be alone here, nor at Cutthroat Pass, where day hikers also flock in substantial numbers. Before pushing on, take a break at the high mountain gap, soaking up sublime scenery. Jagged giants encircle you, with 8876-foot Silver Star Mountain dominating to the east.

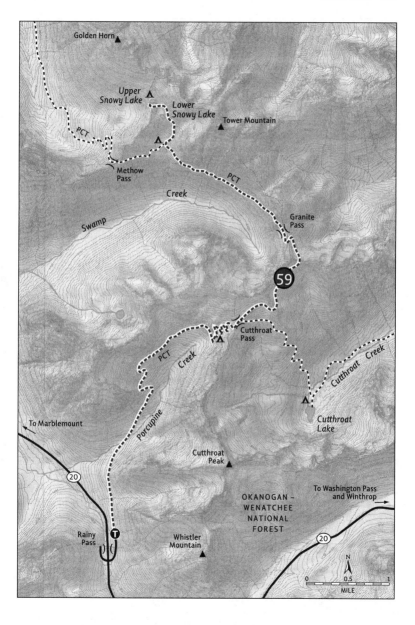

Ignore the trail down to Cutthroat Lake (an alternative approach), and continue north on the PCT instead, an airy arterial for the next 4 miles, hugging high steep slopes. Traverse rock gardens, blueberry patches, and beneath outcroppings of shiny granite shards. Views are breathtaking along this catwalk, especially east out to the Tiffany Highlands.

About 1.4 miles from Cutthroat Pass, round a steep ridge (elev. 6900 ft) and behold pyramidal 8444-foot Tower Mountain and its companion, 8366-foot Golden Horn. The mere presence of this cloud-catching couple is captivating enough. But with their pink and gold feldspars, this dynamic duo emits a golden hue that'll leave you awestruck. When the alpine larches that cling to their sheer slopes don their autumn apparel, you'd swear you were in El Dorado.

The trail now switchbacks down to 6300-foot Granite Pass, where steep lingering snowfields may force you to return another time. From here, the way swings beneath Tower Mountain, dipping another 150 feet as it traverses steep exposed slopes. Occasional rock slides and gullies need to be crossed, which may rattle some hikers' nerves.

At 9.3 miles, cross a creek. The Snowy Lakes lie above, feeding it. Just beyond is a nice campsite (elev. 6250 ft) by a big white boulder. An unmarked trail takes off to the right for the lakes tucked on a high open bench beneath Tower Mountain and the Golden Horn. It's a steep but well-defined path. After 0.5 mile, reach the lower Snowy Lake (elev. 6750 ft); the upper lake (elev. 6850 ft) is 0.3 mile farther.

The lake basin is strikingly beautiful—especially when the small pools reflect the guarding golden giants—and it's extremely fragile. Camp only on ledges and hard surfaces (good campsites can be found above the upper lake), leaving the meadows untrampled.

Don't even think of building a fire. Wood is at a premium here, with just a few larches and pines eking out an existence in this harsh alpine environment. For an evening jaunt, hike up to Methow Pass beneath pointy and prominent 8080-foot Mount Hardy.

Conservationists are campaigning to get this region added to the North Cascades National Park. No formal protection currently exists. Let Congress know how you think this spectacular region should be managed.

TRIP PLANNER	
4.5 miles	Camps below Cutthroat Pass
9.3 miles	Camps at Snowy Lakes junction
9.8 miles	Lower Snowy Lake
10.1 miles	Upper Snowy Lake and camps

60 Twisp Pass–South Pass

RATING/ DIFFICULTY	LOOP	ELEV GAIN/ HIGH POINT	SEASON
***/3	25.4 miles	5475 feet/ 6300 feet	July–Oct

Map: Green Trails Stehekin No. 82; **Contact:** Okanogan-Wenatchee National Forest, Methow Valley Ranger District, Winthrop, (509) 996-4000, www.fs.fed.us/r6/oka, or North Cascades National Park, Lake Chelan National Recreation Area, (360) 854-7200, or Wilderness Information Center, Marblemount, (360) 854-7245, www.nps.gov/noca; **Permits/regulations:** NW Forest Pass required. Backcountry permit required for Lake Chelan NRA, available from Wilderness Information Center, all national park ranger stations, and Winthrop and Chelan national forest ranger stations. Wilderness rules apply. Dogs prohibited in North Cascades NP, permitted on-leash in Lake Chelan NRA; **Special features:** High mountain passes, old growth, wildlife; **Special concerns:** None; **GPS:** N 48 26.360 W 120 31.868

Dagger Lake from Twisp Pass

Deep glacier-carved valleys, lofty ridges and jagged peaks, majestic old growth and alpine wildflower gardens—they're all yours on this trek along and up and over (twice) the high divide between the Twisp and Stehekin river watersheds. Most of this route is lightly traveled most of the season, allowing you an excellent chance for a close encounter of the furry kind. And you get the bonus of side-trip options to lakes, waterfalls, and tiny little Stehekin on Lake Chelan.

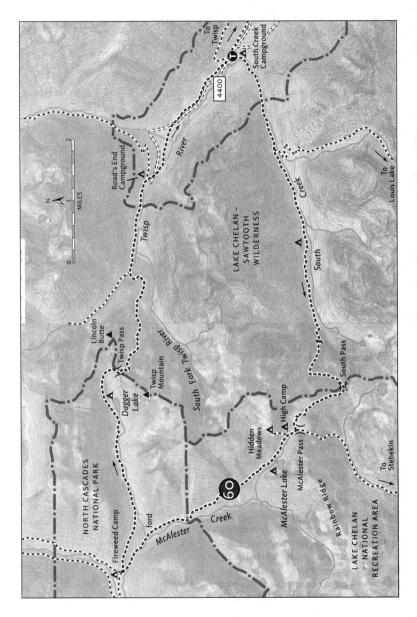

GETTING THERE

From Twisp, follow Twisp River Road west (signed "Twisp River Recreation Area"). The road becomes Forest Road 44 at 10.8 miles and later becomes FR 4400. The pavement ends at 18 miles. At 22 miles, reach the trailhead (elev. 3175 ft) at South Creek Campground. Privy available.

ON THE TRAIL

You get three passes on this loop—that's three passes you have to hike over! The first one is the highest, the second one easiest, and the third is prettiest. Start by heading up South Creek Trail No. 401, immediately crossing the Twisp River on a solid bridge and passing the horse access trail on your left. The trail parallels babbling South Creek through an open forest of big pines, easily marching up the wide valley.

At about 1.3 miles, enter the Lake Chelan–Sawtooth Wilderness. About 1.2 miles farther, reach a junction (elev. 3900 ft) with the trail to Louis Lake, your first side-trip option. Louis can be reached by hiking 3.2 miles and climbing 1400 feet to a big basin beneath 7742-foot Rennie Peak.

For the loop, continue straight ahead through cool groves of old-growth fir and spruce. Avalanche chutes occasionally break the forest canopy and allow good viewing of surrounding lofty mountains. Come late September, aspen and vine maple add touches of bright color to the greenery. At about 4.5 miles, come to a nice camp after crossing a couple of side creeks.

At around 5.5 miles (elev. 5200 ft), the trail begins to switchback out of the valley in an old burn. Views grow. Berries too, in profusion! In summer, however, this stretch can be hot and buggy. Angling along high slopes, the way traverses heat-radiating talus slopes, passes through big larches and spruce groves, and crosses wildflower patches and side trails to old mines and claims.

At 7.3 miles, reach South Pass (elev. 6300 ft) and enter the Lake Chelan National Recreation Area. Scramble the knolls to the right for excellent views down the South Creek valley to 8321-foot Abernathy Peak and to nearby South Pass guardian 7928-foot Mount McAlester. A larch-ringed lake sits in a basin beneath McAlester, reachable from the pass by experienced off-trail travelers.

The trail turns northwest, traversing high meadows and gently descending 1.4 miles to broad, grassy McAlester Pass (elev. 6000 ft). Views along this airy arterial are awesome—especially of the Rainbow Creek valley shadowed by Rainbow Ridge's polished granite slopes and McGregor Mountain's pointy 8122-foot summit. Excellent campsites and reliable water can be found at the McAlester Pass High Camp. For explorations, follow a 0.7-mile trail to Hidden Meadows or scramble along Rainbow Ridge. Extend your nights out by venturing down the Rainbow Creek Trail for 10 miles to Stehekin (camping and ice cream available).

Continue the loop by following the McAlester Trail north through primeval forest, gently descending 1 mile to grassy McAlester Lake (elev. 5500 ft). Good but busy camps can be found here, a popular spot among equestrians, anglers, and biting insects. Beyond the lake, the well-built trail drops through thick timber, crossing numerous side creeks before reaching the North Cascades National Park boundary (no dogs beyond this point) and McAlester Creek shortly afterward. Continue, traversing big avy slopes and a crossing of McAlester's East Fork, which is difficult in high water.

Reach the junction with the Twisp Pass Trail (elev. 3750 ft) 4 miles from McAlester Lake and 13.7 miles from your start. Creekside camps can be found 0.2 mile west at Fireweed Camp. The loop continues right, following the East Fork McAlester Creek 3.3 miles up to forested Dagger Lake (elev. 5500 ft), where there are good camps and a good chance of mosquitoes. Beyond Dagger, reach Twisp Pass (elev. 6100 ft) in 1 mile, where excellent high-meadow roaming can be had by following an abandoned but obvious trail north.

Continue east, reentering the Lake Chelan–Sawtooth Wilderness, descending along ledges and through rock gardens and heather meadows that grant excellent views, and finally coming to a trail junction at the confluence of the North and South Forks of the Twisp River (elev. 4400 ft). Veer right, through forest and brushy avalanche slopes, reaching a trailhead (elev. 3600 ft) at 4.5 miles from Twisp Pass. Pick up the horsey Twisp River Trail here, following it 2.9 miles back to your vehicle and completing the 25.4-mile loop.

TRIP PLANNER	
4.5 miles	Trailside camp
8.7 miles	McAlester Pass High Camp
9.7 miles	McAlester Lake and camps
13.9 miles	Fireweed Camp
17 miles	Dagger Lake and camps
18 miles	Twisp Pass
25.4 miles	Trailhead

61 Oval Lakes

RATING/ DIFFICULTY	LOOP	ELEV GAIN/ HIGH POINT	SEASON
*****/4	20.4 miles	5900 feet/ 7725 feet	July–Oct

Map: Green Trails Buttermilk Butte, WA–No. 83; **Contact:** Okanogan-Wenatchee National Forest, Methow Valley Ranger District, Winthrop, (509) 996-4003, www.fs.fed.us/r6 /oka; **Permits/regulations:** NW Forest Pass required. Wilderness rules apply; **Special features:** Alpine lakes, scrambling opportunities to area summits, larches; **Special concerns:** Difficult creek crossings in early season. Heavy equestrian use; **GPS:** N 48 21.153 W 120 24.427

On this exhilarating loop into the lofty Sawtooth Ridge, visit larch forests, alpine tundra plains, windswept ridges, and one, two—maybe more—sparkling alpine lakes. Scramble an 8000-foot summit and behold a serrated sea of mountains and fjordlike Lake Chelan before you. There's lots of elevation to be gained and lots of heat and biting flies to endure, but the Ovals are worth a round. You can easily turn this weekend outing into an all-week adventure, scouting nearby summits, tarns, and meadowed basins.

GETTING THERE
From Twisp, follow Twisp River Road west. The road becomes Forest Road 44 at 10.8 miles. At 14.3 miles, turn left onto FR 4430 (just after War Creek Campground). Upon crossing the Twisp River in 0.25 mile, reach a junction. Turn left onto FR 4420 and drive for 0.8 mile. Then turn right onto FR 4420-080 (signed "Eagle Creek Trailhead") and continue 1.4 miles to the road's end and trailhead (elev. 3000 ft). Privy available.

ON THE TRAIL
Start on the wide and at times dusty Eagle Creek Trail through an open forest of Doug-fir and ponderosa pine, with Eagle Creek tumbling in a gully below. At 1.7 miles, enter the Lake Chelan–Sawtooth Wilderness, a 150,000-plus-acre wild wedge on the Methow River–Lake Chelan divide. Five hundred feet farther, come to Eagle Creek, requiring a ford that may be difficult and dangerous in early season.

The trail now climbs more steeply, reaching a junction (elev. 4200 ft) at 2 miles. Continue straight up the Oval Creek Trail; you'll be returning on the right. Following good trail, steadily march up the valley through cool pine and spruce forest. At 6 miles, reach a small open basin (elev. 5850 ft) where good campsites can be found by the creek.

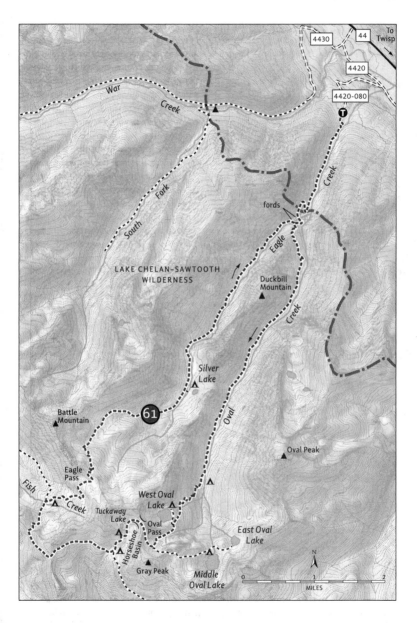

Oval Peak

Beyond this point, the trail gets down to business, climbing steeply and with purpose. At 6.5 miles, hop over West Oval Lake's outlet creek. At 7.2 miles, reach a junction (elev. 6900 ft). The trail right leads 0.25 mile to gorgeous West Oval Lake (elev. 6860 ft), set beneath talus slopes and granite ledges and ringed with larch and whitebark pine, twittering with nuthatches, nutcrackers, and chickadees. Camp away from the lakeshore, respecting areas closed for restoration. West Oval has seen its fair share of overnighters.

If you're intent on doing the loop, return to the main trail, climbing steeply up slopes of rock, krummholz, and tundra and reaching a junction (elev. 7500 ft) after 0.7 mile. The trail left climbs another 100 feet before dropping 900 feet to Middle Oval Lake, set in a big basin beneath Buttermilk Ridge in 1.2 miles. East Oval Lake lies another 0.3 mile away and 50 feet lower. Both lakes are laced with larches that set the basin aglow in gold come late September. There are good campsites at Middle Oval.

For the loop, continue right, climbing to rocky, windswept, and barren Oval Pass (elev. 7725 ft). The views here are breathtaking across the serrated skyline of the Sawtooth Ridge out to Glacier Peak and down below to the golden grassy lawns of Horseshoe Basin. Consider dropping your pack and following a faint track south for 0.5 mile to the open summit of 8104-foot Gray Peak. The view down to Middle and East Oval lakes is stunning.

From Oval Pass, the trail drops steeply in loose shale, reaching tiny Tuckaway Lake (elev. 7400 ft), tucked away beneath a cirque in Horseshoe Basin. Find good campsites here and good bear habitat too, so store food properly. Beyond Tuckaway, the trail drops through flower fields and reaches a forested creekside camp and junction (elev. 7000 ft) at about 9 miles from the trailhead.

Next, head northwest along the Chelan Summit Trail, across slopes of swaying grasses and flowers. Crest a 7350-foot ridge with views to Lake Chelan 6000 feet below. Pass through a forested gap before steadily dropping through old-growth larch and fir, reaching a lovely semi-open basin (elev. 6500 ft) that houses the headwaters of Fish Creek, good camps, and a junction at 11 miles.

Take the Eagle Creek Trail right, climbing steeply out of the basin to meadowed 7250-foot Eagle Pass in 1.2 miles. Drop steeply at first, then gradually, rounding a basin with excellent views out to 8795-foot Oval Peak before entering cool forest. The trail continues, undulating between meadow and forest, eventually meeting Eagle Creek, which it accompanies for 3 miles before crossing (at a tricky ford) on its way back to the Oval Creek Trail and trailhead.

At about 2.5 miles from Eagle Pass, a side trail takes off right to good campsites at shallow, boggy Silver Lake (elev. 5850 ft). From here, it's 3.2 miles back to the Oval Creek Trail junction and 2 more from there to your waiting vehicle.

TRIP PLANNER	
6 miles	Camps in small basin
7.5 miles	West Oval Lake and camps
8.5 miles	Tuckaway Lake and camps
9 miles	Creekside camp at Chelan Summit Trail junction
11 miles	Fish Creek basin camps
15 miles	Silver Lake and camps
20.4 miles	Trailhead

62 Cooney Lake

RATING/ DIFFICULTY	LOOP	ELEV GAIN/ HIGH POINT	SEASON
***/3	16 miles	4440 feet/ 7940 feet	July–Oct

Map: Green Trails Prince Creek, WA–No. 115; **Contact:** Okanogan-Wenatchee National Forest, Methow Valley Ranger District, Winthrop, (509) 996-4003, www.fs.fed.us /r6/oka; **Permits/regulations:** None; **Special features:** Alpine lakes, scrambling opportunities to area summits, larches; **Special concerns:** Part of loop open to motorcycles; **GPS:** N 48 10.748 W 120 15.177

Cooney Lake is one of the famed Golden Lakes, so dubbed by pioneer guidebook authors Harvey Manning and Ira Spring because of the larches that set these alpine bodies of water aglow come autumn. Nestled in a high cirque on the serrated Sawtooth Ridge, on the eastern edge of the North Cascades, Cooney makes for a wonderful weekend adventure or is a good base for days of exploring.

GETTING THERE
From Twisp, drive State Route 20 east for 2 miles. Continue south on SR 153 for 12 miles. At milepost 19, turn right onto Gold Creek Loop Road and drive 1.5 miles to a T intersection. Turn right onto County Road 1034, signed for Foggy Dew Campground. (From Pateros, follow SR 153 north for 17 miles, turn left onto Gold Creek Loop Road, and drive 1 mile to CR 1034.) In 1 mile, come to a junction and continue straight onto FR 4340. Follow this paved road for 4 miles and turn left at Foggy Dew Campground onto graveled FR Spur 200. Bear right at an unmarked junction in 2.3 miles, and at 3.7 miles reach the road's end and trailhead (elev. 3500 ft). Privy available.

ON THE TRAIL
In 1984, Cooney Lake and a dozen-odd other nearby alpine lakes were left out of the 150,000-acre Lake Chelan–Sawtooth Wilderness. While these 100,000 acres of spectacular alpine country are currently managed as a roadless area, most of this wild country is open to motorcycles. Roadless should be motorless! This area is far too ecologically precious to accommodate motors and throttles, far too precious to not be managed as wilderness.

That said, don't let a few motorbikes discourage you from exploring this spectacular corner of the North Cascades. Motorbike use is light and most of these recreationists are decent, friendly folks. They rarely camp, and if you come during the week you'll probably only be sharing the trails with curious deer and ground squirrels.

Start this lollipop loop on the Foggy Dew Trail. Hugging the delightfully named Foggy

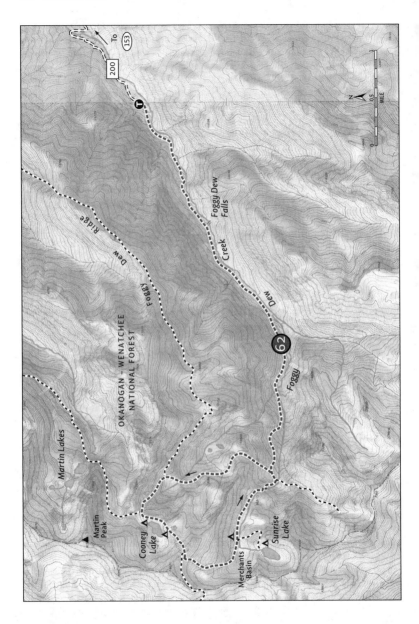

Cooney Lake

Dew Creek for most of its way, this gently graded path passes gurgling chutes and placid pools. At 2.5 miles, admire Foggy Dew Falls (elev. 4900 ft) as it plummets into a narrow cleft. At 4 miles, the trail parts ways with the creek and steepens. At 5 miles, reach a junction with the Martin Creek Trail (elev. 6000 ft).

You'll be returning from the left, so head right on the Martin Creek Trail, gently rounding a ridge. The thick pine and spruce forest soon thins, allowing occasional viewing east. Pass a small pond before crossing a creek and boulder field. At 7 miles, you may miss the junction (elev. 6800 ft) of the hiker-only and in desperate need of maintenance Foggy Dew Ridge Trail. At 7.7 miles, in a small saddle at the edge of a big meadow, come to a horse camp and junction with the hiker-only Cooney Lake Trail.

Head left, soon reaching gorgeous Cooney Lake (elev. 7300 ft), set in a larch-flanked basin beneath the cloud-catching Sawtooth Ridge. Good camps can be found along the lake's west shore. Good fishing can be found immediately in front of you. Good roaming can be found in the meadows west. Good high-country adventure can be found by continuing this loop hike.

On Cooney's east shore, the trail continues, steadily gaining elevation above the sparkling lake. After passing a couple of tarns (or remnants), the trail becomes brutally steep, attacking a heather and rock rib to crest a small gap (elev. 7940 ft) at 8.7 miles. Views are magnificent down to the lake basin (golden in fall) and out across the Chelan ranges and to Mount Stuart. Views get better if you continue on the trail heading right and scramble the unnamed 8321-foot peak just above it.

For the loop, take the trail left, dropping at a sane grade through the meadows and krummholz of sprawling Merchants Basin. Watch for mountain bluebirds. At 9.8 miles, come to a nice streamside camp (elev. 6800 ft) at the junction with the 0.5-mile trail leading to Sunrise Lake (elev. 7228 ft). Lonely and lovely, Sunrise is worth checking out.

The main trail leaves the basin, losing elevation rapidly over increasingly rocky terrain and easing in an old-growth grove of larch and spruce. At 10.9 miles, turn left at a junction—unless you want to continue your travels, in which case follow the trail right for 2 miles to Sawtooth Ridge. Otherwise, in 0.1 mile return to a familiar junction and take the trail to the right—the Foggy Dew Trail leads 5 miles back to your vehicle.

TRIP PLANNER	
7.7 miles	Horse camp
8 miles	Cooney Lake and hiker camps
9.8 miles	Merchants Basin streamside camp
16 miles	Trailhead

63 Corral Lake

RATING/ DIFFICULTY	ROUND-TRIP	ELEV GAIN/ HIGH POINT	SEASON
****/4	33.4 miles	6810 feet/ 7525 feet	July–Oct

Map: Green Trails Billy Goat Mt No. 19; **Contact:** Okanogan-Wenatchee National Forest, Methow Valley Ranger District, Winthrop, (509) 996-4003, www.fs.fed.us/r6/oka; **Permits/regulations:** NW Forest Pass required. Free wilderness permit required, self-issued at trailhead. Wilderness rules apply; **Special features:** Alpine tundra, alpine lakes, scrambling opportunities to area summits; **Special concerns:** Heavy equestrian use; **GPS:** N 48 47.068 W 120 19.082

A long forested approach to a gorgeous larch-ringed lake tucked in a deep cirque beneath windswept ridges carpeted with alpine tundra—all in the center of one of the largest and wildest roadless areas in North America! Journey to the heart of the Pasayten Wilderness, where lynx, wolves, wolverines, and the occasional grizzly still roam. And while Corral Lake is a splendid destination in itself, it makes for a great staging area to further explore this wild and lightly traveled corner of the North Cascades.

GETTING THERE

Follow State Route 20 east to Winthrop. Just before entering the town center, turn left onto West Chewuch Road. In 6.7 miles, reach the junction with the East Chewuch Road (an alternative approach from Winthrop) and continue north onto Forest Road 51. Follow this paved road for 2.6 miles and turn left onto FR 5130 (signed "Billy Goat 17"). Continue for 16.5 miles (the pavement ends in 5 miles; the final 3 miles can be rough but are generally passable to most vehicles) to the

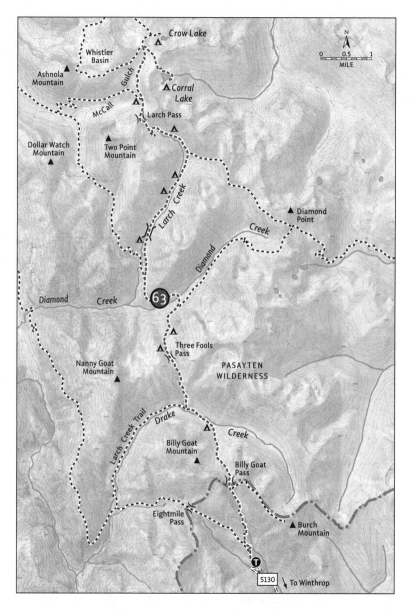

Crow Lake

Whistler
Basin

Ashnola
Mountain

Corral
Lake

Larch Pass

McCall
Gulch

Dollar Watch
Mountain

Two Point
Mountain

Larch Creek

Diamond
Point

Creek

Diamond

63

Diamond   Creek

Three Fools
Pass

Nanny Goat
Mountain

PASAYTEN
WILDERNESS

Latch Creek Trail

Drake   Creek

Billy Goat
Mountain

Billy Goat
Pass

Eightmile
Pass

Burch
Mountain

5130

↓ To Winthrop

N

0   0.5   1
MILE

T

road's end at trailhead (elev. 4800 ft). Privy available.

ON THE TRAIL
The trail starts on an old mining road, passing tailings and old digs. In 0.4 mile, come to a junction (elev. 4950 ft) with the Hidden Lakes Trail, which takes off left for Eightmile Pass (an alternative approach when deep snows linger at Billy Goat Pass). Continue right, twisting and turning under a thin canopy of Douglas-fir, steeply climbing. From forest openings along the way, gaze across the valley to Isabella Ridge's impressive array of summits: Eightmile Peak, West Craggy Peak, and Big Craggy Peak. In early summer, flowers brighten the way. Watch, too, for snowshoe hare—their numbers are indicative of how well the local lynx are faring.

Pass a spring as you climb higher, the valley walls growing tighter. At 2.8 miles, crest Billy Goat Pass (elev. 6600 ft), a deep cleft shadowed by the stark ledges and vertical slopes of Billy Goat Mountain, and enter the 529,000-plus-acre Pasayten Wilderness. Pass a trail heading right that leads to 7782-foot Burch Mountain (a fine side trip), and start descending on muddy tread through meadows alongside a babbling creek (it's possible to camp in the meadows).

Cross the creek and its tributaries several times as you continue descending into the forested valley. At 4.9 miles, come to Drake Creek (elev. 5550 ft), which may be difficult to cross in high water. Find good camps on both sides of crossing. The trail continues, rounding a bluff with good views down glacier-carved Drake Creek valley, coming to another creek crossing by a nice cascade (elev. 5350 ft), again, with good camps nearby. At 5.6 miles, come to a junction with the Larch Creek Trail (elev. 5700 ft). Left heads 3 miles to the Hidden Lakes Trail (an alternative approach). You want to go right, crossing talus and dry meadows, gently ascending the long draw known as Three Fools Pass (elev. 6030 ft).

At the north end of the pass, pass a small spring in meadows and campsites in woods just beyond. Then begin descending in lodgepole pine forest, passing a good but busy camp near a creek crossing before coming to a junction (elev. 5630 ft) at 7.5 miles with the Diamond Jack Trail, which leads to Lake Creek. Stay left and, after crossing Diamond Creek on a bridge (elev. 5500 ft), start traversing warm rocky slopes abloom in midsummer and with good views west to lofty peaks year-round.

At 9 miles, the Dollar Watch Trail (elev. 5625 ft) veers left. Continue right, primarily through forest, reaching a bridged crossing of Larch Creek (elev. 5660 ft) and camps after another 1 mile. Then gradually climb alongside pretty Larch Creek, where pocket meadows soon interrupt the forest. At 11.3 miles, cross the creek and pass more good campsites. Then follow refurbished and new tread built tough for the heavy horse traffic that this trail endures.

At 12.2 miles, a cairn marks an indistinct trail heading to the right toward Diamond Point. This unmaintained trail offers good views and an alternative return (when combined with the Diamond Jack Trail) for experienced backcountry travelers.

The main way carries on left, slowly ascending Larch Pass and crossing pretty meadows (with camps) alongside Larch Creek en route. After making a sweeping switchback, crest the 7100-foot pass adorned with its namesake tree, and then gently descend across talus slopes. Enjoy sweeping views west to distant North Cascades peaks. At 15 miles, reach McCall Gulch (elev. 7025 ft) at the base of long, broad, tundra-covered Ashnola Mountain. There are good camps and water here, and a trail leads left to the East Fork Pasayten River.

You won't feel fenced in at Corral Lake.

You'll want to go right, across spectacular high country denuded of trees and bursting with flowers and views. At 15.7 miles, in a cleft on a lofty tundra-carpeted ridge (elev. 7450 ft), bear right onto the Corral Lake Trail, following it across a high shoulder with far-reaching views that will keep your head spinning. After 0.5 mile on this heavenly path, reach the ridge crest (elev. 7525 ft) and peer down at Corral Lake in a remote basin ringed with larches and shadowed by jagged peaks.

The trail now rapidly drops to that glorious body of water. In early season, cornices may still be present here—in which case, avoid them by following tread left and higher to bypass them. Otherwise, in another 0.5 mile, reach Corral Lake's outlet creek (elev. 7150 ft), where a path diverges left for the horse camp and another one—yours—continues right, to nice camps set on a bluff amid the larches. Set up camp and get the map out to start planning further explorations!

TRIP PLANNER	
2.8 miles	Billy Goat Pass
4.9 miles	Drake Creek camps
6.5 miles	Three Fools Pass and camps
7.2 miles	Busy camp near a creek
10 miles	Camps on Larch Creek
11.3 miles	Camps at creek crossing
13 miles	Camps below Larch Pass
15 miles	McCall Gulch and camps
16.7 miles	Corral Lake and camps

EXTENDING YOUR TRIP

Corral Lake makes for an excellent base camp for further exploration of the central Pasayten Wilderness. Follow an old trail to Whistler Pass across Sand Ridge to Quartz Lake and return via Peeve Pass. Scramble high, gentle surrounding peaks and ridges, or check out Crow Lake (accessible by trail from just beyond where you turned off for Corral Lake) in a nearby cirque. You can easily spend a week here roaming this little-known section of wild Washington.

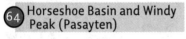

64 Horseshoe Basin and Windy Peak (Pasayten)

RATING/ DIFFICULTY	LOOP	ELEV GAIN/ HIGH POINT	SEASON
*****/3	19.5 miles	3400 feet/ 8334 feet	late June– Oct

Map: Green Trails Horseshoe Basin No. 21; **Contact:** Okanogan-Wenatchee National Forest, Tonasket Ranger District, (509) 486-2186; www.fs.fed.us/r6/oka; **Permits/ regulations:** NW Forest Pass required. Free wilderness permit required, self-issued at trailhead. Wilderness rules apply; **Special features:** Alpine tundra, scrambling opportunities to area summits; **Special concerns:** Portions of route traverse recent burned zones, avoid on hot days and in high winds. Clutch Creek Trail section of loop has brushy sections and fading tread. High-

clearance vehicle required; **GPS:** N 48 54.515 W 119 54.244

You can easily spend weeks exploring this magical high basin in a corner of the sprawling Pasayten Wilderness. Situated in the eastern extremes of the North Cascades, where the sun generously shares its warming rays, Horseshoe Basin is usually hikeable before the summer solstice. But don't discount fall, when Horseshoe's mosquitoes are on hiatus and golden larches warm the basin with their soft glow.

GETTING THERE

From downtown Tonasket, turn left onto Tonasket Bridge Road (signed "Many Lakes Recreation Area"). Upon crossing the Okanogan River, turn right onto the Loomis Highway and follow it for 17 miles to the village of Loomis. Bear right (north) onto Loomis-Oroville Road (County Road 9425), and after 2 miles turn left onto Toats Coulee Road (Forest Road 39). Follow this paved road for 13.5 miles and turn right onto FR 500 (signed "Irongate Trailhead"). Continue for 5.7 rough and slow miles (high clearance necessary) to the trailhead at road's end (elev. 6150 ft). Privy available.

ON THE TRAIL

Following the Boundary Trail (a 73-mile path across the Pasayten), immediately enter wilderness. On an old mine road, gradually descend, passing through a meadow with a good view of Windy Peak before reentering forest. Savor the shade, for the green canopy soon yields to a forest of charred matchsticks compliments of the Tripod Fire in 2006, a conflagration that scorched over 175,000 acres. Much of the way to Horseshoe Basin and around Windy Peak traverses the burn. Greenery is slowly returning. Meanwhile, note that this hike can be hot and potentially

Peaceful camp in Horseshoe Basin

hazardous during strong winds due to falling snags.

At 0.7 mile, come to a junction with the Deer Park Trail, which when combined with the Albert Camp Trail makes for a nice lonely alternative loop return. Shortly afterward, reach the Clutch Creek Trail, the return route described below. Continue straight, and at 1.5 miles cross a branch of Clutch Creek (elev. 6000 ft).

At 3.5 miles, emerge from rows of blackened snags into a verdant meadow of wildflowers. Continuing upward on an easy grade, reach 7200-foot Sunny Pass at 5 miles. Pick Peak lies to your left, an easy scramble. The Windy Peak Trail, your loop return, bears left. Continue right to emerald Horseshoe Basin spread out before you.

In 0.1 mile, pass the Albert Camp Trail, which marches over a high shoulder of Horseshoe Mountain. In another 1.2 miles, reach a three-way junction at Horseshoe Creek (elev. 7000 ft). Decision time. Avail yourself of the good camps here on both sides of the creek? Head right an easy 0.8 mile to little Smith Lake tucked beneath Horseshoe Mountain's larch-covered north slopes? Or head right on the Long Draw Trail to explore silver forests beneath 8076-foot Arnold Peak (an easy scramble)?

Nope. The best choice is to head left 0.8 mile on the Boundary Trail to little Loudon Lake, perched in a rolling lawn beneath Rock and Armstrong mountains (both easy scrambles). Good camps can be found on benches south and west of the lake. Mosquitoes are fierce here in early season but dissipate as the surrounding wetland pools dry out during the summer.

Set up camp and scramble up the tundra slopes of 8100-plus-foot Armstrong Mountain. Check out its two international boundary markers and gape at views north to British Columbia's

Horseshoe Basin and Windy Peak from Armstrong Mountain

Snowy Mountain and Cathedral Park Peaks. Then turn west to admire pointy 8601-foot Cathedral Peak and broader 8685-foot Remmel Mountain. To the east, find the looming summits of the Loomis country—7882-foot Chopaka Mountain dominating—and to the south, hovering above the Horseshoe Basin expanse, is 8334-foot Windy Peak.

When you're ready to continue your loop, retrace your steps back to Sunny Pass to pick up the Windy Peak Trail. Follow this path through the Tripod burn zone, losing about 700 feet to a creek crossing before steeply climbing 1000 feet to a junction with the Basin Creek Trail on a high shoulder of Windy Peak (elev. 7500 ft), about 2.5 miles from Sunny Pass. Tiny Windy Lake (with good camps) can be reached by leaving the trail where it turns sharply away from a small creek (elev. 7050 ft) about 0.4 mile before the junction.

Continue left, climbing through larches, then open ledges and slopes of granite till, as views expand with each step. The trail dips around a knoll and then climbs again to a junction (elev. 7900 ft) 0.9 mile from the previous junction. The trail right heads down Windy Creek to the Chewuch River trailhead. Take the trail left instead, following it a steep 0.5 mile to Windy's aerie-like 8334-foot summit. From this former lookout—one of the highest summits in Washington reached by trail—feast on stupendous views in every direction. You can see almost the entire Pasayten country—and the Kettle River Range, the Sawtooth Ridge, Glacier Peak, and even a tip of Mount Baker!

Retreat to the main trail and traverse Windy's windblown high southern ridge. Just beneath a knoll, before the trail begins to descend, a dangerous snowfield may linger into July. A safe bypass can usually be found to

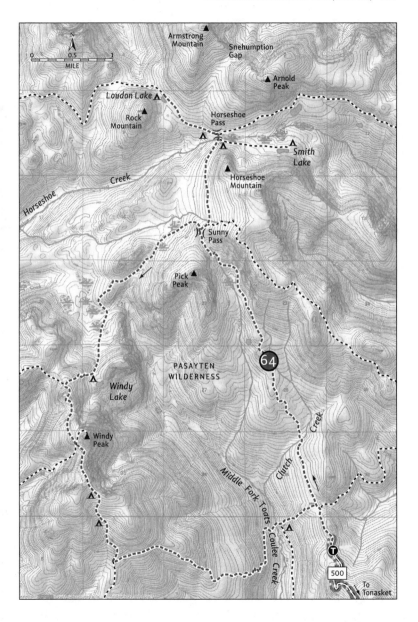

the right. The trail drops rapidly into a lovely basin with good water and camps before reentering burnt forest.

About 1.5 miles from the summit trail junction, reach an easy-to-miss junction with the Clutch Creek Trail (elev. 6900 ft). Turn left (east) here, following this lightly traveled path through lovely meadows before steeply dropping on fading and brushing-in tread. Good trail, however, resumes as the grade eases. At 3.2 miles from the Windy Peak–Clutch Creek trail junction, reach the Middle Fork Toats Coulee Creek (elev. 5400 ft), crossable by a high log bridge. A good but dark campsite is available if needed, otherwise continue. Bear

left at a junction and begin an insanely steep climb of 600 feet, reaching the Boundary Trail after 0.5 mile. It's an easy 0.7 mile back to your vehicle, to the right.

TRIP PLANNER	
5 miles	Sunny Pass
6.3 miles	Camps at Horseshoe Creek
7.1 miles	Loudon Lake and camps
11.3 miles	Windy Lake and camps
12.6 miles	Spur to Windy Peak summit
13.5 miles	Camp after Windy Peak snowfield
18.3 miles	Middle Fork Toats Coulee Creek camps
19.5 miles	Trailhead

Opposite: Blue Mountain Canyon Country from Oregon Butte (Trip 70)

Eastern Washington

65 Kettle Crest South

RATING/ DIFFICULTY	ONE-WAY	ELEV GAIN/ HIGH POINT	SEASON
****/2	13.5 miles	2900 feet/ 6923 feet	late June– Nov

Map: USGS Sherman Peak; **Contact:** Colville National Forest, Republic Ranger District, (509) 775-7400, and Three Rivers Ranger District, Kettle Falls, (509) 775-3305, www .fs.fed.us/r6/colville; **Permits/regulations:** Reservations required for Snow Peak Cabin; **Special features:** Ridgeline hike, extensive views, solitude; **Special concerns:** Car shuttle required. Trail traverses old burn zone, avoid on hot days and in high winds. Limited water sources; **GPS:** Northern trailhead N 48 30.094 W 118 25.290. Southern trailhead N 48 36.516 W 118 28.619

🔪 👫 ⚙ 🏠 ❌ *Kettle Crest Trail No. 13 travels for over 40 miles along the spine of the lofty yet gentle Kettle River Range. One of Washington's finest high-country long-distance trails, it can be hiked piecemeal when combined with its numerous side trails or all the way through on a three- or four-night journey. The southern 13.5-mile section contains some of the range's most dramatic scenery and makes for an excellent two-day trip. Almost the entire way, however, is through the 1988 White Mountain Fire Burn Zone. Shade and water are scarce. But views are nonstop and wildflowers and wildlife are prolific.*

GETTING THERE

For the northern trailhead: From Republic, travel 17 miles east on State Route 20 to Sherman Pass and the trailhead (elev. 5575 ft). (From Kettle Falls, travel 25 miles west on SR 20.) Privy available. For the southern trailhead: Drive SR 20 east from Sherman Pass for 3.5 miles and turn right at milepost 323 onto gravel South Fork Sherman Creek Road (Forest Road 2020). Follow FR 2020 for 7 miles, bearing right onto FR 2014. Continue for 4 miles and turn right onto FR Spur 250. Reach the trailhead (elev. 5200 ft) after 4.2 miles.

ON THE TRAIL

While this trip can be done north to south, it's better to begin from the southern trailhead on FR 250, ascending the dry open slopes of White Mountain early in the morning. This area was the epicenter of the 1988 White Mountain Fire, in which over 20,000 acres burned. Although the forest is regenerating, shade is still at a premium and water sources are scarce. Consider making this trip in early summer, when lingering snows provide runoff. Even then, it's still imperative that you pack sufficient water.

The trail begins by climbing the south slope of White Mountain. Gain elevation steadily on wide switchbacks, alternating between burnt snags and pockets of green. In early summer, wildflowers paint the forest floor in an array of dazzling colors. Admire, too, the various animal tracks in the tread. Coyote, bear, deer, cougar, moose—they've all left their signatures behind.

In 3 miles, find the fading spur trail on the right that leads to White Mountain's 6923-foot summit. It's a 10-minute walk to the old lookout site. The views south to Lake Roosevelt, west to the Cascades, east to the Selkirks, and north all along the Kettle Crest are breathtaking. White Mountain is a sacred peak to the Colville Confederated Tribes. Respect all artifacts on the summit and do not disturb any of the cairns. Many of them were built by young tribal members for vision quests.

Just beyond the spur is a spring. It may be dry by late summer. Open-range cattle make it essential that you treat all water sources along the way. Through beautiful silver-burned

Kettle Crest Trail approaching Sherman Peak

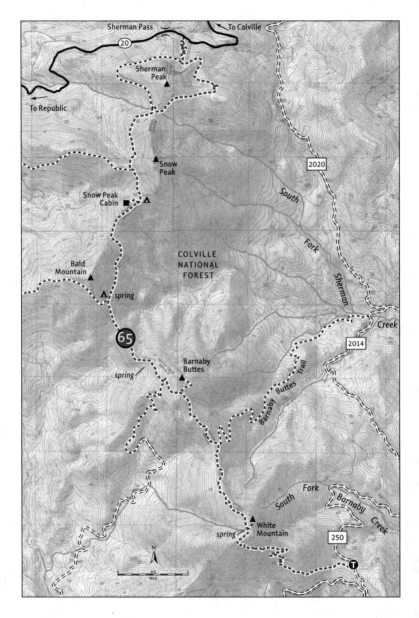

forests, the trail now begins a long but grad-ual descent off of White Mountain. At 5 miles, come to an intersection with the Barnaby Buttes Trail. Now utilizing an old road, the trail works its way between the two buttes. Side trips to the open summits are worthy objec-tives.

At 6 miles, just beyond where Trail No. 7 approaches from the west, there's a spring. Now follow an up-and-down course to the saddle (elev. 5550 ft) between the buttes and Bald Mountain, and then begin a steep climb around Bald's eastern slopes. At 8 miles, at the junction with the Edds Mountain Trail, find another spring in a nice meadow and good spots for setting up camp.

After more ups and downs, great views, and another 1.5 miles, you'll arrive at the Snow Peak Cabin (elev. 6100 ft) and reliable water nearby. The cabin is a great place to spend the night. Be sure to make reservations. Oth-erwise, good camping spots can be found in the vicinity (don't set up camp near the cabin). Beyond the cabin, the Kettle Crest Trail tra-verses meadows and ghost forests, working its way around lofty Snow Peak.

At 10 miles, the Snow Peak Trail branches off west. Continue right, on the Crest Trail, making one last climb to the saddle between Snow and Sherman peaks (elev. 6400 ft) at 11 miles. The Sherman Peak loop trail departs left. Continue right, rounding Sherman and entering cool, mature unburned forest. Finally, after 13.5 miles, reach the northern trailhead at Sherman Pass.

TRIP PLANNER	
3 miles	Spur to White Mountain summit
6 miles	Spring
8 miles	Meadow camp at Edds Mountain Trail junction
9.5 miles	Snow Peak Cabin and camps
13.5 miles	Sherman Pass trailhead

EXTENDING YOUR TRIP

From a base camp at the Snow Peak Cabin you can easily scramble 7103-foot Snow Peak, 7011-foot Sherman Peak, and, 6940-foot Bald Mountain—the second-, fifth-, and sixth-highest summits in the Kettle River Range.

66 Kettle Crest North

RATING/ DIFFICULTY	ONE-WAY	ELEV GAIN/ HIGH POINT	SEASON
****/3	30.5 miles	4600 feet/ 7140 feet	mid-June– late Oct

Maps: USGS Sherman Peak, USGS Cop-per Butte, USGS Mount Leona; **Contact:** Colville National Forest, Republic Ranger District, (509) 775-7400, www.fs.fed.us /r6/colville; **Permits/regulations:** None; **Special features:** Ridgeline hike over high summits, extensive views, solitude; **Special concerns:** Long car shuttle required. Lim-ited water sources, may be contaminated by grazing cattle, treat all water; **GPS:** Southern trailhead N 48 36.516 W 118 28.619. Northern trailhead N 48 51.823 W 118 23.721

Amble along the lofty, lumpy spine of the Kettle River Range, savoring solitude and scenery. Heart of the Columbia Highlands and transition zone between the coastal Cas-cades and interior Rockies, the Kettles are rich in biological diversity and act as a natu-ral bridge between the two mountain ranges. Through unbroken pine and larch forests, and over broad summits carpeted in wildflowers, the Kettle Crest Trail offers some of the finest alpine walking in eastern Washington.

GETTING THERE

For the southern trailhead: From Repub-lic, travel 17 miles east on State Route 20 to

Sherman Pass and turn left (north). (From Kettle Falls, travel 25 miles west on SR 20 to the pass and turn right.) Drive the short spur road to the trailhead (elev. 5575 ft). Privy available. For the northern trailhead: From Republic, drive 3 miles east on SR 20 and turn left onto SR 21. Continue for 18.4 miles to Curlew and turn right onto Boulder Creek Road (County Road 602). Drive 11.2 miles to the trailhead at Deer Creek Summit (elev. 4600 ft). Privy available.

ON THE TRAIL

While this entire 30.5-mile trip has its delights, an out-and-back to Copper Butte is a good idea for those who can't arrange a car shuttle. Also, shorter one-way trips can be made by exiting on any number of the good feeder trails radiating from the crest.

From Sherman Pass, head north on the Kettle Crest Trail, winding through pine and fir groves and weaving through granite shards while gently ascending. Soon, pocket meadows scented in sage and aspen patches golden in autumn greet you—and good views, too, out to the big-sky country west and high Kettle peaks south. At 2 miles, come to a spring (and trough) and a junction (elev. 6150 foot). The trail right—a mandatory side trip—leads 1 mile to a scenic loop and the 6780-foot summit of Columbia Mountain, with its recently restored 1914-built lookout cabin.

The Kettle Crest Trail continues north through big firs and solid stands of western larch that set the range aglow in yellow come October. Some of the finest autumn color displays in Washington are to be found here along the Kettle Crest. At 3.2 miles, after a piped spring (elev. 6200 ft), there's a good camp. After rounding a 6400-foot shoulder of Jungle Hill, the way switchbacks down through stands of lodgepole pine, reaching a small gap (elev. 5850 ft) and the Sherman Trail at 5.5 miles.

Come to a small creek and begin climbing, eventually breaking out into meadows that grant good views east. At 6.8 miles, reach a junction with the Jungle Hill Trail (elev. 6550 ft) at a reliable spring and good camps. Continue north, through flowering meadows punctuated by groves of windswept, contorted whitebark pines and shiny silver snags. Views are excellent up and down the crest and out to the Selkirks east and to British Columbia's Rossland Range north.

At 8.1 miles, intersect the Wapaloosie Trail (elev. 6850 ft) in meadows and rock gardens just below the 7011-foot summit of Wapaloosie Mountain. In late spring, arrowleaf balsamroot speckles this lofty peak's sage-dotted slopes bright yellow. The way then enters a forest speckled with boulders and granite shards and descends to a junction with the Timber Ridge Trail and, shortly afterward, to a rocky saddle (elev. 6350 ft) at 9 miles.

Then up again the trail goes, brushing 7046-foot Scar Mountain. After climbing 300 feet, the trail once again drops, passing dry camps and reaching the exceptionally scenic Marcus Trail in a saddle (elev. 6450 ft) at 10.5 miles. From here, the way winds through open forest and meadows, passing good but waterless camps and reaching the broad open summit of 7140-foot Copper Butte at 11.8 miles. From this former fire lookout site, the highest peak in the Kettle River Range, feast on views up and down the entire range. Enjoy some of the old lookout relics scattered about the peak, too.

Continuing north, the trail rapidly descends through a 1990s burn, where showy fireweed and feisty verdant shoots brighten blackened logs and accent silver snags. Flush grouse and admire woodpeckers in this transitional forest. At 13 miles, intersect the Old Stage Road (elev. 6050 ft), a nineteenth-century transportation route, now a lovely trail across the

A hiker enjoys the view east of King Mountain from near Wapaloosie Mountain.

Kettles. Turn right, following the old wagon track a short way, and then veer left while the old road continues east.

Soon after, pass Midnight Mountain Trail and a spring. Then round Lambert Mountain, traversing lovely meadows to reach a junction with the Lambert Trail (elev. 6150 ft). Then descend, passing through another burnt-over area before reaching a junction with the Leona and Leona Loop trails (elev. 5600 feet) at 16.8 miles. The loop trail veers left to Mount Leona's 6474-foot view-granting summit before reconnecting with the Kettle Crest Trail. It receives little maintenance—so best to stay on the Kettle Crest Trail, swinging east and dipping around Leona, soon coming to a junction with the Stickpin Trail.

Continue north through forest and meadow, crossing a small creek and climbing a little before reuniting with the Leona Loop Trail at 18.5 miles. Then descend to a cool forested gap (elev. 5050 ft) at 19.9 miles, where just beyond, the lightly used Big Lick Trail takes off left, and the Ryan Cabin Trail takes off right. A good campsite and spring can be found near the old cabin about 0.3 mile down the trail.

The Kettle Crest Trail marches on northward, rounding pretty Profanity Peak (I swear that's its name), reaching the rapidly fading Profanity Trail (elev. 5775 ft) at 22.1 miles, and then traversing a beautiful flowering meadow (elev. 5850 ft) that grants excellent views back to Copper Butte. The way then descends, returning to forest and pretty much remaining in the woods for its duration. While this section of trail with its limited views may be monotonous to some, it's excellent bear, moose, and cougar habitat; and a trip here in

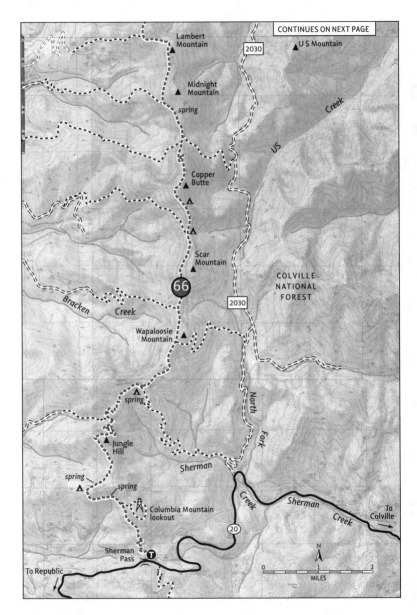

CONTINUES ON NEXT PAGE

Lambert Mountain

2030

U S Mountain

Midnight Mountain

spring

US

Creek

Copper Butte

Scar Mountain

66

2030

COLVILLE
NATIONAL
FOREST

Bracken

Creek

Wapaloosie Mountain

North

spring

Fork

Jungle Hill

Sherman

spring

spring

Columbia Mountain lookout

Creek

Sherman

Creek

To Colville

20

Sherman Pass

T

To Republic

N

0   1   2
MILES

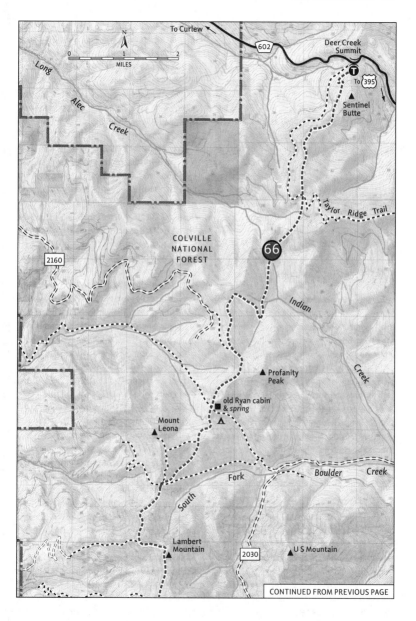

To Curlew

N

0   1   2
MILES

602

Deer Creek Summit

T

To 395

Sentinel Butte

Long

Alec

Creek

COLVILLE
NATIONAL
FOREST

2160

Taylor Ridge Trail

66

Indian

Profanity
Peak

old Ryan cabin
& spring

Mount
Leona

Creek

South

Fork

Boulder   Creek

Lambert
Mountain

2030

U S Mountain

CONTINUED FROM PREVIOUS PAGE

October is through a brilliant tunnel of golden larches.

Cross a few creeks (which often run dry in late season) and, after passing some granite outcroppings (elev. 4850 ft), once again climb. The way then climbs and dips, crosses a boggy area and another creek (hopefully flowing), and reaches an old road and the Taylor Ridge Trail at 27 miles in a grassy saddle (elev. 5400 ft). Proceed north, making one last climb (elev. 5625 ft) before gradually losing elevation through beautiful larch forest to arrive at the northern trailhead at Deer Creek Summit (elev. 4600 ft), at 30.5 miles.

Upon returning home, write to your legislators in support of wilderness designation for the Kettles, which were left out of the 1984 Washington Wilderness Act. A new proposal spearheaded by Conservation Northwest is moving forward.

TRIP PLANNER	
2 miles	Spring and trail to Columbia Mountain
3.2 miles	Piped spring and camp
6.8 miles	Spring and meadow camps at Jungle Hill Trail junction
10.5 miles	Waterless camps
11.8 miles	Copper Butte
20 miles	Junction with Ryan Cabin Trail to camps and spring
30.5 miles	Deer Creek Summit trailhead

67 Little Snowy Top Mountain

RATING/ DIFFICULTY	LOOP	ELEV GAIN/ HIGH POINT	SEASON
*****/3	19 miles	3650 feet/ 6829 feet	July–mid- Oct

Maps: USGS Salmo Mountain, USGS Continental Mountain; **Contact:** Colville National Forest, Sullivan Lake District, (509) 446-7500, www.fs.fed.us/r6/colville; **Permits/regulations:** NW Forest Pass required. Wilderness rules apply; **Special features:** Solitude, high ridge traverse, caribou and grizzly habitat; **Special concerns:** Salmo River difficult to ford in high water. Grizzly habitat, exercise caution and be bear aware; **GPS:** N 48 57.328 W 117 04.890

A wedge of wild land in the extreme northeastern corner of the state, the Salmo-Priest Wilderness protects over 41,000 acres of some of the prettiest and ecologically important alpine country east of the Cascades. Keep your dog close by. Within this wilderness, the only one in the Colville National Forest, are some of the last roaming grounds in the Evergreen State for grizzly bear, mountain caribou, wolf, and wolverine. You'd be extremely fortunate to catch a glimpse of one these rare and elusive megafauna. What you will see along this spectacular loop are miles of wildflower-saturated meadows, vistas of the rugged Selkirks and sprawling Priest Lake, and one of the most impressive old-growth cedar forests this side of the Cascades. And you'll get to visit a remote fire lookout in Idaho!

GETTING THERE

From Metaline Falls, drive 2 miles north on State Route 31 and turn right onto County Road 9345. Drive 4.7 miles and turn left onto Forest Road 22 just before Sullivan Lake. Continue for 6 miles, bearing left onto FR 2220, just after the Sullivan Creek Bridge crossing. Proceed for 13.2 more miles to the road's end and trailhead (elev. 5900 ft).

ON THE TRAIL

This loop is a Washington classic and a pleasure to hike. The trails are well maintained. The grades are gentle. And unlike other eastern Washington hiking destinations, like the Kettle River Range and the Blue Mountains, lack of water is not an issue here. Almost sixty

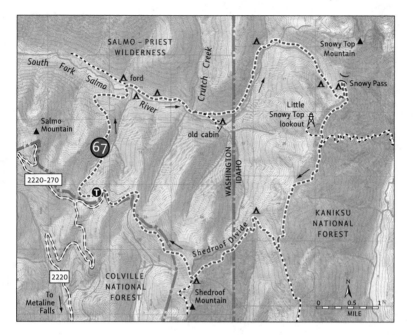

inches of rain fall each year here, making it the wettest spot in the Evergreen State east of the Cascades. However, the second half of the loop along the Shedroof Divide can be dry by late summer. And the South Fork Salmo River can have *too much* water early in the season, making crossing it a tricky affair.

To avoid finishing with an uphill slog, do this loop clockwise, beginning on the Salmo Basin Trail No. 506. You'll be returning via the Salmo Divide Trail No. 535 (which is the start of Trip 68), on your right. Immediately descend, losing 1800 feet in 3 miles, arriving at the South Fork Salmo River (elev. 4100 ft) and good camps. About halfway down, the gigantic ancient cedars begin.

Carefully ford the river (or look for a log crossing) and come to a junction. The trail left is a long-abandoned path to the Canadian border. Head right instead, through a magnificent

forest of ancient giants, slowly regaining lost elevation. With the river nearby, good campsites can be found along the way. At 4.5 miles, cross Crutch Creek, which may also require getting your feet wet. At 5.2 miles, a side trail drops right for 0.3 mile to a dilapidated cabin and good but well-used campsites alongside the river.

Continue the loop, leaving wilderness and Washington to cross into Idaho in 0.25 mile. Conservationists and this author would like to see this 17,500-acre roadless tract of the Gem State added to the Salmo-Priest Wilderness. As you reach higher ground, cedars and hemlocks yield to subalpine firs and Engelmann spruce. At 6.5 miles, pass a good campsite just above the river. At 8 miles, cross a creek—your last reliable water source for the next 5 miles. Continue climbing, and in another 1 mile reach Snowy Top Pass (elev. 6300 ft.) on the lofty

Shedroof Divide. There's a good but waterless campsite here. It's a good base camp if you plan on scrambling nearby 7572-foot Snowy Top Mountain.

The loop continues on the Shedroof Divide Trail No. 512, and views grow with each knoll rounded and ascended. At 10 miles, come to the Little Snowy Top Mountain trail junction. Drop your pack and take this 0.5-mile spur to the old fire lookout. The views from this 6829-foot summit are stunning. Gaze out at Priest Lake and the jagged Selkirks of the Idaho panhandle. Admire the rolling green Shedroof Divide. Marvel at the pointy peaks around Kootenay Pass in British Columbia.

Continuing along the Shedroof Divide, traverse sprawling meadows, taking in breathtaking views of the Priest River valley a dizzying 4000 feet directly below. At 13.5 miles, the lightly used Hughes Ridge Trail takes off left. In another 1 mile, in a low gap (elev. 5600 ft), come to some good campsites and a small creek. Refill water bottles. Then begin climbing, steeply at times, reentering Washington and the Salmo-Priest Wilderness.

Reach a little notch (elev. 6250 ft) between Shedroof Mountain and an unnamed peak at 16 miles, where there's also a junction with the Salmo Divide Trail No. 535. Turn right onto this trail and make one last small climb before gradually descending back to your vehicle. En route, enjoy good views west of the Sullivan River valley and limited views east of the wild territory you just explored.

Gypsy Peak, the highest summit in Eastern Washington viewed from Salmo Divide Trail

TRIP PLANNER	
3 miles	Camps at river ford
3–5.5 miles	Riverside camps
5.5 miles	Old cabin and camps
6.5 miles	Riverside camp
9 miles	Snowy Top Pass and camp
10 miles	Spur to lookout on Little Snowy Top
14.5 miles	Camps in gap
19 miles	Trailhead

68 Shedroof Divide

RATING/ DIFFICULTY	ONE-WAY	ELEV GAIN/ HIGH POINT	SEASON
****/3	19 miles	3200 feet/ 6500 feet	mid-July– mid-Oct

Maps: USGS Salmo Mountain, USGS Helmer Mountain, USGS Pass Creek; **Contact:** Colville National Forest, Sullivan Lake District, (509) 446-7500, www.fs.fed.us/r6 /colville; **Permits/regulations:** Wilderness rules apply; **Special features:** High ridge traverse, caribou and grizzly habitat; **Special concerns:** Car shuttle required. Limited water sources. Grizzly habitat, exercise caution and be bear aware; **GPS:** Northern trailhead N 48 57.333 W 117 04.856. Southern trailhead N 48 47.856 W 117 07.660

A cloud-probing ridgeline hike along the Washington-Idaho border through the Salmo-Priest Wilderness, with old-growth forest, alpine meadows, guaranteed solitude, and expansive views from British Columbia to Mount Spokane. Saunter through bear grass flats and groves of trees scratched by bears through one of the richest bruin habitats in the state.

GETTING THERE

From Metaline Falls, drive 2 miles north on State Route 31 and turn right onto County Road 9345. Drive 4.7 miles and turn left onto Forest Road 22 just before Sullivan Lake. Continue for 6 miles to a junction just after the Sullivan Creek bridge crossing. For the northern trailhead: Bear left onto FR 2220 and proceed for 13.2 more miles to the road's end and trailhead (elev. 5900 ft). For the southern trailhead: Bear right and follow rough-in-places FR 22 for 8 miles to the trailhead just past Pass Creek Pass (elev. 5400 ft).

ON THE TRAIL

This is a great one-way adventure, but out-and-back trips from either direction will satisfy if you can't arrange a car shuttle. A nice 16-mile loop can also be made on the Shedroof Divide from Gypsy Meadows by utilizing the Shedroof Cutoff and Thunder Creek trails.

To minimize elevation gain and maximize prime viewing, begin from the northern trailhead. Follow the Salmo Divide Trail (which starts off as a decommissioned road) east and enjoy excellent views north down to the Salmo River valley and out to British Columbia peaks (notice the border swath?). After gently climbing 100 feet, drop 50 feet and enter old growth at the wilderness boundary at 1 mile.

Now on genuine trail, ascend a 6400-foot knoll, emerging in beautiful meadows that grant sweeping views south of the entire Shedroof Divide and west to Crowell Ridge and 7309-foot Gypsy Peak, the highest summit in eastern Washington. Drop 100 feet, climb 150 feet, and then drop again, coming to a junction with the Shedroof Divide Trail (elev. 6250 ft) and camps at 3 miles. Water can be found 0.1 mile east.

Head south on the divide, traveling through a big-tree grove before steeply climbing to a shoulder (elev. 6475 ft) of 6764-foot Shedroof Mountain. An abandoned and brushy spur leads left 0.4 mile to the old lookout site, with exceptional views of the Idaho Selkirks. Otherwise, continue south and steeply descend, coming to a junction (elev. 5450 ft)

Looking south along the Shedroof Divide from Shedroof Mountain

at 5.4 miles. Here the Shedroof Cutoff travels 2 miles west (water available within a short distance) to FR 2220, and the Hughes Fork Trail travels east into Idaho—like other trails leading into Idaho from the divide, it is little maintained and not recommended for inexperienced hikers.

Continue along the divide through a forest of larch and subalpine fir, enjoying occasional glimpses of Crowell Ridge and the Sullivan Creek valley. Look for tracks of deer, moose, caribou, and bear—especially bear. The divide is teeming with them. At 8.4 miles, crest a 6100-foot knoll. A few minor ups and downs through beautiful old-growth firs await next. The way then wraps around Thunder Mountain, skirting beneath ledges and passing through pine forest and berry patches.

At 9.6 miles, come to an unreliable spring (elev. 5900 ft). After descending another 50 feet, start up again, traversing meadows and

open forest and reaching a good camp (elev. 6050 ft) at 10.4 miles and a reliable spring shortly afterward. Just beyond, at 10.6 miles, a semiabandoned trail takes off right 0.7 mile for Thunder Mountain's 6560-foot summit. Good views can still be had from this former lookout site.

Along the divide, start descending, taking in window views back to Thunder Mountain and out to Idaho and reaching a junction in a narrow saddle (elev. 5500 ft) at 12.3 miles. From here, the Thunder Creek Trail travels 5.5 miles north to FR 2220 and the lightly used Jackson Creek Trail takes off east.

The Shedroof Divide Trail soon crosses Jackson Creek and steeply climbs, passing the Jackson Mountain Trail before entering a recently burned forest. After cresting a gap (elev. 6500 ft) on Helmer Mountain at 14 miles (the open 6734-foot summit is an easy off-trail romp to the right), the way continues

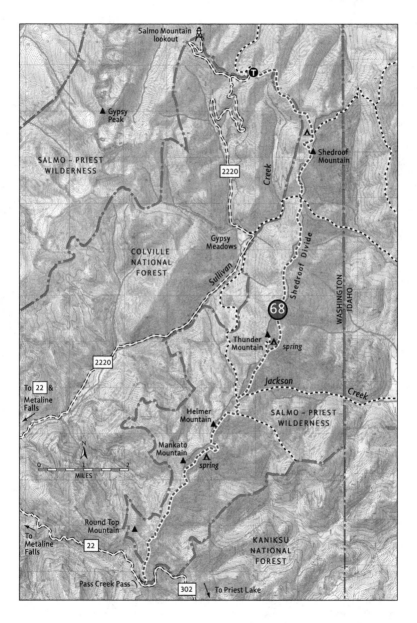

along a high view-granting shoulder before dropping several hundred feet through gorgeous meadows. At 15 miles, come to a spring and camp (elev. 6100 ft). Then ascend a gap and knoll (elev. 6350 ft) on Mankato Mountain at 15.8 miles. The summit of this 6590-foot peak can also be easily bagged.

Continue along the ridge through nice forest lined with bear grass, traveling up and down over several knolls before traversing flowering meadows beneath 6466-foot Round Top Mountain. Like Thunder and Shedroof mountains, Round Top once hosted a fire lookout. But this summit is easier to climb by heading off-trail up the meadows rather than by following its abandoned spur trail (elev. 6100 ft), which you come to at 18 miles.

The final stretch of this trip winds through burn zones, heather, blueberry patches, and Christmas trees punctuated with silvery snags, coming to trail's end at Pass Creek Pass (elev. 5400 ft) at 19 miles.

TRIP PLANNER	
3 miles	Shedroof Divide Trail junction
10.4 miles	Spring and camp
15 miles	Spring and camp
19 miles	Pass Creek Pass trailhead

69 Mount Misery Highline

RATING/ DIFFICULTY	ROUND-TRIP	ELEV GAIN/ HIGH POINT	SEASON
*****/2	17.8 miles	1900 feet/ 6350 feet	mid-June– Nov

Map: USFS Wenaha-Tucannon Wilderness Umatilla National Forest; **Contact:** Umatilla National Forest, Pomeroy Ranger District, (509) 843-1891, www.fs.fed.us/r6/uma; **Permits/regulations:** Wilderness rules apply; **Special features:** Ridge hike across unique canyon country; solitude, abundant wildlife including cougars; **Special concerns:** Ticks

in early summer. Extremely hot at height of summer. Popular hunting area with equestrian parties in midautumn. High-clearance vehicle recommended; **GPS:** N 46 07.096 W 117 31.806

On a crisp September day there is nothing miserable at all about this grand trek across the rooftop of Washington's Blue Mountains. Starting high and staying high, follow the mile-high Mount Misery Trail across meadows and ridges, taking in breathtaking views to the deep canyon country south and out to cloud-piercing peaks in Idaho and Oregon. Except for deer-hunting season, experience absolute solitude on this trek through the Wenaha-Tucannon Wilderness, one of the least traveled wild areas in the state.

GETTING THERE

From Dayton, head east on US 12 for 37 miles to Pomeroy. (From Clarkston, travel west on US 12 for 29 miles to Pomeroy.) Continue through town 0.5 mile past the historic courthouse and turning right onto 15th Street (signed for Umatilla National Forest and City Park), which eventually becomes Peola Road (and Mountain Road after that). At 15 miles, the pavement ends at the national forest, and the road becomes Forest Road 40. After 7.8 miles, bear right at a junction with FR 42, continuing on FR 40. After 7.7 more miles, turn right onto FR 4030. Follow it for 4.5 miles (the last 2.7 miles may be rough for low-clearance vehicles) to the trailhead (elev. 5850 ft).

ON THE TRAIL

With 6366-foot Mount Misery behind you (yes, you start this hike by leaving misery behind!), head west on the Mount Misery Trail (I like to call it the Mount Misery Highline), immediately entering the 177,465-acre

View west from Mount Misery Highline to Oregon Butte

Wenaha-Tucannon Wilderness, one of the largest roadless areas in eastern Washington. Created in 1978 as part of the Endangered American Wilderness Act, it was one of thirteen western wilderness areas created and four expanded for a total of over 1.3 million acres of newly designated wilderness.

Climbing at first on road then on bona fide trail, traverse slopes graced in blueberries and larches, which in fall add vibrant colors to this oft-muted landscape. Pass through a gap, which gives a preview of the sweeping canyon views that lie ahead, ranging from Hells Canyon to the high Wallowa Mountains.

At 0.7 mile, emerge onto the first of many "balds"—flat, open, grassy knobs that sport flowers in summer. Stay left at an unmarked junction (elev. 6275 ft) at 0.8 mile, unless you want to follow the Bear Creek Trail down into the Tucannon River valley. But you may want to follow an unmarked side trail left 0.4 mile to 6379-foot Diamond Peak, the highest summit in Garfield County with sprawling, stunning (especially at sunrise or sunset) views south and west into the Grande Ronde valley, Oregon, and Idaho.

The Mount Misery Trail continues west, dropping into a forested saddle (elev. 6175 ft) at 1 mile, where the Melton Creek Trail begins its long journey to the Wenaha River valley. The way then steeply climbs, cresting a bald knob (elev. 6350 ft), with excellent views east to Diamond Peak. Then carry on undulating between sage-sweetened meadows and groves of fir and larch. Views are good along the way to waves of blue ridges lapping at the horizon.

Check for animal tracks in the granite-pumice-till blanketing the ridges. Lots of deer—cougars too. I saw my first cougar in the wild not far from Mount Misery. At 2.5 miles, after a descent, come to a good camp near Sheephead Spring (elev. 5975 ft). Then climb again. Notice the mountain mahogany growing on ridge ledges. Washington's Blue Mountains are the northern limit for this tree—a species more common in the Great Basin.

After rounding another knob, locally called Sheephead (elev. 6125 ft), with extensive views out to Oregon Butte, descend once more, coming to Squaw Spring (elev. 5975 ft) and a good camp at 3.5 miles. The way then skirts

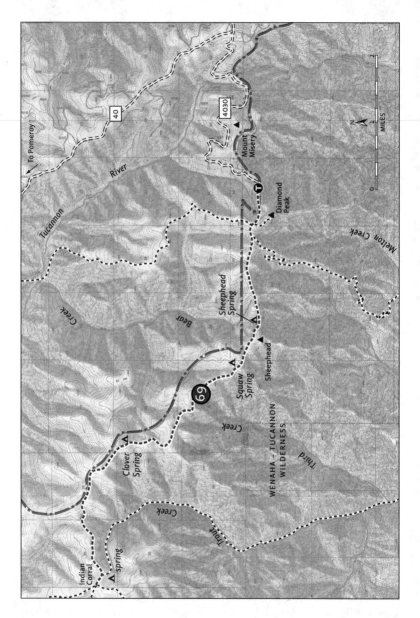

behind a grassy knoll, with more fine viewing, continuing on an up-and-down course before "bottoming out" at 5850 feet in meadows at 5.5 miles.

The trail then enters thick mature forest before traversing a long open ridge, coming to good camps at Clover Spring (elev. 5875 ft), at 6.2 miles, which drains into a trough. The way advances through beautiful open country, reaching a 5700-foot saddle at 7 miles before rising a bit (50 feet or so) and then losing more elevation. Reenter forest after a long meadow wander, coming to a 5575-foot saddle at 7.8 miles. Then once again climb and enter more glorious open country.

At 8.7 miles, come to an unsigned junction (elev. 5700 ft). The Crooked Creek Trail leads left 0.2 mile to Indian Corral, where there are good forested camps and a nearby spring. Set up camp there and rest for the return, or consider side trips down the Trout Creek valley (via Crooked Creek Trail) or west on the Mount Misery Trail for 3.5 miles to the Oregon Butte lookout (Trip 70). Enjoy the solitude!

TRIP PLANNER	
2.5 miles	Sheephead Spring and camps
3.5 miles	Squaw Spring and camps
6.2 miles	Clover Spring and camps
8.9 miles	Indian Corral camps, spring nearby

70 Oregon Butte

RATING/ DIFFICULTY	LOOP	ELEV GAIN/ HIGH POINT	SEASON
****/3	17.4 miles	3400 feet/ 6387 feet	June–Nov

Map: USFS Wenaha-Tucannon Wilderness Umatilla National Forest; **Contact:** Umatilla National Forest, Pomeroy Ranger District, (509) 843-1891, www.fs.fed.us/r6/uma; **Permits/regulations:** NW Forest Pass required. Wilderness rules apply; **Special features:** Solitude, restored lookout, canyon views; **Special**

concerns: Be alert for rattlesnakes in valley. Potentially difficult ford. Popular elk-hunting area; **GPS:** N 46 10.611 W 117 43.163

🔶 👥 ⚙️ 🏠 *The Wenaha-Tucannon Wilderness protects 177,465 acres of the Blue Mountains of southeastern Washington and northeastern Oregon. A land of high tableland ridges and deep forested canyons cut by pristine waterways, the Blues are a wildlife haven traversed by some of the loneliest trails in the Northwest. On this loop to the highest point in the wilderness, enjoy a historical fire lookout, flower-speckled ridges, tumbling creeks, cool evergreen forests, and stunning views of the sun-baked Blues—and the opportunity to see some of the Blues' legendary elk herd.*

GETTING THERE

From Dayton, head east on Patit Road for 14 miles, turning left onto Hartsuck Grade and following it for 4 miles to Tucannon River Road. (From Pomeroy, head 4.5 miles west on US 12, turning left near milepost 399 onto Tatman Mountain Road, and drive 9 miles to Tucannon River Road.) Continue south on Tucannon River Road (which becomes Forest Road 47) for 13.2 miles, bearing right onto FR 4713. Continue 2.5 miles to the Panjab trailhead (elev. 3200 ft). Privy available.

ON THE TRAIL

While this trip can be done from June to November, it's best to avoid in July and August, when temperatures often exceed 90 degrees. Fall is lovely, with western larches painting the Blues gold. But be aware that these trails are busiest then when scores of hunters set up camp. June has the advantage of floral shows and lingering snowfields that keep the shortcut access to Oregon Butte closed, guaranteeing you solitude. And lest you worry that this corner of the Evergreen State may be a little

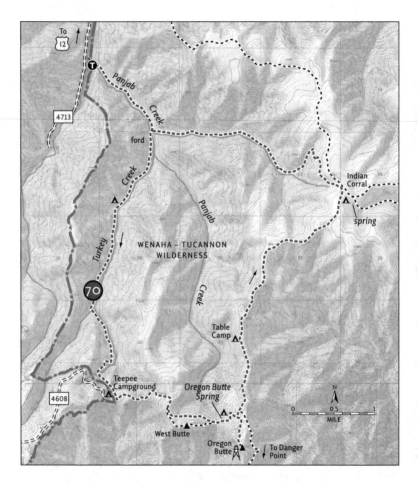

on the dry side, the Blues are blessed with abundant springs and reliable creeks.

Start on the Panjab Trail and immediately cross Panjab Creek on a sturdy bridge, entering the Wenaha-Tucannon Wilderness. The first mile or so is pure delight, a near-level journey along the creek through lush forest that looks like it belongs in the Cascades. Reach a junction and head right on the Turkey Creek Trail. The trail left is the

continuation of the Panjab Trail, your return route.

Immediately ford Turkey Creek, which may be a little tricky early in the season. Then head up a beautiful canyon through a forest of old-growth firs lined with ferns and yews. Plenty of creekside campsites may entice you to set up the tent early.

At about 4 miles, recross Turkey Creek (elev. 4600 ft), steeply climbing out of the canyon. One mile and 900 vertical feet later, reach the Teepee Campground, just outside of the wilderness and reached by the very rough FR 4608. Enjoy good views here south into the Butte Creek drainage.

Just to the east of the campground, find the trailhead for the Mount Misery Trail, a 13-mile ridgeline route across the rooftop of the Blues (see Trip 69). Reenter wilderness to begin a 6-mile journey across alpine meadows and basaltic balds and to overlooks providing sweeping canyon views.

After skirting West Butte, the trail drops slightly to reliable Oregon Butte Spring (elev. 6000 ft) and good camps at 7.2 miles. A short distance beyond, reach the junction with the 0.5-mile spur trail to Oregon Butte. From atop this 6387-foot peak, the highest summit in southeastern Washington, feast on horizon-spanning views that include tabletop ridges in nearby Oregon and cloud-catching peaks all the way in Idaho. Be sure to check out the 1931 fire lookout too, which may be staffed.

When you tire of soaking up the scenery, return to the main trail and continue east, immediately coming to a junction with the Smooth Ridge Trail. For a worthy side trip, follow this trail for about 1.5 miles to 5461-foot Danger Point, and enjoy unique perspectives of the surrounding deeply cut canyons.

The loop continues east on the Mount Misery Trail along high ridge. In about 1 mile, pass Table Camp. Skip it and head 2.3 miles farther to Indian Corral (elev. 5700 ft) instead, where four trails converge and excellent campsites can be found within a serene open setting of basaltic ledges and alpine meadows. Good water can be obtained at Dunlap Spring just south of Indian Corral on the Crooked Creek Trail.

Explore surrounding ridges or head back to your vehicle by following the Panjab Trail

Open canyon country from Oregon Butte

5.6 miles back to the trailhead. Taking off left from the corral, this excellent trail begins its descent following alongside a refreshing tributary of Panjab Creek through cool forest for much of the way.

TRIP PLANNER	
2–4 miles	Creekside camps
5 miles	Teepee Campground
7.2 miles	Oregon Butte Spring and camps
7.5 miles	Spur to Oregon Butte
9.5 miles	Table Camp
11.8 miles	Indian Corral camps, spring nearby
17.4 miles	Trailhead

Appendix I: Recommended Reading

Beffort, Brian. *Joy of Backpacking: Your Complete Guide to Attaining Pure Happiness in the Outdoors.* Berkeley, CA: Wilderness Press, 2007.

Bentley, Judy. *Hiking Washington's History.* Seattle: University of Washington Press, 2010.

Berger, Karen. *Hiking Light Handbook: Carry Less, Enjoy More.* Seattle: The Mountaineers Books, 2004.

Black, Teresa. "Dicentra." *One Pan Wonders: Backcountry Cooking at Its Finest.* Seattle: Black Mountain Publications, 2008.

Curtis, Rick. *The Backpacker's Field Manual, Revised and Updated: A Comprehensive Guide to Mastering Backcountry Skills.* New York: Three Rivers Press, 2005.

Eifert, Larry, and Nancy Eifert. *Olympic National Park Nature Guide.* Port Townsend, WA: Estuary Press, 2001.

Eng, Ronald C., *Mountaineering: The Freedom of the Hills.* 8th ed. Seattle: The Mountaineers Books, 2010.

Filley, Bette. *Discovering the Wonders of the Wonderland Trail: Encircling Mount Rainier.* Issaquah, WA: Dunamis House, 2006.

Kirkconnell, Sarah Svien. *Freezer Bag Cooking Trail Food Made Simple.* Raleigh, N.C.: Lulu.com, 2007.

Manning, Harvey, Bob Spring, and Ira Spring. *Mountain Flowers of the Cascades and Olympics.* 2nd ed. Seattle: The Mountaineers Books, 2002.

McGivney, Annette. *Leave No Trace.* 2nd ed. Seattle: The Mountaineers Books, 2003.

Miller, Dorcas. *Backcountry Cooking: From Pack to Plate in 10 Minutes.* Seattle: The Mountaineers Books, 1998.

Mueller, Marge, and Ted Mueller. *Exploring Washington's Wild Areas.* 2nd ed. Seattle: The Mountaineers Books, 2002.

Nelson, Dan A. *Day Hiking: Mount Rainier.* Seattle: The Mountaineers Books, 2008.

———. *Day Hiking: Snoqualmie Region.* Seattle: The Mountaineers Books, 2007.

———. *Day Hiking: South Cascades.* Seattle: The Mountaineers Books, 2007.

Olympic Mountain Rescue. *Olympic Mountains: A Climbing Guide.* 6th ed. Seattle: The Mountaineers Books, 2006.

Renner, Jeff. *Lightning Strikes: Staying Safe Under Stormy Skies.* Seattle: The Mountaineers Books, 2002.

Romano, Craig. *Columbia Highlands: Exploring Washington's Last Frontier.* Seattle: The Mountaineers Books, 2007.

———. *Day Hiking: Central Cascades.* Seattle: The Mountaineers Books, 2009.

———. *Day Hiking: North Cascades.* Seattle: The Mountaineers Books, 2008.

———. *Day Hiking: Olympic Peninsula.* Seattle: The Mountaineers Books, 2007.

Schaffer, Jeffrey P., and Andy Selters. *Pacific Crest Trail: Oregon and Washington.* 7th ed. Berkeley, CA: Wilderness Press, 2004.

Suiter, John. *Poets on the Peaks.* Berkeley, CA: Counterpoint Press, 2002.

Tabor, Rowland, and Ralph Haugerud. *Geology of the North Cascades.* Seattle: The Mountaineers Books, 1999.

Weisberg, Saul. *North Cascades National Park: The Story Behind the Scenery.* Las Vegas: KC Publications, 1988.

Pasqueflowers brighten up the Pasayten Wilderness (Trip 63).

Whitney, Stephen R., and Rob Sanderlin. *Field Guide to the Cascades and Olympics.* 2nd ed. Seattle: The Mountaineers Books, 2003.

Wood, Robert L. *Across the Olympic Mountains: The Press Expedition, 1889–90.* Seattle: The Mountaineers Books, 1967.

———. *Men, Mules, and Mountains: Lieutenant O'Neil's Olympic Expeditions.* Seattle: The Mountaineers Books, 1976.

———. *Olympic Mountains Trail Guide.* 3rd ed. Seattle: The Mountaineers Books, 2000.

Woodmansee, Mike. *Trekking Washington.* Seattle: The Mountaineers Books, 2003.

Appendix II: Conservation and Trail Organizations

Cascade Land Conservancy
615 2nd Avenue, Suite 625
Seattle, WA 98104
(206) 292-5907
www.cascadeland.org

Conservation Northwest
1208 Bay Street, #201
Bellingham, WA 98225
(360) 671-9950
www.conservationnw.org

Friends of the Columbia Gorge
(503) 241-3762
www.gorgefriends.org

The Lands Council
25 W Main Street, Suite 222
Spokane, WA 99201
www.landscouncil.org

Mazamas
527 SE 43rd Avenue
Portland, OR 97215
(503) 227-2345
www.mazamas.org

Monte Cristo Preservation Association
PO Box 471
Everett, WA 98206
www.mcpa.us

The Mountaineers
7700 Sand Point Way NE
Seattle, WA 98115
(206) 521-6001
www.mountaineers.org

Mountains to Sound Greenway Trust
911 Western Avenue, Suite 523
Seattle, WA 98104
http://mtsgreenway.org

Pacific Crest Trail Association
5325 Elkhorn Boulevard, PMB #256
Sacramento, CA 95842-2526
(916) 349-2109
www.pcta.org

Pacific Northwest Trail Association
24854 Charles Jones Memorial Circle,
Unit #4
North Cascades Gateway Center
Sedro-Woolley, WA 98284
(877) 854-7665
www.pnt.org

Peninsula Wilderness Club
PO Box 323
Bremerton, WA 98337
www.pwckitsap.org

Spokane Mountaineers
PO Box 1013
Spokane, WA 99210
www.spokanemountaineers.org

Spring Trust for Trails
5015 88th Avenue SE
Mercer Island, WA 98040
http://springtrailtrust.org

Washington's National Park Fund
PO Box 4646
Seattle, WA 98194
www.wnpf.org

Washington Trails Association
1305 4th Avenue, Suite 512
Seattle, WA 98101
(206) 625-1367
www.wta.org

Washington Wilderness Coalition
305 N 83rd Street
Seattle, WA 98103
www.wawild.org

Wilderness Society
1615 M Street NW
Washington, DC 20036
(800) 843-9453
www.wilderness.org

Pacific Crest Trail signpost in the Goat Rocks Wilderness

Appendix III:
Short Backpacking Trips

Backpacking Washington is not only meant as a stand-alone volume but also as a companion to the Day Hiking series. Many hikes in the Day Hiking books make fine destinations for short backpacking trips. The following list of hikes from those books are suitable for backpacking. Please refer to the appropriate Day Hiking volume for the full trail description.

 Can generally be backpacked year-round

 Ideal for bringing young children backpacking

![Permit] Permit required; consult land management agency for up-to-date regulations

DAY HIKING: OLYMPIC PENINSULA	365	👨‍👧	Permit
Hike 7	Willapa National Wildlife Refuge: Long Island	•	•	•
Hike 27	Wynoochee Lake	•	•	
Hike 30	Lower South Fork Skokomish River	•	•	
Hike 31	Upper South Fork Skokomish River		•	
Hike 42	Lena Lake		•	
Hike 43	Lake of the Angels			•
Hike 44	Mildred Lakes			
Hike 48	Duckabush River	•	•	
Hike 52	Sunnybrook Meadows		•	•
Hike 55	Tunnel Creek		•	
Hike 57	Lower Big Quilcene River		•	
Hike 60	Silver Lakes			
Hike 63	Tubal Cain Mine and Buckhorn Lake			
Hike 64	Upper Dungeness River		•	
Hike 65	Royal Basin			•
Hike 67	Gray Wolf River	•	•	
Hike 69	Slab Creek Camp and Upper Gray Wolf River		•	
Hike 79	Lake Angeles		•	•
Hike 86	Grand Valley		•	•
Hike 88	Geyser Valley	•	•	•
Hike 93	Appleton Pass			•
Hike 100	North Fork Sol Duc River			•
Hike 102	Mink Lake and Little Divide		•	•

DAY HIKING: OLYMPIC PENINSULA CONTINUED		365	🧍	Permit
Hike 104	Bogachiel River	•	•	•
Hike 105	Hoh River–Five Mile Island	•	•	•
Hike 106	South Fork Hoh River–Big Flat	•	•	•
Hike 107	Queets River			•
Hike 111	Graves Creek			•
Hike 114	Irely Lake and Big Creek	•	•	•
Hike 116	West Fork Humptulips River			
Hike 124	Shi Shi Beach and Point of the Arches	•	•	•
DAY HIKING: COLUMBIA RIVER GORGE				
Hike 34	Soda Peaks Lake			
Hike 39	Grassy Knoll and Big Huckleberry Mountain			
DAY HIKING: SOUTH CASCADES				
Hike 5	Sand Lake		•	
Hike 6	Cramer Mountain Loop			
Hike 9	Clear Lost			
Hike 21	Dark Meadow			
Hike 37	Quartz Creek			
Hike 44	Shoe Lake			
Hike 45	Goat Lake–Jordan Basin			
Hike 48	Walupt Creek Loop			
Hike 51	Packwood Lake		•	
Hike 54	Surprise Lake			
Hike 59	Burnt Rock			
Hike 60	Killen Meadows		•	
Hike 76	Upper Siouxon–Horseshoe Falls			
Hike 110	Butte Camp			•
DAY HIKING: MOUNT RAINIER				
Hike 14	Grand Park		•	•
Hike 15	Crystal Lakes		•	•
Hike 17	Owyhigh Lakes		•	•
Hike 18	Panhandle Gap			•
Hike 19	Glacier Basin		•	•
Hike 23	Palisades Lakes		•	•
Hike 42	Olallie Creek Camp			•
Hike 44	Indian Bar–Cowlitz Divide			•
Hike 51	Gobblers Knob			
Hike 59	Indian Henrys Hunting Ground			•

DAY HIKING: SNOQUALMIE REGION		365	🏃	Permit
Hike 49	Talapus and Olallie Lakes		•	
Hike 50	Island and Rainbow Lakes			
Hike 68	Margaret Lake			
Hike 69	Twin Lakes and Lake Lillian			
Hike 70	Rachel Lake			
Hike 84	Paddy-Go-Easy Pass			
Hike 93	Lake Ingalls			•
Hike 97	Navaho Pass			
Hike 102	Summit Lake		•	
Hike 104	Greenwater and Echo Lakes		•	
Hike 109	Bullion Basin			
Hike 112	Sheep Lakes and Sourdough Gap		•	
DAY HIKING: CENTRAL CASCADES				
Hike 12	Greider Lakes			
Hike 13	Boulder Lake			
Hike 20	Lakes Dorothy, Bear, and Deer		•	
Hike 22	West Fork Foss Lakes		•	
Hike 24	Fisher Lake			
Hike 25	Deception Creek			
Hike 27	Fortune Ponds			
Hike 32	Surprise and Granite Lakes		•	
Hike 34	Trap Lake			
Hike 36	Blanca Lake			
Hike 40	Lake Valhalla		•	
Hike 42	Lake Janus and Grizzly Peak		•	
Hike 47	Lake Ethel			
Hike 49	Larch Lake			
Hike 50	Lake Julius and Loch Eileen			
Hike 57	Colchuck Lake			•
Hike 58	Lake Stuart		•	•
Hike 60	Lake Caroline			•
Hike 62	Lake Edna			
Hike 65	Trout Lake			
Hike 71	Heather Lake		•	
Hike 72	Pear Lake			
Hike 73	Cady Ridge			
Hike 74	Meander Meadow			
Hike 85	Indian Creek		•	
Hike 88	Schaefer Lake			

DAY HIKING: CENTRAL CASCADES CONTINUED		365	🏃	Permit
Hike 89	Rock Creek			
Hike 103	Larch Lakes			
Hike 104	Fern Lake			
Hike 109	Chelan Lakeshore Trail		•	
Hike 116	Ingalls Creek		•	
DAY HIKING: NORTH CASCADES				
Hike 21	Ashland Lakes		•	
Hike 24	Independence and North Lakes			
Hike 32	Goat Lake		•	
Hike 34	Round Lake			
Hike 37	Peek-a-boo Lake			
Hike 42	Boulder River	•	•	
Hike 53	Hozomeen Lake		•	•
Hike 54	Anderson and Watson Lakes		•	
Hike 55	Blue Lake and Dock Butte		•	
Hike 56	Park Butte			
Hike 58	Baker Lake		•	
Hike 59	Baker River		•	•
Hike 67	Yellow Aster Butte		•	
Hike 70	Nooksack Cirque			
Hike 73	Chain Lakes		•	
Hike 76	Lake Ann		•	
Hike 77	Lookout Mountain and Monogram Lake			•
Hike 81	Thornton Lakes and Trappers Peak			•
Hike 87	Thunder Creek		•	•
Hike 91	Canyon Creek			
Hike 92	East Creek			
Hike 101	Windy Pass		•	
Hike 102	Silver Lake			
Hike 107	Scatter Lake			
Hike 108	North Lake			
Hike 113	Crater Lakes			
Hike 114	Eagle Lakes			
Hike 118	Black Lake		•	
Hike 121	Tiffany Lake		•	
Hike 123	Beaver Lake			•

Index

A

Aasgard Pass 191
Al Lake 176
Alder Ridge 210
Alpine Lakes Wilderness
    138–68, 173–76, 177–79,
    180–83, 184–87, 188–91
American Lake 135
American Ridge 100–04
Anderson Glacier 64–67
Anderson Lake 135
Anderson Pass 67
Appalachian Trail 81
Armstrong Mountain 265
Augusta, Lake 183–87
Aurora Peak 122

B

Badlands 183–87
Bald Eagle Trail 222
Basin Lake 109
Bear Lake 141
bears 30–31
Berkeley Park 128
Berry Camp 79–80
Big Basin 103
Big Beaver Creek 235–39
Big Crow Basin 106–10
Billy Goat Pass 262
Black and White Lakes
    68–71
Black Warrior Mine 234
Blue Creek Meadow 209
Blue Lake (Glacier Peak
    Wilderness) 221–24
Blue Lake (Indian Heaven
    Wilderness) 83
Bogachiel Peak 53
Boulder Camp 64
Boulder Lake 55

Boulder Pass 191–94
Boundary Trail 89–90
Brigham, Lake 183
Buck Creek Pass 195–98,
    202, 205
Buckhorn Wilderness 62

C

Cady Pass 171
Camp Mystery 63
campfires 29
camping 22–23
Canyon Lake 206
Cape Alava 42
Carbon Glacier 114, 127
Carbon River 113–14, 127
Carter Lake 186
Cascade Pass 232
Cat Basin Primitive Trail 53
Cathedral Pass 159
Chain and Doelle Lake
    176–79
Charlia Lakes 64
Chilean Memorial 39
Chilliwack River 231
Chinook Jargon 148
Chiwaukum Lakes 179–83
Cispus Basin 94–97
Clarice, Lake 167–68
Cloudy Pass 201
Colchuck Lake 191
Colonnades 124
Columbia Mountain 274
Colville National Forest
    270–84
Conservation Northwest 27,
    97, 278
Constance, Mount 64
Constance Pass 61–64, 66
cooking 29

Cooney Lake 257–60
Cooper River 152
Copper Butte 274
Copper Lake 231
Copper Ridge 228–31
Corral Lake 260–64
Cougar Lakes 132–36
cougars 31–32
crime 34–35
Crow Creek Lake 104–06
Crown Point 110
Cultus Lake 82
Cutthroat Pass 248

D

Dagger Lake 254
Daniel, Mount 159
Deadmans Lake 94
Deception Pass 165
Deep Lake (Alpine Lakes
    Wilderness) 158–61
Deep Lake (Indian Heaven
    Wilderness) 82, 83–84, 87
Deer Lake (Alpine Lakes
    Wilderness) 141
Deer Lake (Olympic National
    Park) 51
Denman Falls 122
Desolation Peak 240–43
Devils Dome 243–47
Devils Garden 85–88
Devils Park 247
Devils Pass 245
Dewey Lake 135
Diamond Peak 285
Dishpan Gap 170–73
dogs 28
Dosewallips River 65
Douglas, William O. 99
Duckabush River 72–74

Dungeness River Trail 64
Dutch Miller Gap 145

E
Eagle Creek 254
East Bank Trail 240–43
East Fork Foss River 173–76
East Fork Quinault River 47–49
Elwha Basin 60
Elwha River Valley 56–60
Emerald Lake 176
Emerald Ridge 122–25
Enchanted Valley 46–49
Enchantment Lakes 187–91
Entiat River Trail 210

F
fees 21–22
Fifes Peaks 105–06
First Divide 72
Flapjack Lakes 68–71
Flora, Lake 183
Flower Dome 196
Foggy Dew Creek 259
Foggy Flat 87
Forest Lake 130
Frosty Pass 181
Frozen Lake 125
Frying Pan Lake 97–100

G
gear 32–33
Gem Lake 150
George, Lake 120
Geyser Valley 57
Giants Graveyard 46
Glacier Peak Meadows 225–28
Glacier Peak Wilderness 191–94, 196–98, 199–203, 204–06, 211–14, 224–28
Gladys Divide 71

Goat Lake (Norse Peak Wilderness) 109
Goat Mountain (Mount Saint Helens National Volcanic Monument) 91–94
Goat Rocks Wilderness 94–97
Gold Lakes 116–19
Goldmyer Hot Springs 142
Grace Lakes 181
Grand Park 128
Granite Mountain Potholes 164
Green River 91–94
grizzly bears 30
Grizzly Lake 90

H
Halfway House 61
Hannegan Pass 230
Happy Lake 55
Happy Lake Ridge 54–56
Hart Lake 74
Hatchery Creek 183
Heart Lake 53
Henry M. Jackson Wilderness 170–72, 218–21, 222
High Divide 48–53
High Pass 197–98
Highline Trail 87
Hoh Head 45
Hoh Lake 53
Hoh River 44, 53
Home Lake 61–64
Home Sweet Home 72
horses 28
Horseshoe Basin (Stehekin River Valley) 232–35
Horseshow Basin (Pasayten Wilderness) 264–68
Hozzbizz Lake 165
Huckleberry Creek 128–32
hunting 30
Hyas Lake 161, 165

I
Ice Lakes 210–14
Icicle Creek 177–79
Ilswoot, Lake 176
Image Lake 203–06
Indian Corral 287, 289
Indian Heaven Wilderness 81–85
Ipsut Creek 113–15

J
Jackita Ridge 243–47
Jade Lake (Mount Daniel) 168
Jade Lake (Necklace Valley) 175
James, Lake 127
Johnson Mountain 224
Jug Lake 100
Junction Lake 82

K
Kaleetan Lake 145–49
Kayostla Beach 41
Kerouac, Jack 240, 243
Kettle Creek Trail 101
Kettle Crest Trail north 273–78
Kettle Crest Trail south 270–73
Kettle Lake 102
Kettle River Range 270–78
Klapatche Park 119–22

L
La Bohn Gap 145, 176
La Crosse, Lake 71–74
Ladies Pass 179–83
Lake Chelan National Recreation Area 253
Lake Chelan–Sawtooth Wilderness 253, 254–57
Laughingwater Creek Trail 135–36

Leave No Trace 26, 29
Lemei Lake 82
Lena Lakes 74–76
Lillian River 57
Little Beaver Creek 235–39
Little Giant Pass 194
Little Snowy Top Mountain 278–81
Locket Lake 176
Loudon Lake 265
Louis Lake 253
Low Divide 60
Lower Tuscohatchie Lake 148
Lyman Lakes 199–203

M
Mad Lake 207–10
Manning, Harvey 26, 119, 207
Marble Meadow 210
Margaret, Lake 60
Marmot Lake (Alpine Lakes Wilderness) 164–68
Marmot Lake (Olympic National Park) 74
Marmot Pass 63
Marten Lake 140
Martins Lakes 60
Mary, Lake 181
McAlester Lake 253
McCall Gulch 262
Melakwa Lake 149
Mesatchee Creek 103
Middle Fork Snoqualmie River 141–43
Middle Ridge 196
Milk Lake 76
Mineral Creek 155
Miners Ridge 206
Monte Cristo 218
Moraine Park 127
Mount Adams Wilderness 85–88

Mount Margaret Backcountry Lakes 88–91
Mount Misery Highline 284–87
Mount Rainier National Park 111–36
Mount Saint Helens National Volcanic Monument 88–94
Mountaineers, The 26
Mowich Lake 113
Muddy Meadows 85
Myrtle Lake 211
Mystic Lake 127

N
Nada Lake 188
Napeequa Valley 191–94
Necklace Valley 173–76
Norse Peak Wilderness 104–10
North Cascades National Park 231, 232–35, 237, 253–54
North Fork Entiat River 214
North Fork Quinault River 60–61
North Fork Sauk River 224, 226
North Fork Skykomish River 68, 72, 170–73
Northern Loop (Mount Rainier National Park) 125–28
Northwest Forest Pass 21–22
Norwegian Memorial 41

O
O'Neil Expedition 48, 71
Obscurity Lake 91
Observation Peak 79
Oil City 44
Olympic Coast 38–46

Olympic Hot Springs 56
Olympus, Mount 51–53
Opal Lake 176
Oregon Butte 287–89
Otter Falls 140
Oval Lakes 254–57
Ozette Lake 42

P
Pacific Crest Trail (PCT) 81, 87, 96–97, 99–100, 109–10, 133–35, 154–55, 159–61, 171–72, 177–78, 226–28, 248–50
Pacific Northwest Trail 239
Painter Creek 186
Panjab Creek 288–89
Pasayten Wilderness 244–47, 262–64, 265–68
Pass Creek 170
Paul Peak Trail 116
Pete Lake 154
Pedro Camp 144
Peggys Pond 159
permits 21–22, 23
Pony Bridge 47
Pratt Lake 146
Pratt River 147
Press Expedition Traverse 56–61
Prusik Pass 188
Pyramid Mountain 214–16

R
rattlesnakes 32
Red Pass 226
regulations 21–22, 23
Rialto Beach 38
road conditions 25–27
Roosevelt, President Franklin D. 48, 71
Roosevelt, President Theodore 66, 71

Ross Lake National Recreation Area 235, 240–43, 244
Ruby Creek 247

S

Saint Andrews Park 121–22
Sally Ann, Lake 172
Salmo-Priest Wilderness 278–84
Sand Point 42
Scout Lake Way Trail 76
Seattle Park 113–15
Semple Plateau 60
Seven Lakes Basin 53
Shedroof Divide 280, 281–84
Sheepherder Lake 106
Shipwreck Coast 38–42
Shovel Lake 91
Silver Lake 220
Smith Lake 71
Snoqualmie Lake 138–41
Snow Lake (Alpine Lakes Wilderness) 149–50
Snow Lake (Mount Saint Helens National Volcanic Monument) 91
Snow Lakes 188
Snow Peak Cabin 273
Snowgrass Flats 96–97
Snowy Lakes 247–50
Sol Duc Falls 51
South Pass 250–54
South Puyallup River Trail 121
Spectacle Lake 152–55
Spider Gap 199–203
Spider Glacier 201
Spider Meadow 200
Spray Falls 115
Spring, Ira 26, 207
Squaw Lake 159
Starbuch Mine 41

Strawberry Point 46
Suiattle Pass 201
Suiattle River 203
Sunny Pass 265
Sunrise Lake 260
Sunset Park 116–19
Susan Jane, Lake 177
Swamp Lake 135

T

Tahoma Creek 119, 122–23
Taylor River 138–41
Ten Essentials 35
Third Beach 46
Three Fools Pass 262
Three Lakes 132–36
Thunder Mountain 282
ticks 32
Toleak Point 46
Tolmie Peak 113
trail conditions 25–27
trail etiquette 27–28
Trapper Creek 78–80
Trapper Creek Wilderness 78–80
Triad Lake 198
Tuck and Robin Lakes 161–64, 165
Tuckaway Lake 256
Tucks Pot 164
Turkey Creek 288
Twin Lakes 218–21
Twin Sisters Lakes 100
Twisp Pass 250–54
Two Lakes 135

U

Umatilla National Forest 284–89
Upper Big Quilcene River Trail 62–63
Upper Florence Lake 181
Upper Lena Lake 74–76

V

Vanson Lake 93
Vanson Peak 93

W

Waptus Lake 155–58
Waptus River 156
Warrior Peak 64
Washington Trails Association (WTA) 26, 65
water 29
weather 23–25
Wenaha-Tucannon Wilderness 284–89
West Fork Dosewallips River 66–67
Westside Road 119, 123
Whatcom Pass 239
White Chuck Cinder Cone 228
White Mountain 270
White Pass 226
Whitepine Creek 180
Wild Sky Wilderness 97, 170
Wildcat Lakes 149–52
Wildcatter Coast 42–46
Wilderness Act 97
wilderness ethics 26
wilderness regulations 22
William O. Douglas Wilderness 97–104, 133–35
Williams Lake 141–45
Windy Gap 127
Windy Lake 148
Windy Peak 264–68
Winthrop Glacier 127
Wonderland Trail 113–15, 116–19, 121–22, 123–24, 125–27, 128

Y

Yakama Indian Reservation 88, 96
Yellow Banks 42
Yellowstone Cliffs 127

About the Author

Craig went on his first backpacking adventure sometime back in the 1970s, with the Boy Scouts in the Lakes Region of New Hampshire. Even though he schlepped an inordinate amount of weight using inadequate equipment, he was hooked. Since those nascent days he has backpacked in various parks and forests from Quebec to Chile, and became an end-to-ender on Vermont's Long Trail.

A resident of Washington since 1989, Craig's first backpacking trip in his new home was Olympic National Park's High Divide. He shared his campsite with a curious young coyote and several bellowing marmots, and five bears and three elk welcomed him along the way. It was magical and he has returned to the High Divide and the Olympics often since.

Craig has hiked and backpacked all over his adopted state, racking up over 14,000 miles from the wild, misty Olympic Coast to the Selkirk Mountains, homeland to grizzlies. He hiked more than 1500 miles over two years just researching this book, encountering countless bears, a cougar, snowstorms,

wind storms, and a forest fire. He braved swollen creeks, steep snowfields, washouts, and brushy, overgrown terrain while on the trail. Mosquitoes, lightning, hail, blisters, and subfreezing evenings—he'd do it all over again in a heartbeat and is excited to be sharing these places, some of the most spectacular in North America, with other hikers.

Aside from hiking, Craig is an avid runner, an occasional cyclist and paddler, and a dedicated conservationist. A full-time writer, he has written for over a dozen publications, including *Adventures NW*, *AMC Outdoors*, *Backpacker*, *CityDog*, *Northwest Runner*, *Outdoors NW*, and *Seattle Met*. He also writes regular content for Hikeoftheweek.com, which he cofounded in 2005. Author of eight books, among them *Day Hiking: Olympic Peninsula* and *Day Hiking: Columbia River Gorge*, and coauthor of two others, Craig is currently working on *Day Hiking: Eastern Washington* (for The Mountaineers Books) with Rich Landers of the *Spokane Spokesman-Review*. Craig's *Columbia Highlands: Exploring Washington's Last Frontier* was recognized in 2010 by Washington Secretary of State Sam Reed and State Librarian Jan Walsh as a Washington Reads book for its contribution to the state's cultural heritage.

Craig holds an associate's degree in forestry, a bachelor's degree in history, and a masters degree in education. He lives with his wife, Heather, and cats Giuseppe and Scruffy Gray in Skagit County, where he enjoys watching swans and snow geese fly overhead when he's not hiking.

Visit him at http://CraigRomano.com and on Facebook at "Craig Romano Guidebook Author."

THE MOUNTAINEERS, founded in 1906, is a nonprofit outdoor activity and conservation organization based in Seattle, Washington. The Mountaineers' mission is "To enrich the community by helping people explore, conserve, learn about, and enjoy the lands and waters of the Pacific Northwest." The Mountaineers sponsors classes and year-round outdoor activities, including hiking, mountain climbing, backpacking, skiing, snowboarding, snowshoeing, bicycling, camping, kayaking and canoeing, nature study, photography, sailing, and adventure travel; these classes and activities are open to both members and the general public. The Mountaineers' conservation efforts support environmental causes through educational activities and programming, and through its publishing division. All activities are led by skilled, experienced volunteers, who are dedicated to promoting safe and responsible enjoyment and preservation of the outdoors. If you would like more information on programs or membership, please write to The Mountaineers Program Center, 7700 Sand Point Way NE, Seattle, WA 98115-3996; phone 206-521-6001; visit www.mountaineers.org; or e-mail clubmail@mountaineers.org.

THE MOUNTAINEERS BOOKS, the nonprofit publishing division of The Mountaineers, produces guidebooks, instructional texts, historical works, natural history guides, and, through partnership with Braided River, works on environmental conservation. Books are aimed at fulfilling the mission of The Mountaineers. Visit www.mountaineersbooks.org to find details about all our titles and the latest author events, as well as videos, web clips, links, and more!

The Mountaineers Books
1001 SW Klickitat Way, Suite 201
Seattle, WA 98134
800-553-4453
mbooks@mountaineersbooks.org

The Mountaineers Books is proud to be a corporate sponsor of The Leave No Trace Center for Outdoor Ethics, whose mission is to promote and inspire responsible outdoor recreation through education, research, and partnerships. The Leave No Trace program is focused specifically on human-powered (non-motorized) recreation.

Leave No Trace strives to educate visitors about the nature of their recreational impacts, as well as offer techniques to prevent and minimize such impacts. Leave No Trace is best understood as an educational and ethical program, not as a set of rules and regulations.

For more information, visit www.lnt.org, or call 800-332-4100.

OTHER TITLES YOU MIGHT ENJOY FROM THE MOUNTAINEERS BOOKS

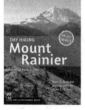

Day Hiking Columbia River Gorge
Romano
100+ fabulous hikes in and around the Columbia River Gorge Scenic Area—plus the Portland region

Day Hiking Central Cascades
Romano and Bauer
125 great hikes in the heart of Washington State—including Lake Chelan

Day Hiking Olympic Peninsula
Romano
125 fantastic hikes on the rugged, wild, and beautiful Olympic peninsula—coast included!

Day Hiking North Cascades
Romano
125 glorious hikes in the North Cascades...and the San Juan Islands, too!

Day Hiking Snoqualmie Region
Nelson and Bauer
125 gorgeous hikes close to the Puget Sound region—includes the Alpine Lakes

Day Hiking South Cascades
Nelson and Bauer
125 superb hikes for the southwest quarter of the state—includes Mount Saint Helens

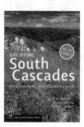

Day Hiking Mount Rainier
Nelson and Bauer
70 spectacular hikes in Mount Rainier National Park, including portions of the Wonderland Trail